Prevention and Intervention in Childhood and Adolescence 5

Special Research Unit 227 – Prevention and Intervention in Childhood and Adolescence

An interdisciplinary project of the University of Bielefeld

conducted by *Prof. Dr. Günter Albrecht, Prof. Dr. Peter-Alexis Albrecht, Prof. Dr. Otto Backes, Prof. Dr. Michael Brambring, Prof. Dr. Klaus Hurrelmann, Prof. Dr. Franz-Xaver Kaufmann, Prof. Dr. Friedrich Lösel, Prof. Dr. Hans-Uwe Otto, Prof. Dr. Helmut Skowronek*

Most of the papers in this volume have their origin in the international exchange network of researchers cooperating with the Research Center "Prevention and Intervention in Childhood and Adolescence" at the University of Bielefeld, of which the senior editor is the director since 1986. We want to express our thanks to all contributors, to the German Research Association *(Deutsche Forschungsgemeinschaft)* for the grant that made the exchange of visits and ideas possible, and to Jonathan Harrow and Liam Gilmour for their careful translation of several articles in this volume.

Klaus Hurrelmann
Uwe Engel

Preface

This volume presents papers that discuss the relative influence of family, school, and peer group as well as leisure and work settings on the process of adolescent socialization in various industrialized countries. The papers document evidence for the fact that the importance of the different areas and contexts of socialization has shifted within the last two to three decades, and thus the social fabric of the "world of adolescents" has changed.

Attempts are made to estimate and evaluate the social and psychological importance of the different socialization contexts in present – day adolescence. The authors discuss the complementary and/or competitive interrelations between these contexts. Where possible, comparative data are included. Different types of methodology are applied. The authors represent various scientific disciplines and different national research traditions in Europe, North America, and Japan.

The papers discuss the social, political, and psychological implications of the changes in the world of adolescents. Questions to be answered are, for example: Who actually are the significant people in the social network of adolescents? What are the consequences of the fact that the peer group and the school, but not family and work, have become very powerful socialization contexts? What is the influence of adults, peers, and mass media on adolescents' lifestyles? What are the implications for the process of cultural transmission, social reproduction, and personality development in adolescence? What are the social milieus and biographical concepts that are important for young people today? Which changes in the pathways from school to work can be observed?

The volume combines more theoretical papers in the first section and more empirical papers in the following four sections. The theoretical papers include sociological, socioeconomic, psychological, systems – theoretical, life – course, and socialization – theoretical perspectives. The empirical papers discuss the situation in different countries as a specific pattern of developments in industrial countries in general. Many papers analyze gender – specific effects and focus on the influence of different regional contexts and biographical stages.

Klaus Hurrelmann
Professor of Education and Sociology, University of Bielefeld

Uwe Engel
Special Research Unit 227, University of Bielefeld

Library of Congress Cataloging in Publication Data

Social world of adolescents : international perspectives / edited by Klaus
    Hurrelmann, Uwe Engel
    p. cm. – (Prevention and intervention in childhood and adolescence ; 5)
    Bibliography: p.
    Includes index.
    ISBN 0-89925-571-X (U.S.)
    1. Adolescence--Social aspects--History--20th century.   2. Socialization--
History--20th century.   3. Teenagers--Social networks--History--20th century.
I. Hurrelmann, Klaus   II. Engel, Uwe.   1954–   .   III. Series.
HQ796.S565   1989
305.2'35--dc 19

Deutsche Bibliothek Cataloging in Publication Data

The **social world of adolescents: international perspectives** / ed. by
Klaus Hurrelmann ; Uwe Engel. – Berlin ; New York : de Gruyter, 1989
    (Preventation and intervention in childhood and adolescence ; 5)
    ISBN 3-11-011996-X
NE: Hurrelmann, Klaus [Hrsg.]; GT

♾ Printed on acid free paper.

The Social World of Adolescents

International Perspectives

Edited by
Klaus Hurrelmann, Uwe Engel

Walter de Gruyter · Berlin · New York 1989

Contents

Contributors

Baethge, Martin
Soziologisches Forschungsinstitut, Universität Göttingen, Friedländer Weg 31, D—3400 Göttingen, Federal Republic of Germany

Baker, David P.
Department of Sociology, The Catholic University of America, POB, Washington DC 20064, USA

Bö, Inge
Hogskolesenteret in Rogaland. Postboks 2557, Ullandhang, N—4004 Stavanger, Norway

Coleman, John C.
The Sussex Youth Trust, 23 New Road, GB—Brighton, BN1 1WZ, Great Britain

Darling, Nancy
College of Human Ecology, Cornell University, Martha Van Rensselaer Hall, Ithaca, NY 14853, USA

Dronkers, Jaap
Department of Sociology, Tilburg University, P.O. Box 90153, NL—5000 LE Tilburg, The Netherlands

Du Bois—Reymond, Manuela
Vakgroep Andragogiek, Universiteit Leiden, Stationsplein 10—12, NL—2312 AK Leiden, The Netherlands

Gaiser, Wolfgang
Deutsches Jugendinstitut. Freibadstr. 30, D—8000 München 90, Federal Republic of Germany

Engel, Uwe
Sonderforschungsbereich 227, Universitätsstr. 25, Universität Bielefeld, D—4800 Bielefeld 1, Federal Republic of Germany

Hendry, Leo B.
Department of Education, University of Aberdeen, King's College, GB—Aberdeen AB9 2UB, Great Britain

Hamilton, Stephen F.
College of Human Ecology, Cornell University, Martha Van Rensselaer Hall, Ithaca, NY 14853, USA

Heitmeyer, Wilhelm
Forschungsschwerpunkt Jugendforschung, Fakultät für Pädagogik, Universität Bielefeld, Universitätsstr. 25, D—4800 Bielefeld 1, Federal Republic of Germany

Hurrelmann, Klaus
Sonderforschungsbereich 227, Universität Bielefeld, Universitätsstr. 25, D—4800 Bielefeld 1, Federal Republic of Germany

King, Alan J.C.
Department of Sociology, McArthur Hall, Queen's University, Kingston, Ontario K7L 3N6, Canada

Matsuda, Sei
Department of Psychology, Aichi University, 1 Hirosawa, Igaya—Cho, Kariya 448, Japan

Melzer, Wolfgang
Forschungsschwerpunkt Jugendforschung Fakultät für Pädagogik, Universität Bielefeld, Universitätsstr. 25, D—4800 Bielefeld 1, Federal Republic of Germany

Meeus, Wim
Vakgroep Ontwikkeling en Socialisatie, Rijksuniversiteit, Heidelberglaan 2, NL—3584 CS Utrecht, The Netherlands

Möller, Kurt
Fakultät für Pädagogik, Universität Bielefeld, Universitätsstr. 25, D—4800 Bielefeld 1, Federal Republic of Germany

Müller, Hans Ulrich
Deutsches Jugendinstitut. Freibadstr. 30, D—8000 München 90, Federal Republic of Germany

Neubauer, Georg
Sonderforschungsbereich 227, Universität Bielefeld, Universitätsstr. 25, D—4800 Bielefeld 1, Federal Republic of Germany

Palazzo, Donato
Director, Giovani Realta, Via 95 Reggimento, Fanteria 31, I—Lecce, Italy

Parsell, Glennys
Department of Sociology, The University of Liverpool, E. Rathbone Building, Myrtle Street, GB—Liverpool L69 3BX, Great Britain

Poole, Millicent
Faculty of Education, Monash University, Clayton VIC, Australia 3186

Rapoport, Tamar
School of Education, The Hebrew University, Mount Scopus, Jerusalem 91905, Israel

Roberts, Kenneth
Department of Sociology, The University of Liverpool, E. Rathbone Building, Myrtle Street, GB—Liverpool L69 3BX, Great Britain

Stevenson, David L.
Office of Research, 555 New Jersey Ave. NW, U.S. Department of Education, Washington DC 20208, USA

Wallace, Claire
Plymouth Polytechnic, Drake Circus, Plymouth, GB—Devon PL4 8AA, Great Britain

Weidman, John C.
School of Education, University of Pittsburgh, 5 S40 Forbes Quadrangle, Pittsburgh PA 15260, USA

Part I
Theoretical Approaches

1.
The Social World of Adolescents:
A Sociological Perspective

Klaus Hurrelmann
University of Bielefeld, Federal Republic of Germany

Adolescence as a phase of the human life course is an historically shaped social "product" that is in a state of constant change. In this introductory section, we first describe the historical emergence of the life phase of adolescence. We then discuss the essential structural changes in this life phase over the past decades. A central topic will be the recent changes within the process of social integration that have occurred as a result of the shifts in educational and occupational opportunities. We postulate that this structural change in the phase of adolescence can be interpretated as a process of restructuring of the phase of life called "adolescence". Finally, we discuss implications for a social policy for adolescents.

1. The Historical Differentiation of the Phase of Adolescence

As the study of social history has shown, adolescence can be identified as a specific and independent phase of the human life course since the second half of the last century. The "emergence" of the phase of adolescence was closely linked to economic, political, and cultural changes evoked by the industrialization process and the accompanying establishment of a compulsory school system (Gillis, 1974).

Among the mostly rural families of preindustrial society, young and old people lived together under one roof and shared many of the same tasks and activities in their daily routines. The child was something like a miniature of the adult (Aries, 1975). Because of industrialization and the beginnings of the process of urbanization, the behavioral domains and action spheres of children and adults were driven further apart from one another. Work outside the family became more and more the norm. As a consequence, new forms of family life arose.

With the industrialization process, adults built up their social relationships around the working place. This development separated children and adults within their daily routines. With most fathers out at work during the day, a first step in the separation of a special life sphere for children was taken. Within the urban regions this process was accompanied and accelerated by a new social and pedagogical definition of the role of children: They were no longer seen as small adults, but as human beings in an independent phase of development that made special behavioral demands, which were no longer identical with those of the adults.

This process of the social separation of the generations was supported by the establishment of a common school system in the second half of the last century. Education, primarily understood as a preparation for occupational demands in the working process, was increasingly taken over by organized and purpose – built organizations. This process accelerated the separation of a specific social world for young people. Through the decades, this dynamic process spread into more sectors of daily life, including leisure time and the use of media. Soon the transition to adulthood was delayed beyond the advent of puberty, at first among middle – class youth. This led to the rise of a new phase within the human life course that became separate from the others: the phase of adolescence.

The emergence of the phase of adolescence

The phase of adolescence emerged at a time when the grade of complexity of job qualifications, which were mainly determined by technological needs, had reached a level which demanded certain skills, attitudes, and requirements. Simultaneously, this stage of societal development saw the emergence of opportunities to grant the younger generation what was considered to be a necessary period for the development of maturity. Because of technological development and the spread of societal welfare systems, human working potential no longer had to be exploited to the same extent as before. At the same time, the restrengthened moral and pedagogical ideas on the necessity and appropriateness of a suitable development of the society's young members had to be met.

Gradually, at first within the middle class, the phase of adolescence grew into an independent phase. The right to the full practice of adult occupation and the connected privilege of becoming self – reliant was bound to the completion of certain stages of education and training. On the other hand, "professional maturity" was generally seen as the prerequirement for granting the right of marriage. Because all societies were interested in providing a sheltered upbringing and appropriate education for their offspring, and the family possessed a virtual monopoly of these activities, the right of marriage was given to men and women only if it seemed that they had learnt enough about the culture of the society and if, in addition, it could be assumed that their material situation guaranteed the security of their own children.

In accordance with this, adolescence was first of all a historical product of the bourgeois middle class. The middle class was wealthy enough to support an extended time of preparation for career life. It also propagated the idealistic picture of adolescence as a psychosocial "moratorium" on the way to maturity, providing protection from the various burdens of adult life. In the course of industrialization, the young members of the working class and the rural families also entered the phase of adolescence step by step.

At least since the 1950's and 1960's, adolescence has become a common cultural good in the societies of the industrialized West. It is no longer only in the possession of the bourgeois male groups of the population. Because the economic conditions and the closely linked living conditions still show a considerable breadth of variation, the phase of adolescence, however, still has several class — and sex — specific features.

As we have mentioned, for all adolescents the social differentiation of the phase of adolescence was realized by extending the general compulsory school attendance over the past hundred years. *Today, in most industrial societies, the typical minimum of 10 years of compulsory school attendance guarantees a certain "minimum of youth" to the members of all social strata.* Many years of the period of adolescence are defined by school attendance. Class — and sex — specific differences are no longer mainly expressed by the single fact of school attendence, but by the kind of school attended, and the long — term prospects for career and life opportunities that are connected with the type and quality of school — leaving certificates and diplomas.

The age of entering a career has shifted considerably in the past two decades, partly as a result of extended school attendance. At the same time, the entry into a social relationship based on marriage, which is a clear indicator of successful social separation from the family of origin, takes place earlier in life. In Germany, for example, at the turn of the century, the average marrying age of the total group of men was 28 years and of women 26; today, men are about 26 and women 23 years old (Jugendwerk, 1981). The average age of entering the world of occupation and gainful employment now stands at about

20 years of age and may have been 15 to 16 at the turn of the century. Thus, these two transitional points in the life course have moved closer to each other.

The same evidence is given in an American study by Modell, Furstenberg and Hershberg (1977), who used Philadelphia census data to make direct comparisons between youth cohorts in 1870 and 1970. They focused on five elements of the transition to adulthood: exit from school; entrance to the work force; departure from the family of origin; marriage; and the establishment of a household. They determined the distribution of ages in young people making these five transitions. They found clear evidence of the extension of formal schooling, and that employment began earlier in 1870. They also found that on average, the five transitions now occur in closer proximity to one another and are completed in a shorter period of time than a century ago. Delayed marriage was more common then. Young people continued to live with their parents longer, and it was common for young married couples to live with parents for several years before establishing their own residence.

What has changed as the 20th century has progressed, therefore, has not been simply a prolongation of youth, but a change in the pattern of transition and of the importance of different elements of this transition:

"No longer are the family transitions the predominant consequential ones: Today school departure and work−force entry are far more important in shaping the subsequent work career than a century ago. And today the familial transitions are not so enduring as was once the case. In the 19th century, the family was a unique institution, standing alone; in the 20th, it is one of many; or rather, one of the many in and out of which individuals have to thread their way (Modell, Furstenberg and Hershberg, 1977, 29).

2.   Structural Changes in the Process of School−to−Work Transition

The decision regarding which position in the social structure a member of the society will occupy when he/she becomes an adult (i.e., how the positioning and placement on the central societal dimensions of power, influence, property, and prestige takes place) is "programmed" at the age of adolescence. The process of integration into adult society is also always a process of social selection for certain status positions (Persell, 1977; Engel, 1987).

Today's industrial societies are achievement−oriented societies in such a way that an individual's economic achievement typically decides the position in the social structure and not − as was the case in preindustrial societies − the social background. For this reason, the main social organizations that determine the process of integration are no longer the families, but the educational and occupational institutions that were specifically established to educate and train the individual capacities of the young members of the society. The educational system possesses a dominant function in the qualification of the offspring of society and the selection according to different levels of prestige and qualification. The final decision about the status attained takes place within the occupational system, but the predecision in the form of presenting school – leaving certificates of different quality is made within the educational system (cf. Poole; Roberts and Parsell; Engel, all in this volume).

This is not to say that the family of origin has no influence on the process of socialization. But the form and shape of this influence has changed considerably within one century. The nuclear family influences its offspring's scholastic abilities in educational institutions by supporting or prompting them. This is an indirect control of the process of status attainment; compared to former times, there has been a decrease in the possibilites of direct intervention.

Educational opportunities and prospects

Because of the great importance that is paid to the structuring of the process of status attainment, we shall now specify the educational and occupational prospects more precisely.

For the "educational market" alone, we can state generally that the opportunity structure has improved continously over the past three decades. We will use the Federal Republic of Germany as a fairly typical example for most of the Western industrial nations. Here the infrastructural weight of the educational system has been reinforced considerably in the last three to four decades. More and more adolescents from all age groups remain in full – time and part – time educational institutions for a longer period of time.

Table 1 gives an impression of the extent of the "educational expansion" that has occured during the past decades. As can be seen, in the last 25 years school attendance has become the dominant characteristic of the phase of adolescence far into the age group of 19 – year – olds. Above all, the attendance of full – time secondary schools and vocational schools has increased considerably during the last two and a half decades.

Schooling in West Germany is compulsory from age 6 to 18: Students must attend school full – time for 10 years in most states and then at least part – time during vocational training for

Table 1: Students aged 16 to 22 in general and vocational schools split according to type of school, sex, and age in percentages of the population of the same age

Age in years	Year	Total	Fulltime general schools		Part–time vocational schools		Full–time vocational schools	
			M	F	M	F	M	F
16	1960	93	23	18	71	65	3	6
	1970	95	29	23	63	58	7	10
	1980	97	47	49	43	33	8	16
	1984	99	57	57	35	25	7	16
17	1960	66	16	11	52	43	2	6
	1970	84	18	13	63	58	7	9
	1980	89	26	27	58	45	8	16
	1984	91	28	29	56	40	11	19
18	1960	32	11	7	24	14	3	5
	1970	47	13	9	40	19	5	8
	1980	70	19	19	49	34	7	12
	1984	78	22	23	53	37	8	14
19	1960	17	7	4	11	5	3	4
	1970	21	7	3	15	6	4	6
	1980	41	10	8	29	19	7	6
	1984	49	10	9	34	25	6	12
20	1960	7	3	1	5	1	2	3
	1970	10	4	1	6	2	3	4
	1980	19	3	2	13	8	4	8
	1984	25	3	2	17	15	5	10
21	1960	3	0	0	2	0	2	2
	1970	3	0	0	2	0	2	2
	1980	9	0	0	8	4	3	4
	1984	13	0	0	8	8	3	6
22	1960	1	0	0	0	0	2	1
	1970	2	0	0	0	0	2	1
	1980	5	0	0	3	1	3	3
	1984	4	0	0	0	0	3	4

(Taken from: Bundesminister für Bildung und Wissenschaft, 1987, 24)

an additional 2 to 3 years. As Table 1 shows, the percentage of those leaving school after compulsory education who go on to full—time vocational schools (trade and technical schools: Berufsfachschule, Fachoberschule, Handelsschule, etc.) for one to three years of further study is rising. Others who leave general school at this point pass directly into vocational training in the "dual system". Under this system they sign on with a firm and are trained in accordance with the vocational legislation applying to a particular trade. They learn on—the—job four days a week and spend one day a week at part—time vocational school (Berufsschule). The classroom time is divided into one—third general studies and two—thirds trade—oriented studies over a period of between 2 and 3.5 years. Students must take a state—approved examination upon completion of their apprenticeships at the age of about 18 years. Students in secondary schools also have to take their final examination (Abitur) at about the age of 18 to 19 years.

Higher education in West Germany, too, has grown tremendously in recent years. Over 250,000 new college places were created between 1970 and 1985. The abolition of student fees and the provision of government grants have made the acquisition of a college education a goal for many young people who, in the past, would not have thought it possible. In the early 1950s, only 6% of each age group attended institutions of higher learning, compared to 22% in 1980. The average length of study at universities is 6.5 years, while at polytechnical schools it is 3.8 years (Bundesminister für Bildung und Wissenschaft, 1987). Since young men have to serve almost 2 years in the army or in obligatory civil service, the average age at which they complete a university education is about 27, for young women 25.

Obviously, the educational success of the disadvantaged groups of adolescents who come from families of low socioeconomic status has improved within the past three decades in West Germany. In grammar schools, for example, the share of these adolescents has doubled between 1950 and 1980, that is, from 5% to 10%. Working—class adolescents have succeeded in increasing their representation in the paths of high—prestige education. But the share of working—class adolescents is still significantly below their share in the general population (about 40%). The higher the level of the educational institution, the smaller the percentage of working—class youngsters.

In the last three decades, working—class adolescents have generally not been able to make any basic improvements in their relative starting position for entrance into the employment system. They are not the only ones who have been able to increase their participation in education; adolescents from the families of white—collar workers, public officials, and the self—employed have done the same. In these classes as well, the general expansion in education has led to a further increase in the proportion of adolescents who complete secondary school education up to university entrance level. For this reason, there has been hardly any change in the class distribution of students in such schools.

Despite the fact that the opportunity structure of the educational system is objectively more favorable than before, the competition for an attractive starting position in the vocational placement process has increased considerably. To retain the social status of their family background, adolescents in the 1980s must obtain qualifications that are higher than those of their parents. Unchanged differences in the starting conditions still characterize the race for the highest qualifications. Adolescents from the middle and upper classes receive more effective support — both material and nonmaterial — when adopting and persevering with the optimization strategy in the education market (Persell, 1977).

Following the period of school education, adolescents pass through a specific phase of vocational training. This phase extends the process of educational qualification with a period that produces the "marketable" skills of the future adult member of society that can actually be offered in the labor market. The period of vocational training is a significant step on the path to one of the key roles of the adult status, namely, employment. It represents a first release from the school as an obligatory and enforced institution of education and thus guides the adolescent into the process of directly productive, qualified work. The transfer from school to vocational training therefore calls for a further important, preliminary decision on the outcome of the placement process and is a decisive crossroads in determining the situation and quality of the adolescent's future life (cf. King; Wallace; in this volume).

Because of the baby boom and contractive trends in the labor market, the fierce competitive pressures in the labor market are already active in the apprenticeship market. The training institutions can select those they consider to be suitable from the now very large group of highly qualified school leavers. A high–quality school education and a good school–leaving certificate qualify as a reference indicating a willingness to adapt and commit oneself to vocational training. School leavers without certificates are forced out of the qualified business, managerial, and technical professions and have to take up manual vocations.

These dislocation processes give adolescents a bitter foretaste of the reality of the labor market that awaits them after the completion of vocational training. Even those among them who successfully complete an apprenticeship are no longer certain of being accepted into the labor market.

Even the highly qualified paths of education have come up against the pressure of contractive trends in the labor market. In the 1980s, a university degree basically no longer guarantees entrance into correspondingly high professional positions. Partially as a reaction to this, in West Germany there has been a continuous decline in the number of students who enter university immediately after successfully completing grammar school: In 1985 this was approximately 70%, while in 1950 it was practically 100%. The proportion of adolescents with university entrance qualifications who first enter business training is increasing (roughly two in ten in 1985).

The training sector "university" also shows clear inequalities in opportunity structures (cf. Weidmann; in this volume). Since the expansion of government service as a traditional labor market for university graduates (teachers, judges, doctors, etc.) in West Germany has dramatically narrowed since the mid–1970s, the internal dislocation processes between groups of adolescents with differing social privileges has grown in the university sector. Here, the same patterns can be found as in the general schools: Various optimization strategies (double degrees, supplementary courses, etc.) are embarked upon and, depending on the material and nonmaterial starting position, are maintained with varying degrees of success.

Placement in the labor market

The placement process comes to an at least preliminary close with the first permanent position in the employment system that is taken up after completion of the educational and vocational qualification process. A consistent extension can be seen in the lines of structural inequality in placement that we reported for the school and training sector. This is reinforced by the contractive trends in the labor market in most Western European countries. Increasing productivity and redundancies due to advances in technology lead to a sinking demand for manpower. The dislocation race thus continues with unappeased ferocity in this section of the placement process as well, with the result that a growing minority of adolescents find no entrance into the employment system.

The increased expansion of the educational system in the last decades can partially be seen as a reaction to this process of contraction in the employment system. The largely state – controlled educational system in Western European countries has become a safety net for the overspill of applicants for entrance into the employment system. By lengthening compulsory education, successfully encouraging adolescents to obtain university entrance qualifications, and expanding full – time vocational schools and vocational education institutions, it has been possible to withhold an increasing proportion of 16 – to 18 – year – olds from the employment system, so that today large proportions of adolescents in this age group are retained in the educational system.

The employed quota, which represents the proportion of employed persons within the same age group in the residential population of a state, has correspondingly sunk in the last decades in the adolescent age group. Baethge, Schomburg and Voskamp (1983) have computed West German figures for the last decades on the basis of available statistical data. As *Table 2* shows, the employed quotas in the group of 15 – to 20 – year – old adolescents have each sunk by over 30% between 1957 and 1980. Even in the 21 – to 25 – year – old age group there are decreases of 10% for males and over 4% for females. These figures show that employment is no longer a typical structural feature for the under – 20s in the 1980s.

Table 2:   Employed quotas of male and female 15 to 35—year—olds in West Germany (as percentages of the residential population) from 1957 to 1980

Age	1957		1974		1980	
	M	F	M	F	M	F
15—20	81	76	57	53	49	41
21—25	92	76	81	68	82	71
26—30	97	52	91	56	90	63
31—35	97	45	97	50	97	56

(Taken from: Baethge, Schomburg and Voskamp, 1983)

The considerable sex—specific differences in the trends of the employed quotas are conspicuous in this table. While female adolescents under 20 have moved out of employed life more strongly than males during the interval covered, this trend is inverted in the higher age groups. The employment behavior of women approaches that of men, or at least the differences in the employment behavior of the sexes have become lower in all age groups. It would appear that young women, and especially those over the age of 25, increasingly strive to earn their own living through employment.

As these figures show, the entrance into the employment system, and thus the transfer to a major subrole of the adult status, has shifted into the third decade of life for the majority of adolescents. At the same time, the problems of starting professional life have become continuously greater: A growing minority of adolescents of both sexes, but particularly female and working—class adolescents, are pushed to the extreme margins of the employment system and into unemployment. The exact number of unemployed adolescents is difficult to ascertain because the official statistics of the unemployment offices are very selective. In West Germany, for example, they only record those adolescents who definitely register as unemployed at the labor office, and thus exclude all those who have not formally registered for some reason or other. Among those who are not registered but could possibly be regarded as additional unemployed are adolescents who help out in their families, casual workers, and those attending vocational courses. The number of unrecorded cases can therefore be estimated as considerable.

Nevertheless, we will look at the official statistics to obtain a picture of the extent of unemployment. They show that since the 1970s, adolescents make up a disproportionately high share of the unemployed in West Germany. This trend has continued to rise: In the mid−1980s, the quota of 15− to 20−year−olds was almost 10% (despite the prolongation of placement in the training system described above), and almost 20% in 21− to 25−year−olds. Female and working−class adolescents are particularly highly represented among the unemployed.

The trends in Western Europe are somewhat different to those in the United States. In the USA, the participation of adolescents under 25 in the labor force has markedly increased and not decreased between 1960 and 1980, as can be seen from *Table 3*.

Table 3: Participation of adolescents in the US labor force (percentage of adolescents employed)

Age	1960		1975		1980	
	M	F	M	F	M	F
16−17	46	29	49	40	50	44
18−19	69	51	71	58	71	62
20−24	88	46	85	64	86	69

(Taken from U.S. Department of Commerce, Bureau of Census, Statistical Abstract, 1984, 407)

These figures reflect the different political strategies for the labor market in Europe and the US. However, the situation for the 1980s is very similar, in spite of the different genesis: *Only a minority of those under 18 years of age are full−time members of the labor force. The proportion of adolescents who are forced into extremely unfavorable sectors of the labor market is increasing.* The surplus of labor has led to the growth of an area with unattractive terms of employment. A sort of two−class system is formed: Alongside the relatively privileged sector with normal terms of employment on the basis of long−term work contracts and the opportunity to take advantage of professional advancement through inservice training, an *underprivileged sector* develops in which employment is provided on the basis of short−term arrangements such as work contracts, freelance contracts, and subcontracts. This sector only offers uncertain employment and merges into the area of nonlegal work. Unemployment benefits or social security are unknown, and there is no permanence in such vocational activity.

As the material and nonmaterial demands of adolescents as a social group are not as fixed as those of adults, and their potential applications are relatively mobile as they are simultaneously more threatened by unemployment than adults, they have no option but to enter into this insecure sector of the employment system. Their relative share of employment in this sector is correspondingly high. As it would seem that the contractive trend in the labor market will continue, unfavorable opportunities of vocational placement must be anticipated for growing minorities of adolescents in the 1990s.

The transition from school to occupation and gainful employment is taking place later in life. At the same time, it has also changed qualitatively: Ways which previously had been relatively transparent and clear have increasingly been put into question, and have become more and more sophisticated; "waiting—loops", "detours" or transitional, alternative occupations outside of training, work, and occupation are increasing; links between education, training, and occupation, which had previously been relatively calculable in Western European countries, become more open and less reliable. The equation "more education equals better career and life chances" becomes less and less true; yet, at the same time less education and less training normally results in relative career disadvantages.

The consequences for the adolescent socialization process are obvious: *Gainful employment, which until the beginning of this century, at least in Europe, was typical for the largest proportion of adolescents, has been replaced by scholastic learning or systematic "training off—the—job".* The experience of being immediately useful to society, of behaving according to the economic norms of rationality and of being responsible for the personal material livelihood can only arrive relatively late in life. School does provide many intellectual and social stimulations, but it is an area which allows only marginal experiences of responsibility and solidarity and, instead, encourages a strong individualistic moral of competition and favors mainly abstract and theoretical learning (cf. Baethge, in this volume). The fact of not being forced to work within the employment sector offers a high degree of individual freedom in the use of time, the selection of communication forms and partners, and the arrangement of everyday life, particularly in the world of media and consumption. As long as young people attend full—time schools, colleges, or universities, however, they are not seen as being "really" adult, regardless of their actual age.

3.   *Structural   Changes   in   Family   and   Peer   Affiliations*

Adolescence is not only a stage of preparation for the transition to work, but also for the status—relevant process of choosing a partner and possibly getting married. For the family of origin, the choice of a partner also determines the social position of its own offspring. As today this is guided by the individualized process of reciprocal affection, the family of origin has little opportunity for direct intervention; the family is dependent on indirect guidance through the arrangement of social contacts. Personal decisions are channeled by the objectively given possibilities. Social conventions, demographic conditions, and other factors constitute a "market for marriages" with rules and opportunities that affect all persons. Typically, adolescents today postpone the formal decision on a marriage partner, but they start partner relations very early (Hurrelmann, Rosewitz & Wolf, 1985).

The family's situation as a central institution for the adolescents' socialization has changed considerably because of the economic, educational, and cultural processes mentioned above. Today, families are relatively small units with only a few members; they are increasingly households of one or two persons. They have become social systems that are highly susceptible to disturbance, mainly because of the rising instability of matrimony, it being the social heart of the family's relationships. In West Germany, some 20% of all households in 1985 were single – parent households. In the USA the percentage is even higher. Obviously, single – parent families and stepfamilies are more likely to have problematic consequences for the interaction within the family and detrimental consequences for the socialization process of young people.

Family relationships in adolescence are of high emotional and social importance. At the same time, one of the developmental tasks at the age of adolescence is to become emotionally, socially, and economically detached from just this important reference group that the family represents. Today this process of becoming detached is structurally very complex: Because of the long – term economic dependence on parents due to prolonged scholastic and vocational education, it takes place later in life than a generation ago. On the other hand, today's adolescents develop a lifestyle which is typically independent from their parents', especially within the area of leisure time and consumption (cf. Du Bois Reymond; Neubauer and Melzer; in this volume). They intend to move earlier into communities with peers or partners of the other sex. (The figures for West Germany are as follows: 18 – to 20 – year – olds living with parents in the parental home: 92% in 1964, 75% in 1981; 21 – to 24 – year – olds: 78% in 1964, 45% in 1981; Jugendwerk, 1981). As the process of becoming detached takes place in the different domains at different times, the relations with the family of origin are complicated. The family's importance as an economic support and also as an institution that adolescents consult for career decisions is very high, whereas its role as a social institution forming the actual cultural lifestyle of adolescence is small.

During the separation process, families negotiate the transition from a primarily unilateral relationship to more of a mutual coalition during late adolescence. Adolescents beyond the age of 13 to 14 spend significantly more leisure time with peers than with parents or alone, but, in overall time (leisure time plus work time), they spend equal amounts of time with parents and peers. The data reveal that parents' and peers' activities mainly center around the completion of a variety of social and household activities, whereas peer time is spent in entertainment, playing games, and talking (Biddle, Bank and Marlin, 1980; Beck 1987).

There is evidence that the influence of parents and peers upon adolescents varies according to types of activities and topics of conversation. In all industrial countries parents' influence seems to prevail in the future–oriented domains, such as choice of school and career plans (cf. Meeus; Dronkers; Baker and Stevenson; Matsuda; all in this volume); peers' influence centers around current events and activities. Daily friendship interactions take up a substantial portion of adolescents' leisure time. Adolescents report spending more time talking to peers than on any other activity and describe themselves as most happy when so engaged (cf. Bo; Hendry; Hamilton and Darling; all in this volume).

Comparative historical studies in West Germany show that at the stage of adolescence the meaning of the peer group as a significant social reference group has increased. In a comparative study, Allerbeck and Hoag (1985) were able to show that the status of peer relations has risen over the past 20 years. Evidently, the social network with peers is more dense today. As the authors report, membership of a group of friends ("clique") was reported by 16% of adolescents in 1962 and 57% in 1983. The status of the peer group appears to increase as a function of adolescents' social detachment from their parents. In this difficult time of separation, the peer group can take over the functions of stabilizing the adolescent socially and psychologically until a new modus of relations between parents and adolescents has been found (Blyth, Hill and Thiel, 1982).

Obviously, the peer group's influence on the organization of consumption and leisure–time activities at the age of adolescence is of outstanding importance. The peer groups give the standards for the orientation in the field of consumption and, while doing so, very often set effective standards for the adolescents' behavior. Parts of them sometimes create their own youth culture, which makes the development of a personal, independent lifestyle possible. Peer groups offer opportunities of equal participation to their members, which family or school do not provide to the same extent. Peer groups are an important medium in which adolescents are able to experience self–determination (Rapoport; Heitmeyer and Möller; in this volume).

Today's adolescents live a life of their own ideas within the area of friends, partners, media, and consumption. Nowadays, they often have more than adequate financial resources at their disposal: The majority of adolescents live in material wealth. They are able to realize many of their wishes in the consumption and leisure field; wishes that their parents would never have thought of and could never have realized. *But adolescents are living their life on a dependent economic basis that is not based on their own active, gainful employment.* This social position allows for a wide spectrum of personal development, and offers a high level of autonomy, spontaneity, creativity, and individuality. Most adolescents enjoy this latitude for decisions, alternatives, and individual shaping of everyday life in a highly imaginative manner. In West Germany, most studies have reported a self−confident way of organizing life beyond the adults' paths when dealing with fashion and dress, taste in music, leisure−time activities, language usage, and political articulation. Adolescents are obviously able to develop forms of acquiring and assimilating social reality that provide them with many facets of sensory, aesthetic, emotional, interactive, and communicative experience.

However, we have to be aware that adolescents develop their spontaneity and individuality in a social context that is insecure, unstable, and hardly accountable. The social position "being adolescent" is always temporary and never concrete and permanently secure. Neither parents, nor teachers, apprenticeship trainers, and friends can reassure the adolescents that opportunities of individualization will also become reality. The occupational future is hardly calculable for adolescents. Reliable future perspectives for the realization of life plans do not exist.

4. Are We Facing a Restructuring of the Phase of Adolescence?

The assessments of the changes in the structure of the life situation in adolescence and its individual and societal significance are controversial. Some authors point out that the liberation from gainful employment that has taken place since the 1950s has for the first time also granted a notably large scope for self−exploration and self−definition to previously underprivileged groups of adolescents. The characteristic scope for self−experience and self−examination and the development of a personal life style in the area of leisure time and consumption, which was traditionally only available for male adolescents from the middle classes, has been enlarged by this general liberation and is now also accessible to female adolescents and those from the working and lower classes (Jugendwerk, 1981).

Other authors point out that the high level of autonomy of action that is now granted to adolescents and even to children in the area of leisure time and consumption has made their behavior, orientation patterns, and life−styles similar and even the same as those of adults. As, in addition, children, adolescents, and adults, regardless of their social situation and their psychological maturity, are addressed and influenced in the same way by the entertainment media, the life and development space that is typical for adolescence disappears according to this concept. Therefore the idea and the reality of the phase of adolescence are drawing apart.

Doubt should be cast on such sweeping interpretations. The same applies to widespread fears that the far—reaching removal of work—related forms of life from the phase of adolescence would lead to the development of value and interest orientations that are foreign to work and career, making it impossible for adolescents to develop suitable orientations in occupational life. In this context, attention is often drawn to the increasing orientation of adolescents toward "postmaterialistic" and even "hedonistic" values. This concept links the orientation toward pleasure and immediate gratification to the strong orientation toward the consumption and leisure—time sector, and considers that this encourages attitudes and life designs that are alien to work and achievement (Inglehart, 1977). Such schematic estimations of the effects of the change in the structure of the phase of adolescence are superficial and unproductive. They concentrate on only one manifestation of adolescent behavior in each case and render it absolute. This leads to an overinterpretation of secondary aspects that can only be analyzed and interpreted meaningfully from a holistic perspective.

The phenotype of the adolescent phase in the 1980s is characterized by deep contradictions that are difficult to comprehend in a closed interpretation. *Our analysis has shown that, for at least the majority of adolescents, the predominant characteristic of adolescent life is an extended school attendance with institution—specific demands on social and achievement behavior and deep biographical significance for the placement in the social structure of society.* The phase of adolescence is above all and in first place a phase of schooling, and because of the hard battle for a favorable starting position in the placement process, a phase of direct coping with life—relevant tasks and problems (cf. Coleman; in this volume).

Alongside the educational sector, with its demands that are normed in a specific way that essentially refer to the employment sector, there are other sectors of activity that open up their doors to adolescents. In these sectors, adolescents also have to follow institution— and system—specific behavior norms, but with a comparatively higher degree of self—determination. They have a relatively large scope for self—determined behavior in the field of leisure time and consumption, in the use of basic commodities and consumer goods including luxury goods, in the field of direct social relationships with peers of both sexes, and in the field of political and religious activity. Early in their biography, they discover an opportunity structure that provides them with broad opportunities for development and freedom and a collectively favorable position as a group in the nonmaterial privilege structure.

However, it must not be overlooked that this collective, relatively large latitude for development and self—determination is partially only an illusion created by the unwritten norms and behavioral demands applying to the leisure—time and consumption sectors that are, to some extent, controlled by commercial interests. It is also often overlooked how much the opportunity to exploit this freedom is influenced by the social situation arising from the adolescent's particular social class.

Internal changes in the structure of the phase of adolescence

Although the phase of adolescence in modern industrial societies has gone through fundamental change from a historical perspective, the constitutive elements for the definition and delimitation of adolescence as an independent phase of life have not lost their meaning. We can talk about a restructuring, a change in the structure of the phase of adolescence; and when we consider the traditional middle – class conception of adolescence, perhaps even about a dismantling of the classical phase of adolescence; but we cannot talk about its disappearance.

Even if adolescents (have to) meet behavioral demands that are similar or even equal to adulthood in some activity sectors, and this even shapes their actual behavior, it does not mean that the phase of adolescence should no longer be assigned an independent status in the human biography. We have characterized the imbalance between independence and dependence, between self – determination and determination by others that is still predominant today as a constitutive element of the phase of adolescence.

Nevertheless, we have to ask whether the prolonging of school attendance and the deferral of the entrance into work as well as the accompanying biographically early adoption of the leisure – time and consumption sphere have led to such radical changes in the internal structure of the phase of adolescence that we can talk about the severance of a "postadolescent phase". In some respect, the classical phase of adolescence is receiving a social "extension". A new, socially regulated age group is arising between adolescence and adulthood. That is, increasingly more adolescents do not enter into adulthood after their adolescent phase as students, but become independent from a social, moral, intellectual, political, erotic; and sexual, to put it shortly, from a sociocultural perspective; yet they do this without developing the economic independence predicted in the historical model of adolescence (Jugendwerk, 1981, 100 – 101; cf. Gaiser and Müller; Palazzo, in this volume).

Without doubt, the extent to which gainful employment is biographically postponed has led to the development of an internally structured life form of postadolescence that helps to cope with and overcome the contradiction between the personal needs for autonomy that are increasing with age and the economic impediments to the realization of this autonomy. Adolescents discover a life space that, though economically insecure, is socioculturally reliable and offers dependable social commitments and value orientations. It is characterized by early departure from the parental home, flexible commitments in unconventional forms of living arrangements other than the family unit, and provisional cohabitation with a steady partner without the legal formalities of family life (Jugendwerk, 1981, p. 105).

However, from a sociostructural perspective, there is nothing historically new about the lack of autonomy or partial autonomy in some areas of action combined with complete autonomy in others presented here. Such a "status inconsistency" is characteristic and constitutive for the phase of adolescence as a whole and particularly for the final phase of adolescence. It is far more the specific expression that this status inconsistency achieves today that is historically new: In broad strata of adolescence, autonomy in the employment sector is only reached biographically late, yet in contrast to former times, it comes earlier in the political, ethical, intimate, cultural, and consumption—oriented fields of action.

This constellation differs from the structure that was typical two or three generations ago. It is questionable whether this specific manifestation of status inconsistency forms the basis for an autonomous and homogeneous lifestyle at the end of the phase of adolescence that takes a consistent form for all adolescents over the age of 18. The social content and societal definition of the different life constellations of postadolescence is very heterogeneous. We cannot talk about a homogeneous life form of postadolescence. Care should also be taken with an attribution of maturity or "majority". A reliable basis for complete autonomy of action and the development of a self—identity can only be considered as given if self—responsibility is achieved in all personally and socially significant areas of action, and therefore also in the area of employment. Sociocultural majority can therefore only be a partial majority that has to be made complete by economic majority.

Characteristic structural features of the change in the phase of adolescence

There can be no doubt that the adolescent phase is undergoing fundamental structural change in recent decades. However, historical and systematic analysis has produced no certain indications for an imminent disappearance of adolescence as an independent phase of life in the human biography. The process of the historical segregation of the adolescent phase of life is not annulled because adolescents and adults are confronted with the same demands and show the same forms of action and behavior in a few everyday fields of action. Instead, it is necessary to take a differentiated perspective and assume that social institutions and organizations are in a process of segregation that is running parallel to the continuing trend in a process of segregation of life phases. This institutional process of differentiation runs at right angles to the process of increasing segregation of life phases and has its own particular influences on the manifestations of the segregation of life phases. It affects the life conditions of all members of society regardless of age.

The manifestations of adolescent behavior that are the subject of the present debate on adolescence can only be explained if we assume an interaction between these two independent processes.

As with the segregation of life phases, the historical origins of this institutional segregation lie in the preindustrial family unit. During the course of industrialization, the societal functional areas of economics, social control, religion, and education that were originally interlinked and restricted to the family unit, as well as more recent functions such as emotional stabilization, entertainment, and information, have, over a period of time that extends to the present day, been transferred to institutions or organizations that each specialize in one of these tasks. The family retains some essential functions, but it is now only one societal subinstitution among many.

Each of the subinstitutions and suborganizations, such as company, church, law, school, commodity market, and so forth, is constructed according to "system—specific" rules and procedures and sets specific demands that differ from the other systems and can rarely be transfered from one system to another. They form self—contained and separated areas of life with specific action and behavior demands.

This institutional segmentation creates similar or equal life conditions for the members of all phases of life. At the same time, a certain bandwidth of special institutions develops; for adolescents, for example, schools, vocational training centers, universities, and children's homes. These extrafamilial authorities of education and socialization take over essential tasks in supporting the process of individuation and integration. The everyday activity of adolescents is decisively characterized by an adjustment to the specific institutions that are standard for their age group. Each of the institutions imposes demands within the framework of its own system—specific conditions and acts according to the patterns of its own functional structures.

Alongside these institutions of education and socialization, which to some extent also include the peer groups, adolescents, just like adults, are involved in further institutionalized areas of activity. Except for the employment system, there are very few sectors in present—day societies to which they do not have access. Particularly in the political and ethical and in the cultural and consumption—oriented areas of activity and communication (including the mass media), they are frequently as involved as adults in the functional procedures of the respective institutions, organizations, and media. To some extent, this applies for children as well.

We can use this approach to explain the specific profile of the forms of activity and behavior that can be found in adolescents today. Because of the institutional segmentation, adolescents have to find their own path of individual development and social integration in the separated activity sectors of education, consumption, politics, information, partnership, and so forth. In many areas, they succeed in coping with these action demands in a similar or equal way to adults. They encounter broad freedoms of action that present them with many personal possibilities at an early stage in their development. In other areas they are excluded from such scopes for development.

Therefore, at different timepoints and under different situative conditions, adolescents achieve the degree of autonomy and responsibility that is characteristic for the adult status in different behavioral sectors. They have to cope permanently with a double inconsistency of action demands: On the one hand, the inconsistent demands of the different behavioral sectors, each with its own specific structure and form; on the other hand, the demands that result from the degree of inclusion and autonomy that is reached in each of the different sectors. Thus, the transfer to the adult status breaks down into a loosely interconnected sequence of single "status passages" that each follow different social and temporal patterns. There is a tense and even contradictory relationship between the different demands of the status passages. To a large extent, each adolescent has to cope alone with these status transfers.

In the end, each adolescent has to bear alone the burdens and the responsibility of coordinating the divergent action demands with their broad variety of options and the necessary decision steps that accompany them. There is no single societal institution that actively assists in this coordination; the entire network of support that is formed by the interplay of the different institutions and organizations in which the adolescent is embedded is important for adolescents.

A differentiated sociological analysis must accordingly arrive at the conclusion that although the adolescent phase is undergoing fundamental processes of structural change that derive from constellations in society as a whole, it remains an independent phase of life as understood in the original definition. It is and remains typical of the structure of adolescence to have in each case a historically specific constellation of "status inconsistency". The particular extent of this status inconsistency can lead to internal substructurings of the phase of adolescence. Such substructurings must not be interpreted ad hoc as an indication for the disappearance or severance of the phase of adolescence. The postponement of the transfer to the employment system, which can be observed among all adolescents in the last decades, is by itself not enough to create, for example, a homogeneous life situation of postadolescence. It is far more the case that there remains a considerable breadth of variation in the configuration of the phase of adolescence that depends on the specific constellations of living conditions and status inconsistencies, on the social network of support, and on the individual forms of processing reality.

5. Implications for Social Support Strategies in Adolescence

We believe that the findings reported in this paper underscore the value of taking a broad ecological and socialization approach to understanding the normal and/or deviant development and behavior of adolescents (Bronfenbrenner, 1979). One of the key implications of these studies involves the importance of interactions with parents, peers, teachers, and other significant partners for the prevention of adolescent involvement in deviant behavior. The findings reported strongly suggest that the maintenance of frequent, constructive interactions with "significant others", including the parents and other significant adults, is very important not only in childhood but in adolescence as well.

From all reports, it becomes obvious that measures to improve adolescents' personal well—being and self—esteem, and measures for improving the material and ecological living conditions and integration in the social network, are of evident significance for the whole process of successful or unsuccessful socialization (Hurrelmann, Kaufmann and Lösel, 1987; Hurrelmann, 1988).

What does this mean for the most important agencies of socialization that have been mentioned in this paper?

1. Regarding the *family area* we can state: The more stable and dependable the relationships between parents and children before entering the phase of adolescence, the better are the starting positions for the further personality development during the age of adolescence. All policies concerned with families must aim to guarantee a minimum amount of economic security and cultural stimulation within the family, as these provide the basis for later satisfactory relationships between parents and adolescents. The erosion of the family as an educational authority at the stage of adolescence makes this task more and more difficult. Parents find themselves in the precarious situation of forcing their childrens' scholastic and vocational career, pushing them into individual competition, but without being able to assure them that these efforts will lead to an acceptable life perspective.

2. Regarding the *peer group and leisure* domains, the great dilemma is that adolescents have a lot of freedom within the social and financial area but are without a real challenge to and satisfaction of their needs and interests: The mass media offer only a superficial fullfilment and a pretence of adventure and experience to them. There is a lack of "serious" personal challenges that would allow them to try out their personal physical power and psychological and social competences, and thus test their personal possibilities and limitations of behavior. There is hardly any freedom permitting a tentative confrontation or experimentation with "law and order" without the immediate intervention of police or control authorities. Our highly civilized and rationalized society has largely filled and leveled out such opportunities. The only plausible alternative is to reactivate these opportunities "artifically" by creating new activities in sports clubs, scout groups, travel groups, and social work groups, while recognizing the problem that today's adolescents only start using these institutionalized offers in a very hesitant way.

3. A key role is taken by the *occupational sector*. Even in our so–called "leisure–time society" this sector constitutes the main area for defining self and prestige. Our society pushes adolescents into enormous difficulties by not giving them a guarantee of future gainful employment after they have successfully finished school. By doing this, the society destroys an essential, minimal calculability of the future, on which adolescents at their specific life phase are dependent. Taking up an occupation – besides getting married and establishing one's own family – has for a long time been the decisive symbolic step toward adulthood. If this is not guaranteed, our societies take away the adolescents' social basis for "becoming adult".

4. What can the specific role of *schools* be in this endeavor? The school is, as has been shown, strongly affected by the structural changes of the life phase of adolescence. As a necessary consequence of this fact, the position of school in the adolescents' everyday life has to be rethought.

    The school's potential for social support should be strengthened. If school, besides being an institution providing knowledge and intellectual training, also becomes a social platform, an encouraging part of the adolescents' everyday life, then it is available for experiences that are important for the personal development in many dimensions. A "good school" in this sense is a society's unsurpassable contribution to youth policies. The school has to offer working and training opportunities with different learning situations for adolescents that they will find meaningful and important. A good school with a pleasant climate can be a social area with a preventive influence on antisocial behavior and health impairment (Hurrelmann, 1987).

    At school, many hours are spent on social communication among students and between students and teachers. The school's potential for social support has to be carefully analyzed. It is helpful to imagine school as just one social institution among others within the entire social network of adolescents. School as a social institution dominates a large sector of the adolescents' social world and has a formative influence on all main sectors of the life course. For this reason, the school is one of the most important institutions reponsible for the competent and healthy development of adolescents. Like hardly any other institution, because of the fact that adolescents are obliged to attend school for many years, school makes contact with practically all members of an age cohort and therefore is principally an ideal location for supportive measures (Hamilton, 1984).

    We have to be aware that the consequences of the heavy emphasis on school during adolescence are ambiguous: On the one hand, the extension of school time "deprives" adolescents of an important field of social experience. Later entry into employment prevents full material independence. Opportunities for earning money, for self–determination, and for leading a life that is relatively independent of the family of origin are no doubt restricted because of the prevailing state of dependence. In many respects, employment is a prerequisite for the acquisition of independence in other areas, because it offers more than just a material basis in view of its substantial psychological and social implications for adolescents and their social environment. Both publicly and privately, the phase of adolescence is mainly defined and interpreted as a process of transition into working life and the economic system.

    On the other hand, the extension of school time offers access to good educational opportunities and large measures of independence and autonomy in a number of action fields, such as leisure, entertainment, consumption, politics, information, and sexual relations. All of this enables adolescents to choose and try out new and individual paths leading toward optimal growth and social integration. It is the task of schools to offer help to adolescents that will enable them to cope with this situation.

Any form of psychosocial and psychosomatic health impairment and antisocial behavior has to be interpreted as an individual way of coping with life stress in adolescence. Therefore, intervention measures have to take directly into account the psychosocial functions that drug abuse, delinquent behavior, and the building up of psychosomatic symptoms possess for adolescents. It is no use developing highly specialized "intervention technologies". We can only provide support and help that is politically, psychologically, pedagogically, and socially effective, if we consider the whole life situation of adolescence. Building up measures such as advisory services, treatment, and therapy on the single symptoms within the psychosocial and psychosomatic domain is necessary, but we must not spend all our energy on this "curing of symptoms". We have to concentrate on the real starting positions for the appearance of the symptoms, which have complex structural origins. In the face of the many facets of this problem, we need a combination and coordination of the activities provided in family and youth work, schools and youth advisory services, public health departments and hospitals, and welfare offices and employment agencies, combined with the setting up of accessible institutions to which parents and adolescents can turn to for advice in their neighborhood.

References

Allerbeck, K.R., & Hoag, W.J. (1985): Jugend ohne Zukunft. München/Zürich: Piper

Baethge, M., Schomburg, H. & Voskamp, K. (1983): Jugend und Krise. Frankfurt: Campus

Beck, S. (1987): Research issues. In Hasselt, V.B., & Hersen, M. (Eds.): Handbook of adolescent psychology. Elmsford: Pergamon Press, 227—241

Biddle, B., Bank, B.J., & Marlin, M.M. (1980): Parental and peer influence on adolescents. Social Forces, 58, 1057—1079

Blyth, D.A., Hill, J.P., & Thiel, K.S. (1982): Early adolescents' significant others. Journal of Youth and Adolescence, 11, 425—450

Bronfenbrenner, U. (1979): The ecology of human development: Experiments by nature and design. Cambridge: Harvard University Press

Bundesminister für Bildung und Wissenschaft (1987): Grund— und Strukturdaten. Bad Honnef: Bock

Engel, U. (1987): Youth, mobility and social integration. In Hazekamp, O. (Ed.): Youth research in Europe. Amsterdam: Free University Press

Gillis, J.R. (1974): Youth and history: Tradition and change in European age relations 1770—present. New York: Academic Press

Hamilton, S.F. (1984): The secondary school in the ecology of adolescent development. In Gordon, E.W. (Ed.): Review of research in education. New York: American Educational Research Association, 227–258

Hurrelmann, K. (1987): The importance of school in the life course. Journal of Adolescent Research, 2, 111–125

Hurrelmann, K. (1988): Social structure and personality development. New York: Cambridge University Press

Hurrelmann, K., Kaufmann, F.X., & Lösel, F. (Eds.)(1987): Social intervention: Potential and constraints. Berlin/New York: De Gruyter

Hurrelmann, K., Rosewitz, B., & Wolf, H.K. (1985): Lebensphase Jugend. Weinheim/München: Juventa

Inglehart, R. (1977): The silent revolution. Princeton University Press

Jugendwerk der Deutschen Shell (Ed.)(1981): Jugend '81. Lebensentwürfe, Alltagskulturen, Zukunftsbilder. Opladen: Leske

Modell, J., Furstenberg, F.F., & Hershberg, T. (1977): Social change and transitions to adulthood in historical perspective. Journal of Family History, 1, 7–32

Persell, C.H. (1977): Education and inequality. New York: The Free Press

2.
Individualization as Hope and as Disaster: A Socioeconomic Perspective

Martin Baethge
University of Göttingen, Federal Republic of Germany

1. The Dilemma of Youth Research

Rarely has a sociological discipline exposed itself to such ridicule through the development of its subject matter as empirical youth research. Youth studies in the Federal Republic of Germany in the 1960s failed to predict the political movement of university students, schoolchildren, and apprentices (Hornstein, 1982). Keniston's (1968) subtle interpretation of the American student movement, for instance, claiming to have discovered through the theory of postadolescence a new style of behavior stemming from structural social change, has not been very convincingly borne out by subsequent developments. Nor have more recent studies, at least not in the Federal Republic of Germany, fared much better. Whereas in the mid−1970s apathy and withdrawal were diagnosed as a new type of socialization (Ziehe, 1975), not long afterwards large numbers of young people became involved in the peace movement and the campaign against the unceasing destruction of the environment. Although this was again interpreted as· a new ideological radicalism and a new social movement in support of alternative life − styles and work structures, only a short time later it was noted with surprise that young people were adopting an unexpectedly reserved political stance and manifesting marked detachment with respect to alternative life − styles.

This is not meant as an indictment of youth research. But the considerable number of scientific blunders that can be laid at its door should make us more careful about interpreting every new empirical snapshot of youth consciousness and attitudes as the expression of a brand new type of young person or of a basic change in values. The public manifestations of youth behavior change too rapidly, and certain trends in the social consciousness of young people that are given much publicity in public debate prove of only brief duration.

In particular, the dominant tendency in the last decade of sociological debate on youth to perceive a general change in values, purportedly spearheaded by young people, seems of problematical validity and in need of rectification. The most frequently invoked proof of such a value shift, Inglehart's (1977) theory, fails to adduce in the research findings on which it is based any unequivocal grounds in support of such a shift. Even if Inglehart's method is accepted and the questionable use of the "materialistic/postmaterialistic" approach is disregarded, during the period under consideration, the 1970s, the so−called "materialistic" value system was still manifestly predominant, even among young people, in all the Western European countries covered by the research, and the trends discernible during the period are extremely varied and also differ completely from one country to another. There can be no question of a stable trend in the development of values, and there is nothing to indicate either that young people perceive a special role for themselves in securing acceptance for postmaterialistic values. The reanalysis of Inglehart's data by Böltken and Jagodzinski (1982) makes this impressively clear.

Rejection of scientific interpretations such as value shifts as empirically unsound does not imply a contrary belief that nothing has changed in young people's value systems, attitudes, and behavior. I am personally convinced that a great deal has changed, and that the traditional foundations of moral consciousness have lost some of their validity. We do not know, however, to what extent this is the case and in what social groups of young people, or what has taken their place. We are therefore in the dark about a great deal that we need to know in order to make assertions about trends in the structures of consciousness and behaviour. In a quandary such as this it seems sensible, instead of limping along in the wake of a youth phenomenon that is very difficult to catch up with through further empirical research, to try to devise a general theory for the interpretation of modes of behavior among young people. This can only be done, however, by examining the social changes that determine the course followed by youth, that is, the transition to adulthood. It therefore calls for recourse to a theory of the development of socialization.

2. The Disappearance of Class − Specific Socialization Structures and the Incomplete Realization of the Bourgeois Adolescence Model

The thesis I would like to develop and throw open to discussion can be summarized in a few words: We are at present experiencing a further development in the changes that occurred in the structure of socialization in adolescence with the transition to a bourgeois society. The general direction of these changes may be characterized as a *trend toward double individualization.*

In this context, the term refers *first* of all to the sociostructural fact that with the increasing differentiation of living conditions and situations in bourgeois societies, patterns of socialization formerly specific to particular classes or strata are disintegrating and becoming individualized (breaking up into subgroups) (Beck, 1982); there is thus less justification than ever for referring to youth as a social unit.

Secondly, double individualization denotes the content and forms of socialization which, with the increasing independence of the socialization process for that agegroup and its release from direct involvement in the work process, are characterized to an increasing extent by factors conducive to the formation of an individualistic identity and less and less by factors through which a collective identity might be forged: I could designate this transformation as the trend away from productionist (i.e., work – incorpated or work – directed) socialization to consumerist socialization. The end of the process for the time being is not fulfillment of the bourgeois social reformer's dream of emancipation of every member of society and the creation of free, self – confident, and educated bourgeois individuals, but a situation in which the increased emancipatory potential discernible in young people in the form of growing sensitivity to communication structures and to the self – destructive tendencies inherent in society goes hand in hand with a weakening of the ability to organize that sensitivity during youth and beyond; this situation can easily contribute to the ultimate destruction of individuality.

In discussing this thesis, I am referring solely to socialization during adolescence and not during the preceding stages. I agree with Erdheim in viewing it as a "second chance", that is, a stage of development not only determined by socialization in early childhood but also capable of developing its own dynamic impetus in the "individual's participation in the changing structures of society" (Erdheim, 1982, 278). Through detachment from the parents, the individual's relationship to society and adult culture becomes clearer during this stage. I shall confine myself below to the aspects central to this process: relationship to work and to the social community.

Among the definitions of adolescence in sociology and socialization theory that seek to clarify the social and personality – related task of development at that period of life, I still find that Erikson's definition is a satisfactory approach to the theory of individual development in a bourgeois society. His classical definition describes the period as a "psychosocial moratorium", during which young men and women, through free experimentation in role playing, seek a place for themselves in some branch of society, a niche that is sharply defined and yet might be specially made for them. In this way young adults acquire a secure feeling of inner and social continuity, the building of a bridge between what they were as children and what they are in the process of becoming; this bridge likewise connects their own self—image with the image that their group and society has formed of them (Erikson, 1973).

We know that Erikson's definition of the inactive period, a time of closely interrelated formation of the inner and outer identity, is very strongly influenced by the model of bourgeois education and reflects the social conditions underlying it. The inactive period, in the sense of a time of free experimental role playing, depends on release from the obligation to work, a situation historically enjoyed first of all by young people preparing for an academic career through upper—secondary and university studies. They were usually the children of the intellectual middle class or in some cases of the propertied bourgeoisie or self—employed farmers and tradesmen; of groups therefore that were later collectively described as the bourgeois middle class. Their extended educational cycle compared with that of other young people and their typical family background gave them the opportunity to engage in active and open discussion with their parents, to experiment freely with their interests and abilities, and to learn to articulate their desires and fantasies while learning a profession.

Of course, the conditions just described represent the ideal case rather than the general run of early bourgeois education (Horkheimer, 1963), but in terms of the trend, they establish a demarcation line between the latter and the conditions in which the overwhelming majority of youth grew up. Their passage into the adult world was usually a much more coercive process than is suggested by the term "free experimental role playing". It was bound up with family—organized work processes (agriculture) or early employment in a firm or factory and was thus subject to the disciplinary norms of productive work and the obligation to earn money, in the form of an individual wage or a contribution to the family income, irrespective of status as an apprentice or a young worker.

Erikson's definition of adolescence reflects the early forms of consumerist socialization and in historical terms referred invariably to a minority of young people. For two reasons, however, it can still justifiably be used as a guide:

1. Its underlying socialization model has become considerably more widespread in the structure of society during the past century as a result of processes of social change which sociologists usually ascribe to the transition from an industrial to a service society and which lead to an increase in intellectual careers and a strengthening of the middle classes (Bell, 1973). Some of its features have also become generalized through the extension of schooling and training periods.

2. I find that this socialization model, although it has less and less of a claim to factual validity as a correct reconstruction of the process of transition to adulthood, none the less possesses continued or even enhanced normative significance in terms of its objective, the development of ego—identity, in the sense that individual capacity for action and achievement in the bourgeois society still depends largely on this kind of integration of ego—identity, however open and incomplete.

Even if the conditions underlying the Erikson model have become to some extent universal — and bourgeois societies have extended adolescence in the sense of work — detached latitude for development to a historically unique and unprecedented degree in terms of time and social structures — it is doubtful whether even now the process leads to the underlying goal of the socialization model, the self — aware individual. It is my fear that the end product will not be an independent bourgeois individual and still less a class — conscious proletarian as postulated by socialist theory, capable of bringing about the collective transformation of society, but rather an increasingly helpless and isolated creature not quite sure where he/she belongs and unable to help feeling apprehensive about the future. The reason for this presentiment is the particular course being followed by the social extension of adolescence.

The history of the changes that have occurred in adolescence in the last couple of centuries cannot be reconstructed within the space of a single article; a central feature obviously is the continual extension of the period of schooling, that is, the time spent by young people in institutionalized learning processes detached from the world of work and other branches of life. It is precisely during the last few decades that schooling and higher studies have been given even futher impetus.

In the Federal Republic of Germany, for example, the gainfully employed ratio, that is to say the ratio of gainfully employed persons to the total population in a particular age group, dropped by over 30% in the case of the male population under 20 between 1960 and 1980, which means that most of the members of that age group are at school or university or doing their military service (Baethge, Schomburg and Voskamp, 1983). The student ratio among females rose even more steeply. If vocational training either in educational establishments or in enterprises is added to this, it is found that the under — 20 age group now spends the bulk of its time, apart from in the family, in institutionalized learning environments. The extension of schooling entails not only restructuring of the field of youth experience so that work experience plays a diminishing role in the socialization process, but also a weakening of the links between the system and life (Habermas, 1981). It reflects the increasing individualization of careers and social — mobility processes, backed up by welfare — state, antirisk, and precautionary measures (unemployment insurance, health protection, etc.) (Beck, 1982).

In applying the term "individualization" to these processes, it must of course be borne in mind that the individualization in question is essentially formal in the sense of individual enjoyment of rights and institutional facilities. As far as socialization is concerned, Beck's important point cannot be overstressed: In the

mass, welfare — state democracies, individualization occurs within the framework
and as the actual manifestation of a process of takeover by the state that makes
individualization (in the sense of attainment of individual independence)
increasingly impossible (Beck, 1982). Who could acquire an education
nowadays without entering school or enjoy the likelihood of a long life span in
the absence of a health system?

The takeover of care and security structures, including education and training,
by the welfare state cannot easily be reversed, since it is linked with the state's
exercise of control over material production. It leads in the final analysis to a
kind of antithesis between the individual and the system that should ideally be
resolved through utilization of the system's facilities by the individual for his or
her personal welfare and development, but in practice almost invariably
produces increased dependency and immaturity in the individual. (This might be
part of the reason for the ironically vehement refusal of old — age pension
schemes and state social services by recent youth protest movements.) From the
point of view of socialization it leads to the general implantation of a
school — based bureaucratic learning environment and to the successive
disintegration of class — and group — specific learning processes, which may be
reconstituted periodically or in the form of subcultural enclaves in particularly
deprived regions as a hopeless form of protest against an imposed learning
system (Willis, 1977). As a rule, however, the combination of the autonomized
nuclear family and the system predominates (Habermas, 1981).

3.   The Change from Productionist to Consumerist Socialization in Adolescence

The salient characteristic of the above brief outline of the social development of
socialization can be considered, from a negative standpoint, to be the fact that
immediate experience of the world of work has been driven increasingly into
the background. The restructuring of the field of youth experience with the
swing from a predominantly directly work — integrated or at least work — related
life — style to a predominantly education — determined life — style must have an
impact on the development, behavior, and opinions of young people and on
their attitudes to society and to work, which remains society's central
institution.

If these structures of experience are compared in the light of an ideal, the longer release of
young people from the world of work implies the following changes in experience of relevance
to behavior and awareness:

1. Later choice of a particular job or career and hence a mental dissociation of learning and working and a tendency toward inner independence of learning.

2. Later confrontation with the business norms of purposive economic rationality, later subordination to them, and later acquaintance with work insitutions.

3. A lengthening of the "psychosocial moratorium", with a greater tolerance or error and failure on the part of young people than is possible in "serious" business situations.

4. Later assumption of responsibility for one's material livelihood, prolongation of the exclusively material responsibility of the parents, and consequent dependence on them.

5. Later experience of one's own social usefulness through a productive material contribution to social reproduction.

6. A longer time spent in receptive activities and learning processes divorced from practice instead of the former early experience of concrete work associated with incorporation in a hierarchical and abstract organization applying standards of performance and selection and controlling the cognitive and mental development process of young people by means of restrictive rule.

7. A longer time spent with members of the same age group and later entry into a world of communication dominated by adults: hence quite different opportunities for developing ideas of one's own concerning life – style and putting them into practice.

8. Above all, a longer time spent in a situation conducive to the development of an individual rather than a collective code of performance and individual identity formation patterns. Learning is in any case primarily an individual act.

The classification of this change in the structure of young people's experience – as a move from productionist to consumerist socialization patterns – draws attention to the implicit shift in the interaction between human beings and the environment and its impact on personality development. Work and consumption represent different and to some extent conflicting modes of reference to oneself and the environment: Work is outward oriented, toward nature and the environment; while consumption is inward and self – oriented.

The term consumption in this context does not refer primarily to material goods but also to ideal forms of assimilation of what the world has to offer (Erdheim, 1982). Consumerist socialization therefore refers to processes of experience dominated by receptive and reflective acts, especially those of learning. Productionist socialization, by contrast, refers to processes of experience dominated by outward – oriented acts reflected in tangible (visible) results, whose success or failure has implications for others and not just for oneself.

The difference in the location of the two forms of socialization (productionist socialization takes place in the context of family or business work processes and consumerist socialization in schools or other educational establishments) is accompanied by differences in the structure of social experience and a different approach to society and the future: In the first case participation in even the most humble form of work is of concrete (perhaps even blindly concrete!) relevance to others and to the further development of society; in the second case the reference is abstract so that the perspective may be wider in some circumstances but at the same time more open and less binding. The entire development process of industrial societies, given their technical and economic rationale, tends to eliminate the socialization of young people in and through work and replace it by ever more abstract learning processes. The trend also seems to be irreversible, since it is also a feature of the new production technologies that the technical characteristics and operating mechanisms can no longer be perceived and learned in the immediate work process.

The change described above is not to be viewed as an unmitigated loss. Productionist socialization under capitalist modes of production has always been subject to the constraints of wage labor and alienation and has frequently offered little opportunity for independent adjustment to the reality of work. Under these circumstances, one might join Marx in viewing work as the realm of necessity, and leisure and consumption on the other hand as the realm of freedom. Although we now know that Marx's viewpoint was somewhat too simplistic and underestimated the influence of the long arm of capital in the realm of leisure (a fact brought to our notice by works of critical theory, especially those of Adorno and Marcuse), the scope for individual control over time and communication is none the less greater outside gainful employment than in it.

But that is only one side of the coin. The other shows a trend toward a weakening and loss of the faculty for social integration. However great individual access to time and money in the field of consumption, we clearly cannot imagine it being channelled into a sense of social usefulness or a movement toward social responsibility, regardless of whether the consumption is material or ideal. No matter how many joint learning and joint leisure – time activities are planned and staged, they are all in the final analysis acts of compensation for the loss of social intercourse through work and real – life situations, and provide incontrovertible proof of the fact that the process of individualization in the form of isolation is well under way. A sense of dependence is gradually developing; people no longer feel firmly rooted in reality and have therefore lost an important prop for their still unstable ego, and less and less time is spent in compulsory interdependence (at work), a form of relationship that imbued even the alienated existence of the proletariat with a meaning outside itself, drawing attention to society and its necessary changeability. Perhaps the crucial unresolved problem of bourgeois society is how to make up for the increasing loss of collective identity formation in the socialization process and prevent it from leading to potentially fatal disintegration.

4. The Destructuring of Adolescence and the Impending Destruction of Subjectivity

While a change from productionist to consumerist socialization patterns more or less correctly describes the situation of adolescents today, it may also be used to explain both the fact that a typical style of youth behavior is becoming relatively widespread and that work principles and standards of performance carry less weight with young people and have been less fully interiorized than was perhaps still the case in the first postwar generation, which experienced a temporary renaissance of the concept of work as a central social integration mechanism because of the task of reconstruction. Lastly, the change in socialization patterns may also explain the considerable instability of modes and styles of behavior and even of political attitudes.

By virtue of their institutionally determined, highly homogeneous age range and isolation, schools have traditionally been important centers for the emergence of new youth trends. The school provides better opportunities than the work place for communication between persons of the same age, and for using leisure time to pursue particular interests, and should therefore increase the social sensitivity and communicative skills of young people, enhance the stability of forms of behavior once they are learned, and hence also continue to exert an influence after school. The fact that schools are being increasingly colonized from within by the constraints of work and the labor market, which generate fear, mounting competitive pressure, and loss of meaning, must be taken seriously and could bring about a permanent change in the character of school – based socialization.

The extension for more young people of the work – free period with its scope for development, together with a general improvement in family atmosphere due to the alleviation of the immediate problems and constraints of the working day as a result of shorter working hours, a relaxation of family authority structures, and a liberalization of the approach to rearing children, should have facilitated the process of detachment from parents for large numbers of young people through open discussion, and led first and foremost to a strengthening of ego – identity.

What is seen in structural terms as a strengthening of individual identity formation in today's prevailing consumerist socialization model could swiftly turn into the opposite, given the already discernible trends in late bourgeois societies. Indeed, it could very well lead to the final disintegration of the classical bourgeois adolescence model rather than to its general implementation, since the structural contradictions are at present escalating at a menacing rate.

Let us therefore take another look at Erikson's definition of adolescence. It implies a correspondence between internal and external development, establishing a specific link between the point of departure and the destination (childhood and adulthood) by first separating them from each other structurally (free role experimentation). In both respects, the inner detachment of youth

experience from both the adult world and the structure of the final objective
(adult status), the model has now, at least in real terms, become problematic in
two ways, though so many external factors support its validity and general
applicability.

The first circumstance, the insufficiently sharp dividing line between the realms
of experience of children and adults, is related to the fact that the prolongation
of adolescence seems to correspond to a general destructuring of age — related
modes of experience. The deeper the media and consumption patterns penetrate
into the daily experience of children and adolescents, the more they take part as
onlookers in the lives and experiences of adults, an insight largely withheld
from them in the past. This should not, of course, make us jump to the
conclusion that childhood and adolescence are disappearing (Postman, 1982),
but the channeling of adult problems and intimacy in a variety of ways into the
living room and children's rooms, and the very early — indeed premature —
initiation of children and adolescents into the world of fully fledged and
vehemently courted consumers by the market and advertisers, can easily lead to
the usurping of demands and modes of behavior that are not backed up by an
internal development process and independent material resources, and can
therefore actually obstruct the process of communication with the adult world.

Although the market and media threat is a general one, the extent to which it is
coped with depends in large measure on the cognitive and pedagogical
resources of the nuclear family. The intensity of the threat is not neutral in
sociostructural terms, and there is no evidence at present to suggest that the
type described as the middle — class "autonomized nuclear family", which
"directly confronts the imperatives of the economic and administrative system
directed at it from without instead of being insidiously media — processed"
(Habermas, 1982, 568), can be generalized from the standpoint of the resources
available for socialization. Along the same lines as the destructuring of
age — related modes of experience, there is also a growing tendency toward
widespread loss of specificity in styles of behavior at different times of life.
Anything with a glow of youthfulness is assured of success and is usurped —
in the opposite direction this time — by adults. Young people's encounters with
adult culture, which is becoming increasingly incomprehensible and
uncomprehended, are made more difficult, if not impossible, by the double
destructuring of adolescence.

The cultural destructuring of adolescence is one aspect stemming from the
dynamics of expanding market economies. The other aspect derives from their
current crises, to which no end is yet in sight, and relates to the basic social
prerequisite for attaining adult status. This status is still closely linked to the

attainment of a firm position in a profession or other form of employment, which both offers material independence as a necessary precondition for assuming all the other adult roles and facilitates the formation of inner bonds between the individual and society (through the exercise of an occupation). But the underlying stability of the employment outlook has been structurally undermined. Today no less than in the past, almost the entire adolescent development process depends on finding a satisfying job or profession. But the experiences that very many young people are likely to face today in almost every highly industrialized Western society are discouraging enough to make them lose faith in society and, perhaps still worse, in themselves and their ability to shape their own lives as adults.

Many studies have shown that the transition of young people from educational establishments to steady employment became considerably more arduous at all levels of education and employment throughout the world in the 1970s and is associated with increased risk, difficulty, and friction. The unfavorable experiences of more and more young people with different kinds of educational qualifications and from all sectors of the population, but particularly from the socially most disadvantaged groups, take the form of unemployment, inferior employment unrelated to previous training, underemployment, and nonattainment of career aspirations. We are familiar with the external consequence of the persistent labor market crisis: prolongation and instability of the transition to adult status for more and more adolescents and an increase in the number of those who are completely denied the social basis for that status in the form of gainful employment and are therefore marginalized. The internal consequences can only be inferred for the time being and will only become fully visible in the future. They have to be analyzed from two standpoints: the identity—building potential of work and the impact of the crisis on society's agencies of socialization.

As adolescents have their first direct encounter with work as a social institution (of great importance for their future) in the search for an occupation or employment after completion of school or university, it would be hard to exaggerate the impact of any disappointments they suffer in the process on their ability to establish a positive identification with work. Whatever form the disappointment assumes in individual cases, outright unemployment, inferior employment, or employment unrelated to previous training, the adolescents concerned perceive it as a radical calling in question of what they have hitherto achieved through their efforts in school and vocational training courses and hence of an important dimension of meaning in that stage of their life.

It seems highly unlikely that such an experience could leave their attitude to work unscathed. On the contrary, I would consider as a plausible assumption in regard to adolescents in that category that the increasing instability of the transition for adolescents from school to a steady job or occupation is making it more and more difficult for growing numbers of adolescents to experience work and career as a suitable basis for the formation of an identity. They lack the experience to make work and career plans with constructive potential for their future, providing them with a sense of direction and considered significant and worthwhile enough for them to organize their life around them. This problem can actually be exacerbated in cases in which adolescents have learned in school to make certain demands with regard to the content of work.

The trends at present observable provide little hope of any spontaneous alleviation of these problems of psychological and social marginalization, for example, through demographic development, in the near future. On the contrary, we may expect an increase in the number of adolescents affected and a further worsening of social imbalances, also among the dependently employed, not only in terms of earning capacity but also in terms of the opportunities for finding an identity and for finding a meaning in work. It looks as though the new dynamics of rationalization, heavily influenced by microelectronics, not only result in considerable labor — saving effects and redundancies but could also in the long run lead to a restructuring of the remaining work processes, leaving little room for Taylor's dequalifying, soul — destroying forms of work and bringing about a further increase in the complexity of the content of work and an enhancement of its status (Kern and Schumann, 1984; Baethge and Oberbeck, 1985).

If our analysis of the trends of gainful employment is correct, the concept of work may be expected to change in the medium or long term in the key sectors of the economy, with a higher value being placed on aspects of individual performance based on self — assured, technically competent, and thoughtful behavior. It is quite possible that this would bring about a closer correspondence between standards of work performance and aspirations and attitudes acquired in preservice training. It would therefore lead to more individualist work styles in privileged sections of the work force.

In this connection, life might even again be given meaning through and in work, and work could thereby acquire a high degree of social acceptability and approval as a social norm because there would be sufficient time for leisure activities and the enjoyment of life. This by no means remote prospect for highly developed capitalist societies assumes a menacing aspect because, as a new social structure, it could be associated with policies of mass exclusion of marginalized individuals from significant work and participation in society, the first signs of which are already discernible.

The impact of the persistent employment crisis on the education system as the most important socialization agency next to the family leads to the gradual separation of educational processes from employment prospects and hence to a paradox that cannot easily be resolved. On the one hand, possession of a good formal qualification is an increasingly important minimum prerequisite for obtaining employment; on the other hand, the traditional correlation between completion of studies and starting out on a career is increasingly losing its validity, so that the whole study process is highly uncertain. The paradox reflects a new degree of escalation in the disintegration of productionist socialization, since the connecting lines within the education system that are supposed to link up study content and spheres of employment are being cut, and the references to work still contained in curricula are loose ends leading nowhere. It is more or less a matter of chance whether a person can use the material learned in school or at a higher level (even through incompany training courses) in a subsequent job.

For more and more young people — and potentially for everyone, because it all depends on the luck of the draw — the social institutions of education and training are losing their primary significance as the key to vocational and social independence. As far as employment and a career are concerned, it has become increasingly difficult to redeem the institutionalized promise of later rewards, which provide a stronger incentive for attending school and conforming to its rules than the compulsory schooling legislation. As a result of the deep – seated economic crisis and the collapse of the traditional correspondence between educational qualifications and career openings, schools and higher education establishments are finding it increasingly difficult to demonstrate that they have a meaning and purpose outside of themselves. In order to fulfil their socializing mission instead of degenerating into detention centres, educational facilities must look for meaning within themselves, in their internal process, and/or in fields unrelated to work. Whether this can be done on an adequate scale is doubtful. Disciplinary problems in many schools and university dropout rates, allowed for in advance by administrations, would seem to indicate that it cannot.

It is an irony verging on absurdity of the logic inherent in the prevailing system that, aside from the resignation of those who are left behind in the race for education, the principal way of escape from this paradoxical situation for adolescents and their parents lies in an intensification of study efforts leading to an enhancement of the prospects for individualistic action. The values of community and cooperation are thus played down, even within the school. The fact that among those who choose this option, the best prospects of individual success lie with young people whose social background offers them the material, cognitive, and emotional support to contend with the (educational) transition to adulthood, which is now a lengthy and unstable process fraught with setbacks and failures, indicates the return to a regressive form of social selection.

The shortcomings of the system of late bourgeois socialization in adolescence cannot be remedied by this form of escape, and the inherent threat they pose to it as a whole cannot be evaded by resorting to tricks, because the option described above, instead of forming an individual in the likeness of Humboldt's humanist, tends to produce a careerist who has learned self – assertion early in life and has lost all sense of cooperation.

The picture drawn above is not exactly optimistic. One may ask in conclusion, therefore, whether this gloomy vision of destruction of subjectivity and sociality must inevitably come to pass or whether the productive potential of more extensive consumerist socialization in adolescence, stemming from an enhanced capacity for intellectual innovation and heightened communicatory sensitivity, can be converted into creative power conducive to the preservation and transformation of society, in other words whether the "second chance" can be used.

Under present circumstances, only an abstract reply can be given in the form of an indication of trends. The transformation of progressive potential is not primarily a project based on new educational and training strategies. Whatever means are adopted to increase the practical relevance of schools and higher education establishments, a return to the productionist socialization model seems out of the question. An ideological change of program involving a revival of religiousness and old values has little prospect of success either (Bell, 1976). Work still constitutes the nucleus of any conceivable transformation. It must be corrected and devalued in terms of its capacity for determining the social structure. This means first of all that the increasing exclusiveness of career and employment openings must be abolished through a redistribution of work embracing every member of society. It means, secondly, that participation in society's wealth, culture, and social and political communication should no longer depend on a person's position in the system of socially organized work. As long as work preserves its capacity for determining the social structure, there is no hope of breaking its actual power to set standards for socialization and utilizing the potential of the new fields of socialization: learning, play, and communication.

Note

An elaborated version of this paper has appeared in International Social Science Journal, 37, 1985, 441–453

References

Baethge, M., Schomburg, H., & Voskamp, U. (1983): Jugend und Krise – Krise aktueller Jugendforschung. Frankfurt: Campus
Baethge, M., & Oberbeck, H. (1985): Zukunft der Angestellten. Frankfurt: Campus
Beck, U. (1982): Jenseits von Stand und Klasse? In Kreckel, R. (Ed.): Soziale Ungleichheiten. Soziale Welt, Special Vol. 2. Göttingen

Bell, D. (1973): The coming of post—industrial society. A venture in social forecasting. New York: Basic Books

Bell, D. (1976): Cultural contradictions of capitalism. New York: Basic Books

Böltken, F., & Jagodzinski, W. (1982): Insecure value—orientations in an environment of insecurity: Post—materialism in the European community, 1970—1980. Unpublished manuscript, Universität Köln

Erdheim, M. (1982): Die gesellschaftliche Produktion von Unbewußtheit. Frankfurt: Suhrkamp

Erikson, E.H. (1973): Identität und Lebenszyklus. Frankfurt: Suhrkamp

Habermas, J. (1981): Theorie des kommunikativen Handelns, Vol.2. Frankfurt: Suhrkamp

Horkheimer, M. (1936): Studien über Autorität und Familie. Paris

Hornstein, W. (1982): Jugendprobleme, Jugendforschung und politisches Handeln. Aus Politik und Zeitgeschichte, 12, 223—229

Inglehart, R. (1977): The silent revolution. Changing values and political styles among Western publics. Princeton

Keniston, D. (1968): Young radicals. New York: Academic Press

Kern, H., & Schumann, M. (1984): Ende der Arbeitsteilung? München: Beck

Postman, N. (1982): The disappearance of childhood. New York: Delacorte Press

Willis, P. (1977): Learning to labour. How working—class kids get working—class jobs. London: Saxon House

Ziehe, T. (1975): Pubertät und Narzissmus. Frankfurt: EVA

3.
The Focal Theory of Adolescence:
A Psychological Perspective

John C. Coleman
The Trust for the Study of Adolescence, Brighton, Great Britain

A consideration of the current literature in the adolescent field indicates sporadic attempts by a variety of authors to propose a model of adolescent development (e.g., Coffield et al., 1986; Violato and Holden, 1988). Unfortunately, however, such models lack a firm theoretical base. Where theory is concerned, social scientists are still drawing on what I have called (Coleman, 1978) the "classical" approaches; that is, those derived from psychoanalysis or sociology, or are anchoring their work in lifespan development theory. In this paper I wish to consider briefly the current status of the "classical" theories, and to review the contribution of the lifespan developmental approach. I shall propose my own model of adolescent development – the focal model – and I shall conclude by linking this model to certain key features of the lifespan approach.

1.   The Classical Theories

While the psychoanalytic view of adolescence and that of the sociologists differ in many respects, they are united in the view that adolescence is a stressful period in human development. According to the psychoanalytic position, the reason for this is to be found in the upsurge of instinctual forces which occurs as a result of puberty. These forces are said to cause a disturbance in the psychic balance, which is believed to lead in turn to regression, ambivalence, and nonconformity. In addition some form of identity crisis is to be expected among older adolescents. As far as the sociologists are concerned, there are a number of factors related to the young person's position in society that may be assumed to result in stress of one sort or another. In the first place, adolescence is a period of both role transition and role conflict. Also, increasing age segregation means less opportunity for young people to be in contact with adult models, making the transition to maturity and the assumption of adult roles more problematic. Furthermore it is argued that teenagers are exposed to a variety of conflicting agents of socialization, with educational institutions, the peer group, the mass media, and political institutions all pulling in different directions. Finally teenagers are often seen as reflecting divisions within society itself. Their position is that of the "marginal man" — being a member of various groups, but belonging to none. Thus they may be said to have an affinity with both conservative and radical forces, owing allegiance to both, but in reality, occupying the battle zone between the two.

Broadly speaking, research provides little support for these traditional theories and fails to substantiate much of what both psychoanalysts and sociologists appear to believe. To take some examples, while there is certainly some change in the self—concept, there is no evidence to show that any but a small minority experience a serious identity crisis (Seiffge—Krenke, 1988). In most cases, relationships with parents are positive and constructive, and young people, by and large, do not reject adult values in favor of those espoused by the peer group (Youniss and Smollar, 1985). In fact, in most situations peer group values appear to be consistent with those of important adults rather than in conflict with them (Coleman, 1980). Fears of promiscuity among the young are not borne out by the research findings (Kendell and Coleman, 1988), nor do studies support the belief that the peer group encourages antisocial behavior, unless other factors are also present (Petersen, 1988). Lastly there is no evidence to suggest that during the adolescent years there is a higher level of psychopathology than at other times (Van Hasselt and Hersen, 1987). While a lot still needs to be learned about the mental health of young people, almost all the results that have become available so far indicate that, although a small minority may show disturbance, the great majority of teenagers seem to cope well and to show no undue signs of turmoil or stress.

Support for this belief may be found in every major study of adolescence that has appeared in recent years (e.g., Kandel and Lesser, 1972; Bandura, 1972; Rutter et al., 1976; Youniss and Smollar, 1985). Most would now agree with the views of Siddique and D'Arcy (1984) who, in summarizing their own results on stress and well—being in adolescence, write as follows:

"In this study some 33.5% of the adolescents surveyed reported *no* symptoms of psychological distress and another 39% reported five or fewer symptoms (a mild level of distress). On the other hand a significant 27.5% reported higher levels of psychological distress. For the majority the adolescent transition may be relatively smooth, however, for a minority it does indeed appear to be a period of stress and turmoil ... . The large majority of adolescents appear to get on well with adults and are able to cope effectively with demands of school and peer groups. They use their resources to make adjustments with environmental stressors with hardly visible signs of psychological distress" (Siddique and D'Arcy, 1984, 471).

There would appear to be a sharp divergence of opinion, therefore, between the "classical" and "empirical" points of view (Coleman, 1978, 1979). Beliefs about adolescence that stem from traditional theory (the "classical" view) do not in general accord with the results of research (the "empirical" view). We need now to consider some of the reasons for this state of affairs. Firstly, as many writers have pointed out, psychoanalysts and psychiatrists see a selected population. Their experience of adolescence is based primarily upon the individuals they meet in clinics or hospitals. Such experience is bound to encourage a somewhat one-sided perspective in which turmoil or disturbance is overrepresented. For sociologists, on the other hand, the problem is often to disentangle concepts of "youth" or "the youth movement" from notions about young people themselves. As a number of commentators have observed, youth is frequently seen by sociologists as being in the forefront of social change. Youth is, as it were, the advance party where innovation or alteration in the values of society are concerned. From this position it is but a short step to use youth as a metaphor for social change, and thus to confuse radical forces in society with the beliefs of ordinary young people (Brake, 1985).

A third possible reason for the divergence of viewpoint is that certain adolescent behaviors, such as vandalism, drug-taking, and hooliganism, are extremely threatening to adults. The few who are involved in such activities therefore attain undue prominence in the public eye. The mass media play an important part in this process by publicizing sensational behavior, thus making it appear very much more common that it is in reality. One only has to consider critically the image of the teenager portrayed week after week on the television to understand how, for many adults, the minority come to be representative of all young people. All three tendencies mentioned so far lead to an exaggerated view of the amount of turmoil that may be expected during adolescence, and thus serve to widen the gap between research and theory.

One other factor needs to be considered in this context. In general, psychologists responsible for large-scale surveys have tended to neglect the possibility that individual adolescents may be either unwilling or unable to reveal their innermost feelings. Much depends on the way the study is carried out, but it is important to remember how very difficult it is for anyone, let alone a shy, resentful, or anxious teenager, to share fears, worries, or conflicts with a strange interviewer. Inhibition of this sort may well result in a bias on the part of those writing from the empirical point of view, and cause an underestimation of the degree of stress experienced by young people. Problems of method, therefore, may also be playing their part in widening the gap between theory and research, not by exaggerating the amount of inner turmoil, but by doing just the opposite, namely, causing research workers to miss the more subtle indications of emotional tension. The divergence of opinion referred to earlier can thus be seen to be the result of a number of factors. Both methods and theories have their weaknesses, and the fault cannot be said to lie exclusively with one side or the other.

It has to be admitted that this divergence of opinion has received relatively little attention in the literature over the last decade or so. By and large those involved in the study of adolescence have not, in recent years, given especial prominence to theoretical issues. This may be partly because it has come to seem a sterile debate — most now accept a formulation broadly in line with that of Siddique and D'Arcy (1984), namely that while a minority experience difficulty during the adolescent transition, the majority cope well and do not exhibit signs to indicate that they are grappling with "storm and stress". Research attention has undoubtedly come to focus primarily on specific topics — according to Van Hasselt and Hersen (1987), subjects of the greatest concern during the 1980's include the peer group and social competence, communication within the family, step — parents and single parents, puberty, and problem adolescents.

2.   The Lifespan Approach

Where theory is utilized as a framework for empirical investigation, it is quite clear that the lifespan developmental approach is considered to be the most useful. Anne Petersen, in her 1988 article for the Annual Review of Psychology, illustrates this trend:

"Recent adolescent — family research is very much in the tradition of contextually based life — span psychology, examining the reciprocal effects of the family on the developing individual, and of the developing individual on family processes" (Petersen, 1988, 25 — 26).

Another example of the same phenomenon may be found in Simmons and Blyth's "Moving into Adolescence" (1987). Here the authors study the impact of pubertal change and school context on a range of outcome variables including self — esteem, academic performance, and involvement in extra — curricular activities. This important study is conceptualized within the life — span approach, demonstrating the advantages of such an approach — it stresses the context of human development; it emphasizes the fact that growth and change come about only as a result of a reciprocal interplay of forces and pressures; and, last but not least, it underlines the necessity for a multidisciplinary approach to development.

Of course the life — span approach also has its limitations. While it may represent a series of important principles, these principles are applicable to human development in general, rather than to adolescence in particular. Such a theoretical stance has no explanation for the adolescent process, nor does it contribute in any way to the debate concerning "storm and stress". Assuming that a majority of young people manage well, while a minority struggle through the teenage years, the lifespan developmental model may indicate the criteria by which we should judge acceptable research on the subject, but it has no explanatory power to help us understand why some cope while others do not, and what is likely to distinguish between the two groups. Finally, and perhaps most significantly, it cannot help us answer the question: "In what way, if any, is adolescence fundamentally different from other stages in the life cycle?"

Let us return for a moment to the two traditional theories originating from psychoanalysis and sociology. Obviously these two theories have some value, and it would be wrong to leave the impression that neither are any longer relevant. Perhaps the most important contribution made by these theories is that they have provided the foundation for an understanding of young people with serious problems and a greater knowledge of those who belong to minority or deviant groups. In this respect the two major theories have much to offer. However, it must be recognized that today they are inadequate as a basis for an understanding of the development of the great majority of young people. The fact is that adolescence needs a theory, not of abnormality, but of normality. Any viable theoretical viewpoint put forward today must not only incorporate the results of empirical studies, but must also acknowledge the fact that, although for some young people adolescence may be a difficult time, for the majority it is a period of relative stability. Nonetheless, there is general agreement that during the teenage years major adaptation has to occur. The transition between childhood and adulthood cannot be achieved without substantial adjustments of both a psychological and social nature; and yet most young people appear to cope without undue stress. How do they do so?

3. The Focal Model

It is this contradiction between the amount of overall change experienced and the relative health and resilience of the individuals involved in such change that now requires some consideration. In earlier papers (Coleman, 1974, 1978,

1979, 1980a) a "focal" model of adolescence has been outlined, in the hope that this will go some way toward resolving such a contradiction. Before this is explained, however, it will be necessary to sketch the background to this model. The model grew out of the results of a study of normal adolescent development (Coleman, 1974). Briefly, large groups of boys and girls at the ages of 11, 13, 15, and 17 were given a set of identical tests that elicited attitudes and opinions from them about a wide range of relationships. Thus material was included on self—image, being alone, heterosexual relationships, parental relationships, friendships, and large group situations. The material was analyzed in terms of the constructive and negative elements present in these relationship situations, and in terms of the common themes expressed by the young people involved in the study. Findings showed that attitudes to all relationships changed as a function of age, but, more importantly, the results also indicated that concerns about different issues reached a peak at different stages in the adolescent process. This finding is illustrated for boys in *Figure 1* in which it can be seen that, simply by considering three of the most important themes, there are peak ages for the expression of each of these various concerns. Similar results were obtained for girls.

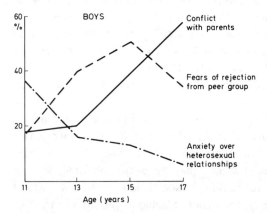

Fig. 1: Peak ages for the expression of different themes. From Coleman (1974)

It was this finding that led to the formulation of a focal model. The model suggests that at different ages particular sorts of relationship patterns come into focus, in the sense of being most prominent, but that no pattern is specific to one age only. Thus the patterns overlap; different issues come into focus at different times, but the simple fact that an issue is not the most prominent feature of an age does not mean that it may not be critical for some individuals. These ideas in association with empirical findings such as those illustrated in *Figure 1*, combine to suggest a symbolic model of adolescent development in which each curve represents a different issue or relationship. This is portrayed in *Figure 2*.

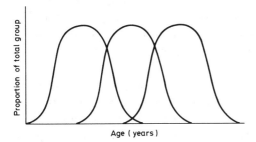

Fig. 2: Focal theory. Each curve represents a different issue or relationship. From Coleman (1974).

In many ways, such a notion is not dissimilar from any traditional stage theory. However, it carries with it a very much more flexible view of development, and therefore differs from stage theory in three important respects. In the first place, the resolution of one issue is not seen as the *sine qua non* for tackling the next. In fact it is clearly envisaged that a minority of individuals will find themselves facing more than one issue at the same time. Secondly, the model does not assume the existence of fixed boundaries between stages and, therefore, issues are not necessarily linked to a particular age or developmental level. Finally, there is nothing immutable about the sequence involved. In our culture it appears that individuals are more likely to face certain issues in the early stages of adolescence and different issues at other stages, but the "focal" theory is not dependent on a fixed sequence, and it would be of very great interest to examine other cultures in the light of this theory of development.

It is my belief that the "focal" model of adolescent development may provide a clue to the resolution of the apparent contradiction between the amount of adjustment required during adolescence on the one hand, and the relatively successful adaptation among the general population on the other. If adolescents have to adjust to so much potentially stressful change, and at the same time pass through this stage of their life with relative stability, as the "empirical" view indicates, how do they do it? The answer suggested by the "focal" model is that they cope by dealing with one issue at a time. They spread the process of adaptation over a span of years, attempting to resolve first one issue, and then the next. Different problems, different relationship issues come into focus and are tackled at different stages, so that the stresses resulting from the need to adapt to new modes of behavior are rarely concentrated all at one time. It follows from this that it is precisely in those who, for whatever reason, do

have more than one issue to cope with at a time that problems are most likely
to occur. Thus, as an example, when puberty and the growth spurt occur at the
normal time, individuals are able to adjust to these changes before other
pressures, such as those from parents and teachers, are brought to bear. For
the late maturers, however, pressures are more likely to occur simultaneously,
inevitably requiring adjustments over a much wider area.

The "focal" model is only one of a number of possible ways of conceptualizing
adolescent development, but it has two particular advantages. Firstly, it is based
directly on empirical evidence, and secondly, it goes at least some way toward
reconciling the apparent contradiction between the amount of adaptation required
during the transitional process and the ability of most young people to cope
successfully with the pressures inherent in this process. Such a model evidently
needs further testing, but since it was first proposed it has come to appear, to
some writers at least, as an important contribution to the understanding of
adolescence (see for example Siddique and D'Arcy, 1984; Meadows, 1986). In
addition, two studies have appeared in the literature providing substantial
support. In the first, Kroger (1984) replicated Coleman's (1974) research on
large samples of US and New Zealand teenagers. The results are quite striking.
They show almost identical patterns of development in the three countries, and
indicate that, in spite of the obvious cultural differences, the same proportions
of adolescents appear to face the same interpersonal issues in much the same
way in each of the three national settings.

The results of Simmons and Blyth (1987) are equally interesting in this respect.
Simmons and Blyth tested the proposition, contained within the focal model,
that those who adjust less well during adolescence are likely to be those who
have to face more than one interpersonal issue at a time. The authors
documented the life changes occuring for the young people in their study, and
related the number of life changes to outcome measures such as self—esteem
and academic performance. Results are illustrated in *Figures 3 and 4*. This is
how Simmons and Blyth describe the results:

"While the timing and level of discontinuity of each individual change is important for the
adjustment of adolescents, also relevant is the cumulation of life changes at one point in time.
Coleman (1974) has advanced the focal theory of change relative to this issue; he has posited
that at entry to adolescence, it is easier to deal with life changes one at a time rather than with
all transitions simultaneously. It is easier if one can focus on one major transition before
tackling the next. For example, it is easier to cope sequentially rather than simultaneously with
environmental changes, physiological differences, the new definition of self as an adolescent,
and the alteration in others' expectations. Findings from this study support the focal theory.
Among both boys and girls, those who experience a greater number of major life changes in
early adolescence are at greater risk in terms of our key outcome variables. ... In sum, in early
adolescence, social—psychological outcomes are affected in interesting ways by the nature of

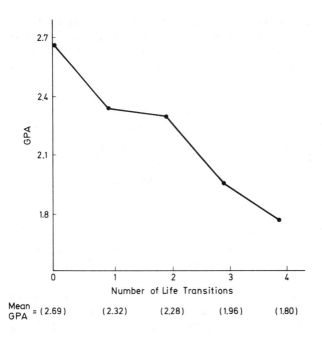

Fig. 3: Grade point average by number of life transitions
for 7th–grade boys (from Simmons and Blyth, 1987)

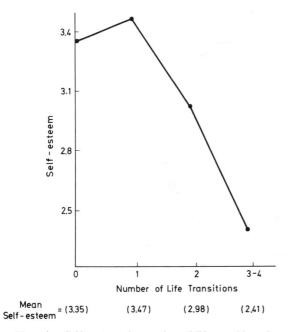

Fig. 4: Self–esteem by number of life transitions for
7th–grade girls (from Simmons and Blyth, 1987)

the changes themselves. There is evidence of detrimental effects if change occurs at too young an age, if it causes the individual to be extremely off—time in development, if the transition place the person in the lowest ranking cohort in the environment, if change is marked by sharp discontinuity, and if many significant changes cumulate and occur close together in time" (Simmons and Blyth, 1987, 350—351).

One other source of support for the focal model comes from an ongoing study of leisure and lifestyles in a sample of 12,000 Scottish adolescents (Hendry, Shucksmith and McGrae 1985). Here it is argued that the model is applicable to social aspects of young people's lives and can be useful in understanding patterns both of leisure and of unemployment. Findings will be reported in due course.

It has to be admitted that the focal model has had its critics too. Coffield, Borrill and Marshall (1986), for example, take exception to the fact that the model makes no attempt to deal with disadvantage and deprivation.

"John C. Coleman's 'The Nature of Adolescence' ends by presenting a new focal theory which shows how far academic psychology is at times removed from the real world of young adults. The theory suggests that adolescents cope with one issue or relationship at a time as they grow

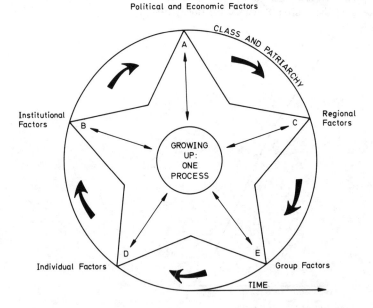

Fig. 5:   An integrating model of adolescence (from Coffield, Borril and Marshall, 1986)

up; it also contains the reasonable deduction that problems are most likely to occur when young people have more than one issue to deal with at the same time. But why is this thought to be particularly true of adolescents? Could not the same be said of younger children, middle — aged parents or old — aged pensioners? Not even the subsequent modifications and improvements of Leo Hendry (1983) can save the theory from the charge of triviality" (Coffield, Borrill and Marshal, 1986, 211).

Coffield et al. present a different model, derived from their experience of carrying out research in the North — East of England with young people, many of whom were unemployed, all of whom were living at the very periphery of British society (*Figure 5*). In their model, class and patriarchy are seen as all — pervading influences that determine to a large extent the options and choices available to young people in this underprivileged section of society. As they write:

"Class and patriarchy are means whereby some gain advantages over others; they are best thought of as relationships between people which accord power, wealth and status to some and deny it to others. Our argument is that *all* of the main factors in our model tend to interact vigorously, creating different patterns of problems and opportunities for individuals. ... In contrast to Coleman, who argues that young adults cope with one issue at a time, we would claim that most of them are struggling to cope with all these different aspects of life, which impinge upon them simultaneously" (Coffield, Borril and Marshal, 1986, 213—214).

Coffield and his colleagues have misunderstood, to some extent, what the focal model is all about. The focal model is to do with the psychological transitions of adolescence, rather than with the economic circumstances of the individual. For example, all young people, irrespective of social background, must negotiate increasing independence from their parents. The focal model suggests that it will be easier to handle the parent issue if the young person is not, at the same time, striving for greater autonomy within the peer group. Nonetheless, Coffield is right to draw attention to the social circumstances of the individual, for these will obviously contribute in a substantial way to the adolescent's psychological adjustment. There can be little doubt that in situations of economic hardship it will be more difficult to manage the adolescent transitions in a satisfactory manner. This point has already been made by Hendry (1983) in his argument that ecological factors are as important as psychological ones in understanding the young person's development. Circumstances, many of them unpleasant, will be imposed on the individual, making it less likely that he or she will feel in control of events. This will in turn complicate relationships with friends and family, presenting the young person with a range of additional stress factors on top of all the normal burdens inherent in adolescent development. At present we know far too little about the way in which the psychological development of the adolescent interacts with environmental circumstances, and perhaps we should be considering both

Coffield's model and the focal model side by side, rather than seeing them as alternative representations of the adolescent process.

A further criticism of the focal model is that it is nothing more or less than the theory of life events (Dohrenwend and Dohrenwend, 1974) applied to adolescence. At one level this is correct. The focal model does imply that the more "issues" the young person has to cope with, the more indications of stress there are likely to be. The research of Simmons and Blyth (1987) provides excellent validation of this view. However, the focal model goes further – for it is in one highly significant respect quite different from life–events theory. While life–events theory implies simply that the more events that occur in the individual's life, the more stress there will be, the focal model suggests that the young person is an *agent* in his or her own development, managing the adolescent transition – where possible – by dealing with one issue at a time.

An important paper by Lerner (1984) entitled "Adolescent maturational change and psychosocial development: A dynamic interactional perspective" is central to this argument. Here Lerner considers three ways in which the adolescent interacts with the environment and thereby affects his or her own development. Lerner draws attention to the adolescent as *stimulus* eliciting different reactions from the environment; as *processor*, making sense of the behavior of others; and as *agent, shaper, and selector*, doing things, making choices, and influencing events. Thus Lerner argues that the adolescent is active in shaping his or her own maturation, and I see this concept as being central to the focal model. Not only does the model imply that the young person copes best when facing one issue at a time, the model implies that in most circumstances the young person may actually be determining his or her own rate of development.

Such an idea seems at first to be rather farfetched. Yet a moment's thought will indicate that the concept is not so extraordinary after all. Consider for a moment the range of choices available to an individual in his or her current relationships. In any one day a teenager may choose whether or not to confront a parent over the breakfast table, to argue with a sibling, to accept the suggestion of a best friend, to stand up to an authoritarian teacher, to conform to peer group pressure, to resist the persuasion of a boyfriend or girlfriend, and so forth. Every one of these situations offers the young person a choice, and all may well have a bearing on the interpersonal issues with which the focal model is concerned. The argument is that most young people pace themselves through the adolescent transition. Most of them hold back on one issue while they are grappling with another. Most sense what they can and cannot cope with, and will, in the real sense of the term, be an active agent in their own development.

I see this concept as providing one of the most exciting challenges for adolescent psychology. It is this notion that forms the bridge between lifespan developmental psychology and the concerns of those who wish to carry forward the understanding of adolescence. The idea also links significantly with the interest currently being shown by social psychologists and personality theorists into self — efficacy and locus of control — topics currently of considerable importance in social psychology. Increased knowledge of this process of active agency could provide essential information to help answer the two key questions: What distinguishes the majority who cope from the minority who experience manifest stress during the teenage years? And: What is it about adolescence that makes it different from other stages in the life cycle?

In my view, the answers to such questions are almost certainly to do with the nature of the transition and the way it is managed. Yet the focal model and the concept of agency provide — at this stage at least — only signposts in the right direction. We need to address ourselves to a variety of issues. Which young people are able to act in this way, and which are not? What are the circumstances that encourage active agent behavior? How does economic hardship, or other environmental trauma, affect the young person's capability in this area? Yet if we can make progress in understanding the way in which young people shape their own development, we will surely be taking one of the most significant steps possible toward clarifying the nature of adolescence.

References

Brake, M. (1985): Comparative youth culture. London: Routledge and Kegan Paul

Coffield, F., Borrill, C., & Marshall, S. (1986): Growing up at the Margins. Milton Keynes: Open University Press

Coleman, J.C. (1974): Relationships in adolescence. London: Routledge and Kegan Paul

Coleman, J.C. (1978): Current contradictions in adolescent theory. Journal of Youth and Adolescence, 7, 1—11

Coleman, J.C. (Ed.)(1979): The school years. London: Methuen

Coleman, J.C. (1980a): Friendship and the peer group in adolescence. In Adelson, J. (Ed.): Handbook of adolescent psychology. New York: Wiley

Coleman, J.C. (1980b): The nature of adolescence. London: Methuen

Dohrenwend, B.S., & Dohrenwend, B.P. (Eds.)(1974): Stressful life events: Their nature and effects. New York: Wiley

Hendry, L.B. (1983): Growing up and going out: Adolescents and leisure. Aberdeen: University Press

Hendry, L.B., Shucksmith, J., & McCrae, J. (1985): Young people's leisure and lifestyle in modern Scotland. Unpublished article on ongoing research project. Dept. of Education, University of Aberdeen and Scottish Sports Council

Kendell, K., & Coleman, J.C. (1988): Sexual behavior in young people: The challenge for adults. Children and Society. (In Press)

Lerner, H. (1985): Adolescent maturational changes and psycho—social development: A dynamic interactional perspective. Journal of Youth and Adolescence, 14, 355—372

Meadows, S. (1986): Understanding child development. London: Hutchinson

Petersen, A.C. (1988): Adolescent development. Annual Review of Psychology, 39, 583—607

Seiffge—Krenke, I. (1988): Developmental processes in self—concept and coping behavior. In Jackson, S., & Bosma, H. : Self—concept and coping in adolescence. New York: Springer

Siddique, C.M., & D'Arcy, C. (1984): Adolescence, stress and psychological well—being. Journal of Youth and Adolescence, 13, 459—474

Simmons, R., & Blyth, D.A. (1987): Moving into adolescence. New York: Aldine de Gruyter

Van Hasselt, V.B., & Hersen, M. (1987): Handbook of adolescent psychology. Oxford: Pergamon Press

Violato, C., & Holden, W. (1988): A confirmatory factor analysis of a four—factor model of adolescent concerns. Journal of Youth and Adolescence, 17, 101—114

Youniss, J., & Smollar, J. (1985): Adolescent relations with mothers, fathers, and friends. Chicago: University of Chicago Press

4.
The Lifeworld of Young People:
A Systems – Theoretical Perspective

Donato Palazzo
Institute of Youth Research, Lecce, Italy

1.   The Concept of Lifeworld

Contemporary sociologists tend to establish a distinction or at times an opposition between the concepts "lifeworld", and "social system". Lifeworld means as much as all personal relationships which precede as well as accompany the reproduction of human life and, in turn, also by means of symbolic forms of communication, a bundle of relationships, that is, familiarity, friendship, or daily interactions based on thorough and mutual comprehension of how to act and how to communicate with one another (Ardigo, 1980).

This definition seems to be so general that it agrees with all the other specifications made of the concept of lifeworld in contemporary literature, from Alfred Schütz to Peter L. Berger, and from Thomas Luckmann to Jürgen Habermas. This concept is opposed by the concept "social system", which is agreed upon as a mixture of relation levels equipped with different priorities. This definition of "social system" is widely approved of and even used by the critics of systems theory. It does not only consider the inner meaning of the system, which is part of this theory, but at the same time agrees with social reality in general. I would like to point out that the theory of systems, particularly as Niklas Luhmann (1984) presents it, allows me to describe my subject of analysis sufficiently as well as to understand it; therefore it is suitable for the complexity of my subject, the lifeworld of young people.

Concerning young people, the concept lifeworld is not something given to them through experience, and it cannot be seen as a social matter of course; it is also not possible to foresee it and reveal it in advance. A generation differentiates itself by its past and its future, and thus constitutes its own way of life. That means, nevertheless, that one generation receives the lifeworld of its predecessors.

Another aspect of the paradox of lifeworlds consists of the difference between the way young people make their own experiences and the way adults deal with these experiences. The experiences of young people are immediately connected with institutions that direct and influence the possibilities of actions young people have. And yet, it is characteristic for young people that they create new possibilities that differ from those they already possess. Adults have less time available than young people, and they rarely make use of the opportunity to create new possibilities that are influenced by their past experience.

2.   Adolescents' Lifeworld: Complexities and Contradictions

Let us try to find a conceptual instrument that enables us to see reality as it appears to young people. Observation and experience help us to describe the various forms that the actions of adult people take. In general, one assumes that certain points of reference belong to specific social roles. Actions gain their value by revealing some of their qualities. In the ideal case, qualities like correctness, rationality, coherency in thinking, the ability of reflection, and careful consideration obviously characterize the ideal adult. The possibilities are limited to the rules and obligations within which the qualities of actions can express themselves. In social interactions these limits are set by guidelines for every action that are supplied within various social systems: politics, ethics, religion, law, love, and so forth.

These guidelines set standards for behavior that enable young people to evaluate concrete actions. Full correspondence with the standard determines the degree of socially conformist behavior. But the behavior of young people does not consist of the negation of characteristics in the behavior of adults; according to them, one is considered young if one shows a behavior opposite to that of adults, if ideal characteristics of adult behavior are not well balanced, or if a behavior gradually transforms itself up to a point at which it reaches the level of the ideal behavior of an adult.

The form of actions one can define on the basis of subjective intentionality, an action to which sense and meaning is given by its guidelines, does not exist in the behavior of young people. The actions of young people do not possess ontological qualities. And besides, to be young is only very relatively correlated with age or fixed biological functions. In the society of today, it is possible to be young and be 40 years old, as well as one can become an adult at the age of 20.

An important issue in the actions of young people lies in the self – representation of actions that the single person elaborates. For example, one can take specific liberties, because one feels young; to a certain extent, one is able to run risks, because one still feels young; if one feels certain that one has much time left, it indicates that one feels young, and so forth.

All these examples do not mean that the actions of young people constitute a universal category of behavior, nor that in terms of socially conformist behavior any other kind of action has to be regarded as a young person's action. The actions of young people – and therefore the fact of being young – constitute themselves in self – representation of every action and in their relations to the systems of expectations that are constituted by society and involve all persons who act the same way. The actions of young people present a form of socially relevant communication. It is the tension between the inner world (self – representation) and the outer world (expectations) that produces this relevance. The lifeworld of young people is nothing other than all the possibilities of actions combined that emerge from the permanent difference between inner and outer world. Lifeworld consists of the continuous creation and overcoming of this difference. This opening and closing down, which is permanently steadied by the needs of single social systems, reproduces the alternation of generations.

The lifeworld of young people shows a high complexity, and, as a result, it offers an abundance of possibilities of actions. These phenomena of innovation and transformation are nothing other than the various structures of possible relations within which the length of time is variable and determination is certainly not subjective. Young people cannot decide whether they are young and for how long they will remain young. Any choice or selection of possible actions inside of social systems shortens the duration of youth. The lifeworld of young people forms the environment for these choices, as well as the circumference within which the sense of actions of young people is created.

On the basis of these conceptual reflections, I shall now proceed to explore some interpretative hypotheses about "life conditions" of young people. But before doing that, we have to consider some fundamental aspects of the daily life of young people.

Aspects of daily life of young people

Recently, a report from an independent commission on "Life conditions of young people in Italy" (IARD, 1985) contained an article with the title "Giovanni anni 80" (youth in the 1980s). This article examines the life conditions of young people in Italy, such as school, family, politics, personal experiences, and plans for the future. The main tendencies in the article are kept very relative, and therefore are balanced by countertendencies that do not permit the elaboration of general perspectives.

In the article two results are predominant: *on one hand a positive attitude in the behavior of young people toward the main socialization institutions family and school, on the other hand the considerable uncertainty that these institutions show in their reaction toward the behavior of young people.* The positive attitude is visible in the acceptance of educational institutions and the willingness to overcome difficulties that derive from the structures of these institutions. Obviously, they are not very helpful in offering young people cultural opportunities in the face of the complexity of contemporary society. At the same time we can observe a strong acceptance of family structures by adolescents, as well as the willingness to live inside of these structures – an attitude the previous generation was not willing to accomplish to the same degree. Also visible are tendencies of social behavior in professional environments that conforms to the organization and structure of these environments. Young people seem to develop mechanisms of acceptance in this area that are more stable than those of adults.

This kind of confidence in social institutions, however, is compensated by the considerable distrust young people have toward all state – related organizations. Whereas they seem to accept the forms of socialization of private and public institutions and the (limited) professional opportunities they have to face, at the same time alienation emerges, an attitude marked by distrust toward systems that organize public life and group mechanisms. Characteristic for this attitude, for example, is the indifference toward politics, the distrust of bureaucracy, the prompt acceptance of consequences created by class distinctions, as well as of different opportunities offered to adolescents, for example, privileges or disadvantages they might experience in the early period of their socialization process.

Institutions react to these attitudes, which are constantly wavering between prompt acceptance and indifference, with permanent insecurity. They do not try to come to meet this behavior of young people efficiently; that is why they do not supply young people with useful guidelines for their actions. Their reaction is based more on their disorientation than on eventual laziness. (This situation, by the way, leads to relief in the relationship between generations: The previous generation typically does not possess the mechanisms that form the characteristic behavior of the present generation; the system, previously marked by representation of strict values and ideologies, is now fading if not vanishing, whereas forms of generally approved adaptations become established while personal motivation decreases.) In spite of these developments, the willingness of institutions to deal with them finally changes into disorientation. Ideas on how to meet this alienation do not exist.

To take an example: The spectrum of long—term alternatives that make it possible to deal with drug abuse shows the wide range from legalization of drugs to imprisonment — even of those who are caught with a microscopic amount of drugs in their pockets. The wide spectrum of reactions shown by the institutions of control demonstrates their disorientation. Traditional attempts to explain the phenomenon of alienation are not convincing; obviously, actions based on these explanations are not efficient. They only produce the opposite of what they intend to achieve: On the one hand, imprisonment creates criminality, whereas the attitude of tolerating every different behavior only creates extreme forms of behavior. On the other hand, disorientated institutions are not able to take rigorous measures; the same points of reference, which are useful to stabilize them, are missing.

Dimensions of the lifeworld of young people

Let us assume that youth indicates a particular social period in the life of every person. It is the very society that determines the richness of this life period. In the same way the society can also renounce what it has determined. And this happens to a great extent in our society: According to analyses of life conditions of young people, one gains the impression *that society increased the life period called youth considerably and did not make any arrangements to control, guide, and direct this period.* And this is the reason for the disorientation we have already talked about. In other words, it is possible to find large amounts of energy available on a communicative level without taking steps to direct them efficiently. Society at this moment does not take the risk of directing young people, because it does not make use of the obvious functionality of coded messages in communication. In turn, a distance rises between young people's forms of self—representation and the expectations of adults, and therefore between developed expectations within systems that are stabilized by social communication and communicative functions expressed in the actions of young people.

We can analyze these phenomena in different areas of adolescents' lives: by analyzing, for example, the extent and consequences of unemployment for young people; considering young people who abandon school and do not try to find suitable professions; considering different forms of alienation and deviance; evaluating the careers of young, alienated people; analyzing the long time young people remain in their families; or the permanent decrease in the number of young people who take the risk of living together as a married couple.

These analyses, however, offer indications that remain undecipherable since they result from observations that are only made in regard to expectations created within systems and stabilized through actions. Also, these analyses do not enable us to conceive the real lifeworld of young people, since they are deprived of component references to actions that usually are given by self — representation. In other words, these analyses indicate signs of something that still has to be deciphered. And what has to be deciphered is the coded message of communication that each new generation determines. This message transforms life experiences within the duration of this very generation.

3. Conclusions

In the young Italian generation of today, for example, one can determine the existence of behavioral patterns that are opposed to one another: Young people are observed to demonstrate both commitment and release from commitment; this happens either on a political or on a social level. Adult people expect widespread amorality in the behavior of young people, a behavior that separates actions from unambigous evaluations. This expectation makes it impossible to describe actions on first sight according to a catalogue of values. Action patterns already seem to change in *status nascendi*. And this happens not because of the rapidity of social transformations triggering actions, but because actions direct themselves according to levels of meaning that appear fragmental to the older generation. Ideologies seem to have no cohesive function any more: They no longer serve as sure guidelines for all actions; they become antiquated like the remains of a past one can only talk about. Only the oral reproduction of ideologies survives.

Since social communication returns to less available resources of values, it removes the difference between public and private affairs. In young people, in their inner as well as in their outer world, the opposition of altruism and narcissism splits up. But it is also remarkable that new guidelines for values do not necessarily cancel old ones and replace them. The problem young people are facing — and they solve it in a way that appears contradictory to adult observers — does not concern values but the definition of the symbolical level of their actions. The explicit code directing behavior is neither ethical nor political but *symbolic*. The young generation of today has found a symbolic universe that stands in contrast to their own actions, and therefore is looking for new forms of producing symbols of the reality they experience.

This pursuit means the *search for their own identity*, which is the identity of one generation. Since the normative structures of action have consumed their resources, the power of young people to assert themselves is given by their ability to reproduce or restore new levels of symbols in reference to their actions. The encounter between generations — if it is an encounter — only happens on a symbolic level. This level alone makes it possible for young people to discover the fact that meaninglessness, the annihilation of sense, offers unlimited possibilities of action. Therefore young people respond to the insecurity of adults by disorientating them without arranging sure references to their actions. On the other hand they continually redefine their own identity, which permanently creates differences and variety, produces a new level of symbols and permanently keeps redesigning a new symbolic environment for their actions.

The young contemporary generation not only achieves a clear differentiation in reference to the previous generation, but its lifeworld allows it to prepare inexhaustible resources for its actions. For the sake of this availability of resources, it permanently denies the expectations adult people confront it with, because these expectations derive from normative trends and tendencies of actions, which, by now, have come to an end. I said that the actions of young people can only be outlined in the perspective of the relation between forms of self — representation (inner world), and forms of expectations (outer world). Young people in contemporary society achieve transformations on a wide scale in their lifeworld. I believe that their lifeworld is characterized and differentiated by their large potential for reproducing actions on a symbolic level.

References

Ardigo, A. (1980): Crisi di governabilita e mondi viali. Bologna
IARD (1985): Secondo rapporta sulla condizione giovanile in Italia (research report)
Luhmann, N. (1984): Soziale Systeme. Frankfurt: Suhrkamp

5.

Adolescent Transitions: A Life—Course Perspective

Millicent E. Poole
Monash University, Clayton, Australia

This article presents an emerging theoretical perspective on the social world of Australian adolescents in transition to adulthood. The perspective is "life course", involving age—related pathways associated with the transition to adulthood in Australian culture, but also the macrosocial, historical, and political contexts that help construct the world of adolescents. In addition, the more microcontexts of family and peers are considered.

1. A Life—Course Perspective on Adolescents in Transition

The life—course perspective is a "combination of some elements from the psychological and sociological, including attention to the interactions between the internal and external factors" (Blackburn and Lawrence, 1986, 268). The perspective has been developed by Elder (1981, 1984, 1988) and brings together a number of important ideas that concern human development: time (social and life histories); context (the influence of settings); and dialectical concerns (interactive processes between individuals and their contexts). The perspective is empirical, ecological, historical, multidisciplinary, and problem — or policy—focused. Three emphases distinguish the life—course approach from the life—span approach: its emphasis on social change and its human consequences; its attention to linkages between social change and life patterns and the effects on differential life paths; and its focus on intracohort processes, as against the comparison of whole cohorts (Elder, 1985).

Blackburn and Lawrence (1986) perceive the key premises of the life course perspective as: (a) theoretical distinctions exist between biographical time (personal experiencing of the life span) and social time (institutional norms that structure the life cycle); (b) characteristics of the individual and her or his social environment interact and result in change over the life course; (c) changes in the environment affect the life—course patterns of individuals or cohorts; and (d) the collective behavior of individuals results in changes in institutional norms (1986, 268).

Blackburn and Lawrence (1986) argue that the life—course conceptualization avoids the psychologistic error of developmental and ontogenetic explanations in the absence of attention to contextual constraints affecting individual behavior and avoids errors sociologists make when they focus on social structures and norms and neglect individual differences and psychological attributes.

The application of this perspective to the study of adolescents in transition to adulthood in Australia is timely, given the pace of social and educational change and the relatively small amount of research resources (financial and human) that have been devoted to studying the social world of adolescents in Australia. Policies and programs, as will be discussed below, have generally been short—term, ad hoc, and problem—focused, and not based on fundamental assessments of the social world of adolescents. The need for long—term planning in society for the transition of adolescence to adulthood has been neglected.

The article will argue that there are major temporal and contextual frameworks that must be considered as part of the process of describing the social world of adolescents in transition to adulthood. The development of the theoretical account within a life—course perspective will occur within the overarching themes associated with the perspective: (a) change and temporality; (b) context and the life course; and (c) cohort processes and intergenerational factors. Finally, the implications of the account for the development of social policies for youth are presented.

2. Change and Temporality: Youth in Transition to Adulthood

Accounts of the social world of Australian adolescents in transition to adulthood increasingly include reference to the changing context — physical, social, and economic (see reviews by Poole, 1987b; Blakers, in press). There is recognition that macrovariables such as social class and culture influence development (Amato, 1987; Poole, de Lacey and Randhawa, 1985). But such recognition is comparatively recent. Goodnow (1986), for example, has described an increasing conceptual awareness, among mainstream developmentalists, that age cohorts matter and that from one historical period to another the very concepts of development have changed dramatically. In effect, one "macro" variable, often referred to as the socio—context, has begun to gain prominence. Future theoretical and empirical work in the contemporary world of adolescence should, therefore, take account of both change and temporality in the "socio — context".

In a trend review of the Australian research on youth in transition, Poole (1987b) examined the "macro" changes that have occured over the past two decades in the economy and examined the impact this has had on the construction of life possibilities for young people, particularly in relation to education, employment, and youth homelessness. Changes in the Australian economy had led to a redefinition of what pathways were available and accessible to young people. In the early 1970s, for example, there was an expectation that all school leavers would enter the labor market; by the mid and late 1970s, major structural changes that had occured nationally and internationally excluded adolescents from labor market participation. Reconfigurations of education, training, employment, and leisure were occuring in the lives of adolescents in transition to adulthood. So great have these changes been, that the difficulties are seen as constituting a major social problem and a destructive break in the "taken — for — granted" smooth transition of young people from education to work (see Poole, 1987b, Blakers, in press, for a comprehensive review and analysis of youth in transition).

The cyclical nature of change, and the policy responses to social problems associated with young people with disjunctions in expected transitions, were examined by Holbrook and Bessant (1987) in their comparisons of youth unemployment in the 1930s and 1980s. Despite a temporal difference of 50 years, many of the policy strategies pursued in the 1980s had their parallels in the 1930s. For example, the notion of traineeships was seen as one way of engaging youth to stave off "a threat to national stability and the social fabric. Youth were seen to be prone to adverse influences while out of work". Government schools were attacked for failing to "keep up with structural changes in the economy." During both periods of history, "governments and the media had quite unrealistic expectations of how quickly the education system at any level could respond to structural or economic movements and meet changing demands" (Holbrook and Bessant, 1987, 40).

That change is occuring in Australian society and that it is having a major impact on the lives of young people has been well documented. Sweet (1978, 1981, 1987), for example, has examined major changes over time in the teenage labor market, charting the disappearance of categories of employment, the disappearance of unskilled jobs, and the growth in part — time jobs for the young. Writers such as Reeders (1986), Sloan and Wooden (1984), and Coventry et al. (1984) have all examined the implications of changes in work patterns for youth. Burke (1987), Windshuttle (1987), and Poole (1984) have examined the impact of technological change in terms of the current and future impact on the lives of young Australians. Byrne and Hazell (in press) in particular considered these changes as they will affect the lives of girls. The changing compositon of Australian culture since World War II has been a dominant theme of social analysis for at least two decades. Poole, de Lacey and Randhawa (1985), in a recent book of readings, examined the implications of change in terms of young people's perceptions of options and possibilities in their lives.

Such studies, and many like them, point to structural changes occuring at both the macro— and microlevels of Australian society. However, inadequate linkages are being made by policymakers between the various contexts in which young people are born and live. This highlights the importance of developing a life — course perspective in which such linkages are perceived in dialectical and dynamic interaction.

The significance of considering notions such as change and sociohistorical context is fully apprehended through an examination of the discourses that construct social expectations of pathways and possibilities for adolescents in a particular historical time frame. Anderson (1980), for example, has outlined major expectations society today holds for youth in transition. These include the accepted and expected pathways of transition to work, to legal and social roles such as spouse, breadwinner, consumer of leisure pursuits, citizen, and voter. Such a list is congruent with the notion of "social life phase" (Higgins and Wells, 1985), in which each phase is associated with particular activities, social roles, privileges, and responsibilities. Social exposure increases social knowledge in terms of what is expected and what is possible at each social life phase.

The argument is developed here that the social world of adolescents is shaped, constructed, and constrained by "messages" from the macrocontext — social, cultural, temporal, historical — as to which are possible and acceptable social pathways, behaviors, and aspirations for the social life phase "youth in transition to adulthood". Johnson (1986), for example, has presented an analysis of the social definition of growing up into a young Australian woman presented to teenage girls from 1930 to 1965. The process was perceived as extended childhood, and as a phase in identity construction with different pathways and prescriptions for girls in terms of educational tracks, curricula, and vocational possibilities. The concept of adolescence was class — and gender — based, and was increasingly linked to "image" creation and consumerism.

The discourse used by key socialization agents in both the micro — and macrocontexts can be used as an index of what the social world of adolescents is like and the roles the society expects of its young people, so that such messages become part of the motives and concerns of young people. Empirical analysis of the kind undertaken by Enright, Levy, Harris and Lapsley (1987), whilst not in the Australian context, provides fragments of social analysis that can be pieced together to present something of a parallel argument. Enright et al. (1987) examine a corpus of literature indicating ideological bias concerning adolescents depending on the economic climate. As they can show, for example, in times of economic depression theories of adolescence emerge that portray teenagers as immature, psychologically unstable, and in need of prolonged participation in the educational system. During wartime, the psychological competence of youth is emphasized and the duration of education is recommended to be more retracted than in depression.

This sociohistorical perspective is found in the work of Kidwell et al. (1986) in their analysis of the factors that contributed to the nature of adolescent research over the past decades. Their research into articles printed in the 1920s and 1930s showed the influence of poor economic conditions on the change in research emphasis within journal articles in the 1930s. Their findings further support the argument by Riegel (1972) that theoretical activity does not take place in a sociocultural vacuum. Rather it is dependent upon the economic and political ideologies that dominate the society. Broughton (1979, 1981a, 1981b, 1983) similarly demonstrates the linkages between psychological theories of the self and structural transformations of society, arguing the salient influence of the two. The arguments that emerge from the Enright et al. paper are that the proper understanding of adolescence requires not only an evolutionary perspective but also an historical perspective as well: and "that societies regulate the status of youth in culturally adaptive ways, so that whether youth will be portrayed as competent to assume adult roles, or as psychologically incapacitated to warrant their exclusion from adult roles, will depend largely on the labor and economic requirements of the society in which they live" (Enright et al., 1987, 542).

The parallelism that can be drawn in Australia emerges from analyses of youth policies and the economic climate over the past decade and the instrumental messages to young people that have been transmitted about their social roles and responsibilities. Such analyses make comparisons involving historical and economic change, and show that "messages" change from attributions of lack of skills, training, and motivation of young people; to attributions of blame to school systems for irrelevance, slow response to change, and lack of vocational training; to universities and institutions of higher education for remoteness from the worlds of science and technology, business and industry. That young people and the socializing systems are blamed during times of economic recession is documented by Holbrook and Bessant (1987) in a comparative analysis of attitudes to youth unemployment in the depressed economic times of the 1930s and 1980s; by Poole (1987b) and Blakers (in press) in an analysis of youth in transition over the past two decades; and in radical critiques of the changes occuring in Australian higher education (Smith, Burke, Smith and Wheelwright, 1988).

A way of gaining a perspective on these changing ideologies, which construct messages about what society expects and what is possible for youth, is contained in the notion of "settlements" (Seddon, 1987). The concept of settlement breaks with the traditional, historical, chronological basis of time or temporality, by identifying qualitatively distinct patterns of human activity that are identified through the analysis of social life (Seddon, 1987). Periods within national histories identified in this way are termed settlements, with qualitatively distinct patterns and relationships, conflicts, and crises. The Keynesian settlement (1940–1960) was characterized by state intervention, emphasis on planning informed by the natural and social sciences, universal social provision, social welfare rather than individual compensation, and the recognition of a hierarchy of talent and environmental conditions (Seddon, 1987). By the 1980s, monetarism had replaced Keynesian economic theory, emphasizing the macroeconomic welfare state, conservative governments, increased unemployment, and an increasing displacement of culturalist concerns of equality and disadvantage by the language of economic efficiency. Such settlements are important macroeconomic, social, and political time—related contexts that construct and constrain the world of youth in transition to adulthood.

3. *Contextual Dynamics*

The social world of adolescents is part of a system of nested contexts that are linked in dynamic interaction throughout the life course. The ecological theorist, Bronfenbrenner (1976), delineates person—environment interactions within four frameworks that are useful in a consideration of youth in transition to adulthood: (1) the microsystems of the immediate family or school settings (e.g., at the dinner table or in a science class); (2) the mesosystems of the interrelations among the major settings containing the adolescent at a particular point and time in his/her life (e.g., the intersections among family, school, peer groups, television); (3) the exosystem, which refers to extensions of the mesosystem into concrete social structures that influence the social world of adolescents (e.g., the world of work, the neighborhood); and (4) the macrosystems, which are the overarching institutions of the culture or subculture (e.g., economic, social, and political systems that are carriers of information and ideology, and contribute to the construction of adolescents' views of social reality).

The evolving complexities of such socioecological factors will not be detailed here but can be found in Bronfenbrenner (1976), Hübner—Funk (1986), and Poole (1987a). Such a framework permits considerations of important contexts that comprise the social world of adolescents, and provide valuable insights into the views of young people themselves concerning their current social realities and possible future.

Family

That the family is an important social context for youth in transition is not largely disputed, for example, for the development of social skills and as a support network. However, recent changes in Australian family patterns and leaving—home rates over the past decade suggest a changing role of the family in the life course of the adolescent.

Various surveys (Edgar and Maas, 1984) have indicated that marriage is no longer the main reason for adolescents leaving home as was the case in the 1970s. Today, the search for independence is a salient factor. An analysis of this trend has led Young (1984) to posit that an additional phase for adolescents has developed that relates to leaving home before the marital phase, that is, a change in the timetabling of social life phases.

The Children in Australian Families Study (Amato, 1987) presents an adolescent perspective on family life and the development of competence. Aspects of parent—adolescent relational processes are examined (e.g., cohesion, control, conflict, responsibility) in terms of various structural arrangements (two—parent, one—parent, and step—parent households). In particular the macrostructures that have an impact on the life of adolescents in families are considered (e.g., family resources, socioeconomic status, and participation in work). The perceptions Australian adolescents hold of their families are generally favorable. There were, however, realities of adolescents living in poverty in some mother—custody families, and under stress in some step—families. There is some linkage out to the world of work (mothers and fathers), and some consideration of socioeconomic status in terms of structures and processes, which serves as a useful assessment of the dynamic between macro— and microcontexts.

Results of surveys found in the work of Edgar and Maas (1984) outline other social trends that point to a changing social environment in the 1980s. These changes have been in respect to changing adult sexual relationships such as older marriage age, an increase in defacto relationships, and higher rates of single—parent families and divorces. Such trends separate adolescents from the earlier more predicatable pathways that typified the life courses in the 1950s or 1960s.

The changing family patterns of the 1980s and the growing need for the contemporary adolescent to seek early independence through leaving home has at one level provided a greater diversity of life choices and experiences for the adolescent. Alternatively it has placed greater pressure on the adolescent to develop the competencies and responsibilities in decision making in order to adjust to this changing social context.

Peers

In the transition to adulthood, the peer group has long been regarded as an important context for the growth to independence. For example, Wearing and James (1985), in their study of employed and unemployed working—class youth, found that friends in both groups, more so than family, were vital for the adolescent's development of identity and personal acceptance. This is contrary to writers like Amato (1985), who argue that the family is the most important social network for the adolescent.

Whilst debates of this sort continue, other literature focuses on the practices and the effects of the peer group on the adolescent life course. Nicholson and Anthill (1981), in their study of the problems faced by Australia's youth, focused on the relationship between peer group acceptance and sex — role identity. Their results found there was a positive relationship between feminine sex — role stereotype and problems experienced by the female samples in the study. In addition, results showed that peer group acceptance had a stronger influence on the behavior of males than females. This was explained by the observation that, since boys congregate in larger groups than girls, the peer group collectively is more important to the boys as a support network.

This trend in gender — differentiated peer group relationships has been confirmed by studies reported by Taylor (1986). Interview responses from teenage girls in these studies outlined their views of how boys "hang around" in larger groups, whilst girls form relationships with one or two others. Taylor (1986) argues that this individualized peer group formation amongst girls is a form of control in their freedom to establish their own subculture and group solidarity. The consequence is the situation in which adolescent girls' behavior and problems, especially in regard to the working class, have been a hidden agenda for academics and policy makers alike. More concentration has been given to the plight of working — class boys' subculture, as they are more noticeable within the social context. There is much in the analysis of social literature on adolescents in Australia to suggest separate peer contexts of development, with more resources having been devoted to an analysis of male peer groups (Walker, 1988).

Studies of peer groups outline their importance in the adolescents' construction of their social world and in their constructions of self and future life — course options. The concern with gender is more recent. Studies of this sort have raised important issues regarding disadvantages of women in school, work, and life paths (Connell et al., 1982; Moran, 1984; Earley, 1981a, 1981b; Poole, 1984; Poole and Beswick, 1987).

Much of the literature in Australia on adolescence and peers has been in relation to a class analysis of the behavior of peer group culture (Roberts 1983; Moynihan 1980; Watson 1985; Connell et al., 1982), implying the dynamic interaction between macro — and microinfluences. Research of this sort has been ethnographic. This approach, whilst not representative, permits more adequate analysis of the construction of the ideas, meanings, and practices that encompass the culture of adolescence in their specific groups (Roberts, 1983). For example, a study by Moynihan (1980) of working — class boys detailed their need for approval within peer groups. The acquisition of status was gained through the performance of daredevil type stunts or risky behavior like vandalism, car theft, or drug taking. Their observations suggest that whilst the peer group provided a sense of self—worth, identity, and of belonging, their involvement in antisocial behavior in order to heighten status within the peer group was adding to the adolescent's alienation from the general community.

Similar research has concentrated on the analysis of working—class subcultures and the meanings and views inherent in their life—styles (Watson 1985; Walker, 1988). Other writers like Connell et al. (1982) in Australia and Roberts (1983) in Great Britain have analyzed the practices of middle—class adolescents in their transition to adulthood. Connell et al. (1982), in his qualitative interviewing of adolescent boys and girls attending private and government schools, outlined how certain variables such as school and parental background have an influence on the life paths of adolescents in terms of career choice and general attitudes to their future. Such class analysis of adolescents in Australia suggests that adolescents are not a homogeneous group, and an emphasis is needed on examining the world of different groups of adolescents in relation to various life settings.

Writers such as Poole and Evans (1988) have similarly examined influences on adolescents in their development of life skills and social competences. In their study, different clusters of influences have been perceived by adolescents as helpful or harmful. The results found the most potent spheres of attributed influence for the adolescent were family, school studies, and peers. Self—determination through one's own constructions — knowledge, actions, attitudes, and experience — or personal traits emerged as an important life influence. Self— or internal attributions were as strong as external ones. The context of learning was an important factor in constructing social worlds, for example, whether young people were at school, in college, or in youth support centers affected life orientations and outlook, as did course type, for example, mainstream academic or vocational alternatives (Evans and Poole, 1988b).

Other research by Poole and Evans (1988) and Evans and Poole (1988b), using a life—skills theoretical framework, developed a set of field studies to identify empirically the major life action areas that were of most concern to adolescents and adolescent competence in coping with these major life areas. The central concerns in the life of adolescents were social relationships, personal development, and careers (Evans & Poole, 1988a). Adolescents perceived themselves as having a fair degree of competence in most of the life action areas. Major educational and work contexts were important in the social construction of perceptions of competence. Emerging from the studies is a clearly "instrumental" set of adolescent concerns focused on education, jobs, and the future. There are, however, areas of more "intrinsic" life concerns and salience such as personal and social relationships and development. Young people are concerned to improve their levels of knowledge and competence in life action areas and in the various social domains, that is, to develop "contextual competence" (Poole and Evans, 1988a).

The findings that are emerging from this program of research are starting to confirm the value of a socioecological perspective in examining the importance of contextual factors that shape adolescent perceptions of their social world. Having emphasized contextual factors, the individualistic perspective that states people ultimately hold their future in their hands (Watson, 1985) is equally important in the analysis of adolescent attitudes and life paths. For whilst they are part of a particular social context, adolescents deal with structures through psychological strategies, and their ideas are expressions of these strategies (see also Poole and Beswick, 1987, 1988).

Other recent studies on the concerns and needs of adolescents have revealed valuable insights into the changing social world of adolescents. Finlayson, Reynolds, Rob and Muire (1987), in their survey of adolescents' views, problems, and needs, attempted to measure a wide range of factors affecting youth as well as the interrelationships between these factors. The importance of the qualitiy of the family relationship was affirmed and shown to have an important influence on adolescent school performance, emotional well–being, and indulgence in problem behavior. Many behaviors of the adolescents in this study reflected a failure of health education and a flaunting of Australia's laws concerning the consumption of substances. The study found that "youth were disenchanted with the key established institutions of our society... . They felt that governments did not understand their needs, and became increasingly alienated from religion as they grew older". Yet, overall, "adolescents were conventional in their aspirations and displayed a general optimism toward their future prospects. Most felt they would obtain a job they liked, and own their own home. The great majority hoped to marry and to raise a family. Sadly, considering the realities of high unemployment and hard economic times, many appear destined to disappointment" (Finlayson et al., 1987, 156).

The Australian National Opinion Polls (ANOP), taken in 1984 and 1986 showed similar results in adolescent concerns: family, personal relationships, social life, money, jobs, education, sport, and hobbies. The results of 1986 did show a change in adolescent unemployment attitudes, which was explained by the fewer young unemployed in that year. In October 1986, the unemployment rate between 15– to 24–year–olds dropped from 17.3% in 1984 to 14.5%. The 1986 report argues that whilst young people still view finding a job difficult, "it has become less difficult to find a job in their own area and there is a greater appreciation of the fact that the Federal government has acted in the employment area to help young people" (p. 9). The government assistance is in relation to the Priority One Project introduced in 1985, which aimed at increasing support for young people, through, for example, training schemes (apprenticeships) and support and information services.

These reported differences in unemployment within a 2–year time span suggest the powerful influence of macrogovernment policies on the discourses and attitudes of adolescents in their microcontext. It further supports the historical−temporal approach that has been discussed in other sections of this paper as a key contributor to the social world of adolescence in Australia.

Such studies show the dynamic interaction between individuals and their life contexts in a way that underscores the importance of both the psychological and sociological approaches. The life−course perspective with its analysis of historical and social contexts and their effects of individual processes aids in a better understanding of adolescent transition to adulthood.

4. *Cohort and Longitudinal Studies*

There have been a number of significant longitudinal studies of young Australians that provide some indications of social trends in the area of youth in transition (to adulthood) and some insight into the changes that have occured in the social world of adolescents.

By the mid to late 1970s, national studies (e.g., Rosier, 1978; Knight 1977; McGaw et al., 1977) were investigating disruptions to normal transitions to adulthood, focusing on the problems faced by young people who left school early or who lived in rural areas in which there were fewer educational and occupational opportunities and in which life pathways were constrained. For example, the transition process was exacerbated by distance, isolation, and transport difficulties. Influences of "setting" and "timetabling" (e.g., of leaving school in the expectation of entering the labor market) were disrupted by a period of high youth unemployment, which was suffered by young Australians as part of a global phenomenon.

The most important longitudinal study undertaken on youth in transition is the Australian Council for Educational Research study "Youth in Transition" based on a 15,000 national probability study of three age cohorts, born in 1961, 1965, and 1970. The study has had various emphases: a comprehensive review and analysis of Australian research on the transition from school to work (Sturman, 1979); school, work, and career, and future prospects for 14−year−olds (Williams, Batten, Girling−Butcher and Clancy, 1981); and for 17−year−olds (Williams, Clancy, Batten and Girling−Butcher, 1980); perceptions by adolescents of the quality of school life (Williams and Batten, 1981); and participation and equity in relation to transition to work (Williams, 1987). Most of the studies are policy−oriented and provide valuable insights into social trends and patterns affecting adolescents. For example, the importance of setting (rural or urban, private school or government school, overseas or Australian born) is assessed for each cohort, and major shifts are documented. More qualitative analyses have also been undertaken: for example, case studies on the quality of school life (Batten and Girling−Butcher, 1981); the psychological consequences of unemployment (Clancy, 1980); and the perceptions of unemployed young people aged 18 and 22 (Blakers, in press). Such studies map out life−course pathways and provide some estimate of the likelihood of being able to follow that pathway. The findings enable questions of participation and access to be addressed in terms of the ideal of social justice between and within cohorts and subgroups.

As the study has progressed, and the emphases in government policies for young people have changed, the orientation of the study has shifted. Currently the major concerns are to look at the social and economic returns to education, the transition itself as reflected in experiences during the first year in the labor force, the net benefits of a private schooling, entry of early school leavers into TAFE (Technical and Further Education), the effects of family economic circumstances in achievement and participation, social and economic influences on quality of life, leisure activities and family formation, and, in each case, differences in these processes over time and between cohorts. A special aspect of the study focuses on unemployed youth, particularly the long—term unemployed, through a review of the literature on youth unemployment and an analysis of the views of youth themselves, both employed and unemployed. Qualitative data obtained through open—ended questionnaires are the focus of these analyses (ACER, 1988). The theoretical emphases of the studies have been based largely on status attainment models, but in more recent years a life—span orientation has been adopted to track the lives of young people over time and to compare cohorts.

The effects of unemployment on young people were examined longitudinally by Feather and O'Brien (1986), using a sample of 3,000 adolescents aged 15 to 17 in 1980, 1981, and 1982. Feather and O'Brian argue an historical—temporal approach that certain social environmental circumstances of a particular time affect the attitudes of adolescents to unemployment. They also argue that different age cohorts experience an alternative view of unemployment, and the authors provide an example of societal change that could affect the unemployment experience, for example, the enactment of new legislation concerning welfare provisions for the unemployed or a worsening economic crisis. The key variables in the study were self—concept, depressive effects, stress symptoms, and work and employment values. Employment status was significant in determining the social construction of self. For example, the adolescent sample who were not able to find employment saw themselves as less competent, more stressed, and less satisfied with life. These results were found in the same adolescent sample while they were at school. The study shows the virtue of the longitudinal method for ascertaining the effects of employment status on youth attitudes over a critical period of the life span, that is, between leaving school and entering the work environment. That the macrocontext led to such negative attitudes in young people while they were still at school is of concern (see also Feather, 1986).

More recently, a major national longitudinal youth in transition study was funded by the Department of Labor. The Australian Longitudinal Survey (ALS) is a panel study of Australian youth aged 15—24 years (2,400 persons registered for at least 3 months for unemployment in 1984) and 16—25 years, selected to provide a representative sample of the transition age cohort (interviewed in 1985, 1986, 1987, and 1988). The survey focuses on labor market, education, and a selection of social issues. Among the many social indices surveyed were: household structure (age, sex, education, employment, income); family background (ethnicity, parents' employment, education, nature of housing, mobility, previous unemployment); marital history and status; schooling (including completed, current, and aspirational in terms of further education); the school/study to work transition; voting; labor market status and activity; child care (usage and constraints); job training, health; attitudes to women and work; income; and housing.

The potential for a life–course perspective to be applied to this data bank is considerable and could help develop a more complete analysis of change, temporality, and context than has ever been available in Australia before. To date, most analyses have focused on structural changes affecting youth in transition: labor market structural changes (BLMR, 1986, 1987; Foster, 1987); transitions from unemployment to employment by youth (Brooks, 1986; Brooks and Volker, 1985; Eyland, 1985); investigations of long–term unemployed youth (McRae and Merrilees, 1987; Eyland and Johnson, 1987); the impact of abolishing certain unemployment benefits for youth (Maas, 1987); and training and the youth labor market (Miller, 1987). Such analyses show how problematic the transition of some youth from school to work has become, and how a socially approved and expected youth rite of passage to adulthood has been dislocated by macroeconomic contexts that influence the direction, options, and possibilities of young Australian cohorts.

An ongoing study by Poole and Beswick (1987, 1988) explores the perception of life–track possibilities by youth aged 17 to 27 years in relation to marriage and career, within a life course framework that acknowledges the power and importance of both intrapersonal and contextual explanations of the life course. So far, the study has examined developmental trajectories both individually and socially constructed and constrained. The studies show, through longitudinal and case study data, some of the conflicts faced by young women renegotiating the conventional pathways concerning young womens' life roles, expectations, and destinations.

Such longitudinal and cohort studies provide a rich data source for further analysis of the lives of adolescents in transition to adulthood. The emergence of such studies and their timing is itself an interesting reflection of changing perceptions of adolescents themselves, their concerns and competencies, and their place in the social fabric. For example, the dominant theme of transition from school to work, with choosing and obtaining a job, and with the duration and consequences of unemployment show quite powerfully the dynamic interaction between individual lives and the social, temporal, and structural pathways that cultures make available to youth in transition.

5. Youth Policies

An index of the changing world of youth is the government educational and
social policies that have been established in the last decade to address youth
issues. The public and political discourse that led to the development of these
programs is also an index of society's expectations concerning youth in
transition to adulthood, and a recognition of the dislocations taking place.

The mid−1970s saw the emergence of policies and programs brought about by serious youth
unemployment. During this period, governments argued that the unemployed could find work if
they really wanted to (i.e., there was a motivational and work ethic deficit among youth). They
also argued that schools had failed to prepare their students for employment through
inappropriate curricula (lacking in relevance and requisite basic and job−search skills). A
major review carried out by the OECD in 1976 focused on the issue of transition from school
to work or further study, and by 1979 transition was a public issue leading to the introduction
of a Comprehensive Policy for Transition from School to Work. The purpose of the policy was
to ensure that all young people in the 15−19 age group would be provided with options in
education, training, and employment (or any combination of these) either part−time or
full−time, so that unemployment becomes the least acceptable alternative.

Blakers (in press, 3) details the criticisms associated with the program: "(1) that it was a
strategy designed mainly to reduce the levels of official unemployment by transferring young
people from the register of the unemployed to education and training programs; (2) that,
focusing as it did on the 'at risk' segment of school students, it merely reinforced the inequities
of the status quo, legitimizing streaming (under another name); and binding schools closely to
the perceived needs of employers; (3) that it accentuated and exacerbated social and class
division within and between schools; and (4) that it focused almost exclusively on education
and training to the neglect of employment creation and other measures".

The policy was very much one of the maintenance of the status quo and a
series of ad hoc solutions to maintaining the social fabric, in the meantime
blaming the victims themselves for their lack of skill and motivation and the
school system for its inadequate socialization of young people for the world of
work.

A change of government, and a rethink of the role, structures, and processes of schooling in
relation to youth in transition, together with a realization of a deteriorating situation for young
people, led to a 1983 OECD review of youth policies and programs (education, labor force
participation, employment and training policies and programs, income support schemes). A
more comprehensive approach to youth policy was initiated. Still with an emphasis on
education and training, but with a different discourse signalling new directions, the government
established the Participation and Equity Program (PEP) to replace the School−to−Work
Transition Program. The program was to reach young people from various social groups who
had been underrepresented in education and training, its aim being to ensure that "at the end of
the decade, most young people complete the equivalent to a full secondary education, either in
school or in a TAFE institution or in some combination of work and education." The

government indicated its apparent concern for youth by initiating a Priority One Program; signalling youth issues as a high government priority.

While education and training remained major emphases, increasingly two problems encountered by youth were addressed through policy provisions — income support and youth homelessness. While it is not possible to document the issues and debates (see Commonwealth Department of Education, 1987, on income support schemes; and Maas and Hartley, 1988, on youth homelessness), it is possible to perceive aspects of the social fabric at risk because of the disruption of social life phases.

Contrasting themes emerging from the major policy perspectives on youth are social integration and maintenance of the status quo versus social transformation. Youth policies have been developed to address potentially dangerous disjunctions in life phases associated with unemployment. For example, alienated youth might become socially disruptive or mobilized against the state. When pathways to adult status are not available, then combinations of work and training and income support schemes have been devised to support the existing structures and patterns, that is, to maintain the status quo. While the rhetoric of participation and equity programs is partly socially transformative, in terms of access and outcomes, the reality is that the programs are being terminated or redirected.

A new discourse is emerging in relation to youth in Australia, epitomized in the discourse of a report "In the National Interest" in which there is a tension between "moral, ethical, social, cultural and educational concerns, on the one hand, and economic concerns, on the other... the report tries to reconcile the democratic and the economic" (Boomer, 1988, 8). In recent times, a new set of economic imperatives have shifted the social and educational discourse concerning youth away from equality and equity, a concern with social and individual rights, to a concern with national economic imperatives and the role that youth must be called upon to play in the new era of science and technology, business and industry. The discourse of "a nation at risk" and "in the national interest", "effectiveness and efficiency", and "relevance" has replaced the former discourse that was more socially rather than economically transformative, which contained a national vision of the construction of a socially just and equitable society in which young people were given a fair start, with a new vision of an economically competitive and industrially restructed society in which economic imperative drive the education of all young Australians. There is a new emphasis on the "productive culture": "schooling has a major part to play in developing young people with the

capacity, individually and collectively to produce in the interest of the nation"
(Boomer, 1988, 9).

Such policies indicate that young people and their life courses have become
inextricably bound up with national and international trends, and that solutions
to problems are influenced by international factors (e.g., OECD influence in
youth policy in Australia, international capitalism and its effects on economic
policies that incorporate youth). This macropolicy level is yet another indicator
of the dynamic interaction between macro— and microcontexts, between
individual lives and society.

Conclusion

This paper has argued the value of the life—course perspective in understanding
the social world of adolescents in transition to adulthood. The perspective,
through its attention to sociocultural and sociohistorical parameters, its advocacy
of cohort and longitudinal analysis, and its emphasis on change — social,
cultural, economic, political, temporal — shows the dynamic interaction of the
dialectic between the individual and society better than the psychological or
sociological perspectives singly. This perspective enables insight to be
developed about the changing sets of expectations held concerning adolescents
as well as the changing views of adolescents themselves. It enables the
pathways from adolescence to adulthood to be mapped for different policy
periods and the life—course trajectories of young people to be examined. It
enables an understanding of different "settlements" and how these affect the
discourse concerning youth and youth policy. It also enables an examination of
overarching themes, such as social integration, maintenance of the status quo,
or social transformation, to be assessed in terms of the macromessages of
societal directions and purposes that constrain or promote the lives of young
people in transition to adulthood.

What has been largely missing from the discourse and action has been a
concern to empower young people; to make them more socially critical or more
able to participate in social transformation or social analysis and questioning.
Although such views have been put by educators and youth workers, their
views have not penetrated youth policy circles (e.g., Ewan, 1987; Poole,
1987b; Poole and Evans, 1988). A life—course perspective would suggest that
such agency and self—empowerment would be of vital significance for
individual and societal futures.

References

Amato, P. (1985): Growing pains. Australian Society, Vol. 4., 6−10

Amato, P. (1987): Children in Australian families: The growth of competence. New York: Prentice Hall

Anderson, D. (1980): Transition from school: A review of Australian research. Seminar on Research in Transition from School. Melbourne, 19−21 October

Australian Council For Educational Research (ACER)(1988): Current Project 1988/89. Hawthorn, Vicotoria

Batten, M., & Girling−Butcher, S. (1981): Perceptions of the quality of school life: A case study of schools and students. Hawthorn, Victoria: Australian Council for Educational Research

Blakers, C. (in press): Youth in transition. Hawthorn: Australian Council for Educational Research

Blackburn, R., & Lawrence, J. (1986): Aging and the quality of faculty job performance. Review of Educational Research, 56, 3, 265−290

BLMR (1986): The first wave of the Australian Longitudinal Survey − Facts and figures about young CES registrants. BLMR Research Monograph, 12

BLMR (1987): Structural change and the labor market. BLMR Research Report, 11, Chap. 9

Boomer, G. (1988): In the national interest and beyond secondary education and youth policy in Australia. Paper presented to the ANU Public Affairs Conference: The Role and Purpose of Education in Australia, Canberra

Bronfenbrenner, V. (1976): The experiemental ecology of education. Educational Research, October, 5−15

Brooks, C. (1986): An analysis of factors influencing the probability of transition from unemployment to employment of Australian youth. BLMR Working Paper, 63

Brooks, C., & Volker, P. (1985): The influence of unemployment duration and homogeneity on the transition from unemployment for Australian youth. BLMR Working Paper, 55

Broughton, J. (1979): Developmental structuralism: Without self, without history. In Betz, A. (Ed.): Recent approaches to the social sciences. Winnipeg: Hignell Printing Co.

Broughton, J. (1981a): Piaget's structural developmental psychology. Knowledge without a self and without history. Human Development, 24, 325−350

Broughton, J. (1981b): Piaget's structural−developmental psychology. Ideology−critique and the possibility of a critical developmental psychology. Human Development, 24, 382−411

Broughton, J. (1983a): The cognitive developmental theory of adolescent self and identity. In Lee, B., & Noam, G. (Eds.): Developmental approaches to the self. New York: Plenum

Burke, G. (1987): Reforming the finance and structure of education in Australia. In Burke, G., & Rumberger, W. (Eds.): The future impact of technology on work and education. London: The Falmer Press, 176−193

Burke, G., & Rumberger, W. (1987): The future impact of technology on work and education. London: The Falmer Press

Byrne, E., & Hazel, E. (in press): Women in science and technology in Australia (WISTA). University of N.S.W. and University of Queensland

Clancy, J. (1980): Youth unemployment: The social and psychological consequences. In Youth, schooling and unemployment. Collected papers of the 1980 Annual Conference, Sydney: Australian Association for Research in Education, 544−549

Commonwealth Department of Education (1987): Support for staying on at school. Canberra: Australian Government Printing Service

Connell, R.W., Ashenden, D.J., Kessler, S., & Dowsett, G.U. (1982): Making the difference. Schools, families and social division. Sydney: Allen and Unwin

Coventry, G., Cornish, G., Stricker, P., Cooke R., & O'Brien, A.M. (1984): Part—time work and youth in transition. V.I.S.E. Research Section, July

Department of Sport, Recreation and Tourism (1984): Young Australians today. A report on a study of the attitudes of young Australians by ANOP Market Research. Canberra: August

Department of the Prime Minister and Cabinet Office of Youth Affairs (1986): A survey of community attitudes to issues affecting young people. Canberra: ANOP

Early, P. (1981a): Girls, school and work: Technological change and female entry into non—traditional work areas. Australian Journal of Education, 25, 3, 269—287

Early, P. (1981b): Girls need jobs too you know! Unemployment, sex roles and female identity. Australian Journal of Social Issues, 16, 3, 202—215

Elder, G.H. (1981): A life—course perspective. Paper presented at the Human Development Colloquium, April 14, Cornell University, New York

Elder, G. (1984): Families, kin and the life course: A sociological perspective. In Parke, R. (Ed.): Review of child development research, Vol. VII, The Family. Chicago: University of Chicago Press

Elder, G. (1985): Human development and social change: An emerging perspective on the life course. Paper presented at a workshop on interacting systems in human development. Cornell University: New York

Elder, G., & Caspi, A. (1988): Studying lives in a changing society: Sociological and personological explorations. Paper presented at the Henry A. Murray Lecture Series at Michigan State University, Lansing, Michigan, April 9—10

Edgar, D., & Maas, F. (1984): Adolescent competence, leaving home and changing family patterns. In XX International CFR Seminar of Social Change and Family Policies, Part 1, 355—426

Enright, R.D., Levy, W.M., Harris, D., & Lapsley, D.K. (1987): Do economic conditions influence how theorists view adolescents? Journal of Youth and Adolescence, 16, 6, 541—559

Evans, G.T., & Poole, M. E. (1988a): The important things in life: Group differences in adolescent concerns. Australian Journal of Education, 32, 2, 203—222

Evans, G.T., & Poole, M.E. (1988b): Adolescent perceptions of life influences. Manuscript submitted for publication

Ewan, J. (1987): The exclusiveness of youth policy. In Marsland, D. (Ed.): Education and youth. London: The Falmer Press, 195—208

Eyland, A. (1985): Young unemployed and the search for work. BLMR Working Paper, 58

Eyland, A., & Johnson, L. (1987): Dynamics of long—term unemployment among Australian youth. Paper presented at the ANZAAS Conference, Townsville

Feather, N.T. (1986): Employment importance and helplessness about potential unemployment among students in secondary school. Australian Journal of Psychology, 38, 1, 33—44

Feather, N.T., & O'Brien, G.E. (1986): A longitudinal study of the effects of employment and unemployment on school—leavers. Journal of Occupational Psychology, 59, 121—144

Finlayson, P., Reynolds, T., Rob, M., & Muir, C. (1987): Adolescents: Their views, problems and needs. A survey of high school students. Hornsby Ku—Ring—Gai: Area Health Service

Foster, W. F. (1987): Some implications of the Australian longitudinal survey calendar data for labor market measurement. Paper presented at the ACET workshop on the ALS, La Trobe University

Goodnow, J.J. (1986): Cultural conditions and individual behaviours: Conceptual and methodological links. Australian Journal of Psychology, 38, 231—244

Higgins, T.E., & Wells, R.S. (1985): Social construct availability and accessibility as a function of social life phase: Emphasizing the "How" vs. the "Can" of social cognition. Unpublished manuscript, Department of Psychology, New York University

Holbrook, A., & Bessant, B. (1987): Responses to youth unemployment in the 1930s and 1980s. Unicorn, 13, 1, 40–50

Hubner–Funk, S. (1986): Major career transitions of youth: Socioecological influences on the status passages from school to work. Paper presented at the American Education Research Association conference, San Francisco

Irving, T.H. (1988): Youth movements in Australia. Report of a working paper to the International Commission for the History of Social Movements and Structures

Johnson, L. (1986): The teenage girl: The social definition of growing up for the Young Australian Women, 1930 to 1965? In Theory, Structure and Action in Education (unpublished manuscript)

Kidwell, J.S., Dunham, R.M., Peppin, T.M., & Passarello, L.C. (1986): The adolescent–in–the–family: The effect of historical influence on the growth of a science. Journal of Adolescent Research, 1, 33–43

Knight, T. (1977): Factors affecting school leaving and work decisions for girls. In Commission of Inquiry into Poverty. School leavers: Choice and opportunity. Canberra: Australian Government Publishing Service

McGaw, B., Warry, R.S., Varley, P.J., & Alcorn, J. (1977): Prospects for school leavers. In Commission of Inquiry into Poverty. School leavers: Choice and opportunity. Canberra: Australian Government Publishing Service

McRae, I. (1984): The Australian National Longitudinal Survey. BLMR Conference Paper, No. 44

McRae, I., & Merrilees, W. (1987): Long–term unemployed youth: Who are they and how do they improve their employment status? Paper presented to the Conference of Economists, Surfers Paradise

Maas, F. (1987): The abolishment of junior unemployment benefit — Who should bear the cost. The Bulletin of the National Clearinghouse for Youth Studies, 6, 3

Mass, F., & Hartley, R. (1988): Living on the outside: The needs of unsupported, homeless youth. Canaberra: Australian Institute of Family Studies

Miller, P.W. (1987): Training in the youth labor market in Australia. Centre for Economic Policy Research, Discussion Paper 172

Moran, P. (1984): Female youth culture and attitudes to education: A focus on social relationships in the school. ANZAAS Congress, 54th

Moynihan, M. (1980): External influences on young people. In Her Keystone Park: Youth in Limbo. Parkside: Service to the Youth Council

Nicholson, S.I., & Antill, J.K. (1981): Personal problems of adolescents and their relationship to peer acceptance and sex–role identity. Journal of Youth and Adolescence, 10, 4, 309–325

Poole, M.E. (1984): Realities and constraints: Pathways for female school leavers. Australian Journal of Social Issues, 19, 1, 43–59

Poole, M.E. (1987a): Youth vocational education and nation–building: Perspectives on SEAMEO Countries. Paper presented at the National and Youth Building Conference, Canberra

Poole, M.E. (1987b): Youth in transition. In Keeves, T.P. (Ed.): Australian education: Review of recent research. Sydney: Allen and Unwin, 286–315

Poole, M. E., & Beswick, D.G. (1987): Marriage and career: The perception of life track possibilities. Paper presented at the National Conference on Girls and Women, Monash University, November

Poole, M.E., & Beswick, D.G. (1988): The transition from matriculation to professional employment: Intra—personal variables influencing the career and family orientations of young Australian women. Paper presented at the XXIV International Congress of Psychology, Sydney

Poole, M.E., & Evans, G.T. (1988): Life skills: Adolescents perceptions of importance and competence. British Journal of Counselling and Psychology, 16, 129—144

Poole, M.E., de Lacy, P.R., & Rhandhawa, B.S. (Eds.)(1985): Australia in transition: Culture and life possibilities. Sydney: Harcourt Brace Jovanovich

Radford, W.C. (1962): School leavers in Australia 1959—1960. Melbourne: Australian Council for Educational Research

Radford, W.C., & Wilkes, R.E. (1975): School leavers in Australia, 1971—1972. Hawthorn, Victoria: Australian Council for Educational Research

Reeders, E. (1986): Influence of economic and political ideologies on the development of developmental psychology. Psychological Bulletin, 78, 2, 129—141

Riegel, K. (1972): Influence of economic and political ideologies on the development of developmental psychology. Psychological Bulletin, 78, 129—141

Roberts, K. (1983): Youth and leisure. London: Allen and Unwin

Rosier, M.J. (1978): Early school leavers in Australia. IEA Monograph Series, 7. Stockholm: Almquist and Wilksell

Seddon, T. (1987): Settlements. Monash University, unpublished manuscript

Sloan, J., & Wooden, M. (1984): Part—time work. School retention and unionization: Aspects of youth labor market. National Institute of Labor Studies, Flinders University, Adelaide, Working Papers 17.71

Smith, B., Burke, G., Smith, G., & Wheelwright, E.L. (1988): Proposals for change in Australian education. A radical critique discourse, 9, (in press)

Sturman, A. (1979): From school to work: A review of major research in Australia. Melbourne: Australian Council for Educational Research

Sweet, R. (1978): The relationship between educational levels and access to apprenticeship in New South Wales over a five year period. Research Report, Sydney: Student Counselling Service, New South Wales Department of Technical and Further Education

Sweet, R. (1981): The teenage labor market: Trends and prospects. N.S.W. A paper delivered at a Public Seminar sponsored by the Victorian Institute of Secondary Education. N.S.W. Department of Technical and Further Education, Student Counselling Research Unit, Melbourne: October

Sweet, R. (1987): Australian trends in skills requirements. In Burke, G., & Rumberger, W. (1987): The future impact of technology on work and education. London: The Falmer Press, 96—117

Taylor, S. (1986): Teenage girls and economic recession in Australia: Some cultural and educational implications. British Journal of Sociology of Education, 7, 4, 379—395

Walker, J.C. (1988): Louts and legends. Sydney: Allen and Unwin

Watson, I. (1985): Double depression: Schooling, unemployment and family life in the 1980s. Sydney: Allen and Unwin

Wearing, B., & James, D. (1985): The adolescent peer group revisited in the 1980s. Australian Journal of Sex, Marriage, and Family, 6, 43—151

Williams, T. (1987): Participation in education. ACER Research Monograph No. 30, Hawthorn, Victoria: Australian Council for Educational Research

Williams, T., & Batten, M. (1981): The quality of school life. ACER Research Monograph, 12, Hawthorn, Victoria: Australian Council for Educational Research

Williams, T., Batten, M., Girling—Butcher, S., & Clancy, J. (1981): School and work in prospect: 14—year—olds in Australia. ACER Research Monograph, 10, Hawthorn, Victoria: Australian Council for Educational Research

Williams, T., Clancy, J., Batten, M., & Girling—Butcher, S. (1980): School, work and career. Melbourne: Australian Council for Educational Research

Windschuttle, K. (1987): New jobs in Sydney, Perth and Melbourne: The organisation of information technology centres. Australian Society, 6, 4, 18—20

Young, C. (1984): Leaving home and returning home: A demographic study of young adults in Australia. Australian Family Research Conference, Proceedings, 2. Family formation, structure, values. Melbourne: Institute of Family Studies, 53—98

6.

The World of Higher Education:
A Socialization—Theoretical Perspective

John C. Weidman
University of Pittsburgh, USA

The purpose of this article is to develop a conceptual framework for understanding salient elements of the socialization process as it occurs in institutions of higher education. The framework builds from both psychological and sociostructural conceptions, drawing upon sociological notions of the socialization process in adolescence and adulthood (Mortimer and Simmons, 1978; Brim, 1966; Wheeler, 1966) as well as approaches to addressing the importance of social structure in socialization and personality development (Hurrelmann, 1988). Important conceptual dimensions of the socialization process are discussed, paying particular attention to those characteristics of both individuals and institutions that are likely to enhance the influence of the higher education experience on students.

The framework incorporates consideration of socializing influences experienced by students in higher education from a variety of sources, both within and external to educational institutions. Even though emphasis is placed on sociostructural aspects of socialization, more interpretive perspectives that focus on the individual student's perceptions of the higher education environment (Huber, 1980) and less on structural aspects of socialization are incorporated, where appropriate, in developing the conceptualization.

1. The Socialization Process

Brim defines socialization as "the process by which persons acquire the knowledge, skills, and dispositions that make them more or less effective members of their society" (1966, 3). While society may be viewed as a generalized social structure composed of smaller units (e.g., families, friends, organizations) within which people behave, it can also be thought of as being composed of groups, "each having a distinct subculture" (Clausen, 1968, 4). Hence, socialization involves the acquisition and maintenance of membership in salient groups (e.g., familial, occupational, organizational) as well as society at large. Consequently, socialization can always usefully be considered from the perspective of the society (or its constituent groups) as well as the individual.

This approach to understanding socialization in higher education suggests two basic questions about the socialization of individuals in an organizational environment. One pertains to social interaction: What are the interpersonal processes through which individuals are socialized? The other pertains to organizational structure: What are the various characteristics of higher education institutions as socializing organizations that exert influences on students? The importance of considering both individual and organizational characteristics in studying socialization can be explained as follows: "Just as individuals may become differently socialized because of differences in past experience, motivations, and capacities, so may they become differently socialized because of differences in the structure of the social settings in which they interact" (Wheeler, 1966, 54).

Hence, it is important to identify social patterns of influence affecting individuals and groups. This is done in the present paper by focusing on the part played by social relationships in the establishment and maintenance of expectations for appropriate member behavior (i.e., norms) and group integration. Dimensions of general socialization theory are then extended to the specific case of student socialization in higher education.

Norms and social integration

From the societal perspective, "socialization efforts are designed to lead the new member to adhere to the norms of the larger society or of the particular group into which he is being incorporated and to commit him to its future" (Clausen, 1968, 6). Norms are important for understanding the process of socialization because, according to Hawkes (1978, 888), "a *norm* may be conceived loosely as a rule, a standard, or a prescription for behavior ... that is in some way enforced ..." Norms provide the basic standards for the regulations of individual behavior in groups as well as in the larger society. Social integration, from this perspective, refers to the extent to which the society or subunit (e.g., institution, organization, group, etc.) is characterized by a shared acceptance of common norms that are reflected in solidary, cohesive, and reasonably stable patterns of relationships among its constituent parts (Parsons, Shils and Olds, 1951, 202—204).

From the perspective of the individual, socialization involves learning the appropriate (i.e., normative) modes of "social behavior and/or role enactment" within the groups in which membership is desired (Mortimer and Simmons, 1978, 422). Role, in this sense, refers to the "dynamic aspects" (Linton, 1936, 14) of positions or statuses in the group, "and may be defined by the expectations (the rights, privileges, and obligations) to which any incumbent of the role must adhere" (Getzels, 1963, 311). Social integration, from the perspective of the individual, refers to the extent to which an individual's behavior in groups is characterized by willing acceptance of group norms and solidary relationships with other members. In terms of socialization, the more fully integrated an individual is into a group, the greater is that group's capacity for assuring a reasonably high level of normative compliance among members.

This is not to say, however, that socialization is a completely deterministic process over which the individual being socialized has little or no control. On the contrary, as individuals mature and move toward the assumption of adult roles, there can be considerable flexibility both in the expectations held of new role incumbents and in the variety of ways in which roles may be fulfilled acceptably (Mortimer and Simmons, 1978). This suggests the importance of incorporating both objective and subjective dimensions when explaining the socialization process (Hurrelmann, 1988). Futhermore, as individuals move toward adulthood, participation in the settings in which socialization occurs tends to be increasingly voluntary. Hence, individuals who do not find the normative expectations in a setting to their liking or who are not welcomed by members may attempt to seek other settings that are more commensurate with personal orientations.

Reference groups and social relationships

An important step in understanding socialization in higher education is to identify those sources of influences that are likely to be the most salient for particular students. Reference group theory is especially useful for identifying potentially important sources of socializing influences. According to Kemper (1968, 32) a reference group can be a person, group, or collectivity that an individual takes into account when selecting a particular course of action from among several alternatives or "in making a judgment about a problematic issue."

A particularly salient social mechanism for the transmission and processing of socializing influences in reference groups is interpersonal relationships, expecially, but not limited to, those that involve close friendships (Shibutani, 1955). According to Brim (1966, 9), this process can be described as follows: "The individual learns the behavior appropriate to his position in a group through interaction with others who hold normative beliefs about what his role should be, and who reward or punish him for correct or incorrect actions."

Anticipatory socialization

General pressures of at least two sorts operate simultaneously. First, students frequently have to make choices concerning their activities after completion of higher education. Second, students need to identify and then to prepare for attaining desirable goals. This process is called "anticipatory socialization," that is, "... the acquisition of values and orientations found in statuses and groups in which one is not yet engaged but which one is likely to enter ..." (Merton, 1968, 438 – 439). Anticipatory socialization prepares individuals for future positions, although much of the preparation is, according to Merton, "implicit, unwitting, and informal."

Many students in higher education attempt to determine not only their own suitability for prospective careers (both in terms of academic skills and perceived job demands) but also the reactions of significant others to their choices. In addition to providing the education and credentials necessary for access to professional, managerial, and upper white – collar occupations, higher education also provides experiences and resources for students to develop more generalized orientations toward work and leisure activities. In this sense, the higher education environment may serve as a context for anticipatory career socialization involving the concomitant influences of students' values and occupational aspirations, because, according to Rosenberg (1957, 24), "in addition to people choosing an occupation in order to satisfy a value, they may choose a value because they consider it appropriate for the occupational status they expect to fill in the future." The choice of an academic major is a central component of this process.

Temporal aspects of socialization

These processes of socialization do not apply only to the late adolescence/early adulthood period of life that is characteristic of traditional students in higher education. Socialization is considered to be a lifelong process that occurs as individuals adapt themselves to a variety of changing circumstances (Bragg, 1976), not the least of which are changes in career demands, family responsibilities, and possibly even the employment structure. There are differences, however, in the basic content of socialization (ranging from the regulation of biological drives to specific group norms), the contexts in which socialization occurs (ranging from the dependent status of the child to the organizational settings of adulthood), and the response of individuals (ranging from the very malleable child to the change – resistant adult) to socializing influences (Mortimer and Simmons, 1978). Because it tends to involve a significant status transition, the higher education experience has been likened to a "rite of passage" (Tinto, 1987). Hence, the study of socialization in higher education should take into account differences in the age and developmental stages of students as well as the cultural and national contexts of higher education systems (Clark, 1983).

A second consideration has to do with the duration of influence. Curtis (1974) has shown, for instance, that the socialization potential of an educational institution increases with the amount of time that a student spends enrolled. The sequential nature of certain types of socialization processes is also important. As formulated by Thornton and Nardi (1975), taking on a role can be described as moving through four stages: anticipatory, formal, informal, and personal. In each stage, there is "interaction between individuals and external expectations, including individuals' attempts to influence the expectations of others as well as others' attempts to influence individuals" (Thornton and Nardi, 1975, 873).

The first of these stages corresponds to anticipatory socialization. The formal stage occurs when the individual begins to assume the specific demands of the role, meeting the group's official or proclaimed expectations of the role. The informal stage occurs when the individual learns the unofficial or informal expectations for the role and adapts behavior accordingly. In the personal stage, the individual reconciles the formal and informal expectations with personal orientations, assumes full membership in the group, and begins to participate in the group's processes of shaping the expectations that will be held subsequently for new role incumbents.

92   *J. C. Weidman*

The essence of this approach as it applies to the relationships among individual and organizational variables in the study of student socialization in higher education can be summarized as follows: Just as students differ in their patterns of interaction and personal orientations upon entrance, institutions of higher education differ in their structuring, intentionally or not, of both normative contexts such as student residences and classrooms, and of opportunities for social interaction among students, faculty, and staff. Furthermore, because socialization occurs over a period of time and is a cumulative process, the relative importance of both institutional settings and significant others may change during the course of the years students take to complete a degree. Hence, it is essential that conceptualizations of socialization in higher education incorporate the longitudinal aspects of change and stability, including personality and social development, over the entire time required for degree completion.

2.   Sozialization in Higher Education: A Conceptual Framework

Figure 1 shows the conceptual framework developed for this article. Underlying this framework, on one level, are concerns for the situational and individual developmental constraints on the choices made by participants in an organizational environment. On another level, the framework explores a set of socialization processes, concentrating largely on the impact of normative contexts and interpersonal relations among an organization's members. It includes consideration of the joint socializing impacts of: (a) student background, (b) the normative influences exerted by the academic and social structure of the higher education environment through the mechanisms of both inter − and intrapersonal processes, particularly as they are reflected in social integration, and (c) the mediating impacts of both parental socialization and reference groups that are not part of the higher education sphere of influence. The framework draws primarily upon the author's own research (Weidman, 1984; Weidman and Friedman, 1984; Weidman and White, 1985) as well as the conceptual work of Chickering (1969), Tinto (1975, 1987), and Astin (1977, 1984).

To summarize the general conceptual framework, socialization in higher education can be conceived as a series of processes whereby the student:

1.   enters a higher education institution with certain abilities, values, aspirations, and other personal goals;

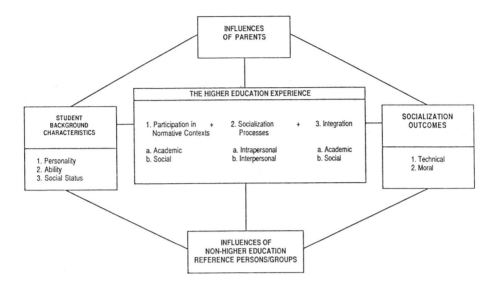

Fig. 1: Socialization in higher education: A conceptual framework

2. is exposed to various socializing influences while attending, including normative pressures exerted via (a) social relationships with faculty and peers, (b) parental pressures, and (c) involvement with non – higher – education reference groups;

3. assesses the salience of the various normative pressures encountered for integration into the academic and social contexts of higher education; and

4. changes or maintains technical (e.g., knowledge and skills) and moral (e.g., values, personal goals, and orientations) attributes.

The dimensions of the model shown in Figure 1 are assumed to be linked in a bidirectional, as opposed to a unidirectional, causal fashion. It is assumed that there is a reciprocity of influences on students such that various dimensions can have greater or lesser importance for socialization, depending upon the outcomes considered as well as both the particular stage of students' lives and of their higher education experience. In the following sections, the dimensions of the framework are described in more detail. Specific attention is also paid to illustrating some of the more important linkages among dimensions.

Student background characteristics

Characteristics of individuals that tend to be correlated with specific types of outcomes must be included in any conceptualization of the socialization process in higher education. The contribution of student background characteristics to understanding socialization in higher education is investigated in at least three primary sources of literature: (a) research examining the broad spectrum of higher education's effects on students (Feldman and Newcomb, 1969; Astin, 1977); (b) research on dropouts from higher education (Tinto, 1975; Pascarella and Chapman, 1983); and (c) research on the sociology of status attainment (Sewell, Haller and Portes, 1969; Sewell, Haller and Ohlendorf, 1970; Alexander and Eckland, 1975; Jencks, Crouse and Mueser, 1983; Hauser, Tsai and Sewell, 1983).

Influence of parents

Explicit in this framework is the recognition that the higher education institution does not, for most students, constitute a totally encapsulated environment. Parents, for example, influence the career preferences and orientations that students bring with them at entrance to higher education (Bengston, 1975). Furthermore, since the effects of parental influences are so very likely to persist during the course of the student's academic program, parental pressures and expectations may serve to mediate the impact of the higher education experience. Two questions are suggested by this approach: How are various aspects of parental socialization and life – styles related to the persistance and change of students' orientations and preferences? How do aspects of the higher education experience and parental socialization (especially as reflected in parent – child relationships) interact with one another in influencing the student?

Sociological research consistently shows that occupational attainment is related to such measures of parental social status as occupational prestige and educational attainment (Blau and Duncan, 1967; Alexander and Eckland, 1975). Other studies indicate that occupational values in work are associated with a middle – social – class position as measured by educational and occupational status, and that these values are transmitted by parents to their offspring (Kohn, 1977; Morgan, Alwin and Griffin, 1979; Mortimer, 1974, 1976). While there are strong correlations between such variables as parental life – style and career orientations of students (Weidman, 1984), there is also evidence that parental influences decline in importance during the course of the higher education experience (Weidman, 1984), especially for those students who move out of their parents' homes to attend an institution of higher education.

It should also be noted, however, that finding no significant parental influences on the career choices of students (Weidman, 1984) may be an artifact of the measures used, especially if they were based on students' self—reports of parental characteristics, expectations, and behavior. Recent studies (Davies and Kandel, 1981; Looker and Pineo, 1983) suggest that adolescents may systematically *underestimate* the importance of parental influences on aspirations. These authors demonstrate the importance of obtaining information about their attitudes and behavior *directly* from parents instead of relying solely on reports by adolescents of their parents' influence.

Non—higher—education reference persons/groups

In addition to relationships with parents, students are likely to maintain ties of various sorts to significant others outside the higher education environment. Because typical education institutions are not encapsulated environments, it is reasonable to assume that performance in higher education may be affected by the student's ability to cope with problems at home (e.g., spouses and children), employers, and other community settings (Weidman and Friedmann, 1984; Weidman and White, 1985; Bean and Metzner, 1985).

Atkins' (1982) finding that dropout among first—year college students is related to concern with "family/personal problems" also supports this extension of the framework, as does Tinto's (1982, 688) acknowledgement that his model did not "... seek to directly address the impact of financial stress or other forces external to the institution's immediate environment (e.g., external peer groups in an urban environment)." The support of noncampus significant others, including friends and other relatives is also important for students (Weidman and White, 1985; Thomas, 1981) who have to cope with many competing expectations and, hence, are exposed to potentially conflicting normative pressures.

The higher education experience

Socialization may be thought of a process that "entails a continuing interaction between the individual and those who seek to influence him" (Clausen, 1969, 3). Socialization, in this sense, "does imply that the individual is induced in some measure to conform willingly to the ways of ... the particular groups to which he belongs" (Clausen, 1968, 4). Socialization in higher education can thus be viewed as a process that results from the student's interaction with other members of the higher education environment in groups or other settings characterized by varying degrees of normative pressure.

This portion of the conceptual framework draws heavily from the seminal structural—functional analysis of American universities by Parsons and Platt (1973). Specifically, the framework focuses on two aspects of their argument as it relates to student socialization. One has to do with what they term the "moral authority of institutions" (Parsons and Platt, 1973, 167). This refers to the normative order (including its mission as well as normative expectations of faculty and staff for students) of the university as a potent agent of socialization. The various aspects of an institution's normative order may then be studied by identifying social contexts that are characterized by especially strong expectations for students. In Chickering's (1969) terms, the greater the "clarity and consistency of objectives," the stronger the normative consensus among members of a particular institution, organizational unit, or group within the institution. The second aspect of the Parsons and Platt (1973) discussion has to do with interpersonal relationships among various members of academic settings. According to Parsons and Platt, these interpersonal attachments make an important contribution to the members' social integration within the university.

Furthermore, interpersonal relationships contributing to the social integration of students into the academic system are related not only to the attainment of institutional goals but also to the personal goals of individual students (Tinto, 1975). Close, personal relationships among members of normative contexts contribute materially to the transmission and internalization of normative influences by members (Moore, 1969). Hence, in studying student socialization in higher education, it is important to explore the impacts of normative contexts as well as the ways in which interpersonal relationships among members serve to either reinforce or counteract the normative influences exerted within various specific contexts (Lacy, 1978).

Following Tinto (1975), Figure 1 divides "Participation in Normative Contexts" into an "Academic" and a "Social" dimension. The academic dimension refers to those aspects of the higher education environment that contribute explicitly to the fulfillment of educational objectives (as stated in the institutional mission), including such things as allocation of resources for the organization of instruction, and student selection in the admissions process. The social dimension refers to the ways in which opportunities for interaction among members are organized and clustered within the institution.

Normative contexts: Academic

Institutional and within–institution program quality, though fraught with problems of definition and measurement (Conrad and Blackburn, 1985), continues to be of considerable interest to scholars, policymakers, and consumers of higher education. The "frog–pond effect" (Davis, 1966; Reitz, 1975) suggests that institutional selectivity decreases students' preferences for seeking educationally high–level careers, largely because the competition between highly able students is greater than in less selective institutions. Other studies (Bassis, 1977; Drew and Astin, 1972), however, found positive effects of selectivity on aspirations and self–evaluations. Solmon and Wachtel (1975) found institutional quality as measured by levels of resource allocation to be positively associated with career income. Institutional reputation or prestige, often used as the primary measure in studies of quality, has also been shown to be related to both degree completion and access to elite careers (Kamens, 1974).

A particularly important locus of both faculty and peer influences on students is the major field (Hearn, 1980; Hearn and Olzak, 1981; Weidman, 1979, 1984), since it tends to be the organizational unit through which degree requirements are formulated and certification of their successful completion is made. Vreeland and Bidwell (1966, 238) assert that the major field "has relatively well–defined goals and expectations for students, and commands powerful normative and utilitarian sanctions."

The major field can be a powerful source of normative influence on student majors, in large part because of the faculty's ability to differentially reward students for their performance in courses, both through the assignment of grades and the encouragement of social interaction (Parsons and Platt, 1973). Faculty evaluation of student's performance in class–related activities as well as in other settings can be a significant influence on students' goals, aspirations, and more general orientations toward such things as political values, use of leisure time, and cultural pursuits (Liebau and Huber, 1985).

The "hidden curriculum" (Snyder, 1971) of higher education can also be a powerful source of influence on students. This refers to the unspoken and unwritten rules defining faculty expectations for students' academic performance. Do examinations, for instance, actually reflect what faculty say is important? Similarly, it could also refer to the unwritten rules of academic behavior as well as to other informal norms about what is acceptable as defined by students (Becker, Geer and Hughes, 1968).

Normative contexts: Social

An important dimension here is the extracurricular structure of the higher education institution. Presumably, those students who participate actively in extracurricular activities may be more likely than their nonparticipant counterparts to look to peers who participate in common extracurricular activities rather than to major field faculty as normative referents. It is also possible that the norms held by others in the extracurricular settings differ from those held by major field peers and faculty.

The spatial location, especially on− versus off−campus, of reference groups can also affect their potential for socialization. The importance for socialization of participation in on−campus activities has been described by Vreeland and Bidwell (1965, 235) as contributing to the power of the institution to influence students because "... the broader the scope of the student's involvement with the college, the more accessible he is to intervention and the more diverse the mechanisms that can be employed (especially mechanisms of indirect manipulation)." Consequently, limited student involvement with on−campus reference groups is likely to reduce the impact of normative pressures exerted within the higher education institution.

Socialization processes: Interpersonal

An important determinant of the socialization potential of social relationships is the degree of intensity of feelings and other affective attachments between the people involved, namely, their sentiments (Homans, 1950). Another critical aspect of interaction is its frequency. The more frequently an individual interacts with specific others, the more he/she is exposed to their attitudes, values, and opinions. Furthermore, as Homans argues, there is often a direct relationship between frequency of interaction with another person and liking that person (Homans, 1961). Homans does not, however, assert this proposition without a qualification, which is that sentiments exchanged may be so negative that frequent interaction may lead to aversion rather than attraction between those involved.

These notions of frequency and sentimental intensity of interaction are basic components underlying this conceptual framework. As Shibutani (1955, 568) asserted, "socialization is a product of a gradual accumulation of experiences with certain people, particularly those with whom we stand in primary relations". Both students and faculty tend to feel that the most enduring academic impacts of higher education result from social interaction between faculty and students outside the formal classroom setting (Thielens, 1966; Wilson, et al., 1975; Pascarella, 1980; Winteler, 1981). Availability of these opportunities may be a significant enhancer of student socialization.

Socialization processes: Intrapersonal

The aspects of the student's higher education experience reflecting his/her subjective assessment (e.g., satisfaction, fulfillment of expectations) are referred to as intrapersonal processes (Weidman and White, 1985). As one critic of the structural—functional interpretation of socialization has argued (Wrong, 1961), socialization encompasses both the transmission of norms and the individual processing of normative influences that result in the development of unique personal orientations to social contexts. Not surprisingly, there is a considerable literature dealing with the related phenomenon of "person—environment interaction" in higher education (Stern, 1970; Moos, 1979).

The general question raised by this approach is: How do the individual's perceptions of participation in various segments of the higher education environment affect its socialization potential? Put in a somewhat different way, the concern is with assessing whether or not favorable student assessments of various aspects of their experience enhance institutional impact. That student satisfaction seems to improve during their years of attendance (Feldman and Newcomb, 1969) suggests that more advanced students may have accommodated themselves better to the demands and expectations of their college, quite possibly reflecting the socializing influence of the campus over time. Another dimension that enhances the institution's socialization potential is the students' images of the campus contribution to the attainment of personal goals (Weidman and Krus, 1979).

Integration: Academic

The student's perceived "fit" or subjective assessment of his/ her degree of social integration into the life of the institution is another dimension of interest in the conceptual framework. In the conceptual model of dropout from higher education developed by Tinto (1975), goal commitments, aspirations, and values held at entrance to higher education are posited to affect both students' academic integration as reflected in grades and intellectual development, and social integration as reflected in peer group and other social relationships within the institution. Academic integration is reflected in the success of students in accommodating themselves to the demands of the formal curricular structure.

Integration: Social

Tinto (1975) described social integration into campus life as being due primarily to interaction with faculty, administration, and peers as well as participation in extracurricular activities. He suggested that these relationships resulted in varying degrees of student affiliation "that modify his educational and institutional commitments" (Tinto, 1975, 107). With respect to students' assessments of impersonal treatment on campus, the expectation is that the less favorable the student is in his/her perceptions of the higher education environment, the less likely that student is to be socialized toward the norms of the institution or of affiliated extracurricular groups.

Socialization outcomes

Vreeland and Bidwell (1966) suggest that the departmental faculty's collective conception of goals for educating students conditions the faculty's conception of the instructional task. This, more than specific subject – matter content, determines the social organization of departmental student – faculty interaction. These authors systematize the structure of departmental faculty influence by dividing faculty goals for educating students into two categories: technical and moral. Technical goals concern transmission of the intellectual structure of an academic discipline as well as more cognitive aspects of career preparation. Moral goals concern such things as the ethical practice of an occupation, the broadening or humanizing effects of education, and the development of social and political values (Bundeszentrale für politische Bildung, 1985).

According to this formulation, the expressed goals of faculty for educating students determine faculty behavior and expectations which, in turn, determine the socializing effects of the department. Vreeland and Bidwell (1966, 241 – 242) posit three conditions that contribute to socialization of students toward major field norms: (a) faculty interest in teaching; (b) student – faculty interaction measured on two dimensions, intimacy and frequency, and (c) faculty and student norms that are "consistent and reinforcing."

3. Discussion

It could be argued that the outcomes of undergraduate socialization during any particular time period are as much a function of the characteristics, values, and aspirations of the students as they are of the socialization processes that occur during the higher education experience. Certainly, there is considerable documentation of the changes in career orientations over the past few decades for students in the United States, with a general increase in the desire to obtain specific occupational skills in higher education rather than a broad, liberal arts education (Hoge, 1976). While this trend holds for both sexes, women have made even greater changes in their career orientations than men, with women now aspiring to high−level careers (Regan and Roland, 1982). There are also rather different patterns of higher education experiences, including career socialization for women (Bressler and Wendell, 1980; Perun, 1982) and mionority students (Willie and Cunnigen, 1981; Thomas, 1981; Nettles, Thoeny and Gosman, 1986). Problems of social and academic integration have also been well−documented for minority students (Fox, 1986; Nora, 1987). This suggests that it is necessary to adapt conceptual frameworks to represent the differing patterns of socialization experienced by members of ethnic and gender groups.

To test empirically the framework that has been developed would require that variables be identified and then operationalized appropriately. Interested readers can see Lenning (1983) or Endo and Bittner (1985) for long lists of potential variables, and Pascarella (1985) for a discussion of some of the measurent problems involved in operationalizing variables. In addition, care must be taken in selecting appropriate statistical techniques, because the model represents multidirectional processes rather than unidirectional causality.

There is, however, one measurement concern of particular importance. Throughout the discussion, it has been emphasized that the characteristics of specific normative contexts should be related as directly as possible to the student, preferably by identifying a linking mechanism of socialization. One of the best examples of research that accomplished this linking is the study of undergraduates at a small, midwestern, liberal arts college done by Wallace (1966). He used sociometric techniques to quantify each undergraduate's "interpersonal environment," aggregating the questionnaire responses from each individual on campus who was named as being a friend of the student. Large sample survey research is not, however, always amenable to such techniques, especially since confidentiality of responses is often of great concern. It may then be necessary to settle for more general measures of membership group attachments based on friendship or interaction not tied to specific individuals, but nonetheless reflecting students' participation in salient normative contexts.

References

Atkins, N.D. (1982): College student performance, satisfaction, and retention. Journal of Higher Education, 53, 32–50

Alexander, K.L., & Eckland, B.K. (1975): Basic attainment processes: A replication and extension. Sociology of Education, 48, 457–495

Astin, A.W. (1977): Four critical years: Effects of college on beliefs, attitudes, and knowledge. San Francisco: Jossey–Bass

Astin, A.W. (1984): Student involvement: A developmental theory for higher education. Journal of College Student Personnel, 25, 297–308

Bassis, M.S. (1977): The campus as a frogpond: A theoretical and empirical reassessment. American Journal of Sociology, 82, 1318–1326

Bean, J.P., & Metzner, B.S. (1985): A conceptual model of nontraditional undergraduate student attrition. Review of Educational Research, 55, 485–540

Becker, H.S., Geer, B., & Hughes, E.C. (1968): Making the grade: The academic side of college life. New York: Wiley

Bengston, V.L. (1975): Generation and family effects in value socialization. American Sociological Review, 40, 358–371

Blau, P.M., & Duncan, O.D. (1967): The American occupational structure. New York: Wiley

Bragg, A.K. (1976): The socialization process in higher education. (ERIC/Higher Education Research Report No. 7). Washington, DC: American Association for Higher Education

Bressler, M., & Wendell, P. (1980): The sex composition of selective colleges and gender differences in career aspirations. Journal of Higher Education, 51, 650–663

Brim, O.G.Jr. (1966): Socialization through the life cycle. In Brim, O.G.Jr., & Wheeler, S.(Eds.): Socialization after childhood: Two essays. New York: Wiley, 1–49

Bundeszentrale für politische Bildung (1985): Politische Sozialisation an Hochschulen. Bonn: Schriftenreihe der Bundeszentrale für Politische Bildung (Band 233)

Chickering, A.W. (1969): Education and identity. San Francisco: Jossey–Bass

Clark, B.R. (1983): The higher education system: Academic organization in cross–national perspectve. Berkeley: University of California Press

Clausen, J.A. (1968): Introduction. In Clausen, J.A. (Ed.): Socialization and society. Boston: Little, Brown & Co, 1–17

Conrad, C.F., & Blackburn, R.T. (1985): Program quality in higher education: A review and critique of literature and research. In Smart, J.C. (Ed.): Higher education: Handbook of theory and research, Vol.1. New York: Agathon, 283–308

Curtis, R.L. (1974): The issue of schools as social systems: Socialization effects as inferred from lengths of membership. Sociological Quarterly, 15, 277–293

Davies, M., & Kandel, D.B. (1981): Parental and peer influences on adolescents' educational plans: Some further evidence. American Journal of Sociology, 87, 363–387

Davis, J.A. (1966): The campus as a frogpond: An application of the theory of relative deprivation to career decisions of college men. American Journal of Sociology, 72, 17–31

Drew, D.E., & Astin, A.W. (1972): Undergraduate aspirations: A test of several theories. American Journal of Sociology, 77, 1151–1164

Endo, J., & Bittner, T. (1985): Developing and using a longitudinal student outcomes data file: The University of Colorado experience. In Ewell, P.T. (Ed.): Assessing educational outcomes. New Directions for Institutional Research, No. 47. San Francisco: Jossey–Bass, 65–80

Feldman, K.A., & Newcomb, T.N. (1969): The impact of college on students. San Francisco: Jossey–Bass

Fox, R.N. (1986): Application of a conceptual model of college withdrawal to disadvantaged students. American Education Research Journal, 23, 415–424

Getzels, J.W. (1963): Conflict and role behavior in the educational setting. In Charters, W.W.Jr., & Gage, N.L. (Eds.): Readings in the social psychology of education. Boston: Allyn & Bacon, 309–318

Hauser, R.M., Tsai, S., & Sewell, W.H. (1983): A model of stratification with response error in social and psychological variables. Sociology of Education, 56, 20–46

Hawkes, R.K. (1975): Norms, deviance, and social control: A mathematical elaboration of concepts. American Journal of Sociology, 80, 886–908

Hearn, J.C. (1980): Major choice and well–being of college men and women: An examination from developmental, organizational, and structural perspectives. Sociology of Education, 53, 164–178

Hearn, J.C., & Olzak, S. (1981): The role of college major departments in the reproduction of sexual inequality. Sociology of Education, 54, 195–205

Hoge, D.R. (1976): Changes in college students' value patterns in the 1950's, 1960's and 1970's. Sociology of Education, 49, 155–163

Homans, G.C. (1950): The human group. New York: Harcourt, Brace & World

Homans, G.C. (1961): Social behavior: Its elementary forms. New York: Harcourt, Brace & World

Huber, L. (1980): Socialization in der Hochschule. In Hurrelmann, K., & Ulich, D. (Eds.): Handbuch der Sozializationsforschung. Weinheim: Beltz, 521–550

Hurrelmann, K. (1988): Social structure and personality. New York: Cambridge University Press

Jencks, C., Crouse, J., & Mueser, P. (1983): The Wisconsin model of status attainment: A national replication with improved measures of ability and aspiration. Sociology of Education, 56, 3–19

Kamens, D. (1974): Colleges and elite formation: The case of prestigious American colleges. Sociology of Education, 47, 354–378

Kemper, T.D. (1968): Reference groups as perspectives. American Sociological Review, 33, 31–45

Kohn, M.L. (1977): Class and conformity: A study in values (2nd Ed.). Chicago: University of Chicago Press

Lacy, W.B. (1978): Interpersonal relationships as mediators or structural effects: College student socialization in a traditional and an experimental university environment. Sociology of Education, 51, 201–211

Lenning, O.T. (1983): Variable–selection and measurement concerns. In Pascarella, E.T. (Ed.): Studying student attrition. New Directions for Institutional Research, No. 36. San Francisco: Jossey–Bass, 35–53

Liebau, E., & Huber, L. (1985): Die Kulturen der Fächer. Neue Sammlung, 25, 314–339

Linton, R. (1936): The study of man. New York: Appleton–Century–Crofts

Looker, E.D., & Pineo, P.D. (1983): Social psychological variables and their relevance to the status attainment of teenagers. American Journal of Sociology, 88, 1195–1219

Merton, R.K. (1968): Social theory and social structure. New York: Free Press

Moore, W.E. (1969): Occupational socialization. In Goslin, D.A. (Ed.): Handbook of socialization theory and research. Chicago: Rand McNally, 861–873

Moos, R.H. (1979): Evaluating educational environments. San Francisco: Jossey–Bass

Morgan, W.R., Alwin, D.F., & Griffin, L.J. (1979): Social origins, parental values, and the transmission of inequality. American Journal of Sociology, 85, 156–166

Mortimer, J.T. (1974): Patterns of intergenerational occupational movements: A smallest space analysis. American Journal of Sociology, 79, 1278–1299

Mortimer, J.T. (1976): Social class, work and the family: Some implications of the father's occupation for familial relationships and sons' career decisions. Journal of Marriage and the Family, 38, 241–256

Mortimer, J.T., & Simmons, R.G. (1978): Adult socialization. In Turner, R.H., Coleman, J., & Fox, R.C. (Eds.): Annual Review of Sociology. Vol. 4. Palo Alto: Annual Reviews, 421–454

Nettles, M.T., Thoeny, A.R., & Gosman, E.J. (1986): Comparative and predictive analyses of black and white students' college achievement and experiences. Journal of Higher Education, 57, 289–318

Nora, A. (1987): Determinants of retention among Chicano college students: A structural model. Research in Higher Education, 26, 31–59

Parsons, T., & Platt, G.M. (1973): The American University. Cambridge: Harvard University Press

Parsons, T., Shils, E.A., & Olds, L. (1951): Values, motives, and systems of action. In Parsons, T. & Shils, E.A. (Eds.): Toward a general theory of action. New York: Harper, 45–276

Pascarella, E.T. (1980): Student–faculty informal contact and college outcomes. Review of Educational Research, 50, 545–595

Pascarella, E.T. (1985): College environment influences on learning and cognitive development. In Smart, J.C. (Ed.): Higher Education: Handbook of Theory and Research, Vol. 1. New York: Agathon, 1–16

Pascarella, E.T., & Chapman, D.W. (1983): A multi–institutional, path analytic validation of Tinto's model of college withdrawal. American Educational Research Journal, 20, 87–102

Perun, P.J. (Ed.)(1982): The undergraduate women: Issues in educational equity. Lexington: Lexington Books

Regan, M.C., & Roland, H.E. (1982): University students: A change in expectations and aspirations over the decade. Sociology of Education, 55, 223–228

Reitz, J.G. (1975): Undergraduate aspirations and career choice. Sociology of Education, 48, 308–323

Rosenberg, M. (1957): Occupations and values. Glencoe: Free Press

Sewell, W.T., Haller, A.O., & Ohlendorf, G.O. (1970): The educational and early occupational status achievement process: Replication and revision. American Sociological Review, 35, 1014–1027

Sewell, W.T., Haller, A.O., & Portes, A. (1969): The educational and early occupational attainment process. American Sociological Review, 34, 82–92

Shibutani, T. (1955): Reference groups as perspectives. American Journal of Sociology, 60, 562–569

Snyder, B.R. (1971): The hidden curriculum. New York: Alfred Knopf

Solmon, L.C., & Wachtel, P. (1975): The effects on income of type of college attended. Sociology of Education, 48, 75–90

Stern, G.C. (1970): People in context: Measuring person—environment congruence in education and industry. New York: Wiley

Thielens, W.W.Jr. (1966): The structure of faculty influence. New York: Columbia University, Bureau of Applied Social Research

Thomas, G.E. (Ed.)(1981): Black students in higher education: Conditions and experiences in the 1970's. Westport: Greenwood Press

Thornton, R., & Nardi, P.M. (1975): The dynamics of role acquisition. American Journal of Sociology, 80, 870—885

Tinto, V. (1975): Dropout from higher education: A theoretical synthesis of recent research. Review of Educational Research, 45, 89—125

Tinto, V. (1987): Leaving college: Rethinking the causes and cures of student attrition. Chicago: University of Chicago Press

Vreeland, R., & Bidwell, C.E. (1966): Classifiying university departments: An approach to the analysis of their effects upon undergraduates' values and attitudes. Sociology of Education, 30, 237—254

Wallace, W.L. (1966): Student culture: Social structure and continuity in a liberal arts college. Chicago: Aldine

Weidman, J.C. (1979): Nonintellective undergraduate socialization in academic departments. Journal of Higher Education, 50, 48—62

Weidman, J.C. (1984): Impacts of campus experiences and parental socialization on undergraduates' career choices. Research in Higher Education, 20, 445—476

Weidman, J.C., & Friedman, R.R. (1984): The school—to—work transition for high school dropouts. Urban Review, 16, 25—42

Weidman, J.C., & Krus, D.J. (1979): Undergraduates' expectations and images of college. Psychological Reports, 45, 131—139

Weidman, J.C., & White, R.N. (1985): Postsecondary "high—tech" training for women on welfare: Correlates of program completion. Journal of Higher Education, 56, 555—568

Wheeler, S. (1966): The structure of formally organized socialization settings. In Brim, O.G.Jr., & Wheeler, S.: Socialization after childhood: Two essays. New York: Wiley, 53—116

Willie, C.V., & Cunningen, D. (1981): Black students in higher education: A review of studies, 1965—1980. In Turner, R.H., & Short, J.F.Jr. (Eds.): Annual Review of Sociology, Vol. 7. Palo Alto: Annual Reviews, 177—198

Wilson, R., Gaff, J.G., Dienst, E.R., Wood, L., & Bavry, J.L. (1975): College professors and their impact on students. New York: Wiley

Winteler, A. (1981): The academic department as environment for teaching and learning. Higher Education, 10, 25—35

Wrong, D. (1961): The oversocialized conception of man in modern sociology. American Sociological Review, 26, 183—193

7.

Adolescents as Productive Processors of Reality: Methodological Perspectives

Klaus Hurrelmann
University of Bielefeld, Federal Republic of Germany

In this paper I shall present a general frame of reference for a comprehensive approach to youth research that considers different "levels" of theoretical analysis. My main aim is to look for those points of consensus that are emerging in the discussion about theory and methodology of youth research. I shall discuss (1) a meta—theoretical model of the subject in youth research, (2) the principles of theory construction in this field, and (3) pluralistic methodological procedures. My plea is for an interdisciplinary approach that will provide for a division of labor between sociology, psychology, and educational science within the framework of an integrative program of research. My starting point is the discussion in sociology.

1.   A Meta — Theoretical "Model of the Subject" in Youth Research

For many years most of the sociological approaches to theory have tended to lose sight of the individual human being. The idea of the social determination of the individual — where it was understood in the sense of a one—sided determination — necessarily led to a shift of research interest to social and material conditions, and ultimately to an elimination of the category of the subject as a self—determining factor in social processes. Accordingly, no significant role was attributed to psychological reasoning.

In recent sociological approaches to youth theory, there has been an increasing tendency to include an explicit elaboration of the subject. Typical of these approaches is, *first*, that they systematically assert that a person is conditioned by society, not in the sense of a mechanistic milieu—determinism, but in the sense of a human being as an acting subject. *Second*, they formulate the central point of any socialization theory, that is, the transition from objective conditions to subjective formations, in concepts such as, for example, appropriation and action, which are rooted both in an external and an internal reality. *Third*, they comprehend social conditions in the context of a theory of a historically developing society (Hurrelmann and Ulich, 1980; Geulen and Hurrelmann, 1982).

These approaches are oriented toward a specific meta–theoretical model, namely that of *the subject who productively processes and manages his/her reality*. This model views personal development and social development in a dynamic perspective and as being mutually dependent on one another.

This model presents a tentative notion of the "object of investigation" in question, that is, human development in adolescence. It provides a point of departure for the choice and derivation of specific theories and methods that are appropriate for the meta–theoretical model. Theories, in this context, are to be understood as systems of sentences that are logically consistent; methods are to be understood as specific procedures for empirical control, correction, and further elaboration of these theories.

The central point of the meta–theoretical model of the subject as described here is the rejection of models of linear, single–factor determination of personality development that assume a passive, receptive formation of the individual, either through socioeconomic or psychophysical factors. It argues that personal development occurs in the process of productively managing both inner and outer reality. The assumption is that, from the beginning, every individual possesses certain capacities for managing reality that he/she uses and develops further. Another central assumption of this model is that the construction of systems of orientation and action takes place as a result of this process, and that the individual reacts to the appearance of reality in its various, situationally determined forms. This leads to changes in the structure of both the person and his/her environment. In other words, what is being proposed here is a model of a "dialectic" relationship between the subject and the socially experienced reality, a model of interdependent relations between individual and social development (Hurrelmann, 1988).

This meta–theoretical model shares many points of contact with models in other social sciences, especially those of developmental psychology (Bronfenbrenner, 1979). Along with sociologists and educationalists, these psychologists are looking for alternatives to the one–sided endogenic and exogenic theories that view development either as a psychophysical system dwelling within the person or as impulses received from outside. Especially in the approach of ecological and life–span psychologists (Baltes, Reese and

Lipsitt, 1980; Oerter and Montada 1982; Lerner 1982), it is the interaction between person and environment as a relation of mutuality, including the active response of a person to the social and ecological environment, that is considered important.

The job of investigating personal development in all its areas and aspects is so many — sided that a variety of theoretical, discipline — based approaches is necessary, even if the fundamental meta — theoretical models have become more similar. The sociologically oriented research strongly stresses the analysis of the societal and material environment as one of the constitutive conditions of personal development. Alongside of the sociologically oriented approaches (including historical and economic approaches), it is reasonable in the sense of a division of labor for there to be a psychologically oriented type of research. The focal points of this approach should continue to be to investigate the intrapsychological mechanisms and the structure of the psychological apparatus at its various developmental stages (Silbereisen, Eyferth and Rudinger, 1986).

This interdisciplinary procedure expresses the fact that the human subject is shaped by psychological and social factors, and that he/she is constituted only in the process of social interaction. In other words, none of his/her functions and dimensions are formed independently of society, but only in the context of a concrete world of experience that is a social and historical reality. The idea of the appropriation and management of inner and outer reality is an inherent element of this conception (Hurrelmann, 1988, 42).

The meta — theoretical model of the adolescent who productively processes and manages his/her reality calls for a fresh look at human development during this phase of life. The adolescent's own perceptions, expectations, goals, and capacities have to be taken into consideration in a much more fundamental way than has been done before.

Modern developmental psychology and socialization theory acknowledge the value of this meta — theoretical model when viewing adolescence and youth as a transitional period in life, a stressful phase of development that poses distinctive tasks and challenges as well as opportunities. During this phase of the life — span, a major disequilibrium in the psychophysical and psychosocial systems of the organism can be observed. One characteristic of his stressful transition or crisis is the general discontinuity with the past situations with which adolescents have previously been confronted (Hamburg, 1980). There is almost no sphere in which it is possible to draw on analogous past experience for support or guidance. Virtually the entire body is involved in the anatomical and physiological changes of pubertal growth, and the psychological development is closely related to the physical development. In adolescence, a totally new programming of behavioral patterns and modes becomes necessary, with a chance of either success or failure in solving these developmental tasks.

In terms of the Havighurst (1972) conception of adolescent development, which is receiving renewed interest, young people have to solve several developmental tasks. A satisfactory solution of these tasks is a prerequisite for the establishment of adequate and secure social relationships and a personal and social identity. Compared to childhood, the expectations of society in relation to adolescence are not clearly defined. Adolescents are faced with the problem that, on the one hand, they do not have enough support from other social groups when coping with developmental tasks, and, on the other hand, they are not allowed to engage in competent and meaningful action because the opportunities necessary for social participation are not available. Adolescents have to pass through a phase of life marked by a high degree of role diffusion (cf. Coleman, in this volume).

The changes in the conditions of life that are due to overall societal and economic changes have made the taking over of the adult role difficult. They have led to increased stress and tension for many young people. Adolescents need to have a great capacity for flexible adjustment to difficult environmental conditions during a phase of development that, in biological and psychological respects, is already demanding a very large measure of coping capacity. Typically, a very high capacity of realistic perception and management of the complex social reality is a prerequisite for solving this task (cf. Poole, in this volume).

2. Theory Construction in Youth Research

Some of the steps necessary and appropriate for transforming the meta – theoretical model of the subject into adequate theoretical constructs will be discussed now.

Components of a comprehensive theoretical model of socialization

The meta – theoretical model of the subject outlined above may be elaborated in various ways with concrete steps leading to the construction of theories. The decision as to which specific theory will be chosen depends largely on the disciplinary training and experience of the researcher and his/her personal preference. My own point of view as a "psychology – oriented sociologist" favors socialization theory with an action – theoretical background. The term "action" offers a transformative construct for the integration of psychological and sociological sets of theoretical statements. The theory of socialization envisages an interdependent relationship between the human subject as a producer and constructor of reality and this reality as his/her product, which, in a process of institutionalization, becomes an objective reality to him/her.

The model of the adolescent as a productive processor of reality requires the construction of a theory that integrates phenomena relevant to the socialization process on different levels of analysis. Ideally, the researcher should be able to include within a single analysis societal processes, the institutionalization process of social organizations and the activities of the formal agencies of socialization, the processes of interaction in small groups and situational contexts, the dynamics of the basic structure of the psychophysical qualities of a person, and his/her conscious, subjective reflection of all these phenomena.

In order to transform the outlined meta−theoretical model into a comprehensive construction of a theory of adolescent socialization, it would be helpful to elaborate a formal conceptual frame for organizing the procedure of theory construction. What I suggest is a conceptual frame of multiple levels of analysis, representing different contexts of socialization, composed of an interindividual/interactional level (small−group context), an organizational level (organization context), and a societal level (social−structure context). The elaboration of levels of analysis will help the researcher to identify interrelated aspects of the process of adolescent socialization in a systematic way, to identify and define the appropriate unit of analysis for each level, to relate the phenomena attached to each level to one another and to the phenomena on the adjoining level, and, if possible, to combine all these phenomena and their interrelations into a single unified structure. *Figure 1* gives an example of a possible construction of levels and appropriate contexts of socialization.

The differentiation of "levels" of analysis merely serves the purpose of summarizing phenomena and concepts that belong together under one single aspect. It would be theoretically worthless to view these levels as isolated and artificial abstractions of reality. It is essential that they should be conceived of as constitutive parts of a comprehensive model in which each level of analysis provides relevant conditions for all other levels. It must be the goal of theory construction to make statements about all levels of analysis and to connect them with each other in a network of mutually related statements. It is the task of socialization theory to analyze developmental processes on each level, and subsequently, to analyze the developmental processes that are specific to each of these levels in regard to their interdependence and their mutually conditioned total relationship, in order to explain human development as the object of investigation.

Which levels of analysis will be considered, according to which criteria, and which conceptual constructions will be used to relate them to one another, depends essentially on the immediate interests of the researcher. It is the researcher who constructs the levels of analysis in order to arrive at a systematic grasp of reality in a systematic way. The procedure for establishing the levels is, for this reason, a question of academic convention.

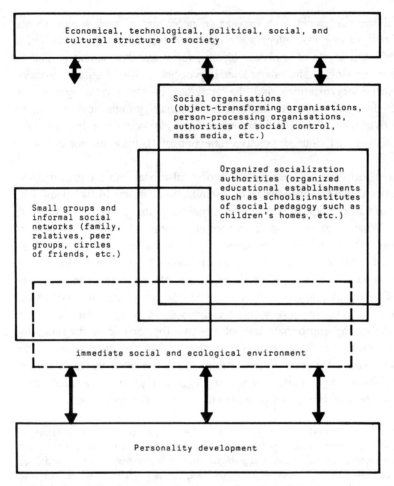

Fig. 1: Levels of analysis, identifying different
         contexts of socialization

Contexts of socialization

In order to explain adolescent development in terms of a productive processing
of reality, it is necessary to identify the different phenomena relevant to the
process of socialization on different levels of analysis and to elaborate the
dynamics of their interrelationships both within a level and between levels. The
basic premise is that the development of the processes of growth of physical
and mental capacities, and of emotions and affects follow their own patterns,
but are overlaid with environmental social factors that affect their temporal
sequence and duration and their organization.

On the *interactional* level, the immediate situational constellation of the social and spatial environment must be taken into consideration. A constitutive part of this environment is small groups and informal social networks with their own dynamics and social rules. Membership in these face – to – face systems plays an important part in the development of children and adolescents. These systems are susceptible to the expectations on the part of the social environment and the systems on the organizational and societal level of analysis. But they are also susceptible to the expectations and actions of the developing adolescent. Thus, they serve as social norms and values and, at the same time, for elaborating the intellectual and social skills of a person in order to manage social reality in a productive manner.

On the *organizational* level, the focus of analysis will be on those social systems that have been established especially for the purpose of the socialization and education of the younger members of society. It seems to be a basic trend in industrial societies to assign the process of socialization to agencies such as kindergartens, schools, and other institutes of social pedagogy. They represent social life worlds that are largely isolated and separated from other spheres of social life, especially those typical of adult life. These educational agencies not only exert an influence on the personal development of their members by way of intentional and conscious educational actions, but also through the manner of their organizational constitution.

There are still other systems on the organizational level that are not educational in character, but nevertheless highly relevant to the socialization process in adolescence: Occupational, political, and religious agencies and the mass media partly supplement, overlap, and correct the influence of the educational agencies. It is typical of industrial societies that all social systems relevant to the function of socialization act side by side in accordance with their own specific systemic problems without concern for the resultant subsidiary problems that might be produced. The rules and perspectives of the various social systems mentioned are partitioned off from one another; they are partly in accord with and complementary to each other and partly contradictory. This has the effect that adolescents are virtually forced to develop a high capacity for a self – reliant management of their own developmental process (Elder, 1975). Since the guiding principles of the conditions of socialization are not necessarily those governing human growth and development, this fact constitutes a big coping problem.

Concerning the *sociostructural level*, political, cultural, social and, above all, economic changes have to be analyzed with their strong repercussions on the process of development during the phase of adolescence and youth. The most recent example of this is the continuous prolongation of the phase of life defined as "adolescence" that we have experienced in the last decades. Because of economic processes, families of all social classes have to get accustomed to adolescence as a kind of social moratorium of a diffuse in−between character within the overall lifespan (cf. Baethge, in this volume).

Another result of these social changes, in historical terms, is the emergence of a new phase of life following adolescence that affects more and more young people and keeps them in a state of at least partial independence: a prolonged period of youth, of "postadolescence", usually lasting from adult age at 18 to the age of 23, 25, or even older, allowing a relatively high degree of independence from parents, independence in peer relations, sexual behavior, moral and ethical orientation, political activity and consumer behavior, but not in the crucial area of vocational economic activity. This phase of postadolescence, which affects more and more young people of all social classes, only ends at the time when full independence from the family is achieved (cf. Gaiser and Müller, in this volume).

3.   Methodological Procedures in Youth Research

The meta−theoretical model discussed does not only have a relationship of appropriateness to theory construction but to methodological procedures as well. The appropriate method is the combination of investigations of objective social reality and subjective interpretations of reality. *Figure 2* shows the interrelations.

Concerning strategies of data collection and research design, the implications of the comprehensive theory of adolescent socialization are that various types of scientifically controllable experience and its systematic documentation have to be applied. Appropriate research designs are those that enable descriptions and analyses of phenomena on one level of analysis related to those on other levels. Thus, we have to look for contextual and organizational variables in conjunction with variables such as cohort, historical, time, and age−related effects.

The existing research strategies necessary for multilevel analysis, especially statistical procedures, are still insufficient. What has been tested so far are versions of two−level analysis that involve connections between the qualities of individual actors and social units. In this way it is possible to ascertain some contextual effects and to avoid drawing inadmissable conclusions on the basis of the connections between variables on one level of analysis and applying them to

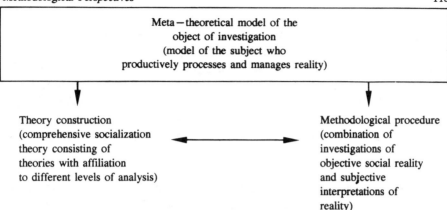

Fig. 2: Interrelations of meta—theoretical model, theory construction, and methodological procedure

connections existing on another. Up to now, we are only able to translate the theoretical model of adolescent socialization into a number of such steps of multivariate analyses. The statistical procedures available permit only a restricted representation of the multilevel theoretical model, in particular the interrelations between variables at different levels of analysis.

One of the methodological requirements of the meta—theoretical model is to carry out not only systematic investigations of the societal, organizational, and interactional aspects relevant to the process of socialization (analysis of "objective" outer reality), but also methodologically controlled investigations of the interpretations and explanations of this reality by individuals (analysis of "subjective" inner reality). The theoretical model outlined requires methodological procedures that permit a description and explanation of the processing and management of reality in everyday situations and at decisive points of the life history of a person; not only from the perspective of the researcher, but also in terms of "from inside looking out", that is, from the perspective of the subject. The researcher has to presuppose the capacity of his/her "object" of investigation to apply qualified, subjective knowledge of a problem competently in a complex situation. He/she has to attempt to reconstruct this knowledge authentically in order to confront his/her scientific theory with it and insert it in the theory (Bogdan and Taylor, 1975).

A "pluralistic" conception of method is the consequent completion of a comprehensive conception of theory, and this would contribute to an improvement in the relevance and applicability of research activities (Denzin, 1978; Jick, 1979). The investigation of the subjective perception of social reality by individuals must always be confronted with and complemented by the results of the analysis of reality carried out by the researcher. The intellectual construction of social reality and the structuring of subjective meaning have to be put into relation to the scientific analysis of socialization contexts: The individual will be understood by me, the researcher, only, if I conceive of him/her in his/her social context, if I imagine him/her in conflict with this social context, and then try to elaborate what room he/she objectively has for subjective interpretations, actions, and developments and how much of this he/she actually uses.

An analysis of the objective social world in which the adolescent lives is the necessary complement to the investigations of the subjective perception of the social world. Only if I do both, can I, as a researcher, relate objective and subjectively perceived possibilities for action and alternatives of behavior to each other, and only then can I gain clues as to the relative value of subjective interpretations of reality. Only then can I relate the problem – solving capacity of an adolescent to the objective situational context and trace the consequences of successful or unsuccessful problem – solving attempts. Only then can I relate the creative, productive potential of the individual who is managing his/her social environment to the objective social and psychological features of that individual and that environment.

In recent years, several research projects have been carried out on the basis of these proposals in the fields of socialization research and developmental psychology. Many of the research reports in this volume follow these lines. Most of these projects try to realize some kind of contextual problem – oriented analysis, concentrating on the socially structured conditions of the actions and the courses of adolescents facing specific developmental tasks, events, or role transitions. Changes in the conditions of life affecting young people that are due to overall societal, economic, and cultural changes are analyzed in terms of the problems they raise for the taking over of the adult role. The individual and collective capacities of realistic perception and productive management of the complex social conditions of life in adolescence and youth are reconstructed and confronted with a detailed analysis of the chances and limitations of unfolding the life course that are objectively given.

To give an example from own research: We analyzed the process of the subjective management of different educational careers by students in different types of secondary schools in West Germany. We started our analysis by describing the sociohistorical development of the West German educational system and than asked for the subjective interpretation of the objectively given socioeconomic constellation of educational and vocational opportunities. For this purpose we carried out interviews with adolescents of the age groups born between 1962 and 1964 from 1977 on. As the analysis shows, West German educational expansion has brought an improvement of the educational opportunities for adolescents in all social strata.

Even children and parents whose background is traditionally not conducive to education have reacted to the change in social values and, above all, the changes in the labor market by recognizing the increased demand for education. At the same time, however, contractive tendencies are becoming predominant in the labor market, and, additionally, the demographic "wave" of the "baby boom" has now reached the labor market. All these factors taken together mean that young people without a socially valuable school leaving certificate find themselves in a hopeless situation on the labor market (Hurrelmann, 1984, 1987).

In order to analyze the subjective interpretation of the objectively given socioeconomic constellation of educational and vocational opportunities, we carried out in—depth interviews with adolescents who, at school, had been either extremely successful or (the other half of the sample) extremely unsuccessful. We were able to confirm an instrumentalistic and "finalistic" nature of the criteria of interpretation by which "significance" is attached to learning at school. Students cling to a criterion according to which the real reason for what happens at school will only manifest itself later on in life, and thus attendance at school has a hidden rationale that is difficult to grasp while they are still at school. The "educational expansion" is not regarded as an improvement of educational opportunities by the birth cohorts questioned. On the contrary, young people perceive themselves as being in a stressful situation with a specific demand placed on them: to hold or even improve the social status of their parents. During the last years of compulsory schooling, many of them live with an undercurrent of fear that the transition from school to employment might not result in a socially acceptable position. Even those who make an effort at school cannot be certain of achieving the social status of their parents, let alone bettering it.

Research projects of this kind offer a chance to overcome the unfruitful split between the paradigms of "quantitative" and "qualitative" methodology. They mark the points of consensus that should find expression in the recent developments in the fields of the psychology and sociology of human living conditions. They allow us to correct, control, and elaborate empirically the theories of socialization that follow the notion of adolescents as productive processors and managers of their reality.

In order to gather more experience with "mixed" and "pluralistic" conceptions of method and design in socialization research, we need more practice with various types of data collection, documentation, and interpretation. Concerning research design, we must not only look for purely nomothetic strategies in which the individual cases are subsumed under general laws. In view of the enormous variety of social conditions that transcend cultures and subcultures, and time and age, greater attention must be paid to the development of idiographic methods and case studies. We need a documentary analysis in the tradition of sociohistorical research as well as large—scale survey research and — possibly within the same survey as a subsample — case studies in the tradition of biographical interviews and interpretative analysis (Clausen, 1986).

References

Baltes, P.B., Reese, H.W., & Lipsitt, L.P. (1980): Life span developmental psychology. Annual Review of Psychology, 31, 65–110

Bogdan, R., & Taylor, S.J. (1975): Introduction to qualitative research methods. New York: Wiley

Bronfenbrenner, U. (1979): The ecology of human development. Cambridge: Harvard University Press

Clausen, J.A. (1986): Early adult choices and the life course. Zeitschrift für Sozialisationsforschung und Erziehungssoziologie, 6, 313–321

Denzin, N.K. (1978): The research act. New York: McGraw–Hill

Elder, G.H. (1975): Adolescence in the life cycle: An introduction. In Dragasin, S.E., & Elder, G.H. (Eds.): Adolescence in the life cycle. Washington: Hemisphere, 1–22

Geulen, D., & Hurrelmann, K. (1982): Towards a programme for a comprehensive theory of socialization. Education, 26, 39–82

Hamburg, B.A. (1980): Early adolescence as a life stress. In Levine, S., & Ursin, H. (Eds.): Coping and health. New York: Plenum Press, 121–143

Havighurst, R. (1972): Developmental tasks and education. New York: McKay (3rd edition)

Hurrelmann, K. (1984): Societal and organizational factors of stress on students in school. European Journal of Teacher Education, 7,181–190

Hurrelmann, K. (1987): The importance of school in the life course. Journal of Adolescent Research, 2, 111–115

Hurrelmann, K. (1988): Social structure and personality development. The individual as a productive processor of reality. New York: Cambridge University Press

Hurrelmann, K., & Ulich, D. (Eds.)(1980): Handbuch der Sozialisationsforschung. Weinheim: Beltz

Jick, T.D. (1979): Mixing qualitative and quantitative methods. Triangulation in action. Administrative Science Quarterly, 24, 602–611

Lerner, R.M.(1982): Children and adolescents as producers of their development. Developmental Review, 2, 342–370

Oerter, R., & Montada, L. (Eds.)(1982): Entwicklungspsychologie. München: Urban & Schwarzenberg

Silbereisen, R.K., & Eyferth, K., & Rudinger, G. (Eds.)(1986): Development as action in context. New York: Springer

Part II
Significant People in the Social Network

8.

Mentors in Adolescents' Lives

Stephen F. Hamilton and Nancy Darling
Cornell University, Ithaca, New York, USA

The word "mentor" evokes the image of a wise counsellor — someone who is at the same time nurturant, challenging, and experienced. At a more concrete level, the mentor relationship connotes a special bond between an inexperienced or naive student and someone more skilled than himself or herself who is willing to act as a guide in a new or unfamiliar situation. The prototypic mentor is an unrelated adult who takes on the responsibility of socializing a youth above and beyond the extent required by his or her social role. A professional teacher or counselor may become a mentor, but the two roles are not identical; being a mentor entails a depth of commitment and breadth of involvement that exceeds professional norms. Parents ordinarily do many of the same things unrelated adult mentors do, but because they are obligated by kinship to teach and counsel their progeny, the term "mentor" is usually reserved for unrelated adults. Mentoring relationships are considered to be beneficial in promoting competence and providing self – assurance and support in the face of new situations. This chapter will primarily discuss mentoring relationships with unrelated adults, but will also examine the extent to which adolescents' relationships with parents, other relatives, and peers have similar characteristics.

This chapter reports on a current project investigating the contribution of mentors to adolescent development. The project has three components: a retrospective study of important people in American adolescents' lives; an international comparison to the retrospective study; and an experimental study in which American adolescents are paired with unrelated adults who try to establish a mentoring relationship, and both the impact of that relationship and its development over time are closely monitored. Our emphasis here is on initial results from the pilot retrospective study, but the conceptual basis for all three components is presented, and the empirical results are discussed in terms of their implications for the other two components.

1.   Mentors and Adolescent Development

The Soviet psychologist, Vygotsky (1978), identified people and activities as the engines of human development. If mentors engage in activities with adolescents that expand their competence, encourage them to engage in other such activities, and extend the range of people with whom they interact, then they should have a positive impact on adolescents' development. Bronfenbrenner drew upon Vygotsky's, Lewin's, and others' ideas in his book *The Ecology of Human Development* (1979) to construct a framework for understanding human development that emphasizes contexts and interactions. Our research is guided by Bronfenbrenner's proposal that "activity, role, and interpersonal relation" (22) are key elements of the ecology of human development and his hypotheses that development is facilitated by participating in "progressively more complex patterns of reciprocal activity" (p. 60) in an environment characterized by a "balance of challenge and support" (288).

More recently, Bronfenbrenner (Bronfenbrenner and Crouter, 1981) has stressed the importance of research guided by what he terms "person – process – context" models; that is, studies that not only examine differences in developmental indicators among subgroups of people but that also document the processes responsible for creating these differences and how these processes may vary depending upon characteristics of the developing person and the person's environment. Applying these criteria, it is not enough to identify differences in school performance, for example, between adolescents of different social classes; the researcher must also determine what features of the environments inhabited by adolescents of different social classes account for differences in school performance and how those differences operate to produce different outcomes for different people. Heyns' (1978) study demonstrating higher rates of learning loss over the summer among disadvantaged children is an example of this kind of research, though it lacks the attention Bronfenbrenner urges to characteristics of the person.   The person – process – context model has been particularly influential in the design of our experimental study and has guided our analyses of the retrospective data from the pilot study.

Previous research

The empirical literature on adolescents' interpersonal relations is limited primarily to descriptive studies and to relations with peers and parents. Two of the most substantial contributions are by Garbarino, Burston, Raber, Russell and Crouter (1978) and by Blyth, Hill and Thiel (1982). Both reported adolescents' responses to questions about the most important people in their lives. Both found that parents, other family members, and peers were the most consistently listed, in that order. A recent review of these and related studies (Galbo, 1986) pointed out that parents remain the most important people in most adolescents' lives, but unrelated adults become increasingly important in later adolescence.

By its scant reference to the developmental effects of significant others, Galbo's (1986) review demonstrated the need to move beyond descriptive studies to assessments of impact, as Foster—Clark and Blyth (1987) have done by showing drug abuse to be related to the characteristics of adolescents' social networks. Using data from our pilot study, Darling (1987) has confirmed the value of examining the developmental impact of adolescents' significant others. She found that eighth and eleventh graders who reported the presence of a challenging adult in their lives performed better on tests of verbal, quantitative, and reasoning abilities, after other factors had been controlled. Challenging parents of the same gender had the strongest impact, but parental influence declined while nonparental influence rose as a function of subjects' age.

While much has been written about the benefits of mentors, there is little empirical evidence about how often they appear in the lives of adolescents, their influence, or even agreement as to how they should be defined. The term "mentor" has been used many different ways. There is confusion as to what a mentor is and what they do — they have been operationally defined as everything from the most influential professor a student had in college (Erkut and Mokros, 1984), to a professional a young student is assigned to during an internship (Borman and Colson, 1984), to someone who fosters a young adult's development by "believing in him, sharing the youthful Dream and giving it his blessing, helping to define the newly emerging self in its newly discovered world, and creating a space in which the newly emerging self can work on a reasonably satisfactory life structure that contains the Dream" (Levinson, 1978).

It is important to distinguish the use of the word "mentor" as it describes a social role from its use describing a functional role. The title "mentor" has been used by several authors to describe an adult who participates in programs designed to initiate adolescents ("protégés") into the world of adulthood by providing youths with career internships (Booth, 1980; Borman and Colson, 1984; Colson, 1980), serving as advisors to college students (Daloz, 1980; Brown and DeCoster, 1982), or helping students work on areas of personal growth (Blyth, Bronfenbrenner, Ceci, Cornelius, Hamilton, and Voegtle, 1987). When used in this way, the word "mentor" describes a social role — who the people involved are — rather than a functional role — what the people involved do. When the word "mentor" is used to describe a social role, any two people involved in such a program would be defined as mentors and protégés, regardless of the extent to which their relationship was characterized by the qualities such a relationship connotes.

On the other hand, the term "functional role" refers to a role defined by its content rather than by its structure. Used in this way, a mentor is one who performs the act of mentoring. The social roles of the participants — whether the experienced person involved is a college professor or a janitor — are irrelevant. Thus in the social role "mentor", the participant's functional role is ignored, while in the functional role "mentor", the participant's social roles are ignored, only their behaviors and the emotional relationship within the dyad are considered. Edlind and Haensly (1985) highlight the tension between these two types of roles in the following statement about a "mentoring" program: "Mentorships, however, are difficult to establish; it might be more appropriate to say that educators arrange for two individuals with similar interests, a student and a professional, to come together in order to provide an opportunity for a mentorship to develop." The social role is easily established, but the functional role may not follow. It is the latter concept with which we will be concerned.

The functional role of "mentor"

Following Bell (1970), we can distinguish two major components to the functional role of mentor: the interaction the mentor engages in with the student, and the mentor's provision of a role model. Interviews with mentors and their protégés have furnished some information concerning the objective behavior evidenced by mentors. First, they are involved in a one — on — one relationship with a younger person. This relationship is characterized by teaching, both in terms of the general transmission of skills and information, but also in terms of the mentor specifically pointing out areas in which the student can improve performance. Moore (in Edlind and Haensly, 1985), describes this as an attitude of "You ought to do this, I'll show you how." Teaching may be formal, as in the case of a piano teacher or athletic coach who is a mentor, but it may also be informal, occurring incidentally as an adult and a young person pursue common interests together. Teaching occurs naturally when an adult and a younger person tinker with an automobile engine, go camping, or talk about personal relationships, fishing, or future plans. In addition to conveying specific knowledge or skills, a teacher opens new vistas and provides new perspectives on familiar scenes. When a mentor shares her stamp collection with a young person, the content of the protégé's learning may be facts about philately, but it may also be the geography of exotic nations or the fine points of engraving and color printing.

Mentors also challenge protégés (Daloz, 1986). This entails both pushing protégés to perform at their best level, but also pointing out possibilities that they may not have recognized as possible for themselves. A mentor's challenging behavior is related to a protégé's goals and their attainment, though often those goals may be unstated, perhaps even unrecognized. More specifically, mentors encourage young people to set goals, and to set them high. They help their protégés make plans for achieving their goals, and help them to evaluate their actions in terms of their contribution to meeting those goals. The challenge provided by mentors is complemented by their teaching, in that one provides the impetus and the other the means of achievement. Evaluation of actions might occur at the conclusion of an explicitly goal—directed activity, but it might also occur when a mentor urges a protégé to try harder at something she or he has been doing, such as school work or playing a musical instrument.

Immediate goals are inherent to certain kinds of activities. When a mentor plays anagrams with a protégé, for example, the immediate goal is for the protégé to come up with as many different words as possible. In the long—term, this may be associated with the goal of increasing cognitive competence, but neither the mentor nor the protégé need to have such a goal foremost in their minds; it may be more salient that they are jointly engaging in an enjoyable activity. In other words, the long—term goals related to some challenging activities may be subordinated to the more immediate goals inherent in the activity and to the immediate goal of enjoying each others' company.

Characteristics of the mentoring relationship

The characteristics of a mentoring relationship described thus far could be objectively observed and are demonstrated by the person playing the mentor role. However, another component of that role is not dependent on the mentor, but on the protégé. In order for an adult to act as a mentor, he or she must be acknowledged by the protégé as a role model (Daloz, 1987; Erkut and Mokros, 1984; Torrance, 1983).

As defined by Kemper (1968), a role model is one "who demonstrates for the individual how something is done in the technical sense ... (The role model) is concerned with the 'how' question. The essential quality of the role model is that he possesses skills and displays techniques which the actor lacks (or thinks he lacks) and from whom, by observation and comparison with his own performance, the actor can learn". A role model provides a protégé with observational learning opportunities that include imitation of new behaviors, inhibition of unsuccessful behaviors through observation of negative consequences, and the disinhibition of formerly constrained behaviors and increasing use of successful behaviors through observation of positive consequences (Bandura, 1971).

Although a mentor cannot make him or herself a role model, because of the importance of role modeling to effective mentoring, good mentors conduct themselves as if their protégés regard them as role models. This requirement carries three implications.

1. Mentors behave in a manner that they would wish their protégés to emulate. Mentors cannot be expected to be saints, but they should demonstrate exemplary character and integrity. When they fall short of their own ideals, it is not for lack of trying.

2. Mentors tell their protégés about challenges, moral dilemmas, and difficult situations they have faced. They describe these and their responses in order to help young people appreciate the need to struggle, not to glorify themselves or to proselytize for their own particular values. Describing a situation that, in hindsight, might have been better handled can be as instructive as describing one in which a mentor made the best decision.

3. As they interact with their protégés, mentors exemplify how mature, thoughtful adults think about issues, solve problems, and confront challenges. Exemplification is not limited to moral issues but also includes the whole range of challenge and support discussed above. With respect to all issues regardless of their moral weight, the purpose of exemplification is not to teach specific values to young people but to demonstrate to them one way to be a responsible and competent adult.

The mentoring role, then, is defined both by behaviors enacted by the mentor – challenging, teaching, and supporting – and by the adoption of the mentor as a role model by the protégé. It is thus the relationship between the two participants that defines mentoring, not simply the behaviors or the psychological events experienced by either participant.

The type of relationship described by mentoring is of particular relevance to adolescents and young adults. One factor contributing to the emotional force of mentoring relationships may be the young person's discovery of an adult who "sees me as I really am" (Daloz, 1986) at a point of identity formation. Erikson (1986, 130) suggested that "adolescents look most fervently for men and ideas to have faith in, which also means men and ideas in whose service it would seem worth while to prove oneself trustworthy". Mentors provide both the ideals that are necessary for identity formation and the skills that allow those ideals to be realized. Through their very existence, they also provide proof that a transition can be made. Identification with the mentor may help students believe that they can successfully negotiate the transition as well.

During adolescence, the importance of nonparental adults in general, and nonparental adults playing mentoring roles in particular, may increase. Several factors contribute to this. First, the adolescent's drive to differentiate him or herself from parents may make the adolescent more open to the influence of an adult other than a parent. Second, as the student's contact with the world outside of the immediate environment increases, the expanded social network that unrelated adults have the potential to bring to the relationship becomes more valuable. Third, for the same reason, skills and knowledge that an associate might have that differ from those possessed by family members become more valuable as they offer insight into the larger world. Fourth, a close, meaningful relationship with an adult other than a parent allows the adolescent to be involved in a more informal adult relationship in preparation for the time when they too will be an adult. Lastly, as children become adolescents and young adults, they gain opportunities to initiate relationships with associates who are interested in the students' own interests. We begin by describing the frequency and content of these relationships.

2. Design and Methods of the Empirical Study

Retrospective accounts of important people were collected from 126 (57 male and 69 female) 3rd−year students at Cornell University who were recruited from three majors: business, natural sciences, and the humanities. Approximately equal numbers of males and females were recruited in each major. Comparable data were collected from a second sample of 40 eighth and 34 eleventh graders (respectively, 13− to 14− and 16− to 17−year−olds) in a small town in rural New York State. The secondary school sample will be used here only to make an age comparison regarding the prevalence of unrelated adult mentors.

Procedure

Students filled out several questionnaires in group settings. Four types of information were collected: (a) a list of the important people in their lives before entering college; (b) a description of their relationship with each person listed; (c) activities they had engaged in and with whom; and (d) background information. In addition, college students completed a battery of cognitive tests.

These data gave us two ways in which to describe our subjects' significant others or "associates." Their responses indicating whether the people they named were related and in what connection they knew them defined associates' social roles: mother, brother−in−law, teacher, coach, and so forth. Statements describing the relationship defined what we call associates' functional roles.

Defining functional roles

Associates' functional roles were derived from subjects' dichotomous responses to 26 questionnaire items describing relationships. Iterated principal component factor analysis was employed to identify six functional roles defined by these items, which we labelled: Mentor, Supporter, Companion, Dependent, Antagonist, and Challenger (Darling, 1986). The PROMAX method was used to rotate the factors. Loadings of the functional role items on each factor are presented in Table 1. An arbitrary decision was made that loadings higher than or equal to .30 would be considered nonzero.

The six factors are correlated (see Table 2). Students who describe associates as mentors are unlikely to feel that they have taught the associate a great deal (i.e., that the associate was a dependent). On the other hand, mentoring and support are related, as are companionship and support. The associates whom students describe as dependents are considered to be companions as well. All of these associations seem sensible, lending face validity to the derived factors.

Conceptual reworking of derived factors

Because mentors are the focus of this paper, only the Mentor factor will be discussed. On conceptual grounds discussed above, this factor was divided into three dimensions, captured by the following questionnaire items:

Teacher

I learned how to do things by watching this person do them
I acquired knowledge, information, or skills from this person

Challenger

This person challenged my ideas
This person pushed me to do a good job
This person pushed me to do things on my own
This person gave me constructive criticism

Role Model

I got a lot of my values from this person
This person served as a role model of achievement for me
I admired this person as a human being.

Table 1:   Loadings of functional role items on six factors

	F1	F2	F3	F4	F5	F6
Factor 1: Mentor						
44. I learned how to do things by watching this person do them	.74*	.07	.03	−.13	.10	−.09
53. I acquired knowledge, information, or skills from this person	.71*	.03	−.01	−.10	.01	.09
46. This person pushed me to do a good job	.62*	−.21	.04	−.06	.03	.37*
51. This person pushed me to do things on my own	.58*	−.16	.02	.04	.01	.20
65. I got a lot of my values from this person	.57*	−.12	.09	.28	−.02	−.11
57. This person served as a role model of achievement for me	.49*	.04	−.12	.00	−.07	.05
59. I admired this person's qualities as a human being	.47*	.19	.09	.14	−.27	−.07
63. This person gave me constructive criticism	.42*	.13	−.00	.06	−.03	.39*
Factor 2: Companion						
49. This person was fun to be with	.07	.72*	.04	−.05	−.16	−.02
56. We shared a lot of interests in common	−.00	.69*	.08	−.02	−.01	−.06
48. We did things that were new and exciting	−.03	.61*	.02	.01	.06	.04
50. We talked together and shared ideas	.00	.61*	.07	.11	−.09	.23
43. This person introduced me to new ideas, interests, and experiences	.29	.34*	−.18	.09	.02	.11
Factor 3: Dependent						
52. I helped this person learn how to do things	.05	.12	.67*	−.03	.09	.05
47. When we did things together, I usually took the lead	−.13	.09	.64*	−.10	−.06	.02
68. I taught this person quite a bit	.06	−.00	.63*	.12	.12	−.04
Factor 4: Supporter						
62. This person protected me from getting hurt emotionally	.10	−.05	−.02	.61*	.01	−.06
64. I served as a source of emotional support for this person	−.13	.15	.31	.43*	.13	−.02
45. This person gave me emotional support, security, and encouragement	.24	.15	.01	.40*	−.09	.08
54. This person gave me advice about my personal life	.06	.33*	−.06	.34*	.10	.16
66. I was physically attracted to this person	−.15	.08	.08	.16	.07	.09
Factor 5: Antagonist						
58. This person had some negative influence on me	−.10	−.15	.02	.04	.53*	.10
67. This person and I would get angry at each other	.18	−.02	.25	.04	.50*	.04
55. When we did things, this person usually took the lead	.29	.13	−.33*	.08	.36*	−.04
60. I competed with this person	−.19	.35*	.14	−.14	.34*	.04
Factor 6: Challenger						
61. This person challenged my ideas	.24	.14	.01	−.05	.19	.39*

* Nonzero loadings

Table 2: Interfactor correlations

	Mentor	Companion	Dependent	Supporter	Antagonist	Challenger
Mentor	—	.16	−.34*	.42*	−.03	.17
Companion		—	.38*	.42*	.21	.09
Dependent			—	.08	.16	−.06
Supporter				—	−.04	.26
Antagonist					—	−.02
Challenger						—

* Nonzero correlations

Assigning functional roles to associates

Associates were classified as performing a particular functional role when the number of items the subject identified with them exceeded the sample median for the factor that represents that role. Operationally, then, a Mentor is an associate identified with four or more of the seven items comprising the Mentor factor. (Such associates will be denoted as "Mentors" throughout the text to distinguish use of the operational definition from other definitions of the word "mentor"). To be classified a Teacher, an associate must be identified with both of the items defining a Teacher, a Challenger with three of four items, and a Role Model with two of three. This procedure reflected our interest in the people in adolescents' lives rather than in the total or average quality of the adolescent's relationships with a range of people. We wished to know about the individuals who could be classified as Mentors, not the sum total of mentoring performed by various people. We recognized the argument against classifying associates dichotomously as either Mentors or not Mentors; however, in reality the characteristics of a Mentor are found to a greater or a lesser degree in different associates. Alternative methods, which treated functional roles as linear variables characterizing either associates or social environments, yielded similar results, but greatly complicated interpretation and presentation. Using a median split to define functional roles operationally simplifies interpretation of the data and assures that only associates who are strongly identified with the relevant items are classified in the role.

Questions

The empirical results that follow address five questions:

1. Who has Mentors? What proportion of the sample identifies unrelated adult associates as performing the Mentor role? Are there gender and age differences?
2. What components of the Mentor role are reported most frequently? Do these vary by gender?
3. What activities do Mentors engage in with adolescents?
4. To what extent do parents, other relatives, and peers interact with adolescents as Mentors do?
5. Are adolescents whose parents act as Mentors more or less likely to have an unrelated adult Mentor?

3. Results: Mentors in the Lives of American Adolescents

Eighty—two percent of the 127 college students in our sample named at least one unrelated adult as an important person in their lives (i.e., as an associate). Of those subjects, 45% had at least one associate who qualified as a Mentor by our criteria. Twenty—four percent of the students described more than one unrelated adult associate as a Mentor.

Who has Mentors?

Females are less likely than males to have an unrelated adult Mentor (37% vs. 54%, $p < .05$). Because females are more likely than males to name an unrelated adult as a significant other, this difference is further exaggerated when we look only at those students who name an unrelated adult. Seventy—two percent of males who named an unrelated adult describe at least one unrelated adult as a Mentor, but only 43% of females who named an unrelated adult do. Thus, although males are less likely to have an unrelated adult in their lives, an unrelated adult who becomes significant to a male is more likely to be a Mentor.

The sample of secondary school students allows us to explore age trends in adolescents' descriptions of their relationships with unrelated adults. Approximately the same proportion (about 60%) of eleventh graders and college students who named adult associates described at least one of them as a

Mentor, but eighth graders were less likely to do so (25%). The proportion of students who named an unrelated adult as a significant other grew larger with age as well. Few eighth graders (53% of girls but only 6% of boys), a larger number of eleventh graders (61%), and a still larger number of college students (82%) named an unrelated adult as a significant other. The rarity of students', especially male students', involvement with unrelated adults during early adolescence suggests that mentoring may be associated more strongly with middle and late adolescence.

What components of the Mentor role are most commonly reported?

The three components of the Mentor role are distributed almost equally, Teacher being somewhat more frequent (68% with at least one in this role), followed by Role Model (67%) and Challenger (56%). However, the picture changes when the components are arrayed by gender, as in Figure 1. Males are more likely than females to have unrelated adult associates who fulfill the instrumental dimensions of the mentoring role — Teacher and Challenger — but are no more likely to see their unrelated adult associates as Role Models.

What activities do Mentors engage in with adolescents?

In view of Vygotsky's observation that people and activities are the engine of human development, activities must be examined along with relations. Do unrelated adult Mentors participate in a greater variety of activities with adolescents than other unrelated adult associates do? Our data indicate that Mentors engage in a greater range of activities with students than do unrelated adults not classified as Mentors, but the difference is not statistically significant.

Unrelated adults, then, are not described as Mentors simply because of the number of activities that they engage in with students. We have no data indicating the intensity with which Mentors engage in activities with adolescents compared to other associates, or the importance adolescents place on this participation. However, there are some activities that unrelated adults who are Mentors participate in more frequently than do unrelated adults who are not:

1. Talking about personal matters you cared deeply about.
2. Talking about family and friends.
3. Talking about ideas, politics, the news, the future, and so forth.
4. Playing word games.

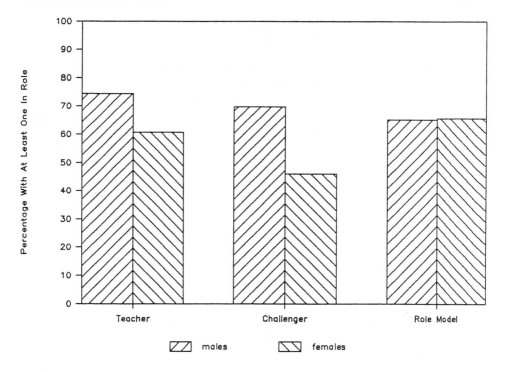

Fig. 1: Percentage of males and females who describe at least one unrelated adult associate as a Teacher, Challenger, or Role Model. (Includes only subjects who named at least one unrelated adult associate.)

5. Listening to music.
6. Cultural experiences (going to classical music concerts, plays, lectures, museums).
7. Outdoor activities other than games.
8. Doing organized activities in or out of school.

The verbal and cultural content of these items is notable. It is unclear whether this is true of all Mentors or whether this is simply characteristic of our student sample. It may be that the kind of adolescent who enrolls in Cornell University is more likely to participate in such activities with adults who challenge, teach, and act as role models for them than are adolescents who become skilled machinists. Analyses now in progress of the activities of Mentors with our secondary school sample, which is more diverse, will shed light on this issue, but the nature of activities engaged in with Mentors may hold the key to explaining why having a Mentor appears to foster cognitive development.

Do other associates relate to adolescents as Mentors do?

Although we began by defining Mentors as unrelated adults who act as informal teachers and counselors, our operational definition of a Mentor in terms of a functional role leaves open the question of whether persons in other social roles are also described by adolescents as Teachers, Challengers, and Role Models. The answer to that question is yes. Of the 563 adults that students named as significant others, 52% were classified as Mentors. The majority of adult associates filling the role were parents, who accounted for 58% of adult Mentors (see Figure 2). Unrelated adults were the next largest category, 34%, while relatives other than parents made up only 7% of the Mentors.

That most people who relate to adolescents as Mentors do are parents is unsurprising in view of our operational definition; one way of defining a Mentor is as someone who stands in loco parentis (as the original Mentor did with Telemachus on behalf of Odysseus). One might suspect that the prominence of parents among mentoring associates results from the fact that most subjects named their parents as important people in their lives. Parents who were listed were also more likely than any other associates to be classified as Mentors. Unrelated adults were next in the frequency with which they were listed as adult associates, followed by relatives. Hence, there are more parents and fewer relatives in the pool of adult associates who might be described as Mentors. However, most parents named as associates (67%) were also classified as Mentors. Of the unrelated adults named as associates, 44% were Mentors, while only 27% of relatives other than parents fit our definition of a Mentor.

Subjects named 843 peers and siblings as associates. Peers who were no more than one year older or younger than subjects were classified as same – age peers. All siblings (n = 247) were coded as peers regardless of age, on the ground that they belong to the same generation as subjects. Nearly all siblings who were named were either close in age or older than the subjects. No younger peers were described as Mentors. Siblings and same – age peers were described as performing the mentoring role in nearly equal proportions (about 48%), with the balance accounted for by older peers.

Mentoring parents and unrelated adult Mentors

The predominance of parents among adolescents' associates who fill the functional role of Mentor raises the question of whether adolescents whose

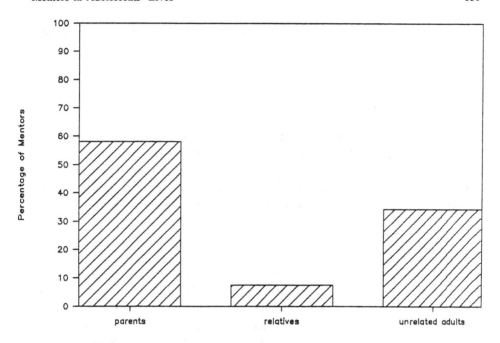

Fig. 2:   Percentage of adult Mentors who are parents, adults, and nonparental relatives.

parents function as Mentors are more or less likely to have unrelated adult · Mentors than adolescents whose parents do not function as Mentors. According to one line of reasoning, unrelated adult Mentors complement parents; they reinforce the kinds of things most parents already do. A competing hypothesis is that adolescents whose parents do not do what Mentors do seek out other adults to perform those functions. In this case, unrelated adult Mentors substitute for parents. Males who describe at least one of their parents as a Mentor are more than twice as likely to describe an unrelated adult as a Mentor than are males whose parents are not Mentors. This is not true for females, however.

If unrelated adult Mentors substitute for parents, then adolescents whose parents are divorced would be more likely to have them than those in two – parent families. However, this is not the case; students who come from divorced families are no more likely to have an unrelated adult Mentor than students from intact families. These findings suggest that nonparental Mentors complement parents, rather than substitute for them. We suspect that males' parents who are Mentors are more likely to encourage their sons in the formation of positive relationships with other adults than are females' parents; the fact that more of the boys we have invited to join the experimental mentor program have accepted and received permission from their parents supports this assumption.

4. Discussion

These results are useful for their descriptive content. Knowing as little as we do about adolescents' relations with adults, we need to begin simply by learning how many and what kinds of adults they consider to be important. The comparisons by gender, parental role, and age yield important findings. Chief among the findings are that younger adolescents and females are less likely to have unrelated adult Mentors than older adolescents and males and that unrelated adult Mentors appear to complement rather than substitute for parents.

The age relationship seems easily explainable. It is consistent with the vision of the developmental process in which adolescents gradually enlarge their social networks to include more persons outside their families. The difference between males and females is less easily explained, though it is also consistent with what we know about gender differences in adolescent social relations. It is interesting to note that females were just as likely as males to describe their parents as Mentors. In fact, the principal difference between boys' and girls' descriptions of their nonparental adult associates was that girls identified fewer relatives and unrelated adults as being Teachers and Challengers, though they were equally likely to describe them as Role Models. These data suggest that some differences in male and female socialization might be attributable less to parental relations or to what adolescents contribute to their interpersonal relations than to how other relatives and unrelated adult associates act toward adolescents. Our design is not powerful enough to support firm conclusions on these matters, but the suggestion is tantalizing.

Finding that unrelated adult Mentors appear to complement rather than substitute for parents confirms results from the studies cited above (Garbarino, et al., 1978; Blyth, et al., 1982; Galbo, 1987) finding that adolescents continue to regard their parents as the most important people in their lives even as their social networks expand. It also constitutes a warning that unrelated adult Mentors are unlikely by themselves to fill the gap left by absent or unavailable parents, at least in naturally occurring relationships. It is possible that Mentors introduced to adolescents as part of our experimental program could compensate for absent parents or parents who for other reasons do not function as Mentors. The scarcity of compensatory Mentors in our sample, however, suggests that this may not be easily accomplished.

The finding that early adolescents have few unrelated adult Mentors also bears directly on our experiment, because we are trying to link unrelated adults with eighth and ninth graders (13— to 15—year—olds). It tells us that we are not only introducing a new adult into adolescents' social networks, but that we are fostering a mentoring relationship quite early, if our eighth grade sample is typical. On the one hand, this may make it difficult for those adults to become Mentors. On the other, if they do establish a mentoring relationship, they may have a more powerful developmental effect because of their early presence. Assuming that Mentors are good for adolescents, as the association reported by Darling (1987) implies, one of the critical questions to be tested in the experimental mentoring program is whether Mentors introduced by a program can, first, establish close relationships with younger adolescents, girls as well as boys, and, second, boost protégé performance on various measures of school and psychosocial development and problem behavior.

Consistent with Bronfenbrenner's person—process—context model, our experimental study is designed not only to assess the developmental impact of having a Mentor, but also to document the course of that relationship. We hope to be able to determine what ingredients contribute to an effective mentoring relationship and how those ingredients might differ as a function of such personal and contextual factors as gender, level of previous problem behavior, city compared to a small town environment, and parental functioning.

Although our international comparison has just begun, communication with colleagues from other countries has revealed some intriguing contrasts. For example, West German apprenticeship places a majority of older youth in workplaces where they are taught by unrelated adults, some of whom may come to function as Mentors. Japanese teachers traditionally take responsibility and exercise authority over far more aspects of their pupils' lives than their behavior in school. They are expected to chastise boys and girls holding hands while walking down the street, for example. They might visit a student's home late at night to assure that he or she is still studying. The Norwegian government routinely sponsors a wide range of youth—initiated organizations and activities, which involve nearly all teenagers, some of whom come into close contact with potential Mentors as a result. These and other contrasts will deepen our understanding of how the process of mentoring operates in widely diverse contexts. Because the United States has particularly few structural supports for establishing close interpersonal relationships between adolescents and unrelated adults, these comparisons will also add to our understanding of how societal support for such contact might be instituted.

Note

An earlier version of this paper was presented at the International Symposium on Unrelated Adults in Adolescents' Lives at Cornell University, March, 1988. It is one product of a larger project supported by grants from the New York State College of Human Ecology, the Spencer Foundation, and an anonymous donor. Dale Blyth, Urie Bronfenbrenner, Stephen Ceci, and Steven Cornelius have been involved in that project, which is now directed by the first author. Secondary school data were collected by Dr. David Smith and his students at Potsdam State College. A number of Cornell students have assisted in data collection, reduction, and analysis. All these people and others deserve our thanks. We would especially like to acknowledge the help and guidance of Urie Bronfenbrenner in this effort.

References

Bandura, A. (1969): A social learning theory of identification process. In Goslin, D.A. (Ed.): Handbook of socialization theory and research. Chicago: Rand McNally

Bell, A.P. (1970): Role modelship and interaction in adolescence and young adulthood. Developmental Psychology, 2, 123–128

Blyth, D.A., Bronfenbrenner, U., Ceci, S., Cornelius, S., Hamilton, S.F., & Voegtle, K.H. (1987): Linking up: An experiment in building teenage competence. Unpublished manuscript

Blyth, D., Hill, J.P., & Thiel, K.P. (1982): Early adolescents' significant others. Journal of Youth and Adolescence, 11, 425–250

Booth, L. (1980): An apprentice–mentor program for gifted students. The Education Digest, December, 38–43

Borman, C., & Colson, S. (1984): Mentoring – An effective career guidance technique. Vocational Guidance Quarterly, 32, 192–197

Bronfenbrenner, U. (1979): The ecology of human development: Experiments by nature and design. Cambridge: Harvard University Press

Bronfenbrenner, U., & Crouter, A.C. (1981): The evolution of environmental models in developmental research. In Mussen, H.P. (Ed.): Handbook of child psychology, Vol. 1. History, theory, and methods (W. Kessen, Volume editor). New York: Wiley, 357–414

Brown, R.D., & DeCoster, D.A. (Eds.) Mentoring–transcript systems for promoting student growth. San Francisco: Jossey–Bass

Colson, S. (1980): The evaluation of a community–based career education program for gifted and talented students as an administrative model for an alternative program. Gifted Child Quarterly, 24, 101–106

Daloz, L.A. (1986): Effective teaching and mentoring: Realizing the transformational power of adult learning experiences. San Francisco: Jossey–Bass

Darling, N. (1986): The functional roles played by important people in developing lives: An exploratory factor analysis. Unpublished manuscript

Darling, N.E. (1987): The influence of challenging and supportive relationships on the academic achievement of adolescents. Unpublished Masters Thesis. Cornell University

Edlind, E.P., & Haensly, P.A. (1985): Gifts of mentorships. Gifted Child Quarterly, 29, 55–60

Erikson, E.H. (1968): Identity: Youth and crisis. New York: Norton

Erkut, S., & Mokros, J.R. (1984): Professors as models and mentors for college students. American Educational Research Journal, 21, 399–417

Foster–Clark, F.S., & Blyth, D.A. (1987): Predicting adolescents' drug use: The role of personal and social network characteristics. Paper presented at the Biennial Meeting of the Society for Research in Child Development, Baltimore, MD

Galbo, J.J. (1986): Adolescents' perceptions of significant adults: Implications for the family, the school, and youth serving agencies. Children and Youth Services Review, 8, 37–51

Garbarino, J., Burston, N., Raber, S., Russell, R., & Crouter, A. (1978): The social maps of children approaching adolescence: Studying the ecology of youth development. Journal of Youth and Adolescence, 7, 417–428

Heyns, B. (1978). Summer learning and the effects of schooling. New York: Academic Press

Kemper, T. (1968): Reference groups, socialization and achievement. American Sociological Review, 33, 31–45

Levinson, D. (1978): The seasons of a man's life. New York: Knopf

Torrance, E.P. (1983): Role of mentors in creative achievement. Creative Child and Adult Quarterly, 3, 8–15,18

Vygotsky, L.S. (1978): Mind in society: The development of higher educational processes. In Cole, M., John–Steiner, V., Scribner, S., & Souberman, E. (Eds): Action and activity. Cambridge Harvard University Press

9.

The Significant People in the Social Networks of Adolescents

Inge Bö
Rögaland University Centre, Stavanger, Norway

Introduction

Important spheres of life — like family, work, local environment, learning, and leisure — need to be interconnected to give maximum potential for socialization (Bronfenbrenner, 1977, 1979). The substance of these links is *relations between people*. According to social observers, these previously intertwined areas are, as a result of urbanization and industrialization, being split into segregated life domains. Thus, people are becoming alienated — and also age — stratified — in relation to each other (Handlin and Handlin, 1971). In particular, it is maintained that adolescents have been cut off from the adult world and abandoned both to age — segregated peer groups and to exploitive commercial interests (Coleman, 1971; Bronfenbrenner, 1973; Condry and Siman, 1974; Montemayor and Van Komen, 1980).

Several scholars express concern about this situation and argue that the alleged isolation of adolescents may lead to a host of detrimental consequences. For example, it has been suggested that the main cause of the impaired well — being of so many young people in terms of mental health, social behavior, and declining academic performance, is a breakdown of the social ecology in which they live (Bronfenbrenner, 1973, 1974, 1979; Coleman, 1974; Magnussen, 1983). At the same time researchers have become increasingly aware that pivotal to this ecology are children's relationships with people of various ages and roles, particularly people outside the immediate family considered "significant others", "role models", "mentors" and so forth (Mead, 1952; Erikson, 1968; Sherif and Sherif, 1964).

1.   Previous Research

Systematic studies of children's and adolescents' social relationships date back
to extensive mid−20th century parent−child research, Moreno−inspired
sociometric approaches, and (mostly) postwar research on friendship and peers.
(For literature reviews, see Rubin, 1980; Foot et al., 1980; Epstein, 1983;
Serafica and Blyth, 1985).

Although age and role segregation are assumed to be widespread, and despite
the long−standing speculations about the nature and consequences of the
composition and effects of adolescents' social worlds, very few direct empirical
attempts to describe them have been accomplished (Blyth et al., 1982, 427;
Montemayor and Van Komen, 1980). Research on adolescents' social relations
has rather been limited to more fragmentary issues like the relative influence of
parents versus peers, peer group popularity, status effects, and friendships −
or to the effects of parental practices upon adolescent behavior (Tietjen, 1982;
Blyth et al., 1982; Serafica and Blyth, 1985; Cooper and Ayers−Lopez, 1985).
Research has focused largely on the direct effect of single environmental factors
or personal categories on the developing person − without taking into account
the total setting in which both physical factors and persons are embedded;
neglecting "aspects of the environment beyond the immediate situation
containing the subject" (Bronfenbrenner, 1977, 514). Accordingly, proposed
preventive and/or remedial measures have to a great extent been "atomistic" −
that is, isolated actions aimed at isolated problems, taking into focus one
problem at a time (Bronfenbrenner, 1974, 1979).

During the 1960s and 1970s a number of investigations (reviewed by Galbo,
1984, 1986) were also carried out regarding who young people rate as
significant in their lives. According to Galbo's review, most of these studies
may have limitations in terms of depth, breadth, and methodology. For
example, they have tended to be based on survey instruments and, occasionally,
structured interviews (as distinct from in−depth ones). Also, they have largely
been restricted to important *adults*, sometimes even to a limited number. Often
these adults were *putative*, that is, determined as significant by the researchers
before the study started rather than left to the free choice and perception of the
subjects. No attempt has been made to regard the meanings and implications of
various adolescent responses. Finally, many of the studies are now obsolete,
bearing in mind that youth's values and lifestyles have changed considerably
during the past two decades (Galbo, 1984, 957).

Certainly, these and other previous studies have identified a number of important aspects and functions of adolescents' social relationships. But though a large amount of data exists, whether taken separately or together, the studies do not provide a satisfying and comprehensive picture of young people's social worlds. Adolescents' relations with children (e.g., siblings), extended family members, coaches, adults in youth serving agencies, and other "caretakers" (other than parents) for the most part have been ignored in empirical studies Blyth et al., 1982). There also has been a tendency to overlook the importance ᵒ the adolescents' own determination of salience, and to ignore the erconnections between adolescents' significant people and the larger social ironment to which their social bonds are tied.

In recent years more holistic approaches to the study of social landscapes have been introduced to meet these shortcomings. One key to conceiving this situation is the use of social network concepts: Adolescents live within a network of relations and experience their social world with a variety of persons comprising their network. These are the persons with whom the adolescent's knowledge of social reality is co−constructed.

During the last 20 years there has been an extensive interest in the assessment of social networks in general, in recent years also interest in networks of young parents and in the social ties of preschool and young elementary school children (Cochran and Brassard, 1979; Tiller, 1980; Tietjen, 1982; Feiring and Lewis, 1981; Gunnarsson, 1985; Cochran et al., 1984). Despite this fact, and despite all research on whom teenagers rate as significant adults or role models, only very recently have researchers begun to apply *network analysis* in empirical studies of *adolescents'* social relations, based on more open−ended approaches, and particularly directed at those perceived as "significant others".

Garbarino et al. (1978) used this technique in a 3−year longitudinal study to map who preadolescents listed as important people in their lives during the transition to adolescence (core family members were omitted). The work showed that during this period, the individual's social world is increasingly made up of peers. In−depth analysis was, however, restricted to the top ten most significant relationships. Further support for age segregation during adolescence was provided by a naturalistic study (observations) conducted by Montemayor and Van Komen (1980). This study showed that adolescents were most often observed with peer friends, next with adults, and least frequently with children.

The project of Blyth and his colleagues (1982) is so far probably the most extensive study of youth's social networks. These investigators invited more than 2,400 seventh to tenth graders to identify the significant people in their lives, using a modified social network approach. They found that the single most frequent type of significant other listed was nonrelated peers of the same sex (about 31% of the total). Opposite−sex young people were more likely to be listed as significant others by older adolescents. Nonkin peers of both genders made up only approximately 40% of all the significant others listed by both males and females. However, this percentage rose to 57 when teenage siblings and teenage extended family members were also included.

In an exploratory study Galbo (1983) asked 31 mid—teen males and females to list their most significant *adults*. He found that parents were the adults most frequently chosen, though some youth selected no parents at all. Nonkin adults were preferred over kin at a ratio of nearly two to one. Male subjects chose an average of 4.79 significant adults, while females chose an average of 4.47 adults. Boys tended to prefer male adults, whereas girls chose females, but at a lower rate.

Another interesting network approach to understanding parts of adolescents' social landscape is the "whom—to—turn—to" technique. Using an instrument developed in Czechoslavakia by Jurovsky, Asne Gardsjord (1972) assessed the "social proximity" of 318, 14— to 18—year—old Norwegian students. These youths responded to questions about whom they would turn to for advice or support in various kinds of daily—life situations, with whom they would share their joys and sorrows, and so forth. Altogether 25 person categories and 21 issues/situations were prelisted. Gardsjord's main findings suggest that (a) as a whole, across all the issues, parents exceeded all other person categories in importance, with best friend and other peers rated second and third, (b) to whom youths go depends to a certain extent on the seriousness and context of the issue at stake: the more important the issues, the more they sought their parents.

Klagholz (1987) reports a similar network study of 223 adolescents aged 15 and 18 from rural and urban locations. She found that social network size and diversity varied significantly by sex and location. Boys and rural students had smaller and less diverse networks than girls and urban students. Regarding choice of person, the overall pattern was — as opposed to Gardsjord's findings — that *peers* were the most frequent choice and mother the second. Klagholz's data also showed that person preferences varied not only by issue — as in the case of the Norwegian study — but also by sex and place of residence: Girls chose peers more frequently than boys, whereas boys chose parents and unrelated adults more often than girls. Rural students, particularly the boys, relied on their parents, especially fathers, more than urban students. Urban adolescents rarely chose fathers at all and instead chose peers, siblings, and unrelated adults more frequently.

So far, the referred network studies have largely been descriptive in design. It is generally agreed that personal networks might be looked upon as "social capital", that is, as a resource needed to promote cognitive development as well as social skills and mental health (Garbarino et al., 1978; Cochran and Brassard, 1979; Epstein, 1983; Galbo, 1986). In recent years we also have seen analytical research considering relations between aspects of adolescents' social networks and behavior. For example, Blyth and Traeger (1985) and Coates (1985) have looked at connections between young person's self—esteem/self—concept and their personal networks. Vondra and Garbarino (1985) have examined such relations with respect to adolescent psychological adjustment, whereas Fischer et al. (1986), in a short—term longitudinal study, have focused on the possible *causal* effects of social network variables on self—esteem and social competence. Also Klagholz (1987) relates social network variables to behavior; in her case to "societal understanding".

The broad descriptive network study directed by Blyth, referred to above, has also been supplemented with an analytic part: Blyth, Durant and Moosbrugger (1985) and Foster—Clark and Blyth (1987) have analyzed how the different sets of significant others, including both peers and adults, operate for groups of nonusers and moderate to heavy, regular marijuana users. Their focus is rather on the quality than on the quantity of the relationships with others; for example, frequency of contact and the perceived intimacy and quality of the relationships are included in their analysis model.

While Blyth and Traeger, Vondra and Garbarino, and Fischer et al. fail to identify clear and substantial relationships between network characteristics and psychological outcomes, Coates and Klagholz reveal complex sets of relationships between measures of network features, both quantitative and qualitative, and self—concept and societal understanding (respectively). The Blyth teams found that drug users had less intimate relationships with their parents and other adults. Drug users were also much more oriented to older youth than were those adolescents not involved with drugs; this was particularly the case for junior high school boys. Also the type of leisure contexts from which the adolescents derive peer intimacy appeared to be related to both own drug use and to the tendency of having drug—using friends: the stronger involvement in adult—supervised activities, the less use and the greater tendency to have nonusing friends. The study also shows that the patterns of mediational effects were rather intricate.

Although most of these studies suffer from methodological shortcomings (e.g., they fail to control for socioeconomic status (SES) and other social structure factors), the lines of research show considerable promise.

2.   Research Questions and Methods of the Norwegian Studies

The objective of the present study has been to examine who are the significant people in the lives of teenaged Norwegians. With Bronfenbrenner's conception of the ecology of human development as the guiding theoretical perspective, stressing the importance of a phenomenological orientation, social network was used as the central approach. This paper has primarily this double focus:

1.   Present a technique of mapping young people's social world.
2.   Present a picture of who 15— to 16—year—olds rate as important people in their lives.

A subordinate purpose of the present paper will be to illustrate by examples how aspects of the personal networks relate to their behavior.[1]

Research questions

The presentation of results will concentrate on the following questions:

1. How many people do youngsters at this age perceive as significant?
2. Which age groups do the significant ones belong to?
3. To whom do adolescents feel most strongly attached?
4. To what extent do parents know their offsprings' network?
5. With whom do adolescents most frequently interact?
6. In which roles do adolescents know their salient network members?
7. Which SES factors contribute the most to their social networks?
8. Which connections can be found between their networks and school related variables?

Whereas the first six questions are descriptive in nature, the two latter are analytic.

Settings

The research reported here actually includes two studies: The main study was conducted in the oil—boom city of Stavanger, on the southwest coast of Norway, with an area population of about 200,000. The other one, originally a pilot study succeeding two prepilots, was done in a nearby fjord village of about 5,000 inhabitants, labeled here by the pseudonym "Fjordvik".[2]

The Sample

In Fjordvik, 82 students — 37 girls and 45 boys — belonging to the village junior high school's catchment area participated in the study. This was practically all the 15— to 16—year—olds in the village. The Stavanger sample consisted of 92 sixteen—year—old boys attending the 9th grade classes in two junior high schools selected because they could provide a cross—section of Stavanger youth.[3]

Measures

As pointed out, researchers have been slow to adopt the network paradigm for understanding the social world of adolescents. Due to the lack of (knowledge of) both empirical studies and measures at the start of the study, the problem was approached in an exploratory manner. Three main instruments were developed: a *Network Interview Form* (NIF), a *Background, Attitudes, and Behaviors Questionnaire (BAB)*, and a *School Rating Scale (SRS)*.

The Network Interview Form (NIF) was developed via two prepilots and finally tested in the Fjordvik study. When interviewing people about their social networks, one becomes confronted with the following methodological issues (Blyth, 1982):

1. How to define social network; in the present case how to delimit the "significant others".
2. How to operationalize the definition.
3. How to help the respondents elicit the relevant contact persons.

These issues are interrelated — and also crucial in terms of what kind of data one receives. In the prepilots much effort was therefore invested into the testing of all the three issues.

Concerning Item 1, in the final two studies five criteria were selected. The respondents were asked to identify people

1. Who had significance for them and/or for whom the respondent felt important.
2. Whose name they knew.
3. Who knew their own name.
4. With whom they did something.
5. With whom they were in regular contact.

The criteria were thoroughly explained; examples given included, for instance, friends of the family, relatives, friends from school and other settings, neighbors, teachers, and club leaders. Probes also mentioned people of different ages, the possibility of telephone and letter contact, and the fact that the contact person did not have to be liked to have significance for the adolescent.[4]

Concerning Items 2 and 3, the problem was to word the instructions and the network interviews in such a way that they listed network members consistent with the given criteria. A vital part of this problem was to make sure that the respondents not only included in their significant others the persons *most* salient — those whom they *recalled* immediately — but also those more hidden ones, whom they would *recognize* on the basis of the eliciting words and who make a difference in their lives. Another problem was to prevent the network interview from becoming a memory test. As far as can be seen, much of previous network research might have stumbled into pitfalls of these kinds.

To accomodate these demands, a network interview form was constructed in which a number of kinds of information were gathered for each network member, including sex, age, length of time known, perceived importance of the relationship, and the role(s) occupied by the person (sister, mother, neighbor, friend, etc). This gave maps of relations with adults, youths and children living both inside and outside the nuclear and extended family.

The Background, Attitudes and Behaviors Questionnaire (BAB). The BAB contained a number of different measures, from which only selected data are included in this paper; measures of
1. SES variables;
2. time spent in direct contact with parents and with peers; and
3. to what extent the respondents wanted contact with adults and elderly.

The School Rating Scale (SRS) had several sections. The main section consisted of two parallel Likert—type rating scales, completed separately by two teachers. These scales contained a large number of items with content relating to personality characteristics and various kinds of school behavior such as school motivation, general conduct, discipline, absenteeism, and so forth. Another section of the SRS provided space for the fall term grades in four core subjects taken from school records. Factor analysis was used to derive new analysis indices.

Variable list

The following indicators were selected for use in the analytic part of the paper: *The Family's Socioeconomic Status (Family's SES)* is an index combining the father's (mother's) number of years of schooling with a score representing the prestige of his (or her) occupation (intercorrelation $r = .61$).[5] *School Achievement* is an index composed of grades in four theoretical subjects (Cronbach's alpha $= .92$). *School Adaptation* combines ten ratings including discipline, general conduct, class conduct, "social risk", and disruptive behavior (.94). *Personality Traits* provides ratings of six personality characteristics, for example, diligence, independence, emotionality, helpfulness (.88). *The Neighborhood Milieu Index* is a composite score created by combining separate ratings of school staff members, the city police department, and the department of social services. They rated the 18 residential areas in which the subjects lived along a 5—point scale according to their general perceptions of the areas as having more or fewer problems (rang correlations between raters: .52, .53, and .61).

Data collection process

The study was explained to all students collectively prior to data collection. The BAB was administered to the students in groups of 10 to 15 students in their classrooms. Separately from this setting, an orientation to the network interview was given to all the participants.

Students were then called from the classroom in pairs, and given an hour of detailed instruction and interview by a trained data collector. During this hour the students completed interview protocols for 10 to 30 of their network members under the auspices of the collector. To get away from the interview being a "snap—shot—type" and to make sure that also important network contacts beyond those off the top of their heads were included, the students took blank network forms home and completed them during the next 10 to 14 days. After this, on the day of delivery, each individual was debriefed extensively for another hour by the original interviewer. In the debriefing session the network forms (and also the questionnaires) were checked for any missing information. A set of additional probes asked the students about their network to make sure that significant relationships had not been overlooked.

The School Rating Scale and The Neighborhood Milieu Measure, completed by the respective groups of school staff members, police, and social welfare personal, were conducted by the study director during visits.

3.   Results: The Significant People in the Social Network

Network size

Size refers to the number of contacts in a person's social network. As previously indicated, the size and other properties given of an individual's social network depend on the phrasing of the definition and the operationalization. To give an idea of the effect a difference in phrasing can make, data from the prepilots are included in *Table 1*. In this study the first item (the one on significance) in the network definition was skipped (cf. Note 4).

The means are all surprisingly high compared to the very limited amount of network research on teenagers that is known. The figures demonstrate that young Norwegians in their mid–teens interrelate with quite a few people. The prepilot data suggest that the number of acquaintances increases substantially if the nonimportant, looser ties are also calculated. Other data (not shown) suggest that the range is large, from an extreme of 409 network contacts of a well–adjusted 15–year–old girl in the first prepilot to the contrasting extreme of 3 of an isolated boy in Fjordvik.

The table also indicates that the youths in the "rural" village incorporate a substantially larger number of people in their group of significant others than the Stavanger youth — a mean of 69 versus 51. This has probably to do with density, which means that people in Fjordvik are interconnected to each other — "everybody knows everybody" — to a larger extent than people in the more metropolitan city of Stavanger.

A comparison between the two genders in Fjordvik indicate that girls have a larger circle of significant people than the boys — a mean of 74 against 65. In both Fjordvik and Stavanger the adolescent boys list more male contacts than females: means of 40/31 males versus 25/20 females respectively. However, girls in Fjordvik include males and females equally in their network, an average of 37 of each.

Table 1:   Number of contacts in the social networks of adolescents

Sample	n	Network contacts Number	Mean
Prepilots[1]	20	3.175	159
Fjordvik girls	37	2.748	74
Fjordvik boys	45	2.925	65
Fjordvik total	82	5.673	69
Stavanger[2]	92	4.709	51

[1]   10 girls and 10 boys
[2]   boys only

To which age groups do network members belong?

The mean age of network members in the two samples is 25.8 (Fjordvik) and 27.3 (Stavanger), with standard deviations of 3.1 and 5.1 respectively. In the Stavanger group the "youngest" network was only 17.5 years on average, whereas the "oldest" one was 48. (The boy with the oldest network reported only adults.) The Fjordvik girls' networks are a bit older than the boys'. The distribution is shown in *Table 2.*

The table confirms our expectation that the largest age group in the adolescents' social network is made up of peers. The data point to the interesting fact, however, that a *majority* of their significant network members does *not* belong to the peer group. The Fjordvik females tend to incorporate into their circle of significant people slightly more adults than the male students.

Zone assignment

By zone we here refer to the degree of importance the individual network member has for the anchoring person. Zone placement might therefore be looked upon as a measure of intimacy. The primary network (Zone 1) contains contacts rated by the students as the most intimate, whereas those next in terms of emotional ties and importance constitute Zone 2 ("the secondary network"). The third zone ("the tertiary network") is made up of those people in the network who are perceived to be less important than both Zone 1 and Zone 2 members (but where members still are felt to have significance for the person).

Table 2:   Adolescents' social network members, by age (means)

	Fjordvik girls	Fjordvik boys	Fjordvik total	Stavanger
n	37	45	82	92
Age				
0−6	3,1	1,9	2,4	1,3
7−12	4,1	3,5	3,8	3,0
13−17	30,0	29,3	29,7	24,0
18−24	6,6	4,8	5,5	4,0
25−39	14,3	10,6	12,2	7,8
40−64	13,3	12,5	12,9	8,4
65 +	2,6	2,0	2,3	2,6
Total	74,3	65,0	69,2	51,2

The social network members' distribution in zones shows that about one in four (Stavanger) and one in five (Fjordvik) network members are assigned to the primary zone. In numbers this means that each Stavanger and Fjordvik youth on average is surrounded by 13 and 15 (respectively) intimate persons.

A natural question in this connection is to which age groups the subjects feel emotionally closest. The Stavanger data show that 80% of all the children and 75% of all the adults 25 years and older are placed in Zones 1 or 2. The contrast to this is that 85% of their peers are placed in Zone 2 or Zone 3. The tendency is in other words evident: The 16−year−olds are more emotionally tied to the children and adults in their networks than to the peer group. Peers are significantly underrepresented in their intimate zone.

Network overlap

In this study, network overlap refers to the degree to which mother and/or father also know (by names and otherwise) their child's network contacts. Mother *and* father are reported to know a mean of as many as two−thirds of all the network members. As expected, we find that the network overlap is more common in the village. Mother knows the most − in Fjordvik she knows 9% of the contacts in *addition* to those father also knows. That Fjordvik is a more interconnected community than the Stavanger neighborhoods, is shown by the fact that only 17% of the students' significant others in this town are *unknown* to both mother and father. The corresponding figure in Stavanger is 27%.

The fact that peers are underrepresented among youths' significant others is reinforced if we look at it from another vantage point: Of all the contacts simultaneously reported as known by their parents *and* as Zone 1 people — the "VIPs" in their lives — only 25% belong to the peer group (a mean of 2.3), whereas the rest (mean = 7) belong to the other ages. As many as 30% (mean = 2.7) of these "VIPs" are uncles, teachers, coaches and so forth aged between 25 and 55; 20% are older.

Contact frequency

How often they have contact with their network members is shown in *Table 3*.

Table 3:   Frequency of contact (percentages)

	Fjordvik girls	Fjordvik boys	Fjordvik total	Stavanger
n	37	45	82	92
Frequency				
Daily	49	58	54	49
Weekly	24	17	20	21
Monthly	10	9	10	13
2–5 months	7	5	6	8
6 months +	8	8	8	10

According to the table, the subjects touch base with about half of their network contacts "daily" (defined as at least 4 days each week). These are primarily members of the core family, friends, and schoolmates. If we add those contacts whom they meet "weekly" (at least every 2 weeks, most of whom are club friends, sport chums, coaches, etc.), we approach three–quarters of the total networks.

Which age groups do they most regularly exchange with? Splitting the various age groupings on frequency of contact (as we did for the Stavanger sample), shows that of all the network members our adolescents encounter daily, 70% are peers (13– to 17–year–olds), about 20% are adults over the age of 25, and 6% are children below 7. This indicates that a normal (working) day for a teenager is filled with exchanges with peers on the various outside home arenas — school, sports, street corners and so forth.

Tables from the BAB questionnaire also confirm that the mid–teen group spend much time interacting with their peers, but also that the time spent with their parents, in particular with their mother during the working days, is notably extensive in comparison. During weekends the subjects report spending similar amounts of time with both groups.

When asked how often the subjects in the two samples communicated with adults other than parents and with people older than 60 years, the answers indicate a surprisingly high contact frequency. In Fjordvik, for example, half of the students touched base with the elderly at least once a week. In Stavanger the corresponding figure was 28%. Only 6 to 7% of the students in the two locations reported no contact with this age group.

Relationships

How are the subjects related to their network contacts, that is, in which role(s) do they know them?

Taken as a whole, relations dominate the networks of significant people: 38 to 40% of the total network members belong either to the nuclear or to the extended family. Next in size thereafter come schoolmates, own friends, and neighbors. Large groups are also the family's common friends, hobby friends, teachers, and so forth. But here we should be aware of the role multiplexity: Network connections whom they know in two or more roles are counted in all roles (Table 4).

Socioeconomic level and network size

An individual's network is not formed in a social, cultural, or economic vacuum. In our studies we attempted to trace links between a series of demographic conditions on the one hand (like neighborhood qualities, length of dwelling time, etc.), and characteristics of a youth's social networks on the other. *Table 5* is restricted to the connections between the family's SES and network size.

Father's work prestige turned out to be the strongest of the single SES variables.[5] It appears likely that the higher the parents' job prestige and education, the more people their offspring are exposed to, and the more they (probably also) are trained in network building skills.

Table 4:　Network contacts split on role categories

	Fjordvik	Stavanger
n sample:	82	92
number of network contacts:	5,672	4,707
	%	%
Core family: parents and siblings	7	8
"Near" family: aunts, uncles, cousins, grandparents	30	24
"Remote" family: other kin members	3	6
Family's common friends, parents' workmates, etc.	8	12
Own friends (minus pure sport and school friends)	16	30
Own friends' family members and friends of friends	3	5
School and workmates	29	28
Neighbors, vacation neighbors clerks, postmen, etc.	12	13
Known through hobbies, sport club, band, confirmation, etc.	8	16
Teachers, school staff, coaches, leaders, etc.	13	6

Note:　When reading the table, it should be borne in mind that a relationship can be "multiplex", i.e., the respondent might know the same person in two or more roles — e.g., as uncle, neighbor, and coach. This is also why the sum of the column percentages amounts to more than 100.

Table 5:　Relationships between network size and the family's socioeconomic level. F= Father's; M= Mother's; Pearson Correlation Coefficient.[1]

	Occupation[2]		Education[3]		Income[4]		SES[5]	SES[6]
	F	M	F	M	F	M	F	F+M
Network size	.37	.10	.24	.15	.15	.21	.36	.31

[1] probability: .19 p < .05; .25 p < .01; .32 p < .001
[2] measured by a Norwegian version of Treiman: *Occupational prestige in comparative perspective*
[3] education measured by a six−level scale
[4] taxable income offered by the taxation authorities
[5] sum of father's occupational prestige score and educational level
[6] sum of father's and mother's prestige score and educational level

Connections between networks and school variables

The analysis model consists of three variable groups: *Background Variables:* Family's SES and Neighborhood Milieu Index; *Process Variables:* Social network variables including time spent with parents and peers; and *Effect Variables:* School achievement, school adaptation, and personality traits.

Table 6, column A, shows some of the relationships found: In accordance with our expectations, the family's socioeconomic level contributes to school – related behavior. It is also interesting to see how the other ecological background factor – the neighborhood quality – connects with the outcome variables, particularly to school adaptation. The two clusters of network variables (variables 3 – 5 and 6 – 9, column B in Table 6) also relate quite extensively to the chosen school indices, but in opposite directions:

Size appears to have strong *positive* effects "in itself" (see below). The data also suggest that there is no difference in power between size of the peer and adult groups. (Other data, not shown, indicate that the size of the network group "younger than 13 years" contributes to the same extent as these other age groups.)

Multiplexity, frequency, zone, and overlap, however, all show a consistently *negative* correlation with the outcome variables. This means that the stronger the ties, the more frequent exchange, the more intimacy, and the higher degree of density, the *poorer* the school behavior. The relationships between time spent with parents and peers on the one side, and behavior on the other side, have opposite directions: the more time spent with *peers* – the more *negative* school ratings; the more time spent with *parents* – the *better* ratings.

There are, however, a number of interesting intercorrelations between all the variables used (not shown), for example, between the two demographic variables (.19), and between demographic variables and network variables. Since the demographic factors enter the arena temporally prior to the networks, this relationship might indicate *causal* links. This might mean that the demographic factors influence behavior both directly and indirectly – via the networks. In the model, therefore, the demographic factors are perceived as independent variables, whereas the network measures are seen as process variables.

Because of the danger of attributing to one variable predictive power that may in fact be more appropriately assigned to other variables with which variance is shared, it makes sense to partial out some of the shared variance before attempting to interpret these relationships. This process was undertaken with 1st and 2nd order partial correlation procedures as shown in Table 6. Partialing out family's SES, the correlation between neighborhood on one side, and the network and behavioral variables on the other, leads to slight decreases (mean drop across all process variables = .06). When controlling for the neighborhood risk factor, the same

Table 6:   Relationships of background and network variables with outcomes.[1]

Column A: Pearson correlation coefficients (without controlling).
Column B: Correlation coefficients between network/process variables and outcome variables controlling for the two background variables.[1]

Probability: .19 p < .05; .25 p < .01; .32 p < .001.

	School achievement		School adaptation		Personality traits	
	A	B	A	B	A	B
Background variables:						
Family's SES	.49	–	.27	–	.43	–
N'hood milieu index	.28	–	.37	–	.30	–
Network variables:						
Size of network	.50	.36	.53	.45	.56	.45
Size of peer network	.45	.33	.46	.40	.50	.40
Size of adult network	.43	.33	.49	.39	.48	.39
Multiplexity[2]	−.32	−.32	−.42	−.36	−.17	−.10
Frequency[3]	−.24	−.09	−.25	−.10	−.13	−.05
Zone[3]	−.10	−.17	−.25	−.32	−.14	−.20
Overlap[3]	−.29	−.27	−.17	−.20	−.24	−.27
Time with parents	.25	.10	.36	.26	.30	.17
Time with peers	−.26	−.14	−.28	−.18	−.28	−.16

1. Direction of scoring: High score means "good" (from the point of view of the establishment). For example, a high Milieu Index Score means low degree of social problems ("low risk"); a high School Adaptation Score means positive behavior (perceived by the school); etc.
2. Multiplexity gives a mean measure of the strength/weakness dimension of an individual's social network. The larger the mean, the stronger the ties between the anchor person and his/her network. See Footnote 1 and text under Table 4.
3. The scores for contact frequency, network zone, and overlap have been made linear by weighting. For example, a network person ascribed "daily exchange" or "belongingness to the primary zone", or "known by both parents" was assigned top score. A person seen only once a year or belonging to the tertiary zone or known by none of the parents, was weighted lowest, etc.

picture emerges (a mean drop of .05). This means that both family's SES and the quality of the neighborhood contribute separately and weakly to the network characteristics, the parent/peer involvement, and the school behavior outcome.

The next relationships of interest are those between the intermediate social processes – time with parents/peers and network involvement – and the various clusters of school outcome variables *when controlling for both background variables.* (Compare columns A and B in Table 6.) The emerging pattern shows an overall drop in the correlation coefficients (mean about .09), with the exception of zone and overlap. This means that when the effect of the background variables (SES and neighborhood) is withdrawn, there is still a relatively strong connection between the network indicators and school – related behaviors.

Finally, multiple regression analysis has also been utilized. Here both the two background and the nine process variables were put into the model simultaneously (see *Table 7*).

Table 7: Multiple regression model (stepwise regression)[1]

	School achievement			School adaptation			Personality traits		
	Beta	F	R^2	Beta	F	R^2	Beta	F	R^2
Family's SES	39	18.6	11	14	–	–	19	4.0	2
Network size	30	10.2	25	43	23.2	28	41	18.0	31
Overlap	−17	3.7	–	−11	2.6	–	−24	7.0	4
Multiplexity	−29	10.3	7	−21	4.1	3	02	–	–
Zone	−01	–	–	−26	5.9	9	−06	–	–
Time with parents	10	–	–	18	4.0	–	22	6.1	7
Time with peers	−16	3.4	–	−13	–	–	−14	–	–

1. Probability F= 4.0 p < .05; F= 2.6 p < .10. Only factors significant on the 10% level are included in the table.

In every case, the R^2 shown is the amount (%) of variance explained when controlling for all other variables. The overall picture is that the network indices, particularly size, overlap, multiplexity, and time with parents, appear to be the best predictors of school – related behavior for 16 – year – old boys. Family's SES is also a relatively strong contributor, especially to school performance, while the milieu index – and also size of the peer and adult groups – are expelled as nonsignificant from the pool of possible factors. Please note from the beta coefficients that some relationships are negative.

4.   Discussion

There are many myths about teenagers in contemporary societies. One of these maintains that their contact networks are not only meager, but also "kinship — alienated" and strongly peer centered. This paper attempts to shed light on certain aspects of adolescents' social landscape. It also provides examples of how demographic and social network factors directly and indirectly link to adolescents' school behavior.

Referring to our first research question, the data document that the mean number of network members in the pilot and in the main study turned out to be 69 and 51 respectively, with a huge range. Young Norwegians — at least in urban and semiurban areas — know, appreciate, and exchange with a surprisingly *heterogeneous* array of people, who at the same time are reported as being of significance to them. The contrast in terms of size between the networks of the prepilot group (Stavanger youth) and the two other groups is probably due to the different criteria sets for the network definition, whereas the distinction between the Fjordvik and Stavanger groups relates to the degree to which people are interconnected on the two sites.

The other conclusion to be drawn is that definition, operationalization, and choice of data collection technique turn out to be of crucial importance when mapping people's social networks. This relates to the determination of both size and other characteristics, and also to the problem of finding the point of balance between not making the network listing interview a test of immediate recall — and the other pitfall of pressing the respondents to include people who do not fulfill the criteria.

These issues make comparisons with other studies problematic. It might seem as if both Blyth et al. (1982), and to a certain extent also Coates (1985), have used "eliciting techniques" similar to the ones utilized in the present study. Blyth's research team found a mean of 15.6 persons in suburban neighborhoods, whereas Coates reported 29.1. Garbarino's team (1978) found means of 16.8 (rural area), 12.2 (city) and 11.1 (suburban), with nuclear family members excluded. Galbo, in his 1983 study, reported averages of 4.79 for boys and 4.47 for girls, but he asked for significant *adults* only.

The Americans, however, based their network interviews on the "snap — shot technique" as distinct from our combination of "interview — supervision — logbook technique". In addition, two of the teams had (other) built — in limitations in their approaches. These methodological distinctions are probably of vital importance and might explain the reported difference in network size between American and Norwegian youth. It might also reflect genuine differences between young people's social landscapes and lives in the two countries.

Data from Fjordvik indicate that girls maintain more contacts than boys and also that they have more heterogeneous networks. Girls include more children and more members of the opposite sex; their networks are also a bit older than the boys'. All this probably mirrors attitudinal and cultural differences between the sexes, girls' stronger sociability, and also girls' higher level of maturity at that age.

Findings also suggest that "rurban" villages of the Fjordvik size encourage the formation of larger networks than big city areas. The density measured by the degree of parents' overlap is also larger. This tendency might be curvilinear in the sense that smaller cities and towns mean a maximum environment for network formation, whereas the conditions are less favorable when cities grow larger and villages smaller. Table 3 also shows a tendency on behalf of the Fjordvik students to "push" their significant network members toward the outer circles. This again might suggest that adolescents living in dense villages of this size, know and appreciate many people, but also that they are less selective or less "inclusive" than young persons living in larger cities. An alternative interpretation would be that in some way, everybody is more intimate in the village, so it makes sense not to seek individual intimacy.

Turning to our second question, it seems to be a common aspect of both the American and the Norwegian studies that the young subjects include in their networks people representing a complexity of ages and roles, but with peers as the single dominating group. In the present study, however, most of the peers are rated as secondary and tertiary network members (Question 3), whereas the most intimate zone is mainly made up of core family, some selected extended family members, and also a close friend or two. No one in our samples excluded their parents or stepparents from the primary zone. These tendencies seem to be in good accordance with the findings of Gardsjord (1972), Blyth et al. (1982), and Galbo (1983): Core family members — and especially parents — are rated as surprisingly important to young people of this age group. While respondents in Gardsjord's and Blyth's studies gave increasing salience to peer friends with increased age, at no point did peers overtake parents as the most significant people in the lives of these teenagers. In addition to these people, youngsters appreciate the contact and exchange with teachers, leaders, coaches, neighbors, sales staff, and so forth (for other references, see Galbo, 1986; Blyth et al., 1982; Serafica and Blyth, 1985).

It is also evident (Question 4) — even in "metropolitan" Stavanger — that there exists a substantial overlap between parents' and their offsprings' social networks. In line with this, data from the questionnaire indicate that there is an extensive exchange between friends of Norwegian adolescents and their parents. Likewise, the respondents also seem to spend a considerable amount of time in their home setting in contact with their parents. Between 30 and 50% of the students reported "weekly" contact with elderly persons, and half of them also expressed a wish for more contact with adults; only one girl living in Fjordvik wanted less contact with adults. These findings correspond fairly well with results in a study quite recently conducted in a suburb of Stavanger. Among girls and those of both genders living in single—parent households, even a substantial *increase* in the wish for closer contact with adults was found from age 13/14 to 15/16 (Hauboff et al., 1988).

Together with research focusing on adolescents' norm orientation, preferences, standards, to whom they would turn in need for advice or comfort, and so forth, the results from this study question stereotypes maintaining that adolescents in general live in a separate world — a teenage culture — detached from the adult society (Brittain, 1963; Andersson, 1982; Henricson, 1973; Befring, 1972; Bö and Boysen, 1984). The present study confirms that people of various ages and roles are rated as important, and that they feel a stronger emotional connection to adults and children, particularly kinship members than to peers. We also recognize — as Blyth and his colleagues do (1982) — that frequency of contact does not necessarily relate to the level of importance, the quality or the intimacy of the interaction.

This should not be mixed with identity formation, which we did not look at, and should also be balanced against the *effect* of the contact frequency: Both our and the American studies demonstrate that adolescents have much more frequent exchange with the peer group, and also that friends are seen in more settings than any other age group (except parents and siblings). These are interactions and situations that undoubtedly expose them to relatively strong conformity pressure.

This high level of contact with peers may account for the difference found between data on young people's social worlds collected by observations, questionnaires, and interviews: Studies employing direct observation (Montemajor and van Komen, 1980) tend to find adolescents associating mainly with peers, but those which ask adolescents to list the significant others, or use a "whom–to–turn–to" approach, show a much more differentiated picture of the adolescents' social world. When literature reviews as a whole offer partly a blurred and partly a complex picture of this world, it might be caused by the fact that the perception of who is a significant contact is situational, and also that their influence on youth's self–concept, attitudes and behavior is situational. In other words, that it depends — as phenomena in the psychosocial world always do — on the ecology surrounding the subjects: macrostructures, SES, ethnicity, nationality and so forth.

So, from an ecological point of view, in order to construct the "correct" picture of adolescents' social landscape, we need a more comprehensive approach (Serafica and Blyth, 1985, 274), for example, simultaneous studies of who youth *rate* as significant others, whom they *turn to* for advise, comfort, sharing of feelings, exchange of goods, and so forth, and with whom they actually *associate in their daily interaction*, in the various arenas on which they live their lives. We also need to assess changes in their relationships with significant agents over time — both as a function of age and of contextual factors such as ecologically contrasting environments (Garbarino et al., 1978).

Bearing in mind that one's personal network contains a rich potential for growth and well—being, it is also important to disentangle the links connecting aspects of the network with formation of the self, with attitudes, and with behavior. This paper points to one possible approach to such research questions, also illustrating some connections to school—related behavior. These findings suggest that both demographic factors, like SES and neighborhood quality, together with social network factors exert influence. Partialing out the demographics, the network factors in themselves appear to correlate quite highly with all the three outcome indices. In the regression analysis, total network size came out as the most powerful single factor. Likewise, partial analyses (not all shown) indicate that the size of network subgroups (i.e., the quantitative aspects of the networks) like size of different age and kin groups, zones, and so forth, all correlate significantly, but not equally strongly, with school variables. For example, the Pearson correlation coefficient between "Size of primary zone" and "School adaptation" is .23, while the coefficient between "Size of tertiary zone" and the same outcome variable is .45, when controlling for the two background variables. This tendency might confirm the importance, emphasized by so many scholars, of exposing children to an array of significant others, representing a heterogeneity of roles, ages, occupations, lifestyles, and so forth, because such encounters stimulate identity and nourish development. (Brim, 1965; Bronfenbrenner, 1979; Coser, 1982).

Blyth and his team underscore the positive connections between qualitative network features and drug related indicators. With this as a background, it might be perceived as remarkable to find in the present study that the more *qualitative* aspects of the networks — multiplexity, frequency, zone, and overlap — correlate *negatively* with the school variables. This might mean that a personal network distinguished by a (too) high degree of strandedness, closure, density, intimacy, and contact frequency is a less fertile seedbed for personal growth than a more open, unstranded, and heterogeneous network. If this is a correct interpretation, it confirms Granovetter's theory about "the strength of weak ties" (1973). We hypothesize, however, that further analyses will indicate that both types of networks are needed in order to stimulate growth — a certain amount of *both strong and weak ties:* Perhaps the sparse, uniplex relations have the strongest potential for the development of instrumental/cognitive skills, whereas the dense, multiplex relations have the strongest potential for development of emotional/expressive social skills?

When focusing on the relationship between social networks on the one side, and behavior and personality on the other, one is confronted with the problem of causality. With the exception of the two background variables, the influences between network and behavior are probably reciprocal. Thus, being well—adjusted to school standards and in addition a high achiever in school might well develop sociability, friendship, and popularity and produce a big network as a result, which in turn stimulates growth.

More research is needed before conclusions can be reached on these questions. We believe that the network interview technique used in the present study has proved to be a promising way of getting a better bird's—eye perspective of adolescents' social landscape, of tracing the links along which influences are flowing back and forth between individuals and their significant network members, and also of unravelling the substance of these influences.

Acknowledgement

Acknowledgements are expressed to Dale Blyth and Moncrieff Cochran, Cornell University, Ithaca, for sharing their considerable competence in network research. Appreciation is also conveyed to the Norwegian Ministry of Cultural and Scientific Affairs, the Norwegian Ministry of Consumer Affairs and Government Administration, the Norwegian Research Council for Science and Humanities, and Högskolesenteret i Rogaland for their support of this research.

Notes

1. The study presented in this paper is part of a more comprehensive project, the main focus of which is to trace the possible links between aspects of young people's social networks and selected behavioral variables such as self—reported attitudes, crime, alcohol comsumption, and school achievement and teacher—reported social behavior. The data from this section are still in the process of analysis (Cochran and Bö, 1988).

2. For several reasons the Stavanger sample was limited to boys: First, the pilot study had shown very little variation from the girls' antisocial behavior — reported both by the girls themselves and their teachers. Second, financial limitations restricted the overall size of the sample. The arguments for including some data from the pilot study here are based on the following:
   1. The approach was the same as for the main study, except for some insignificant changes in the layout of the interview form.
   2. The study was carried out without any difficulties.
   3. The study offered the opportunity to make comparisons between Fjordvik and Stanvanger.
   4. The pilot study also includes girls (which the main study does not).

3. Of the total number of students in the classes (90 in Fjordvik and 97 in Stavanger) 8 in the pilot study and 5 in the main study did not join — partly because of absenteeism (4 and 1 respectively) and partly because they refused to participate, either on their own initiative (2 and 3) or at their parents' request (2 and 1). Data from the school protocols suggest that the 5 "decliners" in the Stavanger study are slight underachievers. Otherwise no information (grades and teachers' ratings) indicate that the attrition groups deviate from the two achieved samples.

4. In the prepilot studies the first item in the definition (on the significance of the person) was omitted — partly for curiosity reasons: to get clues about the possible "maximum" circle of acquaintances with whom young people in their mid—teens had some kind of interaction.

5. The combination of *father's* work prestige and educational level was chosen, due to high intercorrelation and because this combination appeared to excel other SES combinations in terms of predictive power (when tested in a correlation matrix). Of the 92 Stavanger boys, 9 lived in a single—mother family. In these cases, mother's SES was used. Due to this, the factor is called "Family's SES".

6. New, promising approaches to the study of relationships between a broader ecological context and adolescents' development and "contranormative attitudes" are now under way in Berlin directed by Silbereisen. These studies (to a certain degree inspired by G. Elder's 1974 study of the developmental effect of the great depression) include macrostructures, SES variables, leisure settings, etc. in the analysis models (Silbereisen et al., 1986; Walper and Silbereisen, 1987).

References

Andersson, B.−E. (1982): Generation efter generation. Om tonarskultur, ungdomsrevolt och generationmotsätningar. Malmö: Liber Förlag

Befring, E. (1972): Ungdom i et bysamfunn. En sosialpedagogisk studie av Oslo−ungdom. Oslo: Universitetsforlaget

Blyth, D.A. (1982): Mapping the social world of adolescents: Issues, techniques, and problems. In Serafica, F.C. (Ed.): Social−cognitive development in context. New York: Guildford Press, 240−272

Blyth, D.A. et al. (1982): Early adolescents' significant others: Grade and gender differences in perceived relationships with familial and nonfamilial adults and young people. Journal of Youth and Adolescence, 11, 6, 425−450

Blyth, D., Durant, D., & Moosbrugger, L. (1985): Perceived intimacy in the social relationships of drug and non−drug using adolescents. Paper presented at the Society for research in Child Development Biennial Meeting, Toronto, April 27

Blyth, D., & Trager, C. (1985): The impact of quantity, frequency of perceived other relationships on early adolescents' self−esteem. Paper presented at conference entitled Social Connections from Crib to College, City College of New York

Bö, I., & Boyesen, M. (1984): Pa jakt etter "ungdomskulturen". En sosialpssykologisk studie av holdninger og normoppfatninger hos 15−aringer i en fjordkommune pa Vestlandet. I serien Arbeidspapirer fra Rogaland distriktshögskole nr. 10, Stavanger

Brim, O.G. Jr. (1965): Adolescent personality as self−other systems. Journal of Marriage and the Family, 27, 156−162

Brittain, C.V. (1963): Adolescent choices and parent−peer cross−pressures. American Sociological Review, 28, 358−391

Bronfenbrenner, U. (1973): Two worlds of childhood: US and U.S.S.R. New York: Pocket Books

Bronfenbrenner, U. (1974): Developmental research and public policy. In Romanyshyn, J.M. (Ed.): Social science and social welfare. Council on Social Work and Education. New York, 159−182

Bronfenbrenner, U. (1977): Toward an experimental ecology of human development. American Psychologist, 32, 513−531

Bronfenbrenner, U. (1979): The ecology of human development. Experiments by nature and design. Cambridge: Harvard University Press

Bronfenbrenner, U. (1980): On making human beings human. Character, 2, 1−7

Coates, D.L. (1985): Relationship between self−concept measures and social network characteristics for black adolescents. Journal of Early Adolescence, 5, 3, 267−283

Cochran, M., & Brassard, J.A. (1979): Child development and personal social networks. Child Development, 50, 601−616

Cochran, M. et al. (1984): The social support networks of mothers with young children: A cross−national comparison. Research Bulletin, 25. Department of Education Research. University of Gothenburg

Cochran, M., & Bö, I. (1988): Connections between the social networks, family involvement and behavior of adolescent males in Norway. Manuscript submitted for publication

Coleman, J.S. (1971): The adolescent society. The social life of the teenager and its impact on education. New York: The Free Press

Coleman, J.S. (1974): Youth: Transition to adulthood. Chicago: University of Chicago Press

Condry, J.C., & Siman, B. (1974): Characteristics of peer— and adult—oriented children. Journal of Marriage and the Family, 65, 543—554

Cooper, C.R., & Ayers—Lopez, S. (1985): Family and peer systems in early adolescence: New models of the role of relationships in development. Journal of Early Adolescence, 5, 1, 9—21

Coser, R.L. (1975): The complexity of roles as seedbed of individual autonomy. In Coser, L. (Ed.): The idea of social structure: Essays in honor of Robert Merton. New York: Hercourt Brace Janovich, 237—263

Elder, G.H.Jr. (1974): Children of the great depression. Chicago: University of Chicago Press

Epstein, J.L. (1983): Examining theories of adolescent friendships. In Epstein, J.L., & Karweit (Eds.): Friends in school: Patterns of selection and influence in secondary schools. New York: Academic Press

Erikson, E.H. (1968): Identity, youth and crisis. New York

Feiring, C., & Lewis, M. (1981): The social networks of three years old children. Paper presented at the Society for Research in Child Development Convention Boston, April 1981

Fischer, C.S. et al. (1977): Networks and places. Social relations in the urban setting. New York: Free Press

Fischer, J.L., et al. (1986): Social networks in male and female adolescents. Journal of Adolescent Research, 6, 1, 1—14

Foot, H.C., et al. (Eds.)(1980): Friendships and social relations in children. New York: Wiley

Foster—Clark, F.S., & Blyth, D. (1987): Predicting adolescents' drug use: The role of personal and social network characteristics. Paper presented at the Biennial Meeting of the Society for Research in Child Development, Baltimore, Maryland, April, 1987

Galbo, J.J. (1983): Adolescents' perceptions of significant adults. Adolescence, 70, 417—427

Galbo, J.J. (1984): Adolescents' perceptions of significant adults: A review of the literature. Adolescence, 76, 951—970

Galbo, J.J. (1986): Adolescents' perceptions of significant adults: Implications for the family, the school, and youth serving agencies. Children and Youth Services Review, 8, 37—51

Garbarino, J. et al. (1978): The social maps of children approaching adolescence: Studying the ecology of youth development. Journal of Youth and Adolescence, 7, 4, 417—418

Garbarino, J. et al. (1985): Adolescent development: An ecological perspective. Columbus: Merrill

Gardsjord, A. (1972): Ungdom og sosial naerket. Hovedoppgave i psykologi. Universitetet i Oslo. (Klausul)

Granovetter, M.S. (1973): The strength of weak ties. American Journal of Sociology, 78, 6, 1360—1380

Gunnarsson, L. (1985): Sociala nätverk, familiestöd och utveckling. Bö, I. (Ed.): Barn i miljö. Oppvekst i en utviklingsökologisk sammenheng. Oslo: Cappelen, 110—133

Handlin, O., & Handlin, M.F. (1971): Facing life: Youth and the family in American history. Boston: Little Brown

Hauboff, A.L. et al. (1988): Ungdoms behov for voksenkontakt. Kandidatoppgave. Stavanger: Högskolesenteret i Rogaland

Henricson, M. (1973): Tonaringar och normer. En undersökning av tonöringars normklimat. SO—rapport 4/1973, Utbildningsförlaget, Stockholm

Klagholz, D.D. (1987): Adolescent social networks and social understanding. Paper presented at the Biennial Meeting of the SRCD. Baltimore

Magnussen, F. (1983): Om a bli voksen. Universitetesforlaget Oslo

Mead, G.H. (1952): Mind, self and society from the standpoint of a social behaviorist. Chicago: University of Chicago Press

Montemayor, R., & Komen, van R. (1980): Age segregation of adolescents in and out of school. Journal of Youth and Adolescence, 9, 371−381

Rubin, Z. (1980): Children's friendships. Cambridge: Havard University Press

Serafica, F.C., & Blyth, D. (1985): Continuities and changes in the study of friendship and peer groups during early adolescence. Journal of Early Adolescence, 5, 3, 267−283

Silbereisen, R.K. et al. (1986): Place for development: Adolescents, leisure settings, and developmental tasks. In Silbereisen, R.K., Eyferth, K., & Rudinger, G. (Eds.): Development as action in context. Berlin: Springer−Verlag, 87−107

Sherif, M., & Sherif, C. (1964): Reference groups: Exploration into conformity and deviance of adolescents. New York: Harper & Row

Tietjen, A.M. (1982): The social networks of preadolescent children in Sweden. International Journal of Behavioral Development, 5. North−Holland Publishing, 111−130

Tiller, P.O. (1980): Barns "sosiale landskap". Delrapport fra prosjektet "Sosial endring og oppvekstmiljö". INAS rapport 80:1. Institutt for anvendt socialivitenskapelig forskning, Oslo

Vondra, J., & Garbarino, J. (1985): Social influences on adolescent behavioral problems. Paper prepared for the conference on social connections from crib to college: Studies of the Social Networks of Children, Adolescents, and College Students. City College of New York

Walper, S.U., & Silbereisen, R.K. (1987): Economic loss, strained family relationships and adolescents' contranormative attitudes. Paper held et the Biennial Meeting of the Society of research in child development, April 23−26, Baltimore, MD

10.
Parental and Peer Support in Adolescence

Wim Meeus
University of Utrecht, The Netherlands

1. Parent — Peer Conflict: Some Empirical and Theoretical Notions

Since World War II the status of "youth" has become institutionalized throughout Western Europe (Gillis, 1974; SCP, 1985). Formerly, a relatively prolonged adolescence and the opportunity to develop a (youth—) cultural style of their own was the prerogative of young people from the higher echelons of society alone. Nowadays all youth has this opportunity; adolescence has become an identifiable stage of life for virtually every young person.

One consequence of this is that, far more than before, youngsters seek each other's company and have developed group consciousness. In their conceptual replication of a 1962 youth survey Allerbeck and Hoag (1985) found a marked increase in the number of young people moving within small groups or cliques: from 20 % in 1962 to 60 % in 1983. A similar figure is reported by Zinnecker (1982), who noted that some 45 to 50 % of the young regularly pass the time in their peer group. Allerbeck and Hoag add that in 1983, young people identify themselves with their own age group more explicitly than they did in 1962, and that to most of them adults constitute a negative reference group, which thinks poorly of traits appreciated positively by the youngsters displaying them.

In the relation between adolescents and their parents this state of affairs is of great psychological importance. For young people it means that they have access to a major point of reference in addition to that provided by the parents. For parents the implication is that their influence may be neutralized or thwarted by their children's friends. In the psychology of adolescence this problem is known as the "parent — peer conflict". Several investigations have been carried out to determine the areas in which the influence of peer and parent are incompatible, whose influence is the greater, and so on.

The situational hypothesis of the parent — peer conflict

One of the earliest studies in this connection was conducted by Bowerman and Kinch (1959). Ten to 16 — year — olds were asked whether their normative orientation and their identification was geared primarily to that of their parents or to their peers. Bowerman and Kinch's "normative orientation" covered views held by juveniles on a great many topics, while "identification" was defined as the degree to which the respondent felt to be understood by parents or friends and the measure in which, as adult, the youngster would wish to emulate either parents or friends. Regarding normative orientation, the results revealed a marked difference between the youngest and the oldest respondents. In the group comprising the youngest, 82 % oriented themselves to parents and 12 % to peers, whereas among the oldest these figures were 30 % and 50 % respectively. No such tendency was found in connection with identification. In every age group, orientation was mostly in terms of the parents, although parents were accorded less authority by older adolescents than they were by younger juveniles. In short, the work of Bowerman and Kinch showed that the balance of influence exerted by parents and peers is domain — specific; parental influence dominates in one area, while peers have greater impact in another realm.

The results gained by Bowerman and Kinch were confirmed in Brittain's study (1963). He presented a group of 15— to 17—year—old girls with a number of hypothetical dilemmas, simultaneously indicating for each dilemma which choice would be made by parents and which by young people. Brittain found that, depending on the content of the dilemma, either the choice of the parents or that of the peers was adopted. On the basis of these data, Brittain later (1968) formulated his "situational hypothesis", which states that in some situations parental influence on adolescents is the greater, while in other cases peers provide the frame of reference.

Kandel and Lesser (1969) sought to determine whether the educational plans of high school students were in conformity with the wishes of their mothers or rather tended to correspond to the ideas of their best friends. These researchers arrived at two essential findings: (1) Agreement between youngsters and their mother regarding educational plans was greater than agreement with their best friend. (2) Agreement with the mother and with the best friend respectively pointed in the same direction, that is, youngsters who agree with the educational future as envisioned by their mother also agree to a large extent with the ideas of their best friend. Evidently, the influence on adolescent educational intentions exerted by the mother is greater than that accruing to the views of peers. Moreover, in this domain the influence deriving from these categories is not incompatible — a datum which goes a long way toward relativizing the parent—peer conflict hypothesis. Kandel and Lesser (1969) interpret their results against the background of Brittain's situational hypothesis. They argue that the parent—peer conflict may obtain in some domains but does not apply in others. In a number of domains parental influence will predominate, in other areas the views of contemporaries will prevail.

The most incisive criticism of the situational hypothesis was formulated by Larson (1972). He sought to demonstrate that the choices made by adolescents in the hypothetical dilemmas are based on material arguments; parental or peer preferences are relatively unimportant in this. Table 1 in Larson (1972, 70) allows one to deduce, however, that with respect to the choice of a school, approximately 70 % of the respondents conform to the wishes of the parents, while in the case of two other dilemmas related to spare—time activities, the correspondence is far less: from 50 to 55 %. The situational hypothesis would predict precisely this kind of outcome.

Subsequent research resulted in reasonably unequivocal support for the situational hypothesis. For three domains it is possible to indicate whose (parent or peer) influence is the greater. The studies by Kandel and Lesser and by Larson show that parental influence is greatest for the domain of school. In a cross – cultural study Kandel and Lesser (1972) found this to hold for vocational aspirations and occupational plans on the part of youth both in the US and in Denmark. Biddle, Bank and Marlin (1980) also report that with respect to school, parental influence is greater than that of peers. In a review article, Kandel (1974) shows that for many leisure – time activities, peer influence is greater than parental influence. This is true for the use of alcohol and drugs, smoking, sports, and delinquency. Reed et al. (1986) arrived at the same results regarding the use of alcohol and drugs, and Biddle et al. (1980) for the use of alcohol.

Kandel and Lesser's study (1972,) reveals that in the area of personal relationships (problems with parents, personal problems not involving parents, dating, choice of friends), American youngsters are influenced by parents and peers in about equal measure; among Danish youth the influence of peers is the greater.

In view of these results, I conclude that Brittain's assumption proves correct: When the future of adolescents (school, occupation) is at issue, parental influence preponderates; in connection with more peripheral questions relating to the youth period as such (leisure), peers are the more influential. More recently research into the parent – peer conflict received renewed inducement on account of the German survey Jugend '81 (Jugendwerk, 1982) and a series of small – scale studies by Youniss and Smollar (1985).

Youth centrism as an indicator of parent – peer conflict

The variable in "Jugend '81" – and in its sequel, "Jugendliche und Erwachsene '85" (Fischer, Fuchs and Zinnecker, 1985) – central to my theme is "youth centrism". Youth centrism is measured in terms of a 25 – item scale and qua content stands for (1) aversion to parents and a marked orientation toward peers; (2) a critical attitude regarding adult institutions (family, state) and their representatives (parents, teachers, police, politicans); (3) a generation gap; and (4) reliance on the ability of youth to resist the "adult world". Psychologically, youth centrism implies ingroup – outgroup differentiation (Rabbie and Horwitz, 1969), that is, young people constitute the valued ingroup; adults are the outgroup opposition. The other processes which Tajfel

(1978) takes to be related to such social categorization, the construction of social identity and social comparison, are also included in the concept of youth centrism . Young people who score high on youth centrism ("youth centrists" for short) compare themselves favorably with adults; hence their own group constitutes for them the basis of a positive identity. It appears, then, that the concept of youth centrism is theoretically well – founded. Indeed, the results of Jugend '81 showed the validity of the youth – centrism scale to be great. The scale was demonstrably relevant in the domains of family, school, job, and youth – cultural behavior (Zinnecker, 1982). I offer a brief summary of the main points.

On the whole, the relationship between youth and parents or other adults is less satisfactory than it is in the case of their counterparts, the "adult centrists". They do not talk to adults as much and offer them less opportunity to recount their experiences. The degree of psychological support young people receive from their parents proved of crucial importance. Youth centrists do not experience such support nearly as much as adult centrists do. A recent Dutch study (Meeus, 1987) found confirmation for this: The scale "Lack of psychological support on the part of parents" correlated highly with youth centrism (r = .53).

Relatively early in adolescence (ages 15 to 17), youth centrists lay claim to certain adult privileges. They desire to apply their own norm in the areas of sex, timetables of going out and coming home, control of their own funds, and choice of living quarters. But this does not mean that they aspire to adult status in other domains; in fact, compared to adult centrists, they put a much later date to the point in time when they would want to attain complete adult status. These data support the conclusion that youth centrists put greater stress on the importance of adolescence as an independent phase of life than adult centrists do. They are not out to reach adulthood quickly; on the other hand, they wish to possess a number of adult privileges rather than wait until they reach formal adult status.

At school and on the job youth centrists experience greater difficulties than their counterparts. They repeat the year more often, have more trouble acquiring an apprenticeship, and more frequently quit school without diplomas. Unemployment is more widespread among them. It is not the case that youth centrists have more social contacts or operate more in peer groups than adult centrists. They do, however, shape their contacts differently; they tend to consort with informal, spontaneously organized bands of friends, whereas adult centrists are more likely to meet their peers in established associations and have recourse to school and job for group contact.

These results combine to paint a consistent picture: Youth — centrist adolescents distance themselves from adults both personally and socially. Their resistance to (the rules governing) the institutions of education and employment seems to be an extension of the poor relationship with their parents. This is why adolescence as such and the self — regulated peer group necessarily gain importance in the estimation of these youngsters. Yet this does not mean that youth centrists have more frequent or more intensive contact with their peers. Their relatively unsatisfactory relationship to their parents is not automatically compensated for in such ways.

Relating to parents and to peers: Different interaction structures

Youniss and Smollar (1985) report eight small — scale studies in which they researched various aspects of the relationships between adolescents and parents or friends. In a continuation of earlier research conducted by Youniss (1980), these authors apply a Sullivan — Piaget approach. According to this theoretical perspective, people are involved in essentially two kinds of relationships in the course of their life. The first type of relationship is with the parents and is characterized by unilateral authority on the part of the parents relative to the child. The specific interaction structure in this relationship is: request — obedience — approval, or: request — disobedience — disapproval — obedience — approval. The parents decide what the children ought to learn and how they are to behave. The children, in turn, submit to the superiority of their parents.

During adolescence this parental omniscience is questioned. Also, a second type of relationship develops, a relationship vis — a — vis one's peers. According to Youniss and Smollar, this relationship is characteristically one of symmetrical reciprocity. The interaction structure is basically different from the one which marks the relation to parents. In symmetrical reciprocity, positive actions are met with positive reactions, negative behavior evokes negative responses, and neutral acts engender acts of the same kind. Symmetrical reciprocity, then, implies the principle of fair treatment. Once people apply this principle, Youniss and Smollar (1985) assert, they have entered into friendship. Acceptance of the principle of fair treatment entails important consequences for the development of the interaction partners: They must design rules and procedures to take care of possible differences of opinion, since no (unilateral) authority is available to resolve differences directly.

Adolescents are faced with both types of relationship. How does the one kind influence the other? For example, does becoming acquainted with symmetrical relationships lead to adolescent rejection of parental authority?

The following data are reported by Youniss and Smollar: In general, the relationships beween parents and adolescents are asymmetrical or at any rate more asymmetrical than those between adolescents and their peers. This is true for the domains of school, vocation, and relationships. Moreover, parents make more frequent use of unilateral procedures, while peers prefer to have recourse to symmetrical procedures. This does not mean, however, that adolescents reject parental influence. Youniss and Smollar's data show that the influence of parents is domain—specific. In the context of school performance, planning for the future, and determining career goals, parental influence exceeds that of peers. But in connection with relationships, sex, and dating, the influence of peers is greater.

I interpret these data as follows: Adolescents accept the unilateral authority of their parents in the domains of school and vocation. In these realms parental influence is decisive for them, which is not the case in the area of personal relationships. These are determined more by peers and by the principle of symmetrical reciprocity. Parental influence is restricted because in this domain a basis for symmetrical reciprocity between parents and adolescents is lacking. Few parents discuss their personal and emotional problems with their children. Relations among adolescents, on the other hand, are typically symmetrical.

This description can be given additional nuance. In connection with symmetrical reciprocity, these differences in the personal relationships of adolescents with parents and with peers apply more to the father than they do to the mother (Youniss and Smollar, 1985). There is a degree of symmetrical reciprocity with the mother, while such reciprocity with the father is virtually nonexistent.

2.   Research Questions

Reviewing this brief survey of the literature, we can draw the following conclusions:

1.   Support for the situational hypothesis regarding the parent—peer conflict is reasonably unequivocal. Support for it can be derived even from a study by its most outspoken critic, Larson. Research reveals that parental influence is greater with respect to school and education, and that peers may be more influential in the domain of personal relationships (Youniss and Smollar, 1985). Youniss and Smollar offer a developmental—psychological explanation for this difference. When preparation for future social roles is at stake (schooling, career), adolescents recognize parental insight and allow themselves to be led in a unilaterally authoritarian way.

A different principle, that of symmetrical reciprocity, obtains for individual development in the areas of relationships and sex. Since parents seldom discuss their problems in these areas with their children, adolescents in turn lack a basis to address questions of this sort to them. Among their peers they have openings to do so. In the area of leisure time, too, peer influence is greater than that of parents.

2. The (psychological) supports which youngsters get from their parents and their peers need not be mutually contradictory. Kandel and Lesser's study shows that the influence of parents and friends with respect to educational plans points in the same direction.

3. Among youth—centrist juveniles, a poor relationship with the parents seems to lurk behind a general distrust regarding the world of adults. Among such young people, the likelihood of a faulty or failing social integration is greatest. For youth centrists, the self—regulated peer group provides the medium in which to shape their resistance to the world of adults. Youth centrists have neither more extensive nor more intensive contact with their peers. In this respect the group offers them no compensation for the poor relationship with their parents.

In the present study, I seek answers to the following questions:

What is the physiognomy of the personal social networks youngsters have in the domains of leisure time, school, and personal relationships? In view of the investigative data recounted above, I formulate the following hypotheses:

Hypothesis 1: In the life sphere "school", parental social support will be the more important factor.
Hypothesis 2: In the life sphere "social relationships", peer support will be the more significant.
Hypothesis 3: In the life sphere "leisure time", peer support will be the more influential.

Are there differences in the way boys and girls, and youth centrists and adult centrists, experience social support in these three spheres? Against the background of research into gender—related differences in perceived social support (Fisher and Oliker, 1983; Peplau and Gordon, 1984) and on the basis of results of "Jugend '81", I formulate the next hypotheses:

Hypothesis 4: Girls will experience greater social support than boys.
Hypothesis 5: Youth centrists will receive less social support from their parents

than adult centrists. (In addition, I seek to determine whether youth centrists receive more support from their peers than adult centrists would.)

Next, I concentrate on the life sphere "school" to determine the following: Is perception of social support structured in a two—dimensional way? Do parents and peers fit in different slots in this structure? How do gender, educational level, youth centrism, and social support from parents or peers influence school performance? On the basis of the data of "Jugend '81" I come to:

Hypothesis 6: I expect youth centrists to have more difficulties at school than adult centrists. In connection with social support from parents or peers, I investigate whether such support functions as a buffer against poor school performance.

3.   Method

Subjects

The results presented below are based on a survey involving 2,837 students — aged 15 to 17 — from the 4th grade of secondary schools. All the regions of the Netherlands and the four most important types of secondary schools were included in the sample: vocational schools (LBO), low level high schools (MAVO), high level high schools (HAVO), and high level high schools preparing for university (VWO). Half of the subjects were boys, the other half girls; a further sampling criterion was level of urbanization. The survey made use of questionnaires, which were completed in 45 minutes by the students in the classroom.

Variables

Youth centrism was measured by a Dutch version of the original German scale of 25 items (Zinnecker, 1982). Using factor analysis, I eliminated 8 unstable items (factor loadings < .30) from the scale. As in earlier Dutch studies (Raaijmakers, 1987; Meeus, 1988), the resulting scale proved to be sufficiently reliable (Cronbach's alpha = .81).

Personal social networks and social support. To delineate the personal network, a version of the "role—relation approach" (Fischer, 1982; van Tilburg, 1985) was used. In this method, the subject indicates to which extent he/she feels socially supported by a standard set of persons who have different role positions to him/her. The standard set of persons included: father, mother, brothers and sisters, classmates, friends, and acquaintances. The subjects delineated their personal networks three times: for the life spheres of school, personal relations, and leisure time.

School performance. One item was used to measure the subject's perception of his/her school performance. This three—point item was adapted from Van der Linden and Roeders (1983), with Category 1 indicating that the subject was performing generally well at school, Category 3 that he/she was performing generally poorly, and Category 2 that performance was average.

4. Results: Patterns of Parental and Peer Support

The personal networks for the three socialization contexts are presented in Figure 1.

Figure 1 shows the personal networks in the three contexts to be very different. For personal relations, the mother is the most important person in the subject's personal network, while the father has this position for the school context, and the friends for leisure time. These results are clearly in favor of the situational hypothesis of Brittain (1963). The three contexts together show that, overall, mother, friends, and father are the most important persons in the networks.

Social support in social relations, school, and leisure time

Hypothesis 1 is clearly confirmed by the results: Parents (father and mother) are the most important persons as regards school.

Hypothesis 2 must be specified. It holds for fathers but not mothers. In the domain of personal relations, peer support indeed is more important than the support of fathers. The social support of mothers, however, seems to be more important than peer support.

Hypothesis 3 is confirmed; in the context of leisure time the social support of peers is the more important factor.

The results of Kandel and Lesser were more or less confirmed by my study. Kandel and Lesser found a positive concordance on educational plans between adolescent and mother and between adolescent and best schoolfriend. I found low but positive correlations for the school context between the social support provided by mothers and friends (.18) and by fathers and friends (.24). For relations and leisure time, the correlations between father and friends were .14 and .18, and between mothers and friends .04 and .09. So, the hypothesis of Kandel and Lesser seems not to be valid for leisure time.

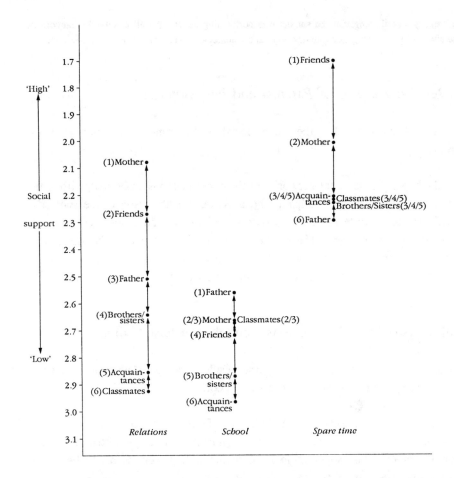

Fig. 1:   Personal networks in the domains personal relations, school, and leisure time. The
numbers between brackets indicate rank positions (1 = first position, etc.). Positions
linked together by arrows have significantly different levels of social support. For
reasons of presentation, I do not give statistics.

Social support, gender and youth centrism

For each domain separately I determined who, either the boys or the girls,
experience more social support from the members of the personal network. To
this end 18 t tests were made (3 socialization contexts and 6 network
members). Hypothesis 4 is clearly confirmed: Girls generally experience greater
social support than boys. In 14 of the 18 t tests this proved to be the case. In
two comparisons no gender—related differences were found: for classmates in
spare time and for father in the context of school. In two cases boys

experienced greater social support: from the father in the domains of personal
relations and leisure time (see Figure 2).

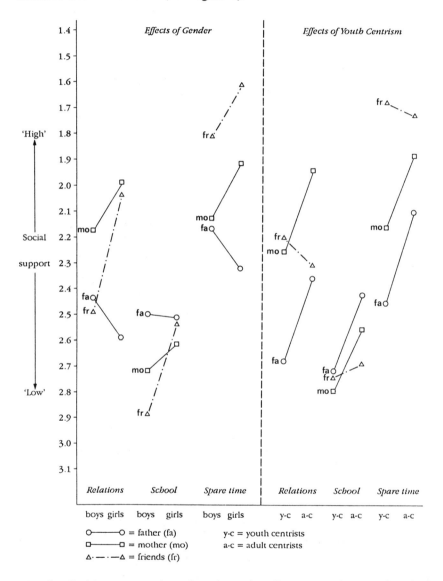

Fig. 2: Social support, gender and youth centrism. For reasons of presentation, the lines for
brothers and sisters, acquaintances, and classmates are omitted; for the same reason
I do not give statistics.

In both domains a same – sex identification takes place: Girls feel more
supported by mothers; boys by fathers. This process has the result that for girls
the difference in support from father and mother is far greater than for boys.

This result was not found for the school context. Another remarkable result is that girls experience far more support from friends in all the three domains. Friends are definitely more important in the personal networks of girls than in those of boys.

Generally, youth centrists experience less social support than adult centrists: This proved to be the case in 11 of the 18 comparisons (t tests), in 5 comparisons no differences were found, and in 2 comparisons youth centrists experienced more support. Thus Hypothesis 5 is confirmed. In the three contexts, youth centrists experience less support from both parents than adult centrists (see Figure 2). The same applies to brothers and sisters; apparently because they are experienced by youth centrists as part of a nonsupportive, paternal entity: the family.

In each of the three contexts youth centrists feel no more supported by acquaintances and classmates than adult centrists. The opposite is true for friends in the contexts of personal relations and leisure time. Youth centrists feel more supported by them than adult centrists. We may conclude that for youth centrists less support from parents and brothers and sisters is counterbalanced by more support from their friends.

Parental and peer support in the socialization context of school

A factor analysis was performed on the social support scores of the personal network in the school context (see Table 1).

The factor analysis shows that social support has a two−dimensional structure in the domain of school: Parental support and peer support are experienced as two independent forms of social support.

On the basis of this factor analysis, factor scores were calculated for parental and peer support. Subsequently an ANOVA was carried out to determine the effect on school performance of the independent variables parental support, peer support, youth centrism, gender, and level of education. The results are shown in Table 2.

Four main effects are observed. Parental and peer support both lead to improved school performance. Boys perform better at school than girls. This confirms Hypothesis 6 : Youth centrists perform worse at school than adult centrists.

Table 1: Factor matrix of six social support scores of the context school. (Varimax rotation, extraction criterion: eigenvalue > 1)

Support scores	Factor 1	Factor 2
Father	.14	.72
Mother	.18	.75
Brothers/sisters	.28	.28
Friends	.73	.13
Acquaintances	.53	.27
Classmates	.64	.12
Variance explained	41 %	19 %
Names of the factors	Peer support	Parental support

Table 2: ANOVA — effects of parental support, peer support, youth centrism, gender, and level of education on school performance (n = 2,837). Only significant interactions are given.

Effects	DF	F	P
Main effects			
Parental support (A)	1,279	8.20	.004
Peer support (B)	1,279	4.20	.041
Gender (C)	1,279	10.10	.002
Youth centrism (D)	1,279	34.25	.001
Level of education (E)	3,279	1,80	.145
3 — way interactions			
A * B * D	1,279	5.83	.016
A * C * E	3,279	3.70	.011

Two three — way interactions are found. The first interaction concerns parental support, gender, and educational level. Essentially the interaction shows that for girls a low level of parental support leads to worse school performance, while this is not the case for boys at the lowest (LBO) and highest educational level (VWO). The negative effects of low parental support are the strongest for boys at the intermediate educational levels (MAVO, HAVO) and for girls at the highest educational level (VWO). The second interaction concerns parental support, peer support, and youth centrism. This interaction is shown in Figure 3.

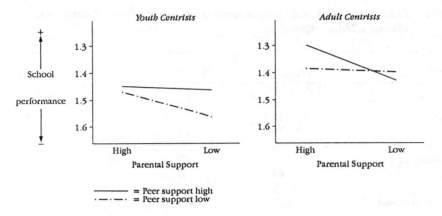

Fig. 3:   Three — way interaction of parental support, peer support, and youth centrism on
school performance.

Figure 3 shows the three main effects: (1) Youth centrists perform worse at
school than adult centrists; (2) high parental support leads to better
performance; (3) the same applies for peer support. The interaction shows that
for youth centrists differences in peer support have the greater effect when
parental support is low, while for adult centrists the effect is more pronounced
when parental support is high. For youth centrists, then, high peer support can
be a buffer against poor school performance in the absence of parental support;
for adult centrists peer support positively influences school performance when
parental support is present.

5.   Summary and Discussion

A central assumption in this article has been that parental and peer support can
be taken as indicators for parental and peer influence. My results favor the
situational hypothesis of the parent — peer conflict. The relative influence of
parents and peers on adolescents differs for the various socialization contexts.
Mothers are the most important in the context of personal relations, fathers in
the context school, and friends in leisure time.

The results show the classic gender — specific division of educational tasks.
Fathers are the most important persons in giving support regarding school, and
of low importance for the contexts personal relations and leisure time. They
seem to concern themselves especially with the preparation of their children for
future tasks and the attainment of social status. Mothers are important
generally, but more so in the domain of personal relations. They especially

look after the socioemotional development of their children. This female preoccupation with personal relations comes forward also in the higher level of social support generally experienced by girls as compared to boys. I take this to indicate that even today Dutch girls orient themselves more than Dutch boys to the field of personal relationships. Also, it is clear that girls cannot learn much from their fathers in this respect.

Youniss and Smollar (1985) see unilateral authority of the parents as characteristic for the relationships between parents and adolescents, and symmetrical reciprocity as typical of the relations between peers. Although my data cannot provide a direct test of this theory, one comment can be made. From the data of Youniss and Smollar (1985) we can infer that unilateral parental influence is domain – specific; it applies especially to school, future plans and career goals. So, one could expect parental support to be greater in the school context in comparison to peer support. My results indeed show that parental influence — mainly of the father — is greatest for school. This is in agreement with the theory of Youniss and Smollar. My data, however, are not in agreement with Youniss and Smollar on symmetrical reciprocity as a unique characteristic of the relations among peers.

If we take social support as a fundamental requirement for symmetrical reciprocity, the theory of Youniss and Smollar would predict that in the domain of personal relations adolescents experience more peer support than parental support. This theory holds with regard to the father, not to the mother. Adolescents feel supported more by the mother than by peers. I conclude that symmetrical reciprocity must be at least as important a characteristic of the relation adolescent – mother as it is of the relation adolescent – peers. On the other hand one might say that my results confirm more explicitly Youniss and Smollar's finding that in the domain of personal relationships symmetrical reciprocity is a feature of the relation between adolescents and their mother.

Table 1 shows that parental and peer support are experienced by adolescents as two independent dimensions of social support. As expected, youth centrists experience less parental support than adult centrists; as a compensation they experience more support from their friends. The hypothesis that youth centrism leads to poorer school performance is confirmed as well.

The results of Kandel and Lesser (1969) were confirmed: Parental and peer support correlate positively for the domain of school; also, they both have the same (positive) effect on school performance. Parental and peer support interact in different ways in youth centrists and adult centrists. In youth centrists, adolescents who orient themselves mainly to peers, peer support has relatively strong negative or positive effects in the absence of parental support. In this group, in which school performance is relatively poor, peer support becomes an important buffer against even worse performance. In adult centrists, adolescents who orient themselves mainly to parents, peer support is most effective in the presence of parental support. So, for youth centrists, peer support has positive effects on school performance when parental support is absent, for adult centrists peer support has added positive effect in conjunction with parental support.

References

Allerbeck, K.R., & Hoag, W. (1985): Jugend ohne Zukunft. München: Piper

Biddle, J.R., Bank, B.J., & Marlin, M.M. (1980): Parental and peer influence on adolescents. Social Forces, 58, 1057–1079

Bowermann, C.E., & Kinch, J.W. (1959): Changes in family and peer orientation of children between the fourth and tenth grades. Social Forces, 37, 206–211

Brittain, C.V. (1963): Adolescent choices and parent–peer cross–pressures. American Sociological Review, 28, 385–391

Brittain, C.V. (1968): An exploration of the bases of peer–compliance and parent–compliance in adolescence. Adolescence, 13, 445–458

Fischer, C.S. (1982): To dwell among friends. Personal networks in town and city. Chicago: Chicago University Press

Fischer, C.S., & Oliker, S.J. (1983): A research note on friendship, gender, and the life cycle. Social Forces, 62, 124–133

Fischer, A., Fuchs, W., & Zinnecker, J. (Eds.) (1985): Jugendliche und Erwachsene '85. Opladen: Leske

Gillis, J. (1974): Youth and history: Tradition and change in European age relations. New York: Academic Press

Jugendwerk der Deutschen Shell (1982): Jugend '81. Opladen: Leske

Kandel, D.B. (1974): Inter– and intragenerational influences on adolescent marihuana use. Journal of Social Issues, 30, 107–135

Kandel, D.B., & Lesser, G.S. (1969): Parental and peer influences on educational plans of adolescents. American Sociological Review, 34, 213–223

Kandel, D.B. (1972): Youth in two worlds. San Francisco: Jossey–Bass

Larson, L.E. (1972): The influence of parents and peers during adolescence: The situation hypothesis revisited. Journal of marriage and the family, 34, 67–74

Linden, F.J.van der, & Roeders, P.J.: Schoolgaande jongeren, hun leefwereld en welbewinden. Nijmegen: Hoogveld Instituut

Meeus, W. (1987): Jeugdcultureel verzet en politiek. Comenius, 7, 305–315

Meeus, W. (1988): Adolescent rebellion and politics. Youth and Society, 19, 426–435

Peplau, L.A., & Gordon, S.L. (1984): Women and men in love: Sex differences in close heterosexual relationships. In O'Leary, V.E., Unger, R.K., & Wallston, B.S. (Eds.): Women, gender and social psychology. New York: Erlbaum

Raaijmakers, Q. (1987): The work ethic of Dutch adolescents. In Hazekamp, J., Meeus, W. and Poel, Y.te (Eds.): European contributions to youth research. Amsterdam: Free University Press, 117–130

Rabbie, J.M., & Horwitz, M. (1969): The arousal of ingroup—outgroup bias by a chance win or loss. Journal of Personality and Social Psychology, 69, 223—228

Reed, F.W., Mc Broom, W.H., Lindekugel, D.M., Roberts, V., & Tureck, A.M. (1986): Perceived value similarity in the transition to adulthood. Youth and Society, 17, 267—285

Sociaal Cultureel Planburo (1985): Jongeren in de jaren '80. Rijswijk: Staatsuitgeverij

Tajel, H. (1978): Social categorization, social identity and social comparison. In Tajfel, H. (Ed.): Differentiation between social groups. London: Academic Press, 61—76

Tilburg, T. van (1985): De betekenis van ondersteuning in primaire sociale relaties. Amsterdam: VU—uitgeverij

Youniss, J. (1980): Parents and peers in social development: A Sullivan—Piaget perspective. Chicago: University of Chicago Press

Youniss, J., & Smollar, J. (1985): Adolescent relations with mothers, fathers, and friends. Chicago: University of Chicago Press

Zinnecker, J. (1982): Die Gesellschaft der Altergleichen. In Jugendwerk der Deutschen Shell (Ed.): Jugend '81. Opladen: Leske

11.

Working Mothers and the Educational Achievements of their Children

Jaap Dronkers
Tilburg University, The Netherlands

My Mother is looking for a job! Now I could end up a delinquent roaming the streets and all that. And what will I do during the holidays? I expect I have to sit in a laundrette all day to keep warm. I will be a latch—key kid, whatever that is. I think my mother is being very selfish. (Sue Townsend, The secret diary of Adrian Mole, aged 13 1/2, 1982, 20)

1. Introduction

The number of mothers with school—age children who have paid jobs outside their homes is increasing in the Netherlands as in most postindustrial societies, although the Dutch number is still smaller than in most comparable European countries. This phenomenon has both social and scientific consequences. First of all, there can be a clash of interests between women wanting paid jobs and children wanting their mothers to stay at home. What it often comes down to is that a woman has to make a choice between a paid job outside her home and having children. Children would be neglected if the mother were to work outside the home, particularly social—emotionally, which would have a negative effect on their educational achievement. This negative effect would be clearer in the Dutch case, because in the Netherlands an elaborate system of daytime child care institutions inside or outside the schools does not exist.

However, empirical evidence for this dilemma between a job on the one hand, and children on the other hand, is not available for the Dutch situation. Very little research has been carried out on the effect women's jobs have on their children (an exception is Bosman and Louwes, 1984). Outside the Netherlands, where we generally find higher levels of labor—market participation among married women, more research has been carried out dealing with the effects of women's jobs. A good example of this research valid for the USA is given in the book edited by Kamerman and Hayes (1982). In this book Heyns (1982) provides an interesting review of the research on the effect of women's jobs on the educational achievement of their children.

Most of the studies reviewed found that the educational achievement of children of women with paid jobs hardly differs from that of children of women without paid jobs. If some differences are found (like among children from poor or minority families and among middle – class boys), there are plausible reasons for assuming that other family characteristics than the women's jobs are responsible for these differences.

This conclusion is not undisputed however, as becomes apparent in the recent sharp discussion in the American journal "Sociology of Education" (Millne, Myers, Rosenthal and Ginsburg, 1986; Heyns and Catsambis, 1986). It is striking that the political context of this discussion is very different in the USA: The focus is on the possible negative effects of the social policy of the Reagan administration which by forcing (single – parent) mothers to go out to work might injure their children's educational opportunities. The political context of the debate on working mothers is quite different in the Netherlands: The focus is on the right of mothers to enter paid jobs and the effect on the well – being of their children. The social and fiscal policy of the Dutch governments (which have been dominated by Christian – Democratic parties since the end of the last century) discourages mothers from having jobs outside their homes. The European regulations for equal rights of men and women are only being implemented at a very slow pace and with many exceptive clauses.

The second, scientific consequence of the growing number of women with paid jobs is that the usual way of establishing the social class of a family, based on the occupation of the mostly male wage earner, has become even more disputable than in the past. In the Dutch research the parental class of students until now is mostly defined by the occupation of the father and the educational level of both parents. Within sociology, and in particular among those who study social stratification and mobility, there has been a long – standing debate on the concept and measurement of parental class in relation to the mother's job. One of the main issues is whether the addition of the mother's occupation improves the already existing measurement of parental class (see, e.g., the debate in the British journal "Sociology": Goldthorpe, 1983; Erikson, 1984; Goldthorpe, 1984; Heath and Britten, 1984. See also Abbot and Sapsford, 1987). This issue could be solved if one could prove that the educational careers of children whose mothers have paid jobs differ from those of children whose mothers have no paid job; or that the educational careers of children whose mothers are in a certain type of job differ from those of children whose mothers are in other jobs.

2.   An Analytical Framework

The central question of this article is: Does the educational attainment of students whose mothers are in a paid job differ from that of students whose mothers are not in a paid job outside their home, after controlling for the occupational level of the father, the educational level of both parents, and the age of the mother? If there is any difference, is this difference linked to the level of the mother's paid job or to the number of hours worked outside the home? Are the effects for boys and girls in any way different?

From the existing literature and on the basis of common sense one can explain the direction of the possible differences:

1.   *The socioeconomic process.* Mothers with paid jobs contribute to the social class of their families in the same ways as their husbands do. Both working parents have their own working experiences and conditions which influence their way of life and the upbringing of their children. This would mean that only *certain* jobs held by mothers have a positive effect on the educational attainment of their children, because of their content, conditions, and experiences. Other jobs have no effects or even a negative effect on the educational attainment of their children. These positive and negative effects should be more or less analogous to those of jobs held by fathers, and they should also be the same for boys and girls, but they increase as the mother works more hours in these jobs. The number of hours worked can influence the impact of the experiences, content, and conditions of the jobs.

2.   *The social – psychological process.* For mothers having a paid job, irrespective of its occupational level, means an emancipation from the confinement of the household. The fact that mothers have paid jobs promotes a more equal balance between the two married adults. The woman can make a larger contribution to the family and she can be a model for her daughter(s), despite the double burden of the paid job and the household. This would mean that *in all cases* paid jobs held by mothers have a positive effect on the educational attainment of their children. This positive effect should be independent of the number of hours of paid work and the occupational level, because emancipation from the confinement of the household constitutes a qualitative change, not a quantitative one. This positive effect should be more pronounced for girls than boys.

3. *The social—pedagogical process.* Paid jobs, irrespective of the occupational
    level, imply less attention for the family, and a bigger chance for lower
    educational attainment of the children. This negative effect is believed to
    increase as the mother works more hours outside her home, and also
    accordingly, that the attention she pays to the family decreases. This
    negative effect can be as pronounced for boys as for girls, and independent
    of the occupational level.

4. *The generation process.* Paid jobs of mothers is less self—evident for older
    generations than it is for the younger. After a low level of participation of
    married women in the labor force in the Netherlands during the 1950s (7%
    in 1960; Berends and Boelmans—Kleinjan, 1979) there has been a strong
    increase during the 1970s to about 30%. This means that women of the
    older generation had to overcome more opposition and had less possibilities
    for adaptation. The supposed positive and negative effects should therefore
    be clearer for children of older women than for children of younger
    women.

It does not have to be mentioned that the various processes can operate at the
same time. The measured differences in the effects of mother's paid jobs can
tell us something about the degrees to which these four processes are active.

Besides these four processes, there are other factors that can affect the
educational attainment of students of mothers with or without paid jobs. Heyns
(1982) lists a large number of them: the quality of the attention paid to the
family when the working mother is at home; the presence of other persons
(husband, elder children, neighbors, family, organized care) looking after the
children's school hours during the mother's absence; the womens'
self—selection in their choice to work outside their homes; the effect of the
characteristics of their children on this choice; and so forth.

If the mother with a paid job spends the remaining hours with her family more
effectively and in a better way than the mother who only works at home (e.g.,
because of a justified or unjustified sense of guilt; because a mother with a paid
job can organize her activities more effectively, or by self—selection or by
training) the third, social—pedagogical effect can be neutralized. The same is
valid if mothers with paid jobs succeed in organizing child care adequately by
having others taking over during their absence. If the working hours of the
mothers with paid jobs are well adjusted to the presence of their children, the
third social—pedagogical process can hardly appear. If mothers take the wants
and needs of their children into account when starting or continuing paid jobs,
this self—selection will make it almost impossible to measure the negative
effect of the third social—pedagogical process.

Finally, the contrast between work inside and outside the home is too simple. The effects of the social — psychological, the social — pedagogical, and the generation processes can be affected by the conditions under which the mothers make their choice for or against jobs outside their homes. Are most mothers who have paid jobs forced to do so for financial reasons? If this is the case, the second social — psychological process cannot be very relevant. Do most mothers stay at home only because they cannot find a suitable job and a suitable form of care for their children? Here the second social — psychological process can be very relevant. Unfortunately, operationalizations of these factors are not available from the data used in this study, nor from any other Dutch data on educational attainment. Moreover, several of these factors are very difficult to measure, especially in retrospect.

This means that the results presented here should be considered provisional, that is, it was not possible to control for all the relevant factors. This does not mean that the results are insignificant. The comparisons made with the added controls are more reliable than the impressions that have had to be relied on so far.

3.   Data and Methods

The data used on educational attainment are well known in the Netherlands; the SMVO — cohort (Social Milieu en Voortgezet Onderwijs; Social Origin and Secondary Education). In 1977, the Dutch Central Bureau of Statistics (CBS) started collecting this panel or cohort of about 30,000 students entering secondary education for the first time (Smulder, 1979; CBS, 1982). The average age of students entering secondary education in the Netherlands is about 12 years. This cohort can be regarded as a nationally representative sample. The CBS have gathered information on the social conditions of these students in 1977 (e.g., the paid and unpaid jobs and the educational levels of both parents). Since this start, the CBS has also recorded the educational attainment of these students during secondary and tertiary education up to the present. Here we only used the data on the educational careers of these students until 1981, when they were about 16 years old (the end of compulsory education in the Netherlands).

In this study we only took into account those students who in 1977 lived with two adults, of which the male adult worked more than 35 hours per week in a paid job. This selection was made to avoid distortion of the results by special family situations like unemployment of the father, one — parent families, and so forth. Bosman and Louwes (1988) have analyzed the effects of one — parent families on educational attainment with the same data. Grotenhuis and Dronkers (1989) are also using the same data to study the effects of the fathers' unemployment on educational attainment.

The independent variables available and used were:

1. Paid jobs outside the home of the mother (WORK).
2. Occupational level of the father (OCFA). We distinguished the usual CBS classification of occupational level: (1) higher white — collar job; (2) middle white — collar job; (3) lower white — collar jobs; (4) self — employed farmers and shopkeepers with employees; (5) self — employed farmers and shopkeepers without employees; (6) skilled laborers; (7) unskilled laborers.
3. Educational level of the father (EDFA) and of the mother (EDMO). The highest certificate was used as its indicator. We used the internationally accepted Standard Education Index of the CBS (CBS, 1976) to make a fourfold classification: (1) only primary education; (2) secondary education at the lowest level (junior vocational education, lower general education, junior general education and unfinished secondary education at the highest level); (3) secondary education at the highest level (middle vocational education, grammar school, senior general education); (4) tertiary education (senior vocational education, university education).
4. The mothers were divided into two groups on the basis of their age: younger than 40 years in 1977, or 40 years or older in 1977 (GEN).
5. The sex of the students (SEX).
6. The paid occupation of the women was classified by the CBS into six occupational sectors (SEC). This classification is not based on the social prestige of the occupations but on the similarity in the nature of the activities of the occupations. The occupational sectors are global fields of activities rather than specific kinds of occupations. In view of the problems presented by other classifications of occupations, which mostly are derived from classifications on male occupations and are not suitable for female occupations (e.g., for the Dutch situation see Van Doorne — Huiskes, 1984), we believe that this occupational sector classification is useful in this phase. The following occupational sectors (SEC) were used (CBS, 1971): (1) Scientific occupations and other professional specialists, artists. Mothers work mostly as trained nurses or teachers in secondary or primary education. (2) Policy — making and higher management occupations. Mothers work mostly as managing directors. (3) Clerical occupations. Mothers work mostly as secretaries, ticketclerks, or in unclassifiable clerical posts. (4) Commercial occupations. Mothers work mostly as shop assistants or self — employed shopkeepers. (5) Service occupations. Mothers work mostly in caring functions or as cleaning ladies. (6) Agrarian occupations. Mothers work mostly as agricultural laborers. (7) Trade — , industrial, transportational occupations. Mothers work mostly as seamstresses of ready — made clothes. (8) We added an eighth sector: household occupation. This contained all women without paid jobs outside their homes.
7. The number of hours per week spent in a paid job were divided into three categories: (1) less than 15 hours; (2) 15 to 25 hours; (3) more than 25 hours (HOURS).

The dependent variables indicating the educational careers of the pupils, were:

1. The total score on a school aptitude test (a combination of a linguistic and an arithmetic test, developed by the national institute for school aptitude tests, CITO), measured in 1977. The number of correct answers was counted (TEST).

2. Teacher's advice, given in 1977. In the top grade of Dutch primary education, each
    student is given official advice by the headteacher of his/her school which states for which
    type of secondary education the child is best suited. This advice is the best indicator for
    success in secondary education (see Faasse, Bakker, Dronkers and Schijf, 1987). The
    score had the following categories from low to high: (1) junior vocational education; (2)
    junior general education; (3) senior general education; (4) preuniversity education
    (ADVICE).
3. The educational level attained in secondary education in 1980/81, that is, after 4 years
    when the students were about 16 years old. The score included the following categories:
    (1) junior vocational education; (2) junior general education; (3) senior general education;
    (4) middle vocational education; (5) preuniversity education (LEVEL).
4. An undisturbed career in secondary education until 1980/81. A student had an undisturbed
    career if he/she reached the 4th grade of his or her school in 1980/81. The score was:
    (0) disturbed career; (1) undisturbed career (UNDIST).

4. Results

A global comparison

Table 1 compares the average scores on the dependent educational attainment
variables of students with mothers who had paid jobs with those of students
with mothers who only worked at home.

Table 1:   The average scores of TEST, ADVICE, LEVEL and UNDIST of students with
             mothers with and without paid jobs outside the home.

	Work			No work		
	M	SD	n	M	SD	n
TEST	42.54	12.05	5525	41.41	12.02	16053
ADVICE	2.66	.99	6286	2.69	.98	18232
LEVEL	2.39	1.35	6325	2.39	1.35	18389
UNDIST	.62	.48	6561	.67	.47	18970

Note: Means in italics differ more than 1.96 in t−test.

It is clear from *Table 1* that the differences in educational attainment, as
measured with the four indicators, were only small between the two groups of
students, and that only two differences were statistically significant. This is
even more astonishing when one realizes that small differences between both
groups of students will be immediately significant because of the large numbers
involved in the analyses. These two significant differences, however, were both
to the disadvantage of students with mothers in paid jobs.

The general conclusion from this first comparison seems to be that no important differences existed between the educational attainment of students with mothers in paid jobs compared to students with mothers working only at home. However, it is possible that more striking differences can be found after controlling for the differences of paid work outside the home by mothers from different social classes, educational levels, generations, and so forth.

Multivariate analysis is one of the ways of controlling for the interfering effects of those other variables. We used ANOVA (SPSS−X2) to control these effects. The independent variables were introduced as factors in the four analyses, one for each dependent variable. In the ADVICE−analysis we aded the variable TEST as a covariate and in the LEVEL and UNDIST analyses both TEST and ADVICE were included as covariates. These additions can give us a clear picture of the effect of the other factors after earlier scholastic achievement has been controlled. ANOVA also gives significant interaction terms. *Table 2* shows the significant interaction terms of the third order. (I did not look for interaction terms of higher orders.)

Table 2 shows that the effect of mothers with paid jobs on the educational attainment of their children was small. Together with the age of the mother (GEN) the variable WORK had the lowest F−values in the four analyses. Again, because of the large number of students involved, even these very small effects were statistically significant.

Table 3 shows that in practice, however, the effects were very small. It gives the corrected deviations from the average scores on the four dependent variables indicating the educational attainment of the students.

Table 4 shows the standardized regression coefficients of all factors and the explained variances (R^2). In comparison to the large significance of the educational level of the mother (EDMO) the effect of having a paid job outside one's home was small. For instance, students with mothers with paid jobs controlled for all other factors scored on the average half a question more wrong, while students with mothers with only primary education scored on the average 1,74 questions more wrong than the students with a mother with an average educational level. It is only on the educational achievement variable (UNDIST) that a paid job by the mother had some effect. However, the total explained variance (R^2) was not big (5%) and the corrected difference between students with and without mothers who had paid jobs outside their homes was only 0,04; that is to say 68% of the students with mothers only working at home had undisturbed educational careers versus 64% of the students with mothers who had paid jobs outside their homes. Almost all of the interaction

Table 2: Variance — analysis on TEST, ADVICE, LEVEL and UNDIST with all relevant factors and covariates and the significant interaction terms.

Sources of variance	Sum of squares	Degrees of freedom	F	P
A. TEST				
WORK	1397	1	11	.001
SEX	1787	1	14	.000
OCFA	19951	5	32	.000
GEN	2495	1	20	.000
EDFA	38701	3	104	.000
EDMO	44844	3	120	.000
B. ADVICE				
TEST	8191	1	18916	.000
WORK	1	1	2	.175
SEX	15	1	34	.000
OCFA	62	5	12	.000
GEN	1	1	2	.170
EDFA	78	3	60	.000
EDMO	54	3	41	.000
Work X EDFA	4	3	3	.041
SEX X EDFA	5	3	4	.010
C. LEVEL				
TEST	1103	1	1736	.000
ADVICE	6098	1	9595	.000
WORK	9	1	14	.000
SEX	15	1	24	.000
OCFA	20	5	6	.000
GEN	0	1	0	.841
EDFA	99	3	52	.000
EDMO	73	3	39	.000
WORK X SEX	8	1	12	.000
EDMO X SEX	6	3	3	.017
OCFA X GEN	11	5	3	.005
EDMO X EDFA	12	9	2	.033
D. UNDIST				
TEST	108	1	510	.000
ADVICE	8	1	37	.000
WORK	4	1	20	.000
SEX	15	1	20	.000
OCFA	12	5	12	.000
GEN	2	1	9	.002
EDFA	1	3	2	.075
EDMO	1	3	1	.491
SEX X OCFA	2	5	2	.045

Table 3:   Deviations of the average educational attainment scores, controlled for all other factors and covariates in the four analyses for each category of the variable WORK.

	TEST	ADVICE	LEVEL	UNDIST
Paid work outside home	−0.46	−0.01	−0.04	−0.03
Only work at home	0.16	0.00	0.01	0.01

Table 4:   The corrected standardized regression coefficients of the factors in the four analyses and the explained variances (R^2).

	TEST	ADVICE	LEVEL	UNDIST
Factors				
WORK	.02	.01	.02	.03
SEX	.03	.03	.02	.06
OCFA	.10	.07	.03	.06
GEN	.03	.01	.00	.02
EDFA	.15	.09	.07	.02
EDMO	.15	.06	.05	.01
R^2	.10	.52	.65	.05

terms of WORK with other factors were nonsignificant. Those few going above the standard significance level of 0,05 are too small to warrant further attention.

Summarizing, we can conclude from this second global analysis that there were no pronounced differences between the educational careers of students with mothers who had paid jobs and those of students with mothers who only worked in their households, even if we take into account social class, education, age, sex, and so forth. But it is still possible that the nature of the mother's paid job affects the educational careers of the children, as is the case with fathers'. This question will be addressed in the next section.

The nature of the job

Again we applied ANOVA−analyses on the four dependent variables in the same way as in the last section. But the factor WORK was replaced by the independent variable SECTOR with household job (SEC 8) as an additional factor in the analyses. We could not analyze for interaction terms because the numbers in certain cells were too small.

Table 5 gives the deviations from the averages for each category of the variable SECTOR, controlled for all other factors and covariates. We also added to Table 5 the F—values of the variable SECTOR in the four analyses to give an idea of the importance of this variable for an explanation of the four dependent variables. From these results we can conclude that if the nature of the paid job of the mother was relevant for the educational attainment of her children, it was not the contrast between a household job or a paid job outside her home. A household job at home (SEC 8) hardly showed any deviation from the average, but some kinds of paid jobs showed a negative deviation from the average, (commercial, service and industrial occupations) indicating a depressing effect on the educational attainment of the children, while other kinds of paid jobs (like scientific, professional, clerical, and agrarian occupations) showed positive deviations from the average, indicating a stimulating effect on the educational attainment of the children.

Not every paid job outside the home had a positive effect. These differences between jobs could be caused by variables we could not control (namely the degree of voluntariness of taking a job outside the home). However, it seems more likely to me that we had the same phenomenon here as is known for men. The market and work situation of men and women affected their attitudes and behavior not only in their jobs but also outside their working hours. This attitude and behavior in turn affected the education of their children. This seems to be true for both fathers and mothers: Both brought in their own market and work situation. A comparison between the F—values of SECTOR and OCFA showed, however, that those of the latter type were always substantially bigger.

Finally, I again repeated the ANOVA—analyses with the extra factor HOURS, indicating the number of hours a week spent in a paid job. These analyses were only carried out with those children whose mothers had paid jobs outside their home. *Table 6* shows that the factor HOURS only had some effect on the dependent variable TEST. Again this effect was not big compared with the other factors.

Table 5: Deviations from the average educational attainment scores controlled for all other factors and covariates in the four analyses for each category of the variable SECTOR and the F—values and the significance of the F—values of the variable SECTOR.

	TEST	ADVICE	LEVEL	UNDIST
SEC1	0.84	0.01	−0.02	−0.02
SEC2	0.63	−0.17	−0.03	0.06
SEC3	1.22	0.12	−0.01	−0.03
SEC4	−0.66	−0.04	−0.06	−0.04
SEC5	−1.97	−0.01	−0.06	−0.03
SEC6	1.80	−0.02	0.02	0.05
SEC7	−1.21	−0.03	−0.03	−0.03
SEC8	0.15	0.00	0.01	0.01
F	11	6	2	4
P	.00	.00	.02	.00

Table 6: Deviations from the average scores, controlled for all other factors and covariates in the four analyses for each category of the variable HOURS and the F—values and the significance of the F—values of the variable HOURS.

	TEST	ADVICE	LEVEL	UNDIST
HOURS 1	0.87	0.01	0.02	0.02
HOURS 2	0.17	0.00	−0.03	−0.01
HOURS 3	−0.78	−0.01	0.01	0.01
F	7	0	2	1
P	.00	.73	.20	.46

5. Discussion

Although this is only a first analysis and caution should be exercised, one may tentatively conclude that the educational attainment of students with mothers who have paid jobs outside their homes hardly differs from that of students with mothers who only work at home. The small differences found rather seem to be due to the nature of the paid job than to having one. The effect of the nature of the paid job of the mother is the same as that of the father. It is the nature of the job rather than having a job itself that can have negative effects on the educational attainment of children.

The socioeconomic process explaining the small number of differences between the educational attainment of students with mothers who have paid jobs and that of students with mothers only working at home can easily be demonstrated. Certain paid jobs have a positive effect on the educational attainment of the child, as is the case with paid jobs held by men. This effect seems to be unconnected, however, with the number of hours worked in the job. A consequence of this result is that the mother's occupation can make a difference — be it small — independent of that of the her husband. Thus, the addition of the mother's occupation will improve the measurement of parent's social class, not only on theoretical but also on empirical grounds.

The social—psychological process was not found. There were too few differences to support the existence of this process. The small negative interaction effect between WORK and SEX (Table 2 panel C), which was negative for boys with mothers with a paid job only seems to offer insufficient support.

The social—pedagogical process can not be proved at all. The same can be stated for the generation process.

Naturally, this is only a first analysis. Many possible factors which can have an effect on the differences of the educational attainment of students with mothers with or without paid jobs were only examined insufficiently. For the present however, I feel free to conclude, on better grounds than merely dominant impressions, that the mother having a paid job outside the home does not necessarily need to have a negative effect on the educational attainment of her child.

References

Abbot, P., & Sapsford, R. (1987): Woman and social class. Tavistock: London

Berends, A., & Boelmans—Kleinjan, A.C. (1979): Beroepsarbeid door vrouwen in Nederland. Den Haag: Staatsuitgevery

Bosman, R. , & Louwes, W. (1984): One—parent family and school—achievement. Paper presented at the Second International Interdisciplinary Congress on Women, Groningen, Netherlands

Bosman, W. , & Louwes, R. (1988): Een— en twee—oudergezinnen en schoolloopbanen. Mens en Maatschappij , 1988, 63, 5—23

C.B.S. (1971): 14de algeme volkstelling, beroepenclassificaties. Voorburg: Centraal Bureau voor de Statistick

C.B.S. (1976): Standaard Onderwisjsindeling. Voorburg: Centraal Bureau voor de Staatistick

C.B.S. (1982): Schooloopbaan en herkomst van leerlingen bije het voortgezet onderwijs, deel 2, cohort 1977, schoolkeuze. Den Haag: Staatsuitgeverij

Doorne–Huiskes, J.van (1984): Vrouwen in mobiliteits– en stratificatie–onderzoke. Mens en Maatschappij, 59, 3, 269–291

Erikson, R. (1984): Social class of men, women and families. Sociology, 18, 500–514

Faasse, J.H., Bakker, B., Dronkers, J., & Schijf, H. (1987): The impact of educational reform: Empirical evidence from two Dutch generations. Comparative Education, 23, 216–278

Goldthorpe, J.H. (1983): Women and class analysis: In defence of the conventional view. Sociology, 17, 491–499

Goldthorpe, J.H. (1984): Women and class analysis: A reply to the replies. Sociology, 18, 491–499

Grotenhuis, H.te, & Dronkers,J. (1989): Bestaansonzekerheid in de verzorgingsstaat. Amsterdams Sociologiich Tydschrift (in press)

Heath, A., & Britten, N. (1984): Women's jobs do make a difference: A reply to Goldthorpe. Sociology, 18, 475–490

Heyns, B. (1982): The influence of parents' work on children's school achievement. In Kamerman, S.B., & Hayes, C.D. (Eds.): Families that work: Children in a changing world. Washington: National Academy Press

Heyns, B., & Catsambis, S. (1986): Mother's employment and children's achievement: A critique. Sociology of Education, 59, 140–152; 154–155

Kamerman, S.B., & Hayes, C.D. (Eds.)(1982): Families that work: Children in a changing world. Washington: National Academy Press

Millne, A., & Meyers, D., Rosenthal, A., & Ginsburg, A. (1986): Single parents, working mothers and the educational achievement of schoolchildren. Sociology of Education, 59, 125–140; 152–154; 155

Smulders, R. (1979): C.B.S.–onderzoek schoolloopbaan en herkomst van leerlingen bij het voortgezet onderwijs. In Peschar, J.L. (Ed.): Van achteren naar voren, achterstandssituaties in het onderwijs. Den Haag: Staatsuitgeverij

12.

Significant Partners in Childhood and Adolescence

Sei Matsuda
Aichi University of Education, Kariya, Japan

In this paper I discuss the general mentor system in Japan. The teachers in formal schools (both public and private) should be psychologically significant partners, but many of them are not recognized as such by their students. On the other hand, many teachers in "juku" (Japanese preparatory schools or cramming institutions) are recognized as significant partners by students who possess voluntary and positive attitudes to learning.

We will discuss the role of these informal schools that sometimes function as supporting and supplementing systems for public education. The intention of these schools is not to encourage the child's general development, but to teach narrow and specific material that will enable the child to pass entrance examinations for further education or training.

In Japan, there are various kinds of apprenticeship systems that teach traditional artistic skills, drama, physical training, and also cognitive skills. However, in recent years these systems have been forced to undergo great changes. The masters in these institutions have found it increasingly hard to find apprentices who they can train to succeed them. For these reasons, it will be necessary to reevaluate these apprenticeship systems in the light of recent changes in the characteristics of youth and to look for new forms of training in these fields.

The main proposal of this paper is that teachers should become more significant and more efficient partners than they are at present, and that their peripheral workload should be reduced in order to attain these goals.

1.   The General Mentor System of Children and Youths in Japan

It is rather common for parents to be the most basic mentors for children in every culture. In addition, the growth of the importance of the nuclear family has made it increasingly difficult for extended family members such as grandparents, uncles, aunts, neighbors, and so forth to function as mentors.

Although the compulsory education system in Japan appears to be very similar to that of the United States and other Western countries, there are many specific differences. Within the compulsory system, the teacher in the public school becomes one of the basic mentors for children from the beginning of their educational careers. As most adolescents attend high school, even after the end of compulsory education (see Table 1), the high school teacher remains an important partner. However, teachers are not always significant mentors in Japan, although they are expected to fulfill this role. I shall return to this topic later.

Table 1:   A breakdown of educational systems and their attendence in Japan for the year 1987

Age group	Institution	Attendance
Childhood	Elementary school	Compulsory
Early adolescence	Secondary (junior high) school	Compulsory
Middle adolescence	High school (senior high school)	93%
	Vocational school	5%
	Other (e.g., employed)	2%
Late adolescence	College (junior colleges and universities)	35%

Schools do not only function as an educational system for the teaching of academic subjects but also fulfill a general role in the training and teaching of cultural knowledge, social skills, and physical training competences.

Table 2 presents the general mentor system in Japan and helps us to understand the roles and positions of the schools. There are three main domains in the school in which the mentor plays a role: cognitive or academic teaching, physical training, and cultural education. The system works differently depending on the developmental stage of the child: childhood, puberty, or adolescence.

Table 2:   The mentor system in Japan (mentor in parentheses)

	Cognitive and academic	Physical training	Cultural
	Childhood		
Formal	School subjects (teacher)	Clubs (teacher)	Clubs (teacher)
Informal — modern	Juku, tutor, academic subjects (private teacher)	Little — league baseball, soccer (coach)	Cultural lessons piano, violin, painting (instructor)
Informal — traditional	Abacus, calligraphy, shodo (private teacher)	Fencing, kendo, judo (coach)	Tea ceremony sado, flower arranging, kado (master)
	Adolescence		
Formal	Junior and senior high school (teacher)	Clubs (older students)	Clubs (older students)
Informal modern & traditional	Juku, entrance examinations (private teacher)	Sports clubs, dojyo, sport centers, private schools (coach)	Clubs, private schools, piano, sado, etc. (master)

The formal aspect represents the public and compulsory system of education that is carried out by teachers in public or private schools licensed by the Ministry of Education. However, one of the informal aspects is performed by private teachers in so−called "juku" (preparatory, supplementary, or cram schools) or tutors who make home visits.

2.   Significant Adults: Public Teachers or Private Teachers?

The national survey by the Ministry of Education NHK (1986) indicated a continuous growth in the proportion of juku attendance: The growth between 1976 and 1986 is shown in Table 3. One half of the ninth graders now attend some type of academic juku. This fact suggests that the juku are expanding their function as supportive and supplementary systems for the public education system, and that the significance of formal education as a comprehensive and dominant organization in the academic field might well be decreasing.

Table 3:   Percentages of Japanese children and adolescents attending juku in 1976 and 1986
(Ministry of Education, 1986)

Grade Year	1	2	3	4	5	6	7	8	9
1976	3.3	4.8	7.5	11.9	19.4	26.6	37.9	38.7	37.4
1986	6.2	10.1	12.9	15.4	21.1	29.6	41.8	44.5	47.3

The mainstream of relationships with significant others changes according to the developmental stage. As Tables 4 and 5 show, cultural juku are very popular in the stages of childhood and late adolescence. However, juku aimed at academic achievement or the preparation for entrance examinations into higher education are more prevalent in the stage of early adolescence (see Table 3).

Some data indicate that junior and senior high school students do not love or like their teachers very much (NHK, 1984). Nowadays, the ties between students and teachers are no longer very strong, especially for almost 11% of these students. This suggests that these students in particular need to search for significant adults among other groups than school teachers.

In their childhood, students were forced to attend some kind of juku because of their parents' belief that the early experience of some new kind of skill was productive and necessary for their children. However, because most of the children spent their time at some juku after school, it was very difficult for them to be with playmates, despite the fact they wanted peer relationships.

Table 4: Leisure−time activities of 4th− to 6th−grade Japanese children (N = 1,661; NHK Survey Division, 1985)(Percentages)

Activities	Male		Female	
	Weekday	Sunday	Weekday	Sunday
Calligraphy	1.6	4.5	2.5	4.7
Piano lessons	1.1	1.2	15.1	16.0
Other musical activities	1.5	2.2	6.2	5.8
Abacus	11.4	1.9	14.9	9.4
Swimming	0.8	1.4	0.7	0.4
Kendo or judo	1.6	2.8	0.0	0.0
Painting	3.9	2.1	4.2	6.8
Sado (tea ceremony)	0.0	0.1	0.4	0.0
Listening to records	1.8	2.5	3.2	5.6

Table 5: Leisure−time activities in adolescence in different age groups (JNN Data Bank, 1986; taken from Suzuki and Matsuda, 1987)

Activities	Male Age group		Female Age group	
	13−19	20−29	13−19	20−29
Enjoying taped music	73.5	66.2	73.8	61.2
Listening to records	55.4	51.0	43.6	38.2
Enjoying movies and films	41.5	42.7	38.2	41.3
Photography	19.6	37.1	21.6	37.7
Playing musical instruments	16.2	11.0	19.1	10.8
Painting drawing	12.3	4.5	22.8	5.0
Going to concerts	9.6	8.9	11.6	13.9
Enjoying the arts	4.6	5.0	10.0	8.9
Going to the theater	3.8	3.9	4.6	4.4
Calligraphy	7.7	1.5	17.8	2.2
Tea ceremony, flower arranging	1.2	0.9	4.1	18.3
Traditional music and/or dance	−	0.3	1.2	1.7

204

Sei Matsuda

Table 6: General relationships with teachers reported by junior and senior high school
students (N = 3,112; NHK, 1984)(Percentages)

Many teachers whom they like or love	18.3
Few teachers whom they like of love	70.2
No teachers whom they like or love	10.8
No answer	6.7

Table 2 suggests that there are three dominant types of afterschool activity for Japanese children. The first is the voluntary afterschool clubs, which are managed and taught by school teachers. Two subtypes exist: physical training and academic teaching. An exception is made for delinquent or bullying children who are compelled to attend physical training clubs, controlled during each daily hour of leisure time, and are disciplined in their attitudes and behaviors through these measures. In these situations, the significant others are the teachers − either in their role as coaches or trainers, or in their role as teachers in the classroom. Peers participate as co−members or co−trainees.

The second type of afterschool activity is the private juku that teach academic subjects. They supplement or compensate for formal school education with the goal of either general improvement in grades or the preparation for entrance examinations to higher−level schools or colleges. The teacher in the juku can only teach a limited number of students who generally have voluntary and positive attitudes to learning. Thus the teachers in the juku can share the same, narrow goals with their students and can develop close relationships without formal regulations.

We must take care when describing their role, because their goal is not to foster the child's growth as a complete personality, but to teach or cram the necessary facts that the students need to pass entrance examinations and advance on to higher levels of schooling.

The third activity is the private juku that train several kinds of skills: physical skills in modern sports (baseball, soccer, swimming, etc.), traditional Japanese skills (kendo, judo, etc.) that are regulated by several associations or leagues with dan or kyu (the formal grades or classes), music lessons (piano, violin, etc.), and traditional but still popular Japanese cognitive skills (abacus and calligraphy, which are also regulated with grades and classes).

Some developmental changes can be seen in the patterns of children's activities. Learning and being trained in cultural and physical skills is insisted upon in childhood by the parents. However, most children give up these traditional disciplines when they reach adolescence. Instead, they are eager to learn in an academic juku, in order to obtain good grades or increase their chances of entrance into higher – level or upper – grade schools. Although the parents suggest and encourage such behavior, the volition and selection by the child is important.

In these situations, the significant others for adolescents are the teachers and coaches in these activities. Children who are able to develop and maintain a close relationship with the teachers in school clubs seem to be contented. However, unfortunately, many students have to search for significant others (mentors) in institutions outside of the schools.

3.   Nature of the Traditional Systems

Japan has always possessed various kinds of apprenticeship systems for traditional artistic skills (painting, calligraphy, etc.) drama (kabuki, nou, kyougen, etc.), physical training (sumo, kendo, judo, etc.), and cognitive domains (go, shogi, etc.).

There is an interesting book entitled "Waza" (traditional skill), in which Ikuta (1987) analyzed the background of the learning process involved in the traditional skills. She not only noted the importance of the skill itself, but also the significance of the surrounding atmosphere, the trivial chores, and other complicated human relationships. In her discussion, she points out that there is a typical learning style in sumo. Sumo wrestlers must learn the patterns (styles or kata) that have spiritual meaning. These patterns are distinguished from the overt forms (katachi).

As Table 5 shows, quite a large number of adolescents learn traditional skills. They are taught the basis of the traditional skills in such areas as kabuki, nou, sado, or sumo.

In recent years, these systems have been forced to change. It has become very difficult for masters to find apprentices whom they can train to become their successors, even when these apprentices are their own children. Adolescents are beginning to demand the right to choose and decide on their own careers. The young generations reject the so – called uchi – deschi (apprentice) system, which insists that they stay in their master's home and do menial work in order to learn both the skill itself and its accompanying background spirit.

A recent event in Japan gained a lot of publicity. This was the escape of the 22 – year – old, grand champion sumo wrestler Futahaguro from his master Oyakata. He felt that his "sumo – do" (belief and technical training system about sumo) was not compatible with his master's.

We must reevaluate these training systems in the light of recent changes in the characteristics of youth and search for new ways of providing training in these fields, though there is only a small number of children and adolescents who want to adopt such traditional skills as their future profession.

4. The Provision of Sufficient and Significant Partners for Adolescents

The school teachers who coach sports clubs in Japan are aware that they are far to busy to be able to care for the private lives of their students in addition to teaching them skills in sport and providing them with the obligatory academic training. Teachers who direct famous sports teams in their districts report that they have no leisure – time, even on Sundays. For example, they spend the whole day with the members in club houses throughout the entire year without taking any vacations.

In the domain of academic studies, some public school teachers will even visit or call on their students at midnight to ascertain how they are studying at this time. They are very eager to make progress in their students' academic achievement, or, in other words, they are competing with other colleagues to gain higher end – of – term grades for their students, and a higher entrance rate for their students into higher – level or upper – grade schools.

However, such extremes are very rare among public school teachers, because their working conditions are organized so that under usual conditions they are able to enjoy their private lives after 5 or 6 o'clock in the afternoon. These teachers have to exercise strict control in the classroom because of the size of classes (average class size: 40 students in elementary school; 45 in senior high school), and because they are expected to teach moral standards and social skills as well as the academic curriculum to such large numbers of students in a restricted number of hours.

It is more the case that the juku teachers are expected to support the hard study courses of their students. They are expected to listen to and answer questions on all current problems, even if a student telephones them in the middle of the night. (One Japanese educational psychologist evaluates his child's juku teacher as being more significant and important than the public school teachers for his child's education on this point.)

These relationships are not formal or public, but tend to be rather private, very close, and intensive. As a result, children really do rely on these teachers, not only for the direct teaching activities, but also for making decisions on future careers and/or with regard to the general attitudes and beliefs in their lives.

Our data from research into mentors in Japan suggest that the most significant others are parents, peers, and juku teachers, though this is only tentative as we are still in the process of analysis.

The above report creates the impression that public school teachers play a very small role in Japan. Must we conclude that the formal role of teachers has been taken over by the juku? Our most recent data on the teachers' influence on the behavior of their students revealed that students reported that their public school teachers had a two−sided role in line with Darling (1987): These are the supportive role and the challenging role. Table 7 presents the responses of 696 Japanese students who are enrolled in a teacher training college at our university.

Table 7: Factor analysis of the percieved traits of the most influential teachers (Matsuda et al., 1988)

Items	Factors	
	1	2
1. Gained my respect	.144	.381
2. Gained my love and affection	.289	− .036
3. Took care of me in many ways	.407	.059
4. Was a good model when I performed something	.013	.327
5. Had a strong impact on making me change my way of life	.029	.216
6. Taught me real new thoughts and experiences	− .064	.261
7. Gave me constructive opinions	.223	.245
8. Supported my emotional stability or my affection	.408	.130
9. Protected me from psychological harm	.302	− .029
10. Was a good counselor in times of trouble	.497	.098

The first factor loads on Items 2, 3, 7, 8, 9, and 10. This factor seems to indicate the supportive relationships of the teachers to their students. In contrast, the second factor loads on Items 1, 4, 5, 6, and 7. This factor suggests that teachers have a challenging nature. These results correspond to the general mentor characteristics reported in Darling (1987).

The results suggest two possible kinds of interpretation: First, that many students have experienced mentor relationships with competent teachers. Second, many teachers are neglected by their students or are not recognized as mentors.

Teachers should be psychologically significant partners for their students, and they should be recognized as such by their students. Unfortunately, and we can sympathize with this, teachers have too many students in their classes. As mentioned above, a teacher has to deal with 40 students in an elementary school class and 45 students in junior and senior high school. With such large numbers, the teachers are simply unable to teach each student according to his or her character or ability. We consider that it is necessary to reduce the number of students per class. Actually, as part of a campaign to reduce violence and vandalism in schools and bullying in the classroom, the Ministry of Education has decided to reduce the number of students per class. We know that a decrease in the size of classes correlates with an increase in the children's level of achievement. Therefore we are certain in our anticipation that such changes will increase the importance of the teachers as significant partners for children and adolescents.

Note

Paper presented at the international conference on "Nonparental Adults in Adolescents' Lives" at Cornell University, Ithaca in March 1988. The author would like to express his gratitude to Prof. Dr. Bronfenbrenner and his colleagues for the invitation to the conference, and also to the Japan Foundation and the Taikou Foundation for the financial support that made his attendence possible.

References

Darling, N. (1987): The influence of challenging and supportive relationships in the academic achievement of adolescents. Thesis: Cornell University
Ikuta, K. (1987): What is learned by "Traditional Skill". Tokyo Daigaku Press (in Japanese)
Matsuda, S., & Suzuki, M. (1987): Parental belief system and efficacy feeling of children. Paper presented at the 29th Meeting of the Japanese Association of Educational Psychology

(in Japanese)

Matsuda, S., Iwai, Y., Takahashi, S., Suzuki, M., & Koyasu, M. (1988): Teachers' aptitude and competency. Retrospective evaluation by the students of a Teachers College. Aichi University of Education (in Japanese)

NHK, The Survey Division (1984): Opinion and attitude of high—school students. Nippon Hoso Press (in Japanese)

NHK, The Survey Division (1985): Time schedule of Japanese. Nippon Hoso Press (in Japanese)

NHK, The Survey Division (1986): The world of the primary school children. Nippon Hoso Press (in Japanese)

Suzuki, K., & Matsuda, S. (1987): Modern psychology of adolescence. Yuuhikaku Co. (in Japanese)

Part III
Contexts of Adolescents' Lifestyles

13.

School and Family in the Lifeworld of Youngsters

Manuela du Bois — Reymond
Leiden University, The Netherlands

1.   Youth Research in the Netherlands

In this first section of my paper, I will go into some aspects of the development of youth research in the Netherlands. Then I will discuss the concept of "life — world" and its applications within youth research. Thirdly, I will present some sociostructural data on Dutch youth and refer to results of research on the life — worlds of school and family. Finally, I will discuss some youth studies in which the concept of "life — world" is further elaborated.

The origin of modern Dutch youth research can be traced back to the year 1948, when the then Minister of Education, Art, and Science commissioned seven leading social — scientific universities and research institutes to investigate the situation of so — called "mass youth". It was intended that this project should entail some proposals for the (re)integration of these youngsters into post — war society. Thirty — nine years later, in 1987, another ministerial order was sent out — this time only to one private institute — to set up an investigation into the situation of Dutch youth. This project, too, was to work out recommendations for modern youth policy. The two dates mark the period in which Dutch youth research evolved.

The first project consisted of some hundred subprojects that were carried out all over the country. These subprojects used methods such as expert interviews (with headmasters, youth workers, clergymen, youth leaders, etc.), participant observation (in youth clubs, working — class districts, rural areas, etc.) as well as interviews with youngsters.

Field researchers adopted the then dominant pessimistic vision of modern culture and "mass youth" rather reluctantly and readily translated it into the definition of "youngsters from proletarian and subproletarian classes". It was this group of young people which the government was seriously concerned with: These youngsters showed (postwar) symptoms of moral degeneration and the pernicious impact of an (Americanized) mass consumer society, which the political and pedagogical authorities already saw appearing on the horizon.

The results of this first investigation into the life situation of postwar youth, however, did not justify the ideology of endangered and morally degenerated youth, and a few years later, postwar panic had relaxed. The project was led by two prominent figures in postwar social pedagogical debates, Father Perquin and the liberal educationist Langeveld. In line with their task, they provided recommendations for the course of future youth policy. This policy, however, was not realized until some decades later, under different social conditions. It included a reformation of a still highly class—rigid educational system, a modernization of the youth social welfare of both the church and the state, and tighter connections between the various socialization fields of family, school, career guidance, and youth work. The final reports raised the question as to what were the exact responsibilities of the educators who guided youngsters on their path to maturity (the title of one of the reports).Thus, this report has already raised the central question of youth educators, that is, how to structure the status passages of youngsters (Meijers and du Bois—Reymond, 1987; du Bois—Reymond and Meijers, 1988).

Ever since the origin of Dutch social sciences in the 1930s and 1940s, it has been taken for granted that research activities should produce data which can be readily applied and which are relevant for the formation of social policy (Gastelaars, 1985). This close — and sometimes tense — relation between social policy and social sciences has been maintained and has been normative for research policy. This — and also the fact that most social science institutes were not founded until after World War II — explains why the first large—scale national youth projects did not lead to a proper development of youth research in the following decades.

The mass youth project of 1948 to 1953 can be regarded as the first investigation into the life—world of Dutch youngsters. Obviously, the present—day concept of "life—world" was not employed as such in those days, but rather the social—psychological theories and sociogeographical approaches of the then leading "Amsterdam School" (Bovenkerk et al., 1978).

As they have had a great impact on the development of youth research, I will mention two other early studies focusing on the life—world of youngsters. At the start of the youth riots in the 1950s, two sociologists investigated the life—world of working—class youngsters from Leiden by means of participant observation and the method of action research. They clearly aimed at challenging the existing prejudices against these youngsters, thus allowing for proposals concerning youth social welfare (Krantz and Vercruisse, 1959). This study can be considered to be a predecessor of subsequent subcultural youth research. The second investigation, carried out by the Dutch youth sociologist Van Hessen, shows a remarkable set — up. Using the oral history method (which was at that time unknown as such), he studied the life — world of the generation of Dutch youngsters at the turn of the century, thus contributing to the development of historic youth research — a discipline which has been ignored almost completely so far (Van Hessen, 1964).

Only fairly recently has academic youth research started to develop as a discipline in its own right, transcending the borderlines of its own field. The reason for this rather slow development (especially when compared to other European countries and the United States) is the relatively young tradition of the social sciences, the continued orientation of pedagogics and social — pedagogics toward the humanities, and finally the dependence on governmental funding that set other priorities for a great number of years. In the 1950s, 1960s and 1970s, youth research was primarily financed by local authorities, churches, or youth societies that demanded concrete knowledge on subpopulations of youngsters that was relevant to their policymaking. (For the development of youth policy after World War II, see Bremer, 1986).

An example would be the investigation into the leisure activities of youngsters (friendship, club life, family life) (Martens, 1962). This kind of commissioned research was mainly concerned with survey research, with little or no need for a theoretical background. In addition, this example also demonstrates the preoccupation of early youth research with recreation, that is, that domain of youngsters which reacts most sensitively to modernizations and avoids the influence of educators. This preoccupation with leisure time had already been predominant in the mass youth project of the 1940s and 1950s. Over the past few years new trends have developed stressing the importance of more coherence and of new theoretical programes in which life — world analyses play an important role. (A useful overview is given by Matthijsen et al., 1986; du Bois — Reymond et al., 1986; Meijer, 1987; Meeus et al., 1988).

2. The Concept of "Life — World" in Dutch Youth Research

The present crisis of the welfare state, which began in the mid — 1970s, increased the public need for and interest in youth research and made researchers aware of the need for more elaborated theoretical frameworks. In traditional youth studies, many problems which youngsters (as well as policymakers and educators) were faced with never came to light: problems in realizing the standard biography and status passages within the school, family life, and labor relations under increasingly insecure life perspectives. The supposed integration of separate fields of life became questionable, and one could observe a disillusion with quantitative analysis methods which shed little light on the concrete day—to—day lives of students, young workers, unemployed youngsters, girls, and other groups of youngsters.

The Dutch Hoogveld Institute, a semi—university catholic research center, is the leading institution in this area today. According to its social—pedagogical and social—psychological tradition, the Hoogveld Institute has always been concerned with the life situation of youngsters. In the "mass youth project", it was the only institute that did not rely on expert interviews or other indirect methods of investigation but employed face—to—face interviews instead. Nowadays, the Hoogveld institute applies a combination of the following theoretical approaches:

1.   A social—psychological approach which is mainly expressed and operationalized by the concept of self—esteem;
2.   The concept of life—world, based on the model of social—ecological zones developed by Baacke (1983).

According to the present manager of the institute, Van der Linden, there is a clear relation between the concept of life—world and Lewin's life—space model; he nevertheless prefers the concept of life—world because, as he put it in one of his recent articles, "explicit attention is paid to the affective quality of experience", whereas Lewin's model is more concerned with perception and cognition and lacks the experience dimension. He even goes as far as to say that he considers the social—ecological concept of life—world to be the most adequate theoretical basis for social—pedagogical youth research, if combined with personality theories (Van der Linden, 1988, 152).

Since the 1970s, the Central Statistics Bureau (CBS) has held national inquiries into the life situation of the population and investigates the satisfaction of various groups of the Dutch population with their family, school, labor, and leisure situation. Whereas the CBS uses quantitative data, the Hoogveld Institute applies semistructured interviews in which the subjective experiences and interpretations of youngsters are taken into account much more seriously. It remains doubtful, though, whether the social—ecologically inspired life—world model can fully compensate for the weaknesses of the inquiry methods. After all, the distinguished social—ecological zones are no more than a pragmatic classification with which the various socialization fields of youngsters can be examined. The implications of the antagonistic relation between life—world and system in Habermas' theory are not exploited for data interpretation (Habermas, 1981). Nor is there a continuation of the phenomenological Utrecht School which also uses the concept of life—world (Lippitz et al., 1986).

Also many small—scale and local youth studies, carried out at universities and using the concept of life—world, are characterized by a lack of solid theoretical frameworks. Life—world has become a "container term", embodying a specific kind of research in which the subjective experiences of particular groups of youngsters are explored, usually by means of unstructured or semistructured interview techniques.

It should be noted, however, that the − albeit diffuse − reception of the concept of life−world has strongly stimulated Dutch youth research and has even made it attractive for commissioned research. Over the past few years, a large amount of data on the everyday life of youngsters have become available, which in previous years could only be produced indirectly by means of inquiries or (educational) mobility studies, or were taken into account only marginally.

The life−world analyses focus primarily on the following fields:

1. School and school cultures;
2. political−cultural youth cultures;
3. youth unemployment and opinions on the meaning of labor;
4. social networks of youngsters (with remarkably little attention to the impact of family life).

Over the past few years, special attention has been paid to the problems of girls, in order to negate the frequently cited paradigm "youth research = boys research". But in spite of an active women's movement and a hard−won increase in academic women's studies over the past decade, Dutch research into the lives of girls is still in its infancy.

3. A Portrait of Dutch Youth

Until we go into recent studies on the life−world of school and family, it seems useful to give some relevant socio−structural data on the present situation of Dutch youngsters. As is the case in other Western European countries, Dutch youth is affected by the transformation of the welfare state and work society. In the course of this process, the status passage from school to work and adult life comes under pressure because of structural unemployment and a rearrangement of the various sectors of production. New models of a youth biography emerge, particularly for girls.

The general level of education has increased tremendously over the past two decades. Girls and young women have been very successful in this process. Yet, the critical situation in the job market reinforces old prejudices against female labor; besides, women are placed at a disadvantage: 25 % of 22− to 25−year−old women still do not have a paid job (Social en Cultureel Planbureau, 1985). At the same time, within the framework of emancipation policy, the government intends to link the entitlement to social benefits with the availability for the labor market of women above 18 years who do not have to care for children. Emancipation policy expresses the changed identity of (many) girls and women. They question their traditional roles and want to realize an economically independent existence. The traditional two—phase model (leaving school and taking up a job/ getting married and having children) is joined by other models: parttime work after the children attend kindergarten and school; several forms of combining childraising and jobbing, for example, parttime work and shared family responsibilities; postponing the birth of children in order to build a career — with the possibility of not having children at all; new models of co—parenthood after divorce, and so forth.

In 1986, 32% of the youngsters under 17 and 22% of those between 19 and 22 were unemployed with only marginal differences between young men and young women (Central Bureau voor de Statistiek, 1987). Today, one third of all youngsters leave school with no diploma at all; 20% finish with a low—prestige general or vocational training diploma. The group of migrant youngsters are hidden behind these general data: These youngsters are heavily disadvantaged in comparison to Dutch youngsters.

According to official statistics, 90% of all Dutch youngsters find a job within one year. There is also a trend toward decreasing youth unemployment (Schoolverlatersbrief, 1988). In cooperation with unions and employers, government has created short—term labor contracts (the so—called job/training schemes: YTS) with which they hope to introduce youngsters into the regular labor system. Yet, first experiences with these YTS demonstrate that older youngsters will become and remain unemployed. Even now, youngsters above 20 who have been unemployed for more than 12 months hardly succeed in acquiring a full—time job. They can be regarded as the "lost generation"; a nightmare which is constantly being referred to by the media (Meijers and Peters, 1987). In spring 1988, 48,000 of all 450,000 youngsters between 18 and 21 and 200,000 youngsters between 22 and 27 were unemployed and not following further education.

Nearly all 18—year—olds still live with their parents; of the group of 24—year—old adolescents, only 25% have left home (Sociaal en Cultureel Planbureau, 1985). The adolescents' prospects for a room of their own have decreased over the past few years, both as a result of cuts in youth income (labor and study) and decreasing family income in case of unemployment. At the same time, the trend toward individualized households and the growing ambitions of young women to become independent continue.

Yet, it would be misleading to picture the situation of Dutch youngsters as a crisis situation. The relation between the generations is not deeply disturbed, neither between parents and children, nor between youngsters and political parties and the state (Meeus, 1986; Dijkman, 1987). Dutch society is characterized by a high level of consensus. The family, the educational system, and work are stable frames of orientation for most of the youngsters in spite of susceptability to crises in certain areas and among certain groups.

4. The Life — World of the School

No other field of youth research draws so much attention as the school. Most research is mainly concerned with the official curriculum and educational mobility and less with students and school cultures. In the years between 1970 and 1980 extensive organizational and curriculum reformations on all levels of education — from kindergarten to university — stimulated commissioned implementation and defined youngsters narrowly in their roles as pupils, irrespective of their relations outside the school.

It is worth mentioning that even before the rise of life — world studies, compensatory education programs shed more light on youngsters outside the school situation. Although evaluation reports on these experiments cannot be looked upon as research into the life — world, they did yield descriptive data on tensions between school and the family situation of children and youngsters.

In the early 1980s, the previously mentioned Hoogveld Institute carried out the first national study into the life — world of 15 — year — old students and their self — esteem. This investigation was commissioned by the Ministry of Education, because of an increasing concern among educators (especially secondary school teachers) over the lack of motivation and radically changed behavior of students.

"Some social factors that threatened the well — being of the youngsters were: the various, rapidly evolving social and cultural changes, changes in norms and values, rising divorce rates, deteriorating economic circumstances along with an increase of unemployment. All these factors have a negative impact on youngsters and endanger the socializing function of school" (Van der Linden and Roeders, 1983, 6).

Some results of the most recent studies carried out by the Hoogveld Institute will be dealt with in more detail. One of them is concerned with group discussions with 16 — to 22 — year — old students and former students, differentiated for type of school, sex, level of urbanization, and geographic region. The second study involves interviews with 24 students between the age of 12 and 16, differentiated for identical criteria (Van der Linden and Dijkman, 1987; Dijkman and Van der Linden, 1987). The respondents were asked to comment upon the following aspects: (1) job experience, (2) family situation, (3) leisure time, (4) social relations, and (5) expectations for the future.

Students have a positive opinion of their (previous) schools; they do not show an "anti — attitude". This overall result does not differ from the study carried out in 1983. However, in — depth questions lead up to crucial points and bring to light the elsewhere noticed dichotomy in school experience (Matthijssen, 1986; du Bois—Reymond, 1986): a dichotomy between the formal and the informal curriculum. Students indicate that they are prepared to bear with school only if there is enough occasion for informal activities (enforced by students) within and outside of the classroom. Having a good time, chatting, teasing teachers and fellow—students and so forth are forms of relaxing which all students use, independent of age, type of school, or sex (Van der Linden and Dijkman, 1987).

Between teachers and students one can observe an interplay which seems to be based on a free market model rather than on the authoritarian model of "adaptation and achievement in exchange for school success" (Willis, 1978). Students, as well as teachers, make school life easier by relaxing the official achievement scheme and "filling it up" with elements of an informal culture. Teachers tend to abandon their traditional professional responsibilities of enforcing school achievement. They shift the emotional and social expenses of ill—spent time on the students and their parents.

Students perceive the laissez—faire attitude of teachers as a form of tolerance. The increasingly enforced formalization of assessment (e.g., numerous tests that are only assessed quantitatively) also contributes to the image of the fair and objective teacher. School conflicts mainly show up when the balance between students and teachers is disturbed, for example, by an oldfashioned, strict teacher, by an authoritarian schoc' climate, or by an assault on leisure time because of excessive homework.

Like their teachers, students make a cost—benefit analysis with regard to the energy they are willing to put into their work at school. They develop a pragmatic approach to learning: They assess the "product of training" on its future value for the job market and have a low opinion of the value of less relevant subjects (humanities). In all, they have a highly instrumental learning motivation.

As a result of the analysis of the quantitative data, the following six, most frequently mentioned reasons for "attending school with pleasure" are reported: (1) cosy, good atmosphere (45%); (2) social aspects (33%); (3) learning, subjects (23%); (4) school as an alternative to boredom, doing nothing (21%); and (5) good relationship with teachers (14 %).

The six, most frequently mentioned reasons for "sometimes not wanting to go to school" are: (1) subjects, lessons, curriculum (43%); (2) long school days, boredom (31%); (3) test, assessments (18%); (4) many subjects, much homework (13%); (5) teachers (13%); and (6) too little sleep (11%).

Clearly, in positive school assessment, the informal aspects of sociability and opportunities to contact peers outbalance the formal aspects. School is not looked upon as a learning institution but as a life space, even if students acknowledge its value for the future (Dijkman and Van der Linden, 1987; Jongeling, 1986; Tillekens, 1986).

The latent tension between school as a compulsory institution and school as a sociable institution becomes manifest in the problem of playing truant which all schools are faced with and which educationists have been seriously concerned with over the past few years. Bernard (1986) studied the truancy strategies of Amsterdam secondary school students and discovered that nearly two—thirds of all students play truant now and again. Students of the highest levels of education play truant most often but also most strategically: They stay away from school, for example, to catch up with subject matter, to prepare themselves for tests, or, more generally, to take a day off because of school stress in order to be fresh the next day. Unlike students from general education, students from vocational schools play truant to protest against school compulsion. With regard to this matter, serious plans which tend toward the free market model propose granting pupils of a certain age a number of truant days which they can take off as they like. As a matter of fact, these measures legalize what happens anyway.

Within the "new sociability" at schools, various subcultural youth styles manifest themselves which coexist peacefully within the school. A great many studies have been devoted to these youth styles elaborating on the investigations of the Birmingham Center on Cultural Studies. De Waal (1987), for example, investigated the dress styles of female students. Te Poel (1982) studied the cultures of domestic school students, and the Hoogveld Institute — within the framework of their school research — collected a large amount of of data on the behavior of students within groups and friendship relations.

Since the increase of structural youth unemployment in the mid—1970s, youth researchers have focused on this field. However, the question in how far the threat of youth unemployment leads to a decrease in school motivation can hardly be answered without longitudinal research. As long as youngsters are not confronted with the concrete problems of the job market, they look upon their career opportunities from an optimistic point of view. Looking back, however, unemployed youngsters realize that this optimism was false. Systematic investigations, which analyze the interaction between sociopolitical aspects, labor market conditions, gender—specific and subjective factors, and motives for the youth biography, are still lacking. Research into youth unemployment is primarily attitude research, which also examines how unemployment is experienced, but which most of all investigates the stability of value orientations (De Goede and Maassen, 1986; Ten Have and Jehoel—Gijsbers, 1986).

With respect to life—world research into school, another important observation can be made. Unlike, for example, West Germany, Dutch research has not produced that many biographically oriented school analyses and school criticism that examine the qualities of school from the points of view of those who are actually involved (teachers and students) (Böhnisch and Schefold, 1985). Teachers in particular have not greatly contributed to this issue. However, if all field reports on compensatory education and other experiments — regularly published in school—related magazines — were subjected to close investigation, a rich variety of data with respect to the school world would come to the surface.

5.   The Life—World of the Family

I have already indicated that studies into family life are not widely available in Dutch youth research. This is probably due to the fact that family life is less accessible with respect to life—world analyses than the school world. In addition, government as well as individual researchers seem to have little need for such studies (Van Leeuwen, 1976). Recently, however, the Ministry of Welfare, Health, and Culture has expressed the desirability of paying more attention to the issue of youth and their life within the family.

Social—psychological and social—pedagogical family studies primarily focus on education styles, identity development, and family climate; family is focussed upon as a field of socialization rather than a life—world of youngsters (Schoorl, 1986). In contrast to this kind of study, the Hoogveld Institute interprets and investigates family as an ecological zone in its own right. Attention centers on the question of how youngsters experience family life.

As many as 90% of the interviewed 12— to 16—year—olds live in complete families; this corresponds to national data (in 1983, 92% off all 12— to 17—year—old youngsters lived in complete families; Sociaal en Cultureel Planbureau, 1985). It is remarkable how many youngsters between 12 and 16 describe their relationships with their parents as good (Jeugd, 1987). Only 2% describe the relationship as not too good and, in all cases, the relationship with the mother is experienced as (even) better. Boys more often mention common interest as a basis for a good relationship with their fathers; girls mention the emotional quality of their good relationship with their mothers (Dijkman and Van der Linden, 1987).

As youngsters grow up, the parent—child relations evolve from dependent, authority—based relations into equal, affective relations which youngsters acquire through independence and self—discipline. The majority of Dutch youngsters of this age group feel that their parents participate in their lives with great interest and support them in case they should have problems. Youngsters would hardly ever keep things secret from their parents; as they grow up, their relationship becomes even more intense. They obey their parents because they identify themselves with them, because their parents set an example to them, or because they acknowledge their greater experience. Only a minority obeys for fear of punishment or because of promised rewards. Regardless of whether or not they have a say in family matters, 96% of all youngsters say that they are satisfied with the situation at home. All these aspects suggest growing tolerance within the context of family life which could be captured in the trend: from an authoritarian family toward a negotiation family (De Swaan, 1982; du Bois — Reymond and Jonker, 1988).

The increased meaning of school and its social value for future professional careers is probably better demonstrated by the parent — child relationship than by the school world itself or by considering the children's answers to the question on what their parents expect from them (see also Boef — van der Meulen, 1987; she directly interviewed parents and came up with similar results). Here, school and education got the highest value — scores (55%) and were therefore ranked above the supposed parental expectations with regard to general values and norms concerning youth behavior, such as, decency and good manners. A longitudinal investigation from the 1950s up to the 1980s would probably demonstrate that the dramatic turning point in parents' views on education lies in the 1970s, that is, at the height of education reforms (Zinnecker, 1987. An earlier study by the Hoogveld Institute, carried out in the mid — 1970s, which posed similar questions as the above — mentioned study, already sketched the same picture: Van der Linden, 1978).

The second Hoogveld study focused on 16— to 22—year—old youngsters. Although it largely confirmed the sunny picture of family life, some problems came to the surface that have to do with the acquisition of independence. Here it can be demonstrated that gender—specific distinctions still play a role. More so than boys, older girls have problems with being dependent on their parents and being under constant family control. They are more strongly involved with household matters and have fewer opportunites to protect their private lives from the family (see also Kooy, 1975).

The data also show that complete faith in and openness toward parents change as youngsters grow up: Parents are no longer involved in the discussion of problems in relationships with friends; instead, these problems are discussed within the peer group because youngsters fear, concerning parents, that they will meet with disapproval rather than good advice. For these precarious issues, youngsters reach a compromise with their parents in the sense that they keep this field of intimacy away from their parents, and that the parents accept this exclusion. Thus, the — generally (very) good — relationship between parents and children remains intact. In addition, children expect their parents to be prepared to learn new things, that is, they should adapt their attitudes and norms to the "spirit of the age". This plays an important role in the relations between siblings; older brothers or sisters "pave the way" for their younger brothers or sisters by pursuing their independence (going out in the evening, time of coming home).

This meets with some opposition from parents, but they more readily accept these desires from younger children (Dijkman and Van der Linden, 1987, 42). By no means do older youngsters prefer to live independently in all cases. They explicitly state that they miss the care and company of their family and weight the advantages and disadvantages of living at home and living on their own.

As the studies show, the importance which parents ascribe to the school career of their children does not diminish for older youngsters. However, parental expectations with respect to the behavior of youngsters within the family play a larger role than was the case with the younger age group. Parents expect good behavior from their older children in exchange for their extended stay at home. This could be an indicator of the fact that the conflict potential between parents and (older) adolescents increases.

Results on the attitudes of youngsters toward raising a family or alternative life plans are controversial. The results of the Hoogveld Institute demonstrated that all 16— to 22—year—old youngsters expect to have a partner and a couple of children, a nice house and a car within the not—too—distant future; they were absolutely certain that they would find a job. To some extent, however, the population of this study is not representative, and the specific problems of youth unemployment or the conflicts of women with gender—stereotyping are not in the centre of attention.

If this had been the case, as for example, in an (albeit not representative) study of unemployed (Rotterdam) youngsters, a completely different picture would emerge. This investigation yielded strongly gender—specific distinctions, leading up to the following classification of young women: young women with a traditional life perspective with respect to family and labor; young women with an antitraditional life perspective: the "ambivalents", the largest middle group (Meijers and Peters, 1987). The "traditionals" want to solve the dilemma of children versus job with the three—phase model (education/job — raising a family — re—entering work as soon as the children have grown up). In contrast, the "antitraditionals" hold on to the compatibility of family and work or consider the option of not raising a family. The "ambivalents" hesitate between these two positions. More interesting than the typology is the finding that *all* young women — much more so than young men — struggle with the conventional gender—stereotyping in trying to strike a balance between work and children/family. Furthermore, *all* young women first of all want to have their own income before starting to think about raising a family.

The most recent national inquiry among 16— to 24—year—old youngsters also provides a somewhat more subtle picture than the Hoogveld Institute: The most important value of life appears to be good health (51%), followed by a good marriage (15%) and a nice family (13%). Nevertheless, youngsters do not regard marriage to be the one and only acceptable life style, and 90% do *not* agree with the statement that married people are generally happier than unmarried people (Sociaal Cultureel Planbureau, 1985).

Summing up, it will be obvious that the present data on youth and family require further investigation, both with respect to inter— and intragenerational relations and with respect to changes in the youngsters' standard biography and the impact of these shifts on the family. Particularly shifts in the female standard biography of mothers and daughters may turn out to be extremely clarifying (Beck—Gernheim, 1983).

6. Research Design and Research Methods of Life—World Studies

As the present youth biography and the relation between the generations are more and more characterized by breaks and dissimilarities, research design and research methods that insufficiently take this complexity into account have their limitations. Therefore, it is a promising development that the interest of Dutch youth researchers in more meaningful theories and more sensitive methods is growing. Biographical, historical, and longitudinal methods in combination with the life—world approach can be expected to yield the best results.

Recent studies investigate the life—world of girls, working—class youngsters, and — which is extremely rare — village youth by means of intensive participant observation and individual and group interviews (Naber, 1985; Miedema and Eelman, 1987; Hazekamp, 1985; ter Bogt, 1987). They focus on the non—school— and non—family—bound life—worlds and activities of youngsters: the street, the playground, the neighborhood, youth clubs, friendship, hanging around, going out, and so forth. The ethnographical tradition proves to be fruitful, especially when it does not merely involve the investigation of the subjective experiences and action space of youngsters and youth cultures but also a description of the material and symbolic environment in which youngsters live. A sociological—criminological study, in which conformist and deviant behavior with respect to more or less serious offences of working—class youngsters is carried out by means of extensive biographical interviews (Miedema and Janssen, 1986) results in a typology that concentrates on the detailed and multiple transitions between conformist and deviant behavior. This typology includes the individual youth biography, peer group life, parents, and class culture. The investigators are not so much led by a social—ecological or psycho—ecological models, nor by the ethnographical tradition. Rather, they connect an actor—oriented socialization theory with subcultural youth theories of the British School and can thus demonstrate the strength of the intergenerational connection between youngsters and their parents in traditional working—class districts. Structural factors such as a low level of education, few or no chances on the job market, and the breakdown of old residential areas produce youngsters with more or less criminal careers.

Finally, I would also like to refer to a project which starts from the concept of the standard biography and which, by means of a longitudinal design, attempts to investigate the status passage school — education — work — family on the basis of repeated biographical interviews. Breaks in the standard biography and status passage (Fuchs, 1983) are most of all expected to occur with girls/young women. Changes in the standard biography should be traced by means of intragenerational comparison between parents and children. At a later point, nonkin educators who guide youngsters (school and professional educators, welfare workers, etc.) are to be interviewed with respect to their capacities and skills (Meijers and Peters, 1988). It is remarkable to notice that state financiers have begun to raise the importance of this kind of research. So far, the only longitudinal studies that have been undertaken are mobility studies within the educational sector.

Historical life—world studies are scarce. A start was made by Behnken, Du Bois—Reymond, and Zinnecker (1988). They undertook an intercultural comparison betwen a German and Dutch town in order to study the life—worlds of children and youngsters in the decades 1900 to 1920 by means of oral history interviews.

Over the past few years, Dutch youth research has surpassed the marginal position within the social sciences and is oriented more and more toward European and international discussions. Thus it follows its object of knowledge, namely youth, which — although it has a national history and life—world — nevertheless also transcends local boundaries. The problems and life styles of youth can no longer be fully understood within a national framework only.

References

Baacke, D. (1983): Die 13— bis 18—jährigen. Weinheim: Beltz

Beck—Gernsheim, E. (1983): Vom "Dasein für andere" zum Anspruch auf ein Stück "eigenes Leben": Individualisierungsprozesse im weiblichen Lebenszusammenhang. Soziale Welt, 34, 307—340

Behnken, I., Bois—Reymond, M.du, & Zinnecker, J. (1988): Stadtgeschichte als Kindheitsgeschichte. Opladen: Leske

Bernard, Y. (1986): Spijbelen, schakel tussen school en vrije tijd. In Bois—Reymond, M.du, Hazekamp, J., & Matthijssen, M. (Eds.): Jeugd onderzocht. Amersfoort: Acco, 75—92

Boef—van der Meulen, S. (1987): Rondom basisvorming. Tijdsbesteding van scholieren. Meningen van ouders. Sociaal en Cultureel Planbureau. Rijswijk

Bogt, J.ter (1987): Opgroeien in Groenlo. Amersfort: Acco

Böhnisch, L., & Schefold, W. (1985): Lebensbewältigung. Soziale und pädagogische Verständigungen an den Grenzen der Wohlfahrtsgesellschaft. Weinheim: Juventa

Bois–Reymond, M.du, Hazekamp, J., & Matthijssen, M. (Eds.) (1986): Jeugd onderzocht. Amersfoort: Acco

Bois–Reymond, M.du, & Meijers, F. (1988): The mass youth project. In search of a "modern" pedagogical norm. In Olk, T. (Ed.): Structural changes of youth. A social–historical and social–cultural perspective. Weinheim: Juventa

Bois–Reymond, M.du (1986): Een essay voor Paul. Schoolcrisis en jeugdcultuur. In Appelhof, P.N., et al.: Naar beter onderwijs. Tilburg: Zwijsen, 195–212

Bois–Reymond, M.du, & Jonker, A. (1988): Relaties in het gezin tussen ouders en kinderen 1900–1930. Een oral history onderzoek in Leiden. Comenius, 8, 2, 175–207

Bovenkerk, F. et al. (Eds.)(1978): Toen en thans. De sociale wetenschappen inde jaren dertig en nu. Baarn: Ambo

Bremer, R.J.B. (1986): Jeugd in opspraak, jeugdbeleid in sociologisch retrospectief. Enschede: Quick Service

Centraal Bureau voor de Statistiek (1987): Statistisch Bulletin, 3. Rijswijk

Dijkman, T.A. (1987): Jeugd, democratie en politiek. Een onderzoek naar de politieke socialisatie in het kader van de leefwereld van jongern van 12 tot 16 yaar. Nijmegen: Hoogveld Instituut

Dijkman, T.A., & Linden, F.J.v.d. (1987): Verslag van de voorstudie betreffende het leefsituatie–onderzoek Nederlandse jeugd. Nijmegen: Hoogveld Instituut

Fuchs, W. (1983). Jugendliche Statuspassage oder individualisierte Jugendbiographie? Soziale Welt, 8, 222–234

Gastelaars, M. (1985): Een geregeld leven; Sociologie en sociale politiek in Nederland 1925–1968. Amsterdam: SUA

Goede, M.de, & Maassen, G. (1986): Werkloos–zijn; hoe beleven jongeren dat? In Matthijssen, M., Meeus, W., & Wel, F.v.d. (Eds.): Beelden over jeugd. Groningen: Wolters–Noordhoff, 156–170

Habermas, J. (1981): Theorie des komminikativen Handelns, Bd. 2. Frankfurt: Suhrkamp

Have, K.ten, & Jehoel Gijsbers, G. (1986): Werkloze jongeren: een verloren generatie. In du Bois–Reymond, M., Hazekamp, J., & Matthijssen, M. (Eds.): Jeugd onderzocht. Amersfort: Acco, 125–140

Hazekamp, J.L. (1985): Rondhangen als tijdverdrijf. Amsterdam: VU–uitgeverij

Hessen, J.S.van (1964): Samen jong zijn. Een jeugdsociologische verkenning in gesprek met vorigen. Assen: Van Gorcum

Institut voor Marktinformatie (1987): Jeugd '87. Onderzoek Interview. Amsterdam

Jongeling, E. (1986): Havo–leerlingen over hun onderwijs. In Matthijssen, M., Meeus, W., & Wel, F.v.d. (Eds.): Beelden over jeugd. Groningen: Wolters–Noordhoff, 31–47

Kooy, G.A. (1975): Sexualiteit, huwelijk en gezin in Nederland. Deventer: Van Loghum Slaterus

Krantz, D.E., & Vercruisse, E.V.W. (1959): De jeugd in het geding. Amsterdam: Bezige Bij

Leeuwen, L.T.van (1976): Het gezin als sociologisch studie–object. Een historisch overzicht van de ontwikkeling van een subdiscipline, speciaal met het oog op de situatie in Nederland. Wageningen (intern report)

Linden, F.J.v.d. (1978): Thuiswonende jongeren over hun gezinssituatie. Jeugd en Samenleving, 161–182

Linden, F.J.v.d., & Roeders, P.J.B. (1983): Schoolgaande jongeren, hun leefwereld en zelfbeleving. Nijmegen: Hoogveld Instituut

Linden, F.J.v.d. (1988): Adolescent lifeworld and youth research: A plea for an eco—psychological approach. In Hazekamp, J., Meeus, W., & Poel, Y.te (Eds.): European contributions to youth research. Amsterdam: Free University Press

Lippitz, W., & Meyer—Drawe, K. (Hg.)(1987): Kind und Welt. Phänomenologische Studien zur Pädagogik. Frankfurt: Athenäum

Martens, J.J.M. (1962): Jeugd en vrieje tijd. Roermond (intern report)

Matthijssen, M., Meeus, W., & Wel, F.v.d. (Eds.)(1986): Boelden van jeugd. Groningen: Wolters—Noordhoff

Matthijssen, M. (1986): De rol van de schoolse socialisatie bij identiteitsontwikkeling. In Matthijssen, M., Meeus, W., & Wel, F.v.d. (Eds.): Beelden van jeugd. Groningen: Wolters—Noordhoff, 11—30

Meeus, W. (1988): Adolescent rebellion and politics. Youth and Society, 19, 426—435

Meeus, W., Hazekamp, J. L., & Poel, Y.te (1988): European contributions to youth research. Amsterdam: Free University Press

Meijer, E. (Ed.)(1987): Alledaags leven; vrije tijd en cultur (2. Vol.). Tilburg: Centrum voor Vrijetijdskunde

Meijers, F., & Bois—Reymond, M. du (1987): Op zoek naar een moderne pedagogische norm. Beeldvorming over de jeugd in de jaren vijftig: het massajeudgonderzoek (1948—1952). Amersfort: Acco

Meijers, F., & Peters, E. (1987): Jugend und Arbeit in den Niederlanden. In Raab, E. (Hg.): Jugend und Arbeit. München: Juventa

Meijers, F., & Peters, E. (1988): When is YTS an alternative for young people? Some results from a Dutch qualitative research project. International Journal of Adolescence and Youth, 1, 3 (in press)

Miedema, S., & Janssen, O. (1986): Respectabiliteit en deviantie in levensstijlen. Universiteit Groningen (Criminologisch Instituut)

Miedema, S., & Eelman, N. (1987): Over pumps en punks. Universiteit Groningen

Naber, P. (1985): Vriendinnen. Amsterdam: VU

Poel, Y.te (1982): Meisjes van het huishoudonderwijs: Hun belevingswereld en socialisatie. In Diekerhof, E. (Ed.): Leren wat moet je er mee? Muiderberg: Couthino

Schoolverlatersbrief (1988). Risjwijk (Ministerie van Onderwys en Wetenscheppen)

Schoorl, P. M. (1986): Regelpatronen in het gezinsleven. Lisse: Swets & Zeitlinger

Social Cultureel Planbureau (1985): Jongeren in de jaren tachtig. Rijswijk

Swaan, A. de (1982): Uitgangsbeperking en witgangsangst; over de verschuiving van bevels— naar onderhandelingshuishounding. In Swaan, A.de (Ed.): De mens is de mens een zorg. Amsterdam: Meulenhoff

Tillekens, G. (1986): Variaties in schoolbeleving. Een onderzoek naar verschillen in individualiteitsbeleving bij leerlingen in het voortgezet onderwijs. In Husken, R. (Ed.): Schoolwelbevinden en voortijdig schoolverlaten. Nijmegen: TS

Waal, M. de (1988): Meisjes: een wereld apart. Amsterdam/ Meppel: Boom

Willis, P. (1978): Learning to labour. Farnborough

Zinnecker, J. (1987): Jugendkultur 1940—1985. Opladen: Leske & Budrich

14.
Experimentation and Control in Family, School, and Youth Movement

Tamar Rapoport
The Hebrew University, Jerusalem, Israel

Research analyzing the intricate socialization process from a sociohistorical perspective (Aries, 1962; Gillis, 1974; Sommerville, 1982) has generally pointed to a movement away from relatively closed socialization arrangements toward more open, permissive, and even lax and overpermissive ones. Accordingly, sociohistorians have suggested that the socialization process has become marked by increasing progressiveness insofar as contemporary agencies allow youth greater freedom and utilize fewer coercive and arbitrary means of socialization than they did in the past. However, by implying that relaxed control inevitably leads to increased experimentation, and vice versa, these studies have overlooked the distinctiveness and independence of each of these socializing dimensions. Furthermore, they have tended to disregard the way in which the dimensions of control and experimentation have been uniquely manifested in each of the major agencies.

The importance of distinguishing between the major socialization agencies in terms of the specific dimensions they comprise and their corresponding effects has been demonstrated by sociologists, particularly structural functionalists (Musgrove, 1966; Parsons and Bales, 1955; Eisenstadt, 1956; Smelser, 1968; Gecas, 1981), who have pointed to increasing institutional differentiation and division of labor between socialization agencies in advanced societies. One of their main assumptions is that different types of agencies (e.g., the school, the family) differ in their organizational structure and consequently in their impact on child development and behavior, beyond the impact of individual socializing agents (e.g., parent or teacher).

This literature suggests that differential socialization effects need to be understood against a background of fundamentally distinctive underlying structures. More specifically, it implies that the differential acquisition of personal resources by adolescents is related to the socialization experiences peculiar to each type of agency in which they participate. Accordingly, such research generally distinguishes between the sentiment – based, intimate family context, the semiprofessional, instrumental – based school, and the expressive, voluntaristic – based context of the informal peer group and youth association. In this respect, the school is considered more influential in the development of general cognitive skills and information (Hurn, 1985); the contribution of the family is viewed predominantly in terms of psychosocial development, especially as regards independence, autonomy and identity formation (see Grotevant and Cooper, 1983; Youniss, 1980); and the informal peer group and youth association is perceived as more effective in developing interpersonal skills and norms of behavior (see Dunphy, 1963) and in fostering sociocognitive, universal orientations (Piaget, 1932; Kahane, 1975).

By concentrating on the unique character of each agency, however, such research has not placed the divergence between agencies within a single conceptual framework. More specifically, it has not paid adequate attention to the differences between agencies in the actualization of common structural dimensions. It is my contention, in contrast, that the differential socialization experiences generated by different agencies may be ascribed to the pattern in which the structural dimensions of control and experimentation coexist in each agency.

The usefulness of a conceptual framework based on the dimensions of experimentation and control becomes clear against the background of the Israeli context. The history of the major socialization agencies in Israel points to a move from a convergence in their socialization patterns (based on high informality) in pre – State Israel to a divergence between them in the contemporary society. While the relatively large pre – State convergence has been ascribed to the voluntary nature of the rather homogeneous society at that time (Ben David, 1954; Kahane, 1986), the subsequent divergence has been attributed to increased complexity and institutionalization in all spheres of life (Eisenstadt, 1971).

Within the socialization system of Israel, youth movements deserve special attention, as they have operated as a rather unique socialization setting[1]. They have been affiliated, officially or unofficially, to political parties, yet cultivate an autonomous youth culture. In their Golden Age (1930 – 1950), when 35% of the 11 – to 18 – year – olds were members, they were described as the core of the Zionist revolution, serving both as a means and an end for achieving national goals. However, it is generally believed that since the establishment of the state they have gradually lost their unique socialization power (e.g., there have been repeated indications of no difference between members and nonmembers in terms of value commitments and social orientation; Alon, 1986). This is attributed, among other things, to their increasing levels of professionalization, on the one hand, and their emphasis on expressiveness and looseness to the point of "childish" orientations, on the other (Kahane and Rapoport, 1986).

There is also reason to suspect that the increased complexity characteristic of contemporary Israeli society has led to a change in the patterns of socialization experiences found in the two other agencies — that is, the family and the school. It thus may be posited that a different pattern of socialization experiences has evolved in each agency. Such a hypothesis can be tested through systematic comparison between the socializing structures of contemporary agencies.

1. A Two–Dimensional Model for Comparative Analysis of Agencies

Recent comparative studies carried out by this author have addressed the socialization structure and effect of the major agencies in Israel. This attempt to systematically compare socialization processes in the three major agencies was based on the reduction of multiple aspects of the socialization process into generic dimensions, which is assumed to help explain the differential and combined effects on child behavior and development in adolescence (Kahane, 1985; Gecas, 1981; Rollins and Thomas, 1979).

In a study that extended the sociological application of institutionalized moratorium (Erikson, 1955, 1963, 1968) to a comparison of the family, the school and the youth movement (Rapoport, in press)[2], a divergence, or a division of labor, was found between socialization patterns in the three agencies. These findings suggested that the family approximates the socialization pattern of institutionalized moratorium, that the school is far removed from it, and that the youth movement falls in between the two, although it is closer to the pattern of the family. Such patterns were examined in terms of five components — suspended obligations, lenient control, free experimentation, extended rights, and quasi–responsibility — which were said to operationalize moratorium as a principle of socialization.

In the present study, socialization processes in the major agencies were compared via a two–dimensional model of experimentation and control, employing a much larger sample and pretested indicators. The utilization of a two—dimensional model both facilitates systematic comparisons and is more useful in constructing typologies.

I contend that "control" and "experimentation", which I conceptualize as coexisting, independent dimensions of socialization, are parsimonious and useful in the comparison of socialization experiences in different types of agencies. Whereas control denotes the imposition of external pressure on the child to behave in a manner that is desirable to the adult, experimentation denotes the child's autonomous trial and error behavior. Thus, while control refers to the passive role of the recipient of socialization, experimentation refers to the active role he or she plays in shaping his or her own socializing experiences.

Although the dimension of control is commonly accepted as applicable to the study of socialization processes, the dimension of experimentation has received little systematic attention. My main aim is therefore to substantiate experimentation as a generic dimension of socialization and to empirically examine whether and how control and experimentation coexist as independent dimensions of socialization within the three major agencies during adolescence.

Theoretical and empirical efforts to develop generic dimensions of socialization have been made by scholars of family socialization who have sought to account for regularities in parent—child relationships, especially with respect to parental influence on the socialization of preadolescents. This literature has stressed the utility of studying two orthogonal, independent variables of parental behavior, namely "support" and "control" (see review in Rollins and Thomas, 1979; Maccoby and Martin, 1983). Support, which operationally connotes emotional, affective behaviors toward a child (such as praise, approval, physical affection), indeed serves as an indispensable organizing principle in the intimate family context (Parsons and Bales, 1955; Laslett, 1978). However, it does not satisfactorily explain the socialization process in the other major agencies (particularly during adolescence), because they are organized, as mentioned earlier, by different orientations (i.e., achievement and competition in the school and social relations and expressivity in youth associations).

The dimension of control, on the other hand, does seem to be generalizable across agencies, particularly as regards settings in which there are accepted and institutionalized status distinctions between the agent and the object of socialization (e.g., parent—child, tutor—tutee and teacher—student interactions). With respect to such settings, on which I focus here, control is commonly viewed as indispensable to the socialization process, although authority and power may be eliminated from it (see Swidler, 1979). Attempts to implement alternatives to "conventional" control mechanisms (e.g., fraternity of peers) tend to be ephemeral, as their employment is too "costly" for the organization to maintain, and they introduce too much uncertainty and risk (Rothschild – Whitt, 1979).

The common conception of control assumes that the object of socialization plays a passive role. It is my contention that experimentation complements control in accounting for socialization processes in that it encompasses the active shaping of experiences on the part of the recipient of socialization. Since experimentation has received little analytical attention as an institutionalized dimension of socialization, I shall now briefly discuss several research directions from which the conception of experimentation is derived.

2. Experimentation as a Dimension of Socialization

"Experimentation" is defined as the utilization of perceived opportunities (by the recipient of socialization) to freely explore a range of multiple alternative behaviors, roles, and tasks before becoming fully committed to them. Thus, it encompasses trial and error and legitimizes regressive behavior. Actors are not required to bear immediate and full consequences for their actions when trying out behaviors and roles.

This definition of experimentation is based on earlier studies that have generally pointed to the essential role played by trial and error behavior in human development. Thus, for example, experimentation is optimally realized in children's free play by enabling the child to actively restructure and transform reality; the play context generates growth and development (for a comprehensive review, see Schwartzman, 1982). Along these lines, scholars of various disciplines have recognized the connection between experimentation, risk taking, and the development of autonomous, innovative, and creative behavior.

From a cognitive – developmental perspective, Piaget and Inhelder (1969) point to the relation between the child's acting upon his or her environment and cognitive maturation. Through this interaction the child creates experiences from which she or he learns specific skills and develops his or her general intellectual competence (Carew, 1980).

From the perspective of the philosophy of education, Dewey, the major proponent of "pragmatism", asserts that social development "does not mean just getting something out of the mind. It is a development of experience and into experience that is really wanted" (Dewey, 1964, 349). According to him, some kind of organized institutional set−up is needed to serve as a frame for regulating socialization experiences. In this vein, believers in "alternative education" in its various forms (e.g., open classrooms, progressive schools), who view educational maladies as stemming from arbitrary, hierarchical control, generally propose the introduction of experimentation in order to promote favorable educational outcomes (see Neill, 1960; Graubard, 1972).

From a psychosocial perspective, Erikson (1963, 1968) points to the relation between institutionalized moratorium − which entails experimentation − and processes of social maturation. Adolescents are allowed to experiment freely with different aspects of social reality and psychological states while being relieved of full adult obligations and responsibilities. Psychological elaboration upon this theory makes extensive use of the idea of experimentation in the analysis of career choice (Grotevant and Cooper, 1988) and ego development in adolescence (Marcia, 1980). Kahane (1975) utilizes the concept of moratorium in a sociological analysis focusing upon the structure of informal youth organizations; he believes that experimenting with different behavioral patterns within a peer context facilitates transition to adulthood.

Other sociologists have also emphasized the importance for sozialization of creating opportunities that enable youth to experiment with a variety of roles and situations. For example, Coleman emphasizes "the importance of encouraging as wide a variety of environments for youth as are compatible with the enforcement of criteria to safeguard their development" (1974, 6). In the same vein, but from an ecological perspective, Bronfenbrenner suggests that "...human development is facilitated through interaction with persons who occupy a variety of roles and through participation in an ever−broadening role repertoire" (1979, 104).

In sum, the different schools of thought view experimentation as crucial in accounting for socialization processes. Nevertheless, little research has been devoted to its systematic study as an institutionalized dimension of socialization. Moreover, scholars have treated experimentation in isolation and have seldom considered the possibility of its coexistence with control, even though their findings seem to suggest such a relation between the two. For example, the literature on family socialization has claimed that a surplus of control leads to blind conformity and dogmatism (see Adorno et al., 1950), while overexperimentation (excessive opportunities for trial and error behavior) is linked to the emergence of insecurity, confusion, and self−indulgence (e.g., Baumrind, 1968). It is therefore suggested that both dimensions are essential for normative child growth and development and, more specifically, for the development of autonomy, individuality, and innovativeness on the one hand, and social commitment and obligations on the other.

3. Variable Specification

Although the dimensions of control and experimentation may be initially viewed as reflections of each other and as mutually dependent, a more thorough analysis of their inner logic leads us to conceive of them as coexisting and empirically independent. Concerning the relation between learning and sanctions, control presupposes that they are linked while experimentation does not, although it does not refute the role played by sanctions in affecting behavior.

More specifically, experimentation allows for self−correction and a temporary disassociation of tasks and sanctions. In addition, while control presupposes the necessity of external rules, unified norms, and hierarchical supervision for regulating behavior, experimentation emphasizes the motivation, responsibility, and curiosity of the learner without denying the importance of an organized set−up. The coexistence of tight control and innate motivation may produce optimal accomplishment of tasks (e.g., in voluntary, crack army units). When experimentation is dominant, the allocation of rewards is based on one's investments and commitment (i.e., equitable distribution of justice); when control is dominant, rewards are allocated on the basis of observed achievements. These criteria of allocation can coexist, as in the kibbutz system.

Finally, the opportunity to err and even to deviate, which is intrinsic to experimentation, embraces uncertainty, while control works to maximize predictability. However, in situations of calculated risks, uncertainty and predictability may operate together. This means that *relaxed control does not automatically lead to experimentation* but rather may develop into anomie and anarchy. Conversely, *the institutionalization of experimentation does not lead to the total elimination of control* (as in a chemistry laboratory) and should not be confused with the emergence of weak and obscure boundaries.

I therefore propose to conceive of control and experimentation as empirically independent, coexistent dimensions. Notwithstanding the distinction between them, the two dimensions work together to generate socialization experiences in the day−to−day arrangements of the major agencies.

The research reported here aims to illustrate an attempt to empirically validate the coexistence of control and experimentation as independent dimensions within each of the three major socializing agencies in adolescence — the family, the school, and the youth movement — and to distinguish accordingly between these agencies.

4. Method

Subjects

The sample consisted of 1,433 Jewish Israeli adolescents who were members of five different youth movements covering the religious and sociopolitical spectrum of Israeli society. Their average age was 13.9 years (SD = 1.3), and 58% of the sample were females. Subjects came predominantly from urban settings (72%) and in general were drawn from the middle—class Israeli population.

Measures

A questionnaire formulated in a 5—point Likert scale format (ranging from very seldom to very often with a midpoint of sometimes) was devised in order to assess levels of control and experimentation. Each of the two dimensions was operationalized by six items formulated as general statements applicable to all agencies (see items in Table 1). Having to choose between general and specific indicators for a comparative study like the one reported here places the researcher in a dilemma. Though general questions allow one to go beyond the bias of agency—specific idiosyncracies, they may also miss the unique meaning of the socialization process in each agency. Deliberate reference to the special character of each agency, on the other hand, may overlook the unifying meaning of socialization processes and emphasize particular traits. On the basis of a previous study (Rapoport, in press), it was therefore decided to employ general questionnaire items [3].

The questionnaire was constructed in three versions, the sole difference between them being that each referred to a different agency (the family, the school, and the youth movement) and that the item order was changed. Each subject was asked to respond to all three versions, and each third of the sample received a different questionnaire version first.

Data Analysis

The data were first processed by means of confirmatory factor analysis (varimax rotation with Kaiser normalization), which was conducted on the subjects' responses for each of the three questionnaire versions (one for each socialization agency). Three tests were conducted for each agency: one for the entire sample, and one for each gender group (nine tests altogether). (It should be noted that the gender subsamples served to corroborate the results obtained for the entire sample. In other words, I do not focus here on gender—differential socialization experiences within and across agencies.) Hotelling's T^2 test was then employed with respect to the entire sample in order to test the difference between agencies in terms of the mean scores obtained for each dimension. In this context, 95% confidence intervals of mean scores were computed and compared.

5. Results

The findings show that in virtually all the analyses the items designated to operationalize experimentation made up one factor while those constructed to reflect control made up another. More specifically, the item loadings obtained from the factor analysis indicate a two—factor solution for each agency (see Table 1).

An examination of Pearson correlations between agencies by dimension (see Table 2) shows that the clear and recurrent distinction between the dimensions, as manifested in the obtained factorial structure, cannot be simply attributed to the personal preferences of subjects for a specific dimension. More specifically, the correlation levels show that many subjects tend to assign different scores to the three socialization agencies regarding both experimentation and control.

The clear—cut differentiation between the two dimensions over all agencies and samples is reinforced by a recurring pattern with respect to item loadings. Hence, the highest loadings in each factor are obtained by identical items, with but a few exceptions, in all analyses. With regard to the dimension of control, the content of these items includes: a straightforward, direct control statement (Item 2), the requirement to report on one's behavior (Item 4), and the statement referring to a direct link between action and sanctions (Item 5). Regarding the factor of experimentation, highest loadings were generally obtained for the item referring to the undertaking of responsibility (Item 9), for that regarding the chance to keep trying until one's mistakes are corrected (Item 12), and for that referring to negotiation over and changing of punishments (Item 7). The above findings point to a clear—cut overall distinction made by the subjects between experimentation and control, empirically validating the two dimensions.

Having discerned two distinct socialization dimensions, the next step was to compare between agencies in terms of the mean scores of each of the dimensions (these analyses were not applied to gender).

Table 1:   Matrix of Factor Loadings

Items	School		Family		Youth movement	
	F1	F2	F1	F2	F1	F2
Control :						
1.Everyone has the same idea about how I should behave.	.29	.06	.28	−.07	.37	−.02
2.I'm told what to do; I'm under supervision.	.71	.16	.47	.23	.54	.21
3.They look the other way if I do something that's not exactly alright.	.20	.06	.17	−.02	.14	−.01
4.I have to report what I'm up to.	.61	.17	.56	.04	.50	.00
5.I get a reaction to whatever I do.	.53	−.10	.53	−.01	.47	−.11
6.I pay a lot for my mistakes.	.47	.12	.35	.30	.38	.11
Experimentation :						
7.I can negotiate and change punishments.	.10	.36	.02	.35	.09	.41
8.I do things my way.	.12	.26	.10	.16	−.00	.52
9.I do things that require responsibility.	.02	.55	−.06	.47	−.06	.52
10.They don't let me do things because I'm too young.	.22	.26	.22	.37	.09	.28
11.I learn from my own mistakes.	−.04	.29	−.12	.34	−.08	.27
12.If I err, I can keep trying until I get it right.	.11	.39	−.04	.52	.04	.39
Explained variance	20.7	12.3	17.4	13.7	16.0	13.6

F1 = Factor 1 (control); F2 = Factor 2 (experimentation)
n = 1,433

Table 2: Pearson correlations between agencies by dimensions, (N = 1,433)

	Experimentation			Control		
	F	YM	S	F	YM	S
Family		.43	.35		.33	.32
Youth movement			.33			.40

F = Family; Y = Youth movement; S = School

Hotelling's I^2 test revealed significant effects for agencies and dimensions (Hotelling's I^2 = 122.85, df = 1,130, p < .001). The comparison between mean scores together with the 95 confidence intervals obtained (see Table 3) reveal significant differences between the agencies according to the level of experimentation. The mean scores show that it was highest in the family, lower in the youth movement, and lowest in the school. When agencies were compared according to the level of control, significant differences were found between the youth movement, on the one hand, and the family and school on the other.

Table 3: Mean Scores, Standard Deviations (in parentheses), and Confidence Intervals for Experimentation and Control, by Agency (N = 1,302)

Agency Dimension	Family	Youth movement	School
Experimentation			
Mean scores	3.74	3.67	3.49
S.D.	(.542)	(.520)	(.556)
Confidence intervals	3.71–3.77	3.65–3.70	3.45–3.51
Control			
Mean scores	3.18	3.29	3.16
S.D.	(.569)	(.574)	(.667)
Confidence intervals	3.14–3.20	3.26–3.32	3.12–3.20

The higher the mean score, the lower the level of control (i.e., the higher the laxity).

6.   Discussion

The findings confirm that the dimensions of control and experimentation are independent and coexisting within all three socialization contexts examined — the family, the school, and the youth movement. They also show that the agencies differ in the extent to which each dimension is present and therefore in the patterns of socializing experiences that they generate.

The conditions specific to Israeli society help explain this divergence. Not only is Israel a complex, advanced, and industrial society undergoing rapid social changes, but it is also continually plagued by acute stress in terms of the economy and security conditions (Breznitz, 1983). The high risks involved, together with the rapid pace of development, require the nurturing of both strong personal commitment to the society and high individual levels of excellence, innovation, and expertise (Breznitz and Eshel, 1983). One may speculate that in cultivating these behavioral orientations, the socialization agencies work in different directions.

The Israeli school therefore seems to react more to constant pressures for high achievement and expertise (Adler, 1986), a trend which is indicated, for example, by the growth of vocational education in the last decades (Kahane and Starr, 1984). Research on schools in other societies points to a similar dominance of control attempts and sanctions in regulating school life and the learning process. More than the other agencies, the school tends to reproduce the social order (Bowels and Gintis, 1976) and therefore employs stronger coercive means and straightforward control.

The Israeli family, in contrast, encourages negotiation and autonomy, which enhance the solidarity of the family unit and help its members to shape personal identities. Similar findings have been obtained in cross–cultural and longitudinal studies conducted in both Japan (Youth Survey, 1978) and Europe (Allerbeck and Hoag, 1985; Young Europeans, 1982; Shell Survey, 1985), which suggest a move toward more permissive familial patterns and opportunities for experimentation.

Finally, the Israeli youth movement is characterized by relaxed control, a finding that may be related to its flexible structure and high level of expressivity (Kahane, 1986). A study conducted on recent changes in three major models of youth movements (the Soviet Komsomol, the British Boy Scouts, and the Israeli Pioneering Youth Movements) suggests a move toward a more expressive and loose setting (Kahane and Rapoport, 1986).

From a more theoretical perspective, experimentation and control are conceived as two complementary yet differentiated structural dimensions, each of which is composed of different premises regarding the nature of the learning process and the agent — learner interaction. Experimentation presumes the active, voluntary role of the learner, his or her ability to choose between alternative behavioral patterns, roles, and tasks, and an implicit contract based on trust between the learner and the socializer regarding the negotiable boundaries of legitimate behavior. It views error and regressive behavior as an integral part of the learning process. Control, on the other hand, does not assume preconditional trust and presupposes the learner's recipient role and the inevitability of hierarchical relations for effective learning. Boundaries of legitimate behavior are largely prescribed, while the contract between the socializer and the learner is based on external legitimation and supervision. Control emphasizes learning outcomes more than the learning process, and puts forward efficient strategies that bear favorable results in the shortest, most parsimonious way.

It should be recalled that experimentation is not identical to boundlessness and excessive behavior, and that the movement away from closed, strict socialization arrangements does not necessarily eliminate control or encourage experimentation. Rather, both experimentation and control may remain present and work together to generate socialization experiences. More importantly, it may be suggested that the coexistence of two complementary yet differentiated dimensions essentially entails a process of mutual mitigation that curbs the dominance of one overruling the other. In this way, the socialization process is kept from turning into either unsanctioned overpermissiveness or excessive strictness accompanied by primarily negative sanctions, thereby restricting the emergence of unfavorable socialization outcomes. It is my contention that this dialectic process facilitates the emergence of an open social arena that combines spontaneity and trial — and — error behavior with regulatory norms and rules.

Going one step further, I propose a preliminary typology based on several possible combinations of experimentation and control (see Figure 1), each of which analytically represents a distinct type of socializing context and as such is assumed to generate a distinct impact on child growth and development. The "moratoric" type, based on the presence of both experimentation and control, facilitates identity formation and the development of autonomy (Rapoport, in press). The "authoritarian" context, in which control is high while experimentation is virtually absent or minimized, is generally believed to encourage the emergence of "closed minds" and dogmatism (Rokeach, 1960). The minimal presence of both experimentation and control characterizes "anomic" contexts, while "permissive" contexts are based on excessive experimentation and random control. "Permissive" socialization contexts are often related to the development of personal disorientation and identity confusion. It should be noted that the above typology is dynamic; the context can change from situation to situation or over time.

Fig. 1: Typology of Socialization Contexts

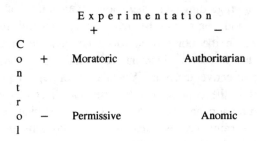

The dimensions of experimentation and control examined here appear to be both useful and parsimonious for the comparative analysis of socialization processes. Further, the analytical and empirical tools tested in the present study may serve as a useful starting point for comparing processes of socialization in different cultures, life stages, and social classes. Additional research in these directions will reveal whether the two dimensions identified here recur outside the Israeli context and with respect to different subgroups of adolescents.

Notes

This research was supported by Grant No. 88−01−014 of the Israel Trustees Foundation. I am very grateful to Reuven Kahane, Eyal Ben Ari, Zeev Rosenhek, Clara Sabaag, and Niza Benner of the Hebrew University for their comments; to Moshe Cohen for his helpful statistical consultation and data analysis; and to Helene Hogri for her indispensable editorial assistance.
[1] For an analysis of youth movements from a historical and cross−sectional perspective, employing a recently developed conceptual model of informal organization, see Rapoport and Kahane (1988) Kahane and Rapoport (1988).
[2] The theoretical basis for this paper has been developed jointly with Prof. Reuven Kahane of the Department of Sociology and Social Anthropology at the Hebrew University of Jerusalem.
[3] The attempt to construct different questionnaires for each agency based on equivalent questions pertaining to issues within specific agencies (e.g., asking about the freedom not to participate in a youth movement hike or a family Passover meal) failed to produce satisfactory instruments.

References

Adler, C. (1986): Israeli education addressing dilemmas caused by pluralism — a sociological perspective." In Rothemund, D., & Simon, J. (Eds.): Education and the integration of minorities. London: Frances Pinter Publishers

Adorno, T.W., Frenkel—Brunswik, E., Levinson, D.J., & Sanford, R.N. (1950): The authoritarian personality. New York: Harper and Row

Allerbeck, K., & Hoag, W. (1985): Jugend ohne Zukunft. München: Piper

Alon, M. (1986): The eternal hope — Youth and social change . Tel Aviv: Sifriat Poalim. (Hebrew)

Aries, P. (1962): Centuries of childhood. New York: Knopf

Baumrind, D. (1968): Authoritarian vs. authoritative parental control. Adolescence, 3, 255—272

Ben David, J. (1954): Membership in the youth movement and its impact on social status. Megamot 5/3, 227—243 (Hebrew)

Bowels, S., & Gintis, H. (1976): Schooling in capitalist America . New York: Basic Books

Breznitz, S. (Ed.)(1983): Stress in Israel. New York: Nostrand Reinhold

Breznitz, S., & Eshel, Y. (1983): Life events: stressful ordeal or valuable experience? In Breznitz, S. (Ed.): Stress in Israel. New York: Nostrand Reinhold, 228—261

Bronfenbrenner, V. (1979): The ecology of human development . Cambridge: Harvard University Press

Carew, J. (1980): Experience and the development of intelligence in young children at home and in the day care. Monographs of the Society for Research in Child Development, Developmental Series 187/6—7

Coleman, J.S. (1974): Youth transition to adulthood. Chicago: University of Chicago Press

Dewey, J. (1964): John Dewey on education , R. Archambault (Ed.). New York: The Modern Library

Dunphy, C. (1963): Structure of urban adolescent peer groups. Sociometry, 26, 230—241

Eisenstadt, S.N. (1956): The social conditions of the development of voluntary associations: A case study of Israel. Scripta Hiersolymitana, 3, 104—125

Eisenstadt, S.N. (1971): Social differentiation and stratification. Glencoe: Scott Foresman

Erikson, E.H. (1955): Ego, identity and the psychosocial moratorium. In Witmer, H.L., & Kotinsky, R. (Eds.): New perspectives for research in juvenile delinquency. Washington DC: U.S. Department of Health, Education and Welfare

Erikson, E.H. (1963): Childhood and society . New York: Norton

Erikson, E.H. (1968): Identity: Youth and crisis. New York: Norton

Gecas, V. (1981): Contexts of socialization. In Rosenberg, M., & Turner, R. (Eds.): Social psychology. New York: Basic Books

Gillis, J.R. (1974): Youth and history. New York: Academic Press

Graubard, A. (1972): Free the children: Radical reform and the free school movement . New York: Random House

Grotevant, H.D., & Cooper, C.R. (1988): The role of family experience in career exploration: A life—span perspective. In Baltes, P.B., Featherman, D.L., & Lerner, R.M. (Eds.): Life—span development and behavior , Vol. 8. Hillsdale: Erlbaum

Hurn, J.C. (1985): The limits and possibilities of schooling: An introduction to the sociology of education (2nd ed.). Boston: Allyn and Bacon

Kahane, R. (1975): Informal youth organizations: A general model. Sociological Inquiry, 45, 4, 17—28

Kahane, R. (1985): Paradigms for a comparative study of educational systems . Jerusalem: The Hebrew University, School of Education (Hebrew)

Kahane, R. (1986): Informal agencies of socialization and the integration of immigrant youth into society: An example from Israel. International Immigration Review, 20, 1, 21–39

Kahane, R., & Rapoport, T. (1986): Four paradigms of youth movements — an analytical comparative perspective. Report submitted to the Konrad Adenauer Foundation

Kahane, R., and Starr, L. (1984): Education and work: Vocational socialization processes in Israel. Jerusalem: Magnes Press (Hebrew)

Laslett, B. (1978): Family membership, past and present. Social Problems, 25, 5

Maccoby, E.E., & Martin, J.A. (1983): Socialization in the context of the family: Parent–child interaction. In Mussen, P. (Ed.): Handbook of child psychology , Vol. IV. New York: Wiley, 1–101

Marcia, J. (1980): Ego identity development. In Adelson, J. (Ed.): Handbook of adolescent psychology. New York: Wiley

Musgrove, F. (1966): The family, education and society. London: Routledge and Kegan Paul

Neill, A. (1960): Summerhill: A radical approach to child rearing . New York: Hart

Parsons, T., & Bales, R.F. (1955): Family socialization and interaction process. Glencoe: Free Press

Piaget, J. (1932): The moral judgement of the child. London: Routledge and Kegan Paul.

Piaget, J., & Inhelder, B. (1969): The psychology of the child. New York: Basic Books

Rapoport, T. (in press): Moratorium as a principle of socialization: A comparative study of three agencies." Youth and Society

Rapoport, T., & Kahane, R. (1988): Informal frameworks and role development. Sociological Inquiry, 58, 1, 49–74

Rollins, B.C., & Thomas, D.L. (1979): Parental support, power and control techniques in the socialization of children. In Wesley, B.R. et al. (Eds.): Contemporary Theories about the Family, Vol. I. New York: Free Press

Rokeach, M. (1960): The open and closed mind. New York: Basic Books

Rothschild–Whitt, J. (1979): The collectivistic organization: An alternative to rational–bureaucratic models. American Sociological Review, 44, 509–527

Schwartzman, H.B. (1982): Transformations . New York: Plenum Press

Shell Survey (1985): Generationen im Vergleich. Jugendwerk der Deutschen Shell. West Germany

Smelser, W. (1968): Essays in sociological explanation. Englewood Cliffs: Prentice–Hall

Sommerville, J. (1982): The rise and fall of childhood. Beverly Hills: Sage

Swidler, A. (1979): Organization without authority — Dilemmas of social control in free schools. Cambridge: Harvard University Press

Young Europeans (1982): Young Europeans: An explanatory study of 15–24 years in EEC countries. Brussels: Report by the Commission of European Communities

Youniss, J. (1980): Parents and peers in social development . Chicago: University of Chicago Press

Youth Survey (1978): The youth of the world and Japan — The findings of the Second World War Youth Survey. Tokyo: Report of the Youth Bureau, Prime Minister's Office

15.

The Influence of Adults and Peers on Adolescents' Lifestyles and Leisure—Styles

Leo B. Hendry
University of Aberdeen, Scotland, Great Britain

1. Introduction: Young People and Society

From the physical and physiological changes that herald the teenage years, the adolescent has various personal and social tasks to achieve. There are at least six tasks to be attempted across the adolescent years (see Hendry, 1983 for elaboration):

1. developing a self—identity in the light of physical changes;
2. developing a gender identity;
3. gaining a degree of independence from parents;
4. accepting or rejecting family values;
5. shaping up to an occupational (or unemployed) role; and
6. developing and extending friendships.

These six tasks are encapsulated in the notion put forward by Erikson (1968) that the chief task of adolescence is identity formation. Yet there are no obvious symbolic "rites of passage" into adulthood in Western society, so the adolescent's route toward adulthood is not marked out by clearly defined signposts that indicate progress in a desired direction. It is perhaps remarkable that so many arrive at their adult destination emotionally and psychologically unscathed.

Thus, the essential concern for the individual adolescent in the process of growing up is between "playing appropriate roles" and "selfhood". It is important for the young person to learn to play appropriate roles in a variety of social settings and to follow prescribed social rules in these situations. It is equally important to be able to maintain elements of individuality. It is the interplay of internal and external forces that contributes to the success or failure of progress toward adulthood. In the process of socialization various adults and peers with whom individuals will interact are important as role models and reinforcers of behavior. But the functions of selfhood, identity, and perceived competence are equally vital, together with the need to make sense of the social world.

It is here that the role of leisure may be significant in creating opportunities for identity development and allowing the exercise of choice in the selection of alternative social and physical contexts and variations of role and rule structures. This is possible because alternative forms of self—presentation and style can be tried out as "non—serious miniature achievement models" (Sutton—Smith et al., 1963). At the same time these (supposedly) individual behaviors are carried out within certain defined roles and norms with relatively expected and predictable subcultural social behaviors and rules. These styles of behavior contain the essential paradox between "selfhood" and "roles" that unites lifestyle and leisure. Both reveal the possible conflict between the young person's need, in a developmental sequence, for self—identity and a range of personal skills, against the constraints of roles, expectations of socializing agents, subcultural norms and values, and so forth.

If leisure pursuits are central concerns in many young people's lives, what do they do? In Hendry's (1983) review, adolescent's main leisure pursuits included activities that were designed to cater almost exclusively for teenagers or were undertaken in groups: dancing, youth clubs, drinking, dating, going on the town, and "hanging around" with friends. Such ideas closely match the findings of major surveys: Visiting friends, pop music, pub going, cinema attendance, discotheques, and dancing appeared to be popular leisure activities for Scottish teenagers, whereas playing sports or going to youth clubs were not so interesting to them (Scarlett, 1975). Dancing, relaxing at home, visiting friends, drinking in bars, together with a lesser interest in swimming and sports were the pursuits of English adolescents (Fogelman, 1976). Emmett (1971) has also argued that though social class is important in the choice of leisure pursuits, so too is type of school attended (though this is likely to be closely linked to social class) and teenage subcultures to which the adolescent is exposed (Brake, 1980).

Emmett (1977) has reported in a follow—up study of over 2,000 adolescents 3 years after leaving school (i.e., at 19 years of age) that factors of gender, social class, occupation, academic attainment, and peer group allegiances continued to exert an influence on recreational involvement. Roughly twice as many boys as girls belonged to organized clubs; girls tended to enter casually into activities without necessarily joining officially. Casual activities which could be undertaken with a friend of the opposite sex — tennis, hill walking, horse — riding — were popular with both sexes, yet there was also some small carry — over beyond school days of organized school activities. Emmett concluded that some of the factors to which postschool leisure interests can be attributed were:

1. Some participation in school sport is compulsory and competitive, and this affects out — of — school interests;
2. Postschool years are courting years;
3. Young people at work have more money and greater freedom from parental control in choosing leisure pursuits; and
4. At 18 years of age they are legally entitled to drink in bars.

This tendency toward social activities was detected by Hendry and Marr (1985): Drinking in public houses (bars) was the most popular activity for late — adolescent males. This activity was ranked second most popular for women, coming behind going out with boyfriends or husbands, but in all probability there would be a strong relationship between the two activities.

Like adults, young people seek out social contexts in which to interact with peers. Nisbet et al. (1984), in a study of both rural and urban locales in a Scottish region, found that over 70% of students in their last years of compulsory schooling had been members of a sports club or team at some time in the past, but only 47% were members at the time of investigation. With regard to nonsporting interests and hobby clubs, 80% had been members in the past, but only 50% were currently involved. The trend was most evident for uniformed organizations like Scouts and Guides in which 75% of adolescents had been members but only 16% had maintained membership into their mid — teens.

2. A Focal Theory of Adolescents' Leisure and Lifestyles

In order to understand the significance of these transitions away from organized leisure activities, it is first of all necessary to examine some general claims about the changing focus of leisure in adolescence.

Leisure activities may be chosen for their personal meaning and for social expression, and these choices are, in turn, colored by influences such as the family, peers, the educational system, the media, leisure promotion industries, and changes in the general social context such as massive unemployment. A crucial point to stress in all this is the way the interplay of factors determining leisure choices varies as the focus of social interests changes across the adolescent years (Coleman, 1979, and in this volume).

If *Figure 1* is examined, the changes and continuities in the adolescent's leisure preferences and behavior (i.e., their focus of leisure interests) can be noted. The main factors influencing leisure pursuits are suggested here to be age, sex, and social class. These are hardly surprising elements, but when linked to the shifting focus of social relationships postulated by Coleman (1979), a framework can be offered to provide insights into a changing and differential pattern of leisure focus in the teenage years. We would want to argue that this leisure focus generally shifts from adult—organized to commercially organized leisure, and that these transitions may occur roughly at the ages when main relationship issues — sex, peers, parents — come into focus.

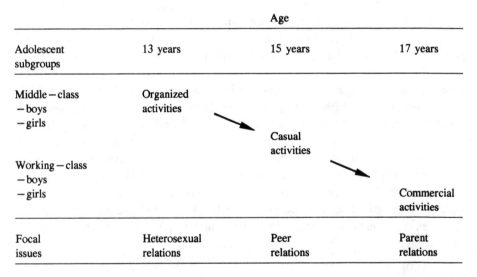

	Age		
Adolescent subgroups	13 years	15 years	17 years
Middle—class —boys —girls	Organized activities	Casual activities	
Working—class —boys —girls			Commercial activities
Focal issues	Heterosexual relations	Peer relations	Parent relations

Fig. 1:   Focus of interest and types of leisure pursuits

The differential effects of sex and social class can influence this general leisure pattern to produce possible patterns of overlap not dissimilar to those postulated by Coleman. For instance, the earlier physical and psychological maturity of girls underpins their relatively earlier transition toward a focus on peers and casual leisure pursuits, and then toward more exclusive courting couples and commercial leisure provision. It may also reflect a more rapid move to social sophistication, if not maturity, and may be linked to what has been called their perceived "career" as girlfriends and wives, though it should be noted that the proportion of teenage brides has dropped considerably (in 1974, one in three single women getting married under 20 years of age; by 1984 the figure had dropped to one in six).

The continued allegiance of the middle classes, and perhaps particularly middle — class boys, to games and organized pursuits, may be indicative of Sutton — Smith and Roberts' (1964) postulations about play — styles and their use as rehearsals for adult lifestyles; and also of their longer dependence on parents (often in conjunction with plans to pursue courses in higher education), which ensures a continuing (and relaxed) relationship with adults and creates opportunities for further socialization toward particular adult values.

The coincidence of an interest in organized and structured leisure pursuits and clubs, with the focus on heterosexual relationships in early adolescence, seems plausible. Conger (1979) has suggested that the increase in the sexual drive that accompanies puberty occurs when close social relationships and leisure activities are largely confined to members of the same sex. It is also a period, Conger points out, when the opposite sex can appear rather mysterious and sometimes anxiety producing. Thus youth clubs and organized adult — led leisure pursuits can provide a safe environment from which to observe and to interact with the opposite sex, but it is a context in which the focus of attention is on the "action", on the activities, and where the social milieu is less central. Further, the adults present contain the social interactions among members, and the pervading values and norms are directed toward conventional socialization (Eggleston, 1976). It is merely a launching pad for the next focal issue concerning peers and casual leisure interests. For example, a number of studies concerning community centers have shown that a very high percentage of girls said they attended for social reasons — especially to "chat up the talent" and to use the amenities as a social meeting place (Hendry and Simpson, 1977; Hendry, Brown and Hutcheon, 1981).

The second leisure focus concerns peer relationships in conjunction with casual pursuits. Because this focal leisure area involves not only peers and casual activities, but also occurs at about the period when the minimal school — leaving age is reached, it contains perhaps the stage of greatest diversity of pattern. In part, this conjunction of peer relations and acceptance of subcultural values with an interest in casual leisure, may offer some additional insights into antischool subcultures (Hargreaves, 1967; Murdock and Phelps, 1973; Willis, 1977). The lure of the peer group in terms of behavior is irresistible. Thus, while conformist youths may continue to be more attracted to organizations and adult influence, such structured clubs do not touch many adolescents, who pursue leisure lifestyles that derive identification from subcultural attempts to resolve the contradictions of school and work situations. It has been suggested that these contradictions are mediations of class differences in society (Murduck and Phelps, 1973). The general feeling among many young people is that official youth clubs are too tame or overorganized to appeal to them and are too much like school.

To go beyond this stage of understanding we need to progress by exploring the dynamics and processes involved in these changes in leisure interests and life — style across the adolescent years. Is change gradual? Are there identifiable triggers in terms of altered perceptions or life incidents that shift individuals on to new ventures and activities? We need, therefore, to ask whether the factors that precipitate change at the various stages outlined are mainly sociocultural, somatic, or psychological. The relative influence of these broad factors may alter across the adolescent years. The crucial questions here relate to understanding the influencing factors and life events which create continuity and change in adolescents' leisure patterns.

Thus, if we look at the preadolescent period, we find that as children emerge from the middle years of childhood they are engaged in play patterns that are basically traditional, conformist, and possibly strongly influenced by family patterns, but that these are slowly eroded by a more adult concept of leisure and recreation. In particular, Hendry and Percy (1981) found that by the upper stages of the elementary school, social pressures and the influence of the media were pushing boys and girls into much more gender — specific roles in terms of, for instance, their leisure activities, reading interests, and their television viewing preferences.

Sociocultural factors would seem to predominate over physical and psychological ones at the juncture between childhood and adolescence. With these social triggers, young people move toward the setting of organized adult — run activities as a context for slowly acquainting themselves with the opposite sex after a childhood in which single sex groupings are the norm. Such activities include clubs run at school, youth clubs, church groups, and so on.

Conversely, the process that triggers the transition from organized activities toward casual activities a few years later is one in which physical and physiological factors may be to the forefront. For girls in particular, the relatively rapid changes in body shape and size and the onset of menstruation may well explain the rapid loss of interest in physical activity and organized games at this stage. The physiological and psychological changes experienced by all adolescents, however, require them to reappraise their self — images, and at this stage it is important for these self — images to be reinforced by peers;

Weinstein (1973) suggested that peer group relationships offer multiple opportunities for witnessing the social strategies of others, seeing how far these are effective, and offering an area for learning self — presentation.

This may result in strong sex differences in leisure pursuits — many girls, for instance, may seem at first to skip this stage of casual peer — oriented activities except in sharing fashion or social strategies with one or two close friends within "the culture of the bedroom" as Frith (1978) has described it. Brake (1980) stated:

"...Women have reality mediated not just by class location interpretation, but also by patriarchy, the system of subordination in a world which is male dominated in sexuality and procreative potential; a system where women's labor is organized economically, ideologically and politically by males. It is a world where sexism is the articulated, as well as the taken for granted unquestioned superiority of men. In this sense women inhabit two locations; their role in their specific social class and their position in patriarchy" (Brake, 1980).

At the next focal stage, an interest in commercial leisure provision is linked to the peak of conflicts with parents:

"Perhaps, indeed, (adolescents) have been kept in even longer subordination just because they *are* more mature and consequently threatening to the old ... Where society does not permit the adolescent to assume a social role compatible with his physical and intellectual development ... adult maturity is come by with more difficulty" (Musgrove, 1964).

Adolescents in this period of their lives are closer to being perceived as adults, and their leisure — time pursuits will be adult — oriented leisure interests. This fact alone will create a climate for intergenerational disagreements, as Musgrove described, even although the actual leisure patterns of adolescents may closely match their subcultural heritage. The factors that lead to an involvement with commercial leisure are more social — psychological than somatic in character and have to do with the growing adolescent's desire to be seen as playing an adult role. Pubs, clubs, discos, commercial leisure facilities, and even foreign travel, all feature in the leisure activities of young people at this stage.

Clearly, participation in these sorts of activities is influenced by occupational status and subcultures, peer group membership, and whether or not by this stage courting dyads have been formed. Hence, again the broad influencing factors are mainly sociocultural values, available cash and employment opportunities, family commitments, and the effects of the broad leisure interests developed in the previous stages.

3. Adolescents and Leisure Education

If we look at the school situation in Britain, evidence is available about young people being shaped in the image of their teachers. As Henry (1966) wrote: "School metamorphoses the child ... then proceeds to minister to the self it has created." In this process, various elements of the school system can combine to differentiate students in terms of their attitudes toward teachers, their self-images, and their scholastic success. It has been suggested by Leigh (1971) that education for leisure within schools should attempt "to increase both the true range of choices available and the ability of the individual to make effective and significant choices". But the majority of schools provide leisure education in very similar ways, usually through a mixture of curricular and extracurricular activities, with the addition of schemes such as the Duke of Edinburgh Award Scheme, which allows young volunteers to develop skills and hobbies and to offer community service for which they are assessed and awarded bronze, silver, and gold grades. Hence the activities that educators often see in terms of the leisure lives of students are sports, games, art, music, and practical subjects such as woodwork, metalwork, and technical drawing — which, even though they may have a vocational bias in a narrow sense, are useful for do-it-yourself and recreation. Often these subjects are also offered to students in extracurricular time.

Yet, in designing leisure education programs schools may well reject ways in which adolescents actually spend their leisure time simply because these do not conform to the school's view of how leisure should be profitably used. Thus it has been found that the range of extracurricular activities that the vast majority of schools provide, in order to substantiate their claim of providing leisure education, is in fact pursued by only a minority of adolescents — mainly middle-class, academically able students (Hendry, 1983; Hendry and Marr, 1985).

It can be suggested that attempts within the extracurricular life of comprehensive schools to educate students toward worthwhile leisure pursuits can be divisive and reinforce differing student groupings. The school system, it has been suggested, may embody certain implicit values in which certain students can share and which other students at best find unfamiliar and difficult to understand or accept (Davie et al., 1972; Hargreaves, 1972; Willis, 1977). Middle-class students who do well in school and stay on and take academic subjects are by and large the students who take part in extracurricular activities, including physical recreation and sports (Start, 1966; Emmett, 1971; Reid, 1972; Hendry, 1978) and nonsporting clubs and pursuits like the school choir or debating society (Reid, 1972; Kind, 1973) or become prefects (Start, 1966; Hargreaves, 1967). As Reid has queried: "Why don't a higher percentage of (academically) able students belong to activities other than the 'prestige' activities (i.e., sports teams, school choir)?" (Reid, 1972).

Such a system creates a changing impetus for the leisure interests of many adolescents (Hendry, 1978), and existing evidence certainly suggests that students are unlikely to perceive themselves as pursuing many school – based activities in postschool life (Emmett, 1977). If it is those adolescents accepting the "good student" role who also associate with school activities (Hargreaves, 1967; Hendry, 1978), for other adolescents school offers few attractions (Sugarman, 1967). As Hargreaves wrote: "The social life of the adolescent in school may have from the teenager's perspective a definite old – fashioned air" (Hargreaves, 1972).

From the above discussion it is clear that school influences provide important constraints and opportunities for young people's leisure. The educational system provides a potentially valuable structure within which interests may be aroused and cultivated; but mainly for middle – class students. There is a possible stifling of interest development that frequently attends early school leaving (Morton – Williams and Finch, 1968; Bone, 1972).

"The influence of thousands of hours in schools given to arts and crafts and to physical education and cultural development is only partially discernible in post – school leisure interests" (Simpson, 1973).

4. *Young People, Adults, and Leisure Contexts*

Adults can play an important part in peer group interactions. Sport clubs, hobby groups, youth clubs, uniformed organizations (Scouts and Guides) all tend to be arranged for adolescents by adults and are often closely supervised by adults. This may be significant because the degree to which adults are directly involved is likely to influence the relationships among adolescents. Adolescents' involvement in such adult – sponsored situations, though nominally voluntary, may not be genuinely self – chosen. Consequently, many adolescents will choose *not* to become involved in such settings (Hendry, 1983).

Youth clubs and organizations touch the majority of young people, however temporarily, and in this way may play an important part in their social and leisure lives. Other voluntary organizations – churches, uniformed bodies, community groups – involve a number of adolescents from time to time.

Further, the potential value of local authority provision has grown with the development of sports and community centers.

It should be remembered, however, that some adolescents join "alternative" groups, often associated with oriental religions or near delinquent activities. This can be seen as part of the variability pattern of peer groupings and as reflecting the variety of subcultural patterns (Milson, 1972).

In studying youth and community centers, one of the models that Eggleston (1976) found to be of major relevance was what he called the "socialization model", in which adolescents are seen to be socialized or made ready for adult society — learning and accepting approved patterns of social behavior, knowledge, and values.

Clearly, not all young people are attracted by such institutions, and Bone (1972) has argued that acceptance patterns are related to academic attainment and social class, in that early school — leavers are less likely to attend organized clubs offering sporting interests or hobbies or being a uniformed service. Jephcott (1976), Scarlett (1975), and also Hendry and Simpson (1977) have all said that the reason why many adolescents do not attend such organizations is because they are too closely linked with school organization and structure, either because of the pattern of discipline or because school buildings are used. Many adolescents, being disenchanted, are only briefly attached to youth clubs:

"Many of the existing organizations, because they have such long histories, frequently display intense self — consciousness about their traditions and never fundamentally question their reasons for existing ... . The older teenager in particular, sensing that ultimate control lies with middle — aged and older adults, seems increasingly to display dissatisfaction by avoiding what youth establishments have to offer" (Davies, 1970).

Scarlett (1975) found that adolescents had mixed feelings about local authority youth clubs and centers. Some stated that they were good because they developed "character" beyond the boundaries of school; others (although complaining about their similarity to schools in organization, leadership, and attitude — a conclusion that agrees with Jephcott's (1967) earlier investigation) admitted disliking clubs and centers because of the occurrence of violence, lack of interesting activities, or lack of organization. For such reasons many adolescents may opt out of active participation and attend as a matter of course, using the center solely as a context for forming social relationships. They tend to receive what clubs provide in a passive way and to leave when the provision loses its appeal (Corrigan, 1979; Hendry, 1981).

It may be that the relatively ephemeral attachment of the early school — leaver is because his/her social requirements can be satisfied outside formally organized groups or within commercial provision. According to Bone (1972), when members of sports — centered and interest — centered activities left, it was mainly because of career demands or lack of leisure time due to study, whereas those attending casually orientated youth clubs were more likely to abandon the center for social reasons (e.g., friends stopped going or other members were perceived as not being particularly interesting or attractive). Leadership, especially in the form of part — time leaders, has been criticized by several researchers (Scarlett, 1975; Eggleston, 1976). The fundamental problem in successfully running a youth center seems to revolve around how authoritarian or democratic a leader should be. Eggleston (1976) argued that many leaders are torn between subscribing to the norms approved by the local authority and the norms of adolescent clients. Consequently, their organizational approach may oscillate between a directive style with clear educational and positive goals, and a nondirective style with a flexible, less authoritarian role. A further demonstration of the basic conformity of club attenders in a study by Hendry, Brown and Hutcheon (1981) was their attitudes to club leaders. Although perceptions of club leaders were mixed, they tended to be favorable rather than unfavorable, and suggest that these "clubbable" adolescents were basically conformist and related positively toward adults with a willingness to subscribe to an acceptance of rule, regulations, and authority.

A study by Hendry and Simpson (1977) and a replication study by Hendry, Brown and Hutcheon (1981) on regular users of an urban sports and community center revealed a differing pattern in terms of leisure pursuits and lifestyles. It was clear from these studies that two distinct and separate teenage groups existed with little or no contact between them: one group following sports activities, the other using the facilities as a social amenity, sitting around the community area, chatting, drinking coffee, and listening to pop music.

This brings us to the important question: Why did the majority of young people in the neighborhood of the center choose *not* to attend the sports area? Many of the community area members complained that there were too many rules surrounding the sports area, that sports area leaders were unable to mix well with young people and were unsympathetic. They agreed with the necessity of rules and were not advocating a sports area without rules. Instead, rather than subject themselves to the strict discipline and rules, they preferred not to attend, thus opting out of the organized atmosphere of sports for the relaxed, informal, less restrictive atmosphere of the community area.

An interesting observation noted by the researchers was that younger users of the sports area were less likely to be reprimanded than older members. It would appear that not only do young people come to an age at which they more critically perceive rules and regulations, but that these written and unwritten rules are likely to be enforced more strictly by leaders as adolescents progress through the teenage years. It became clear during conversations with community users that their dislike of or disinterest in the sports area was often due to confrontations with sports leaders over enforcement of these unwritten rules.

One further observable feature of the sports area was that groups were already formed, creating possible difficulties for such adolescents in infiltrating these activities. In other pursuits, "star" performers were seen as individual attractions with their own band of groupies. For serious sports participants one obvious sign of difference was their "uniforms" of tracksuits, specialized clothing, and equipment, which may create a symbolic barrier between them and other adolescents who might want to follow sports simply for recreation and enjoyment with no great interest in the pursuit of excellence.

Together with an antipathy to organized sports and their trappings, there was also a pull toward the social amenities provided by the community area at a time when many adolescents are exploring the possibilities of relationships with the opposite sex (Coleman, 1979). Several young people interviewed admitted that the main reasons for attending the center were that "it was better than sitting at home", but especially that it provided an opportunity to meet other teenagers of the opposite sex.

The two groups, however, differed in their views of the center, and perceived themselves as clearly different. Feelings of group solidarity were quite clear. They were loyal to their own area and its leaders and revealed a need to belong, to identify, and to support their own particular group, seeing it as a mirror image and reinforcement of their own qualities and characteristics.

With regard to an investigation of a rural center by Hendry, Brown and Hutcheon (1981), it was found that teenage boys in general attended the center for the activities offered, whereas girls claimed to attend to meet established friends or to make new ones. In this there may be some conscious or unconcious subscribing of expected sex roles. The idea that males should be aggressive, dominant, and sports—loving is a potent one (Emmett, 1971; Sharpe, 1977), while Sharpe (1977) argued that girls quickly tune in to things that bring social approval: picking up cues and responding to pressures from inside and outside school to look "sexy", decorative, and alluring. Linked to this, a considerable percentage of nonattenders at the senior youth club stated that they preferred commercial provision to the center — a finding that agrees with Bone's (1972) assertion that girls are the most enthusiastic supporters of commercial leisure provision. Eggleston (1976) also believed that commercial facilities satisfied the older teenagers' need to be independent and were preferred by adolescents for their greater lavishness and unrestrictive, undemanding provision.

Alternatively, it could be argued that their allegiance had changed from the establishment to the values and norms dictated by peers. Whatever reason is more acceptable, these findings are closely aligned to Coleman's (1979) ideas that the adolescent's focus of interest changes across the teenage years.

As the adolescent grows older, he/she becomes more critical, questioning, and sceptical of adult—oriented organizations, and he/she wishes to use his/her peers to reinforce his/her emergent self — image. The need to feel independent may be a vital reason why the older adolescent moves toward commercial leisure provision. Thus, Eggleston (1976) believed that many problems in youth clubs might be solved by allowing a greater measure of shared responsibility between leaders and members.

Those who provide structured leisure activities and who organize them may perceive these organizations differently from the clients. Adolescents may perceive these organizations as being more structured and authoritarian than do the organizers:

"Like the school itself, like the education system as a whole, like the Duke of Edinburgh Award Scheme, like the Scouts, like the Youth Service and like school — based leisure, Youth Clubs describe themselves as non — authoritarian" (Corrigan, 1979).

This involvement provides an opportunity for those adolescents who attend organized clubs and structured activities to associate with adults (beyond the family) on a regular basis. At the same time in pursuing more casual leisure interests they can continue to align themselves with their peers. In this way they can have a foot in both camps so — to — speak: have the opportunity to experience a wide range of social roles, and perhaps are given the chance to develop a greater versatility in their social relations whilst absorbing and accepting adult attitudes and values. It has also been suggested that there are dangers for the teenagers who do not involve themselves in adult — organized groups:

"In turning to commercial enterprises for leisure activities, or in creating their own ... adolescents are in a vulnerable position with respect to commercial exploitation and are likely to reduce the amount of informal contact with responsible and caring adults" (Hargreaves, 1972).

5. Unemployment and Adolescents' Leisure

The impact of unemployment on adolescence is complex and far — reaching. From the study of one Scottish city carried out by Hendry and Raymond (1983) it was apparent that students about to enter the job market were fully aware of the problems of finding a job, and the school's emphasis on this aspect of unemployment had an indirect effect on working adolescents, creating feelings of insecurity about their jobs and forcing them to remain in jobs they found unpleasant and unsatisfying.

But the major impact of unemployment on adolescents seems to be its ultimate effect on the transition from adolescence to adulthood. Being unable to find work appears to frustrate adolescents' expectations of postschool patterns of work and leisure. Unemployment, even in the short term, redefines the individual's conception of leisure time. Parker (1971), for example, saw leisure as a time of freedom bounded by the constraints of work and nonwork commitments. As De Grazia (1962) wrote: "Work is the antonym of free−time. But not of leisure. Leisure and free−time live in two different worlds ... . Anyone can have free−time."

Hendry and Raymond indicated that this relationship determines the attitudes school−leavers have toward leisure: "You can only have leisure when you're working − you'd enjoy yourself more in your free time if you're working". The unemployed adolescents in their study felt that they were being excluded from the more "adult" leisure of their employed contemporaries: "I'm too old for youth clubs now"; "You can't go out with your mates when they're working, they've got more money than you've got".

Hendry, Raymond and Stewart (1984) also discovered that a major consequence of unemployment was the adolescents' conception of their workless status as denying them entry into the package of work and leisure that makes up "adult" lifestyle. In addition, Coffield, Borrill and Marshall (1983) noted how the young unemployed lacked the financial resources to play an active part in the culture of young workers. This isolation from working peers led Roberts (1983) to suggest that the young unemployed are not being socialized into the culture of work. None of the adolescents investigated by Hendry and Raymond (1985) had broken into the "adult" package of work−related leisure identified by Hendry, Raymond and Stewart (1984). Financial constraints meant that only very few visits could be made to pubs or discos. Cheap, informal, and often passive leisure activities were preferred by both boys and girls.

Like adults, unemployed teenagers are cut off from the culture of work, which also curtails their leisure activities. If they continue to visit pubs and cafes they spend less. They are less likely to reduce their frequency of activity than their expenditure. When they go out they usually remain close to their homes. Local discos replace city−center nightspots. Even travelling costs are prohibitive. Yet attendance at youth clubs is perceived as a "childish" pursuit by older adolescents.

There are many reasons why persistent unemployment in the 1980s has not become a social, political, or economic crisis. Many teenagers have devised effective coping strategies, and these are individualistic and involve seeking personal escapes. These coping strategies are usually successful, which may be why the majority of young people out of work at any time do not progress toward collective political action. Francis (1985) warned of the potential political extremism of unemployed individuals denied a purpose in life and treated as worthless. Such a statement is elevated above mere conjecture when one considers that Stokes and Cochrane (1984), in a longitudinal study of redundant workers, found increased levels of hostility and criticism of others and society at large after job loss.

In reality it seems that unemployed individuals are more likely to become isolated, apathetic, and helpless than to collude on some collective rebellion. Where violence does erupt, it would appear to be introjected (Stokes, 1984) or directed sideward rather than upward, in a domestic rather than social setting. Leisure could become the process for self−actualization and "to offer activities which contribute to the growth and development of an individual" (Gordon et al., 1974). The reality of the situation, however, is that an increasing proportion of adolescents may be found with "enforced" leisure time; and the evidence suggests that few teenagers perceive unemployment as necessarily being synonymous with leisure (Jahoda, 1979; Hendry and Raymond, 1983). In such a context, adolescents are all too aware of the problems of boredom and the risks of turning toward crime. Loss of producer roles, and the inability of education and training to guarantee lifetime vocations, make young people more dependent on ascribed statuses, sometimes derived from gender and ethnicity, in establishing adult identities and independence.

Current trends may make young people more dependent on leisure activities and environments to sustain these identities, and to establish and maintain relationships that allow other aspects of the transition to adulthood to proceed despite the impossibility of stepping directly from full−time education to stable employment. Hence, leisure is likely to grow in importance as a source of stability in adults' and young people's lives, when most other aspects of society change rapidly and are beyond individuals' control. Leisure is likely to become one sphere in which people are assured of "returns on their investments". Access to conventional leisure of various kinds − sporting, musical, or political − can assist young people who wish to preserve conventional lifestyles and trajectories. Equally, adolescents who are pioneering less familiar ways of living − as claimants, in marriage, cohabitational relationships, or other households − benefit from leisure environments in which to interact and display their preferred personal and social identities.

6. Concluding Remarks: Young People and the Transition to Adulthood

If we return now to the focal theory of leisure (Hendry, 1983) presented earlier, a framework for analysis can be proposed, and future directions for young people's development toward adulthood suggested. It was argued that the leisure focus across the adolescent years shifts from adult — organized clubs and activities, through casual leisure pursuits, to commercially organized leisure; and that these transitions occur roughly at the ages at which the main relational issues postulated by Coleman (1979) — sex, peers, and parents — come into focus. Additionally, an ongoing longitudinal project of Hendry, Shucksmith and McGrae (1985) demonstrated the strength of peer involvement in mid — adolescence and the greater allegiance of middle — class youth to adult — led organizations and clubs.

Because this focal leisure area involves not only peers and casual activities, but also occurs at about the period when the minimal school leaving age is reached, it contains perhaps the stage of greatest diversity of pattern. Thus, while conformist youths may continue to be more attracted to organizations and adult influence, such structured clubs do not touch many adolescents, who pursue alternative leisure lifestyles, which derive identification from attempts to resolve the contradictions of school and work or unemployed situations.

Without the influence of caring adults at this period of adolescence, and without the contact with adult — organized clubs and activities, various deviant patterns of subcultural lifestyle may begin to emerge in some adolescents' leisure, reflecting particular value systems and reinforced by adult society and identification with peers. These leisure pursuits can include drugs, alcohol, sexual activity, and more general adventurous excitement — seeking and delinquent behavior, often within gangs.

Hamilton (1986) emphasized the importance of building in adolescents the conviction that future opportunities as competent adults and citizens give validity to commitment to the present social order. Cochran and Bo (1987) presented a similar hypothesis when they stated that: "... Boys with good academic skills and 'winning' personalities have the abilities needed to make themselves attractive to teachers, trainers and youth group leaders, and so become socially connected with such people." Adults can provide role models of life in the adult world, the future, and so make concrete an image of long — term goals that may otherwise be too ephemeral to stimulate short — term sacrifices by adolescents.

In this way, social roles are developed in work and leisure, and conformist youths are socialized in the image of their adult mentors. But in its wake, this process of socialization, transition, and absorption of adult values raises questions about self–agency and adaptability in young people who face adult life in a rapidly changing society. As Mundy and Odum (1979) wrote: "Young people need to develop a cognitive, conscious awareness of their own behavior and beliefs ... establish criteria for leisure issues and decisions ... and develop skills related to enriching self–determination, pro–activity and meaningful control over their own leisure lives." In this way, it may be possible to enable young people to make the transition to adult life encouraged and guided by adults, but with a developing sense of self–agency.

References

Bone, M. (1972): The youth service and similar provision for young people. London: HMSO

Brake, M. (1980): The sociology of youth culture and youth sub–cultures. London: Routledge and Kegan Paul

Cochrane, M., & Bo, I. (1987): Connections between the social networks, family involvement and behavior of adolescent males in Norway. Paper presented at the Meeting of the Society for Research in Child Development, Baltimore, Maryland

Coffield, F., Borrill, C., & Marshall, S. (1983): How young people try to survive being unemployed. New Society, 2 June

Coleman, J.C. (1979): The school years: Current views on the adolescent process. London: Methuen

Conger, J. (1979): Adolescence: Generation under pressure. London: Harper and Row

Corrigan, P. (1979): Schooling the smash street kids. London: MacMillan

Davie, R., Butler, N., & Goldstein, H. (1972): From birth to seven. London: Longman

Davies, R.D.S. (1970): Youth service as a part of further education. In Bulman, I., Craft, M., & Milson, F. (Eds.): Youth service and inter–professional studies. London: Pergamon

De Grazia, S. (1962): Of time, work and leisure. New York: 20th Century Fund

Eggleston, J. (1976): Adolescence and community. London: Arnold

Emmett, I. (1971): Youth and leisure in an urban sprawl. Manchester: University Press

Emmett, I. (1977): Unpublished draft report to the Sports Council on decline in sports participation after leaving school. London: Sports Council

Erikson, E.H. (1968): Identity, youth and crisis. New York: Norton

Fogelman, K. (1976): Britain's sixteen year olds. London: National Child Bureau

Francis, L.J. (1985): Young and unemployed. London: Costello

Frith, S. (1978): The sociology of rock. London: Constable

Gordon, T., Lang, C.L., Nixon, J., Rockwood, R., & Wilson, G. (1974): The community education view of health, physical education and recreation. In Butcher, C.A. (Ed.): Dimensions of physical education. St. Louis: C.V. Mosby

Hamilton, S. (1986): Adolescent problem behavior in the U.S. and Federal Republic of Germany: Implications for prevention. In Hurrelmann, K., Kaufmann, F.X., & Lösel, F. (Eds.): Social intervention: Potential and constraints. New York: De Gruyter

Hargreaves, D.H. (1967): Social relations in a secondary school. London: Routledge and Kegan Paul

Hargreaves, D.H. (1972): Interpersonal relations and education. London: Routledge and Kegan Paul

Hendry, L.B. (1978): School, sport and leisure. London: Lepus

Hendry, L.B. (1981): Adolescents and leisure. London: Sports Council/SSRC

Hendry, L.B. (1983): Growing up and going out. Aberdeen: University Press

Hendry, L.B., & Simpson, D.O. (1977): One center: Two sub—cultures. Scottish Educational Studies, 9, 2, 112−121

Hendry, L.B., Brown, L., & Hutcheon, G. (1981): Adolescents in community centers: Some urban and rural comparisons. Scottish Journal of Physical Education, 9, 28−40

Hendry, L.B., & Percy, A. (1981): Pre—adolescents, television styles and leisure. Unpublished memorandum. University of Aberdeen

Hendry, L.B., & Raymond, M. (1983): Youth unemployment and lifestyles: Some educational considerations. Scottish Educational Review 15, 1, 28−40

Hendry, L.B., Raymond, M., & Stewart, C. (1984): Unemployment, school and leisure: An adolescent study. Leisure Studies 3: 175−187

Hendry, L.B., & Marr, D. (1985): Leisure education and young people's leisure. Scottish Educational Review, 17, 2, 116−127

Hendry, L.B., & Raymond, M. (1985): Coping with unemployment. Unpublished Report to the Scottish Education Department, Edinburgh

Hendry, L.B., Shucksmith, J., & McGrae, J. (1985): Young people's leisure and lifestyles in modern Scotland. Department of Education, University of Aberdeen and Scottish Sports Council, Edinburgh

Henry, J. (1966): Culture against man. London: Tavistock

Jahoda, M. (1979): The impact of unemployment in the 1930s and the 1970s. Bulletin of British Psychological Society, 32, 309−314

Jephcott, P. (1967): A time of one's own. Edinburgh: Oliver—Boyd

King, R. (1973): School organization and student involvement: A study of secondary schools. London: Routledge and Kegan Paul

Leigh, J. (1971): Young people and leisure. London: Routledge and Kegan Paul

Milson, F. (1972): Youth in a changing society. London: Routledge and Kegan Paul

Morton—Williams, R., & Finch, S. (1968): Enquiry 1: Young school—leavers. London: HMSO

Mundy, J., & Odum, L. (1979): Leisure: New York: Wiley

Murdock, G., & Phelps, G. (1973): Mass media and the secondary school. London: MacMillan

Musgrove, F. (1964): Youth and the social order. London: Routledge and Kegan Paul

Nisbet, J.D., Hendry, L.B., Stewart, C., & Watt, J. (1984): Participation in community groups. Oxford: Carfax

Parker, S. (1971): The future of work and leisure. London: MacGibbon and Kee

Reid, M. (1972): Comprehensive integration outside the classroom. Educational Research 14, 2, 28−34

Roberts, K. (1983): Youth and leisure. London: Allen and Unwin

Scarlett, C.L. (1975): Euroscot; the new European generation. Edinburgh: The Scottish Standing Conference of Voluntary Youth Organisations

Sharpe, S. (1977): Just like a girl. Harmondsworth: Penguin

Simpson, J. (1973): Education for leisure. In Smith, M.A., Parker, S., & Smith, S.C. (Eds.). Leisure and society in Britain. London: Allen Lane

Start, K.B. (1966): Substitution of games performance for academic achievement as a means of achieving status among secondary school children. Britsh Journal of Sociology, 17, 300−305

Stokes, G., & Cochrane, R. (1984): The relationship between national levels of unemployment and the rate of admission to mental hospitals in England and Wales (1950–76). Social Psychiatry, 19, 117–125

Sugarman, B. (1976): Involvement in youth culture: Academic achievement and conformity in school. British Journal of Sociology, 18, 157–164

Sutton–Smith, B., Roberts, J.M., & Kozelka, R.M. (1963): Games involvement in adults. Journal of Social Psychology, 60, 1, 15–30

Sutton–Smith, B., & Roberts, J.M. (1964): Rubrics of competitive behavior. Journal of Genetic Psychology, 105, 13–37

Weinstein, E.A. (1973): The development of interpersonal competence. In Goslin, D.A. (Ed.). Handbook of socialization theory and research. New York: Rand McNally

Willis, P. (1977): Learning to labor. Farnborough: Saxon House

16.

Changing Sex Roles, Lifestyles and Attitudes in an Urban Society

Alan J.C. King
Queen's University, Kingston, Canada

1. Introduction: Research Questions and Survey Samples

In Canada, as in other Western urban societies, young people are involved in a complex of socialization events, some of which change over time. These events coincide with emotional and physical changes and with the need to establish some career direction. But adolescence is also a long period of attendance in school, which provides young people with time to experiment and explore in circumstances that are both economically and socially supportive.

In this paper we discuss the lifestyles and attitudes of adolescents in Canada. We also explore the changes that have taken place over the past few years and examine the impact of these changes on Canadian youth. We focus on the 13 – to 18 – year – old age range, almost all of whom are in school to age 16 and nearly 70% to age 19.

The data used for the analysis come from three main sources:

1. A comprehensive survey of the in – and out – of – school activities of over 40,000 secondary school students in the largest province (The Adolescent Experience, 1986);

2. A survey of over 4,000 youth in the same province with regard to part – time work and school – leaving patterns (Student Retention and Transition Study, 1988); and,

3. A comprehensive national study providing information from 30,000 young people on self – concept, mental health, relationship with parents and peers, sexuality, school performance, and behavior related to alcohol, drug and

tobacco use (Canada Youth and AIDS Survey, 1988). The sample size by age for these studies appears in *Table 1*.

Table 1:   Sample size in three Canadian studies

	Ages					
Source	13	14	15	16	17	18
The Adolescent Experience	965	7,886	9,366	9,229	8,152	5,067
Student Retention and Transition Study	–	–	252	1,392	1,575	1,067
Canada Youth and Aids Study	–	11,826	–	10,598	–	7,130

Canada, the second largest country in the world, has a small population consisting of approximately 26 million people who are distributed unevenly across its ten provinces and two territories. Although the country as a whole is sparsely populated, over three – quarters of Canadians live in urban environments. The linguistic and ethnic composition of the Canadian population is diverse, but 88% of Canadians report their ethnic origin and mother tongue as English (61%) or French (27%). Indians represent only 2% of the population.

In spite of Canada's size, there is great commonality in adolescent values. Young people from coast to coast feel similarly about their parents, have similar career aspirations, and feel pressured by the same issues. There are some differences between the Francophone and Anglophone adolescents, but these are not substantial differences and are much smaller than they have been in the past. In many areas of social change, Quebec has been in the vanguard (e.g., education and the arts).

There are economic differences that affect the lifestyles of Canadian youth. Employment opportunities are not equal across the country. In some parts, welfare and unemployment become an acceptable lifestyle and actually strengthen family ties, while in others they are responsible for the disruption of family life.

Canadian native people have never been fully integrated into society and manifest many characteristics of alienation and disaffection. Although we have responses in the Canada Youth and AIDS Survey from native adolescents, they represent too small a part in the overall sample to develop in detail.

2. Results: Lifestyle and Attitudes of Canadian Adolescents

Changing sex roles

A remarkable change has transpired in the past few years in the aspirations of young girls. A few years ago when we asked adolescent girls early in secondary school what their future plans were, the majority would say, "I don't know." Now virtually every student offers some career plan with more girls than boys having clarity in their career plans. Girls typically achieve higher marks than boys in Canadian secondary schools. They feel more pressure to achieve in school and appear to suffer more strain because of the value they place on academic achievement. Their attitude is perceived by teachers as more appropriate for learning and they are more inclined to do homework. But because in the past they were less motivated or career – directed than boys, they were more inclined to leave school earlier. This has changed. More girls than boys are now enrolled in university – bound programs in secondary school and more girls than boys are enrolled in community colleges: Male and female enrolments in universities are now quite similar.

There do seem to be some adverse effects of this change in the outlook of girls. In spite of the success girls have in school, they are more likely than boys to have low self – esteem and be concerned about achievement in subjects such as mathematics and science. Girls also are more concerned with their physical appearance. As well, girls seem to experience more strain in their relationship with parents. Part of this is related to parents being unable to provide direction and role models for young women in their search for meaningful careers. Girls seem to be quite aware of the potential of strain in mixing a career with marriage and child rearing. They typically plan to do all three but have some difficulty in working out the logistics. On the other hand, boys, when describing their futures, rarely mention marriage and family as they take this part of their lives for granted and do not recognize that they will have to share family responsibilities with working wives. The potential for conflict is considerable.

Another change among young Canadian women is the increase in importance given to their friendship groups in the latter years of secondary school and into postsecondary education and the world of work. The traditional pattern of female cliques had been one of growth in the early secondary school years, stability in the middle years, and a collapsing in the senior years as male/female relationships increase in priority. The pattern has changed in that the strength of the cliques actually increases in the latter years of secondary school. In fact, dependence on friends for advice on major decisions is so great among some girls that shared misinformation on career possibilities leads to inappropriate course selection in secondary school. *Table 2* illustrates the male — female difference on statements about friendship.

Table 2:   Students agreeing with items about the importance of friends, by gender

	% Agree	
	Male	Female
When I have a big decision to make, I ask my friends.	48	68
What my friends think of me is very important to me.	75	82
I discuss my problems with friends.	57	79
My friends often ask me for advice and help.	59	85
I have a lot of friends.	86	88
If I have a problem, I usually keep it to myself.	52	36

Source: The Adolescent Experience, 1986.

The secondary school social environment provides opportunity for the cultivation of serious male/female relationships. When asked an open — ended question about major concerns, surprisingly few of the respondents indicated any concerns about sexual issues, and the vast majority of young people feel that they get along well with the opposite sex.

Although concerns about sexual issues do not come up spontaneously when young people are asked to describe their major concerns, their level of sexual activity is greater than most parents suspect. Perhaps this is because sexual matters are an aspect that adolescents keep to themselves and parents probably consciously ignore. *Table 3* shows, by age, the percentage of students who have had at least one sexual experience.

Table 3:   At least one sexual experience, by age

		% Agree Age	
Gender	14	16	18
Male	30	52	78
Female	24	48	74

Source: Canada Youth and AIDS Survey, 1988.

The pattern is very similar to that evident in the United States and some European countries. There is clearly a heightened fear in young people about sexual relationships because of AIDS. Many young people talk about monogamous relationships, others about waiting until marriage before becoming sexually involved.

More girls than boys are concerned about protection from disease and pregnancy during sexual intercourse. It is interesting that males are far more homophobic than females, more likely to be afraid of being touched by someone of the same sex, and more antagonistic toward people with AIDS.

There is a heavy burden of expectations the contemporary Canadian adolescent girl must bear. According to our study, a girl feels pressure to be slim, clear — skinned, and physically attractive; she must have a career in mind, preferably one that requires a postsecondary education; she must also plan on being a good wife and mother. She must protect herself carefully to avoid pregnancy and sexually transmitted diseases. All this must be accomplished while trying to attend to the expectations of parents and the influence of a powerful peer group.

Family

The concept of family is important to Canadian adolescents. They are strongly influenced by their parents throughout their school lives and universally declare that what their parents think of them is important. *Table 4* indicates that three — quarters of young adolescents live with their natural parents.

Table 4:   Home status, by age

		Age	
Home status	12	14	16
Mother and father	75	75	75
Mother only	11	10	10
Father only	2	3	2
Mother and stepfather	6	7	6
Father and stepmother	2	2	2
Guardian	1	2	2
Other	3	2	3

Source: Canada Youth and AIDS Survey, 1988

The majority of young people who do not live with both parents are similar in many respects to those who do. Those who live with their mother only are more likely to come from low socioeconomic status homes; more likely to drink alcohol, smoke, and take drugs; but only slightly more likely to have lower marks in school.

Young people's views of marriage and family are different depending on their family background. Those from broken homes say it is less likely that they will marry and that they will raise their children differently from the way they were raised. Girls from broken homes seem more influenced by their home situation with regard to how they would raise their children, but are less influenced than boys in their intention to marry.

The vast majority (80%) of young Canadians expect to marry and have children. These numbers have not changed substantially over the years.

Religion

Nearly half of Canadians are Roman Catholic with just over 40 percent Protestant (Canada Year Book, 1988), but as can be seen from *Table 5*, less than 30% of young people regularly attend church. There has been a steady decline in the proportion of young people who go to church regularly. Table 5 indicates that the proportions also decline as young people get older.

Table 5:   Church attendance, by age

| Attendance | % Attending | | | |
| | Age | | | |
	12	14	16	18
Weekly	30	24	22	17
Now and then	24	21	20	20
Special occasions	21	28	30	35
Never	26	27	28	27

Source: Canada Youth and AIDS Survey, 1988

With regard to many adolescent behaviors, there are sharp differences between young people who attend church and those who do not. Those who go to church regularly are less likely to drink alcohol, smoke, and engage in sex at an early age. Church does appear to have a strong conservative influence on young people's values, and as fewer and fewer are attending church, permissiveness in their values is increasing.

Part—time work

Perhaps the most significant change over the past 15 years in the leisure—time activity of Canadian youth is in the amount of time students work part time. As can be seen from *Table 6*, nearly two—thirds of students at least 16 years of age work part time. Another 20% are actively looking for jobs.

Table 6:   Percentage of students working part time, by age

Age	%
15	51
16	57
17	65
18	70
19	71

Source: Student Retention and Transition Study, 1988

Surprisingly, there are no significant differences by gender, socioeconomic status, or postsecondary career aspirations. Nearly 40% of students who work do so for 21 hours or more a week. Most of the students who work part time spend their money on their own personal needs (about 85%). Very few save, contribute to family spending, or are self–supporting. The money is spent on clothes (probably with the tacit approval of parents who appreciate the saving), records, entertainment, and visits to fast–food emporiums. In fact, the students spend their money in great part in the very places in which they work. What we have, then, is an adolescent subculture designed around activities that need financing; a subculture directly linked to the economy which serves it and fuels it through cheap labor.

The students provide low–cost labor; they present themselves well and are enthusiastic and flexible in the hours they work. As such, they represent an extremely valuable and inexpensive labor resource. They are typically supported in their work efforts by employers with performance reviews involving regular wage increments and recognition in the form of programs such as Employee of the Month. Greenberger and Steinberg (1986) are critical of the amount of part–time work in which students are involved. They argue that it creates bad habits in terms of spending that causes difficulty in the future and gives students the impression of flexibility regarding when and how long they work. There is a counter–argument that working part time increases young people's sense of responsibility and understanding of the world of work. But there is a real intrusion on the young people's time. This influences their involvement in school activities, the time they have for homework, and even time with friends and family.

In Canada, unlike many European countries, the relationship between school and work is not well developed. There is no tradition of business and industry being involved with schools in programs such as apprenticeships. Therefore, the part–time work experience of young people does not translate readily into transition to work. The vast majority of students who work part time do not expect to work full time in the same kinds of jobs. The rapid growth of cooperative education (in which students gain school credits for supervised work outside school) may improve the relationship between schools and the private sector of the economy.

Leisure activities

Young Canadians spend a great deal of time in front of television sets, but as they get older they spend less time watching television and more in part–time jobs and socializing with friends. We found very little relationship between the number of hours young people watch television and the amount of school work they do. However, those who watch 30 hours or more do seem to experience more school – related adjustment problems.

Deviant behavior

The social unrest of the late 1960s and early 1970s did not affect Canadian young people as substantially as it did Americans and Western Europeans. Today, there is very litte evidence of the tradition of picketing or other collective political activity, and most schools are unaffected by political activism. Canadian youth tend to be conservative in their behavior and notably career – oriented. There is a degree of deviance in schools characterized by poor attendance patterns and an unwillingness to perform at a reasonable level. This seems in part to be related to the necessity of secondary schools to sort students and the response of less successful students to this process in the form of a counter system. However, even the socially deviant are relatively placid and are characterized by clothing and hairstyle abberations and music and social interests that are not socially destructive.

The period of adolescence is characterized by sexual experimentation and risk taking. The negative life circumstances experienced by some youths encourage even greater risk – taking behavior. A very small proportion of Canadian youth take to the streets of Canada's major cities. These youths represent a subculture that is steeped in risk – taking. Their everyday life struggle precludes concern over the consequences of their actions. "Street kids" are entrenched in a world that encourages sexual activity, promiscuity, and an excessive use of drugs and alcohol (*Figure 1*).

Today, in Canada, street life is a small but growing subculture, and young people represent a significant part of this lifestyle. These youths are considered lazy and delinquent. In the past, vagrancy was typically associated with economic crisis, poverty, and mental health problems. Today street youths are less likely to be regarded as the product of poverty but more as runaways who have rejected the responsibility of education and employment.

Many of the street youth are not running to the streets but rather from their homes. Furthermore, they are often abandoned or thrown out of their parents' homes. Although some youths are attracted by the exciting lifestyle of the street, the majority are there out of desperation. These young people represent a potential breeding ground for the growth of the AIDS epidemic.

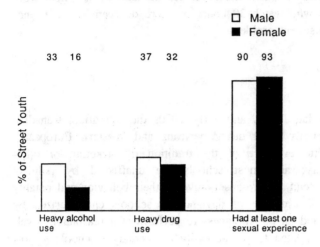

Fig. 1: Alcohol use, drug use, and sexual activity of street youth, by gender

Attitudes

Young Canadians seem disenchanted with their politicians and the way they are responding to issues such as pollution and the proliferation of nuclear weapons. But they are not inclined to take action in any collective fashion. They tend to be accepting of the larger society and anxious to find a place for themselves that involves a financially rewarding career.

The vast majority of young Canadians say they are happy and the majority (86%) like themselves. There is, however, still evidence of strain; depression and loneliness seem to be particularly present in the younger years of adolescence. Those experiencing the greatest strain also seem to have a less than satisfactory relationship with their parents. In fact, negative parental relationships are strong predictors of deviant behavior and mental health concerns in Canadian adolescents.

In our 1986 study we found many young people were concerned about the possibilities of nuclear war and future unemployment, but on both these issues our 1988 study shows a sharp decrease in the numbers of youth concerned about East — West tensions and economic issues.

3.   Conclusions

Canada is a country relatively unaffected by war, violence, and social unrest. Its people can be characterized as conservative and law–abiding. Adolescents share many of the same values as their parents. They value marriage and family, tolerance of others, independence, and friendship. The adolescent subculture is defined by strong friendship grouping with dependence on each other for social interaction and management of the strains of adolescence. The greatest social changes that have occurred in the lives of Canadian adolescents in the past few years relate to (1) the rapid growth of an economy of products and services designed to support their interests and financed by their own part–time work, (2) the expectation among virtually all young girls that they will work outside the home for most of their lives, and (3) the priority placed on educational and career matters over social and political issues.

References

Bibby, R.W., & Posterski, D.G. (1985): The emerging generation: An inside look at Canada's teenagers. Toronto: Irwin Publishing Co

Canada Yearbook (1988): Ottawa: Queen's Printer

Csikszentmihalyi, M., & Larson, R. (1984): Being adolescent: Conflict and growth in the teenage years. New York: Basic Books

Greenberger, E., & Steinberg, L. (1986): When teenagers work: The psychological and social costs of adolescent employment. New York: Basic Books

King, A.J.C. (1986): The adolescent experience. Toronto: Ontario Secondary School Teachers' Federation, 1986

King, A.J.C., Warren, W.K., Michalski, C., & Peart, M.J. (in press): Student retention and transition study. Toronto: Ontario Ministry of Education

King, A.J.C., Beazley, R.P., Warren, W.K., Robertson, A.S., & Hankins, C.A. (in press): Canada youth and AIDS survey. Ottawa: Health and Welfare in Canada

Part IV
Social Milieus and Biographical Concepts

17.

The Importance of Peer Groups in Different Regional Contexts and Biographical Stages

Wolfgang Gaiser and Hans Ulrich Müller
German Youth Institute, Munich, Federal Republic of Germany

1. Introduction

This paper discusses specific conditional structures and patterns concerning the importance of peer groups in various social and ecological contexts (small towns, modern suburban housing, and urban working — class areas). Our empirical survey is based on results of a research project "Socialization and Environment" (Hübner — Funk, Müller and Gaiser, 1983; Müller, 1983) and on a follow — up survey "Socioecology and Biography" (Gaiser, 1985; Gaiser, 1988). Repeated interviews with the same adolescents and/or young adults at various stages of their lives (upper elementary school, vocational training, career) allow us to arrive at statements about continuity and change in the structures and the content of the peer group culture. Our focus is on students in "Hauptschule": the low — prestige secondary school with grades 5 to 9, usually leading into apprenticeship and/or lower level paid work, mostly attended by working — class adolescents.

As a second step we will present considerations and first results from the pilot stage of a project presently conducted at the "Deutsches Jugendinstitut": "Lebenslage (Life Conditions) and Life Management in the Postgraduate Phase: Adolescents and Young Adults in Rural Regions and in Urban Areas" (Böhnisch, Funk, Gaiser and Müller, 1988; Böhnisch and Funk, 1988; Gaiser and Müller, in press). Here we will stress peer groups as a factor in life situations and their function as resources for everyday life management in a time in which adolescence is continuously prolonged and is becoming increasingly complicated.

2.   Peer Groups in the Socioecological Context

The specific importance of peer groups can be explained with reference to the parameters of the biographical phase, the gender – specific roles, and the contexts of family and school in various socioecological environments. In our studies, these parameters have been introduced by the following field approaches:

1.   The basis survey has been established through standardized interviews with a total of 140 students at Hauptschule (73 male, 65 female), conducted in 1976/77 in three different residential areas of Bavaria in West Germany: a modern suburban housing project, an urban working class area close to downtown Munich, and a small town in Lower Bavaria. The students were interviewed 3 months prior to their graduation from the Hauptschule – after 9 years of schooling.

2.   Group interviews were conducted 5 to 6 months after graduation. Because most of the former students were by then apprentices or involved in some kind of vocational training, they were interviewed about their experiences at their jobs and during their training, and about changes in their lifestyles.

3.   At the end of 1981, all of the 140 former Hauptschule graduates were contacted again by mail for a follow – up survey. By now they were almost all fully trained in their professions and were asked for information about their life situations.

4.   In the autumn of 1982, individual biographical interviews were conducted with the young adults – selected on the basis of the data from 1981 – about their further experiences in their private and professional lives.

Toward the end of the Hauptschule, the following social constellations predominate:

1.   Several gender – specific characteristics can be noticed among all three groups of Hauptschule students: During the last year of Hauptschule many girls are already engaged in a relationship with an older boy or young man. Friendships with one good friend are more frequent among girls than among boys. Boys prefer their "cliques" for being among themselves. Boys recruit participants for their recreational activities from the population of their class at school much more than their female classmates. Both female and male students indicated their preference for a mixed "clique" as the context from which to choose their peers. But various kinds of tensions seem to exist between the genders, especially in coed classes: Girls often find their male classmates stupid, childish, boastful, crazy, or weird; to the boys the girls seem too dependent on their families, or too focused

on relationships with older boys. In this way a gap is created in the class that can only be bridged in part through individual contacts.

2. The importance of the Hauptschule as a forum for peer group contact clearly depends on socioecological factors:

    In the *modern suburban housing area* the relationhips of adolescents indicate that traditional social structures, borne by a network of friends and relatives among families, are mostly missing. The recreational needs of adolescents were neglected in the planning of this housing area. Because of a lack of acoustic and visual separation of the spontaneous meeting places, complaints by the residents led to their closing. In this way, the Hauptschule gains an additional function besides its educational relevance, that is, the focus and switchboard for personal relations among peers.

    In the *urban working—class area* adolescents consider school an unpleasant obligation rather than a possibility for contacts with peers, because here they must spend a great amount of time that they would prefer to spend quite differently. Only in this survey region does skipping school class come into play as a means of "creating" extra leisure time. Conditions for recreational activities are heterogeneous and varied: Youth organizations, a swimming pool, public squares, parks, as well as pubs that admit young people and are attractive for them. This situation offers numerous recreational possibilities aside from those organized by the institutions. The ninth graders here belong comparatively rarely to "cliques" recruited from their school classes, and at the same time this is a group that is the least organized in clubs. A substantial number belong to a "clique" independent of the school context.

    In the *small town* area the Hauptschule is a generally respected institution. Contacts among students outside of school are quite natural as they are based on previously established connections between the families. Thus the interaction among adolescents can develop within social structures that are the result of relationships among relatives, neighbors, and of the economic structure in the small town. The individual was either born into this preestablished network, or is an outsider. Transgressions of the border lines are possible, but not a simple matter; a fact that makes itself felt less in the small town itself than in the surrounding villages that the Hauptschule also serves. Recreational activities are predesigned along the lines of local traditions and organizations. Therefore, a frequent consequence of the participation in youth groups is that adolescents adopt the values, the standards of achievement, and the integrational aspects of these rather traditionally oriented organizations.

3. Thus the Hauptschule has little importance as a forum for peer contacts in the urban working—class area, great importance in the modern suburban housing area, and medium importance in the small town. These proportions are also reflected in the organizational degree of adolescent activities: 71% of the young people in the suburban housing project try to compensate for the lack of recreational opportunities and spaces for informal contact through membership in clubs and organizations, whereas 43% of the adolescents in the urban working—class area and only 55% of the respondents in the small town are organized.

Peer support for life management

After their graduation from the Hauptschule, adolescents are more dependent than before on socioeconomic conditions and their own competence in order to build, develop, and maintain a network of social relationships, because the social interaction as a side effect of school life no longer exists for them. However, in this biographical phase of growing up (leaving home, starting a career, finding an own apartment, starting committed relationships) with its complicated changes, peer groups gain an increasing and new importance. Especially informal contacts and informational network and mutual support become more significant, because the institutionalized pathways on the housing and job markets of the 1980s lead to decreasingly satisfying living and working situations.

In this way the peer group gains a function beyond its recreational aspect in offering orientation and concrete support in everyday life management and in serious decisions about the adolescents' future:

1. The importance of a network of friends and peers, already established during the years at the Hauptschule, becomes obvious: Peer groups that support the individual beyond mere recreational activities are characterized by the impossibility to create them when needed. They rather depend upon a previously established basis of trust as the basis on which involvement, mutuality, and adequacy can be expected. This applies especially to situations in which the chances to experience loyalty normally are low. For trainees/apprentices in small companies (usually the most frequent occupational training situation for adolescents in West Germany) the group loyalty that had been or can be developed elsewhere becomes very important. These other contexts are very often the socioecological environment and the former Hauptschule.

2. Graduation from the Hauptschule initiates a considerable difference between female and male adolescents in reference to their peer groups: Among girls the tendency to turn away from the Hauptschule context increases. At the same time they are increasingly oriented toward the peer group of their boyfriend and toward friendships with girls. Boys, however, still prefer gender — homogeneous peer groups that are often recruited from their former classmates or from the members of their youth organizations. Independently from the survey region, boys and girls alike, however, maintain the contact with former classmates. Conversations occurring in casual encounters and questions asked at class reunions reveal some

interest in news also about those not present, their professional and private lives, and about their well – being.

3. The adolescents in the urban working – class area know most about each other. Coincidental encounters in the area are used for extensive conversations. Also here, boys maintain closer contact with former classmates than girls. To the same degree to which the Hauptschule and the classmates had been only one part in a complex social background for adolescents in the small town before graduation, former classmates do not play a specific role in their peer groups afterwards either. This applies to girls and boys similarly. Coincidental encounters among former schoolmates are more rare in the modern suburban housing area, but if they happen they are used extensively for exchanging news. Adolescents here employ the quasi institutional form of class reunions more enthusiastically than adolescents in the other survey regions. A network of new peer groups is least developed in the suburban housing area, and therefore reunions with former friends from school and class are welcomed.

Peer groups and growing up

The character of our survey as a longitudinal study (more than 6 years) allows us to look at the changing importance of peer groups in the process of growing up: Before graduation peer groups played an important role for recreational activities, for the formation of the adolescents' personality and identity, and for experiencing and respecting equal relationships. In the process of growing up the adolescents experience the additional relevance of the peer group for life management: Beyond friendship, sex, culture, fashion, politics, and daily events, now the problems discussed include decisions about larger expenses, the choices of going into debt or saving money, choosing a career and selecting/finding an employer, looking for an apartment, and so forth. Before graduation the parents, the family, and the Hauptschule presented the adolescents with alternatives in an upcoming decision, whereas now the network of friends takes the role of providing advice and help.

When comparing "loners" and "activists" in our survey, the role of friends became especially clear: Loners were finding themselves more frequently than activists in a dead – end road, depending exclusively on institutional help, and being dissatisfied with decisions they had taken.

The increased importance of friends and private contexts must be seen on one hand as the result of the individuals' changing values and goals (Zinnecker, 1987). On the other hand, it is a result of fundamental social changes: In reference to the segmentation of the job market and the tightening of the housing market, social background and connections become increasingly important for an advantageous placement within the existing structures of life. For peer groups this can turn into a stress factor: While individuals and their personal rapport are dominant in the choice of friends and recreational relationships, "material" interests become increasingly part of the structure of these relationships: "Am I approached, accepted, respected as a person or just as the holder of certain social resources?" As a mutual process, this gives room to reservations and scepticism, which can arise and affect the spontaneity and the openness essential for peer relations.

At the same time these ambivalences are embedded in the general pluralization of life concepts and the individualization of biographical developments. Social integration and the formation of the identity become precarious: More complex expectations toward people come into existence together with new demands in reference to the maintenance and the perspectives of social networks. And accordingly, the successful integration requires a highly creative potential on the individual's side. Social psychologists call the resulting phenomenon the "patchwork identity" (Keupp, 1988), for which they acknowledge the possibility of a gain in the potential for a creative life without the loss of inner coherence.

3.   Peer Networking as a Factor in the Life Situation of Young Adults

Our interviews with the former Hauptschule students have already shown several phenomena that have been addressed in the sociological discussion under the terms "prolonged adolescence", and " postadolescence" (Zinnecker, 1981; Hurrelmann, Rosewitz and Wolf, 1985; Hornstein, 1985; Böhnisch and Schefold, 1985; Lutz, 1987; Bertram, 1988).

In general the life situation ("Lebenslage") of young adults can be characterized as follows: We observe a postgraduate phase that, due to changes in and the crisis of the work – oriented society, takes place below the socially accepted status of autonomy. Adolescents in this phase have to cope with processes of searching and the task of finding orientations. They must find ways to combine and connect their own psychological and social development with the available forms and stages of the professional and economic development in society. It might become as essential, however, to disconnect the two, because the conventional transitions into the employment system as well as the standards of the grown – up world have become less smooth and are decreasingly suited to offer orientations. The daily challenge for adolescents in this situation consists in "coping", in developing a life – style that will correspond adequately with their real situation.

Accordingly, structure and meaning of the postgraduate phase of adolescence can no longer be defined by the term "status passage". The traditional concept of adolescence as a period of learning and preparing, as a time of psychological and social development as it has been employed in the theory of socialization no longer quite suffices to describe the postgraduate phase and the social and cultural self – reliance necessary in this biographical stage. The need arises therefore to expand the biographically functional definition of adolescence as a status passage as well as the understanding of the theory of socialization of adolescence as a period of preparation, by introducing another viewpoint that will describe and analyze this "later adolescence" as a set of specific, independent, and differentiated "Lebenslagen".

The term "Lebenslage" offers a concept that allows us to connect and to evaluate the observed changes of life situations and of adolescent behavior on the one hand, with the general contexts of social development and change on the other.

The interaction patterns of adolescents during this phase of their lives must be interpreted as patterns of managing complicated and problematic situations specific for this life phase. Specifically relevant and predominantly important among the parameters of Lebenslage are those of professional qualification and income, socioecological conditions, and gender – specific structures of opportunities.

A structure of requirements, for example, becomes part of the reproductive function of peer relations, due to their increasing relevance for the management of everyday life. They become an important part within the entire network of peers beyond the age group, and the young adults themselves are responsible for maintaining the network. In these structures the peers are potential supporters and users of supportive activities as well as potential competitors. In this way the peer group turns into a multifaceted phenomenon, contradictory in itself.

To the same degree to which institutionalized biographical patterns disappear, the individuals become responsible for shaping and planning their own biography. Therefore, peer groups, as groups of "contemporaries" subjected to the same developments, are relevant as a frame of reference.

These outlines are, of course, still too general: After a temporarily homogenizing process, to which adolescents with different social backgrounds are subjected in the educational system and institutions, social inequalities and differentiations (class—, gender—, region—specific; inequality of social opportunities and disadvantages) reemerge in the postgraduate phase. The importance of the postgraduate existence varies considerably. Even in rather clearly definable groups (e.g., young women and young men, adolescents in rural and in urban areas, etc.) relevant differences can be expected that call for further differentiation.

General factors of the Lebenslage in the city

The following refers to the section "city" of the abovementioned research project; the data used have been acquired in the pilot stage of the project, consisting of the following survey sequence:

1. A representative survey on the "life situations of young adults in Munich".
2. Eight group discussions (with a total of 80 participants) covering the following topics: housing, vocational training, education, careers, job, recreation, infrastructure of the city, life conditions for young women, self—images, life concepts, and plans.
3. Open interviews with 12 young adults.
4. Expert hearings about vocational training, work, and housing.

Several general aspects of life management in the postgraduate phase of adolescence in the city should be acknowledged first: There is a decrease in the idealizing perception of the city as a place where professional career advancement and the realization of social and cultural goals are granted. The multiple odds of the job— and housing market are evaluated quite realistically. The disproportion between cultural events, the variety of possibilities offered by the city's infrastructure, and their own financial resources take a central part in the everyday experience of these young adults. Finally, they clearly perceive the risks and problems of social integration.

We have to understand these perceptions in the context of the increasing disparities of the social and the economic development in the various urban and conurbation areas in West Germany. One of the central sources of disparity is a regionally uneven distribution of "old" and "new" industries, producing the polarization of two types of urban development: On one hand, we find the "winners", prosperous cities like the conurbations of Munich, Stuttgart, and Frankfurt, on the other hand are the "losers": declining cities like Bremen, Saarbrücken, and the cities in the Ruhr area. The regional disparity is reproduced within the cities themselves: Talking about social segregation we are including the social and geographical inequalities between the "rich" and the "poor" neighborhoods of the cities. Even though this type of segregation concerns the declining cities more than others, it cannot be assumed that the conditions of life in the prosperous cities would be equally positive for all social classes and groups. Economic growth can very well coincide with increasing social disparity. Many indicators suggest that a considerable number of young adults are located on the dark side of prosperity.

Among the young adults, processes of segregation take place that are due to the limited access to and the separation among various peer networks. Polarization trends can be observed, separating those who are rather established, advancing in their careers, and making a good living, from those whose background already gave them a more difficult start, who are less successful in their education, and who presently have a hard time making ends meet. The chances of sliding down from the middle into this kind of situation are considered higher than the chances of social advancement. Participation in the glamour of the costly world of leisure is only occasionally possible.

For young adults the major question is to find a balance of integration and life management adequate to the general development and the life conditions in society. For this, some consistent aspects must be considered:

1. Above all, young women encounter more obstacles in opening resources of life management for themselves, professionally as much as privately and socially. More than young men they depend on lower paying professions and jobs, and urban "scenes" of adolescents and young adults are obviously still not unconditionally accessible for single women. In many public spaces, for example, in subway stations, parks, on certain blocks, and in bars, women frequently feel insecure and threatened. They also experience higher pressure toward adjustment in respect to their autonomy and their growing — up.

2. Secondly, we observe in young adults a generally low inclination to concern themselves with long — term plans for their future. A strong sense of the here and now and a concentration on the short — term goals of life management seems significant. This attitude, however, is not at all

hedonistic, nor does the short—term orientation exclude perspectives, only the time concepts are narrower, and the present claims priority in relation to the future. Concentration on the present does not necessarily translate into an easy going attitude toward everyday life, it rather means stress, full schedules, and time pressure on daily scores. Attention has been shifted from the preoccupation with a future adult life — for which certain abstentions in the present seemed acceptable — to the management of the present. The young adults have reported how time—consuming it can be to coordinate and integrate into normal life the demands of their professional work and studies, the search for jobs, the integration of their job into their daily and weekly routine, the realization of their own lives and their independence, the indispensable input into the communication with and maintenance of social networks, and finally the obligations in relationships and friendships. Much energy, creativity, and also money is needed in order to create forms of living that correspond with the desire for autonomy and an independant life—style as well as they enable the young adults to participate in the advantages of the urban environment.

3. Another general aspect is that everyday life is at least influenced, if not dominated, by specific economic calculations: There is the question: "What do I want, what can I afford, which things do I need in my life"; and on the other hand the problem of assuring sufficient financial means. Even if prosperous regions, like Munich, for example, present a large variety of possible occupations, jobs, temporary employment, and substitute or seasonal jobs, these types of income are earned outside of the traditional job market and therefore outside of state—and union—regulated securities and benefits. These circumstances require that the individual is prepared to deal with short—term, partly parallel and intertwining phases of work, achievement, income, qualification, training, continuous learning, leisure, traveling, and consumption. The resulting complex structure of demands leads more often than not to a biased self—image of the young adults, oscillating between optimism and positive self—perception at one time, and insecurity and scepticism in regard to the future at other times. When peers live in similar situations, there is a better opportunity to work through the frequently changing and contradictory experiences; this way the peer group provides the long term effect of supplying some stability, of supporting the development of an individual identity, and helping with further moves.

4. A last general aspect is the relation between generations. Economic support from parents is considered a normal part of the existentially mandatory support system up into the late 20s, for example, in the form of a financial

contribution to the costs of independent living that is justified through the expensive urban housing market. Separation from the parents is not a big topic; as topics of the communication between the generations, we find rather the obligations and the chances for creating an individual way of life management. The young adults describe rather nonconflicting relationships with their parents. They make use of the urban possibilities to create local and social distance by choosing different geographical and communicative areas, and are therefore able to reduce the friction between members of different generations.

4. Patterns of life management

In this section we will outline four tentative patterns of life management as possible responses to specific life situations and life problems of young adults. Lebenslagen of young adults in the city of Munich will be illuminated from the side of the subjective experience of everyday life. We will ask for the terms of interaction with the objective structures of the socioeconomic situation in order to reconstruct a slice of the adolescents' personal reality.

We have constructed these patterns on the basis of the qualitative materials from the group discussions and individual interviews mentioned above. The different patterns of life management can be characterized with the terms "maintaining options", "conventional adjustment", "ritualization", and "withdrawing". It became clear, however, that there are also forms of unsuccessful or only partly successful life management, especially in cases in which a lack of support from family and friends, unemployment, and homelessness create much instability and discontinuity in the daily life. The four above – mentioned patterns of life management provide specific solutions for specific problems; if these problems, however, concentrate in particularly resourceless situations, the young adults facing them become existentially dependent on the support system (social and youth services) of the welfare state.

"Maintaining options"

"Things are only happening in small groups, or if you get involved somewhere politically, or at the cultural center... . I'm working parttime as a social worker for children, from noon to 5 P.M. In the mornings I have a job from 7 to 11.15 helping in the house, like babysitting, cooking, cleaning, whatever comes around. I go there three times a week. On those days I'm really pooped, and I don't feel like doing anything else afterwards. But if I wouldn't do that job I'd have less money than when I was a student... . But then the rent wasn't that high either — actually, I had more money than I have now. Working for the city as a social worker, you don't make a lot of money in the first year, about 10.000 Marks. From that I wouldn't be able to live, paying the rent and everything. Since I took this part—time job, the money is ok, but I don't have much time any more — only on weekends — but during the week I'm glad if I sometimes have an evening for myself." (A 24—year—old social worker who shares an apartment with other people.)

In this pattern we find no vertical life plan, and accordingly the spaces for life management, in equal parts the professional and the reproductive realm, have to be developed. We do not find the segments of an individual life linked with defined and socially normative biographical stages. The point is rather, as we see it, to disconnect traditional transitions and biographical sequences, to combine objectively disparate and seemingly contradictory chances and opportunities, in order to live an individual biography, "to make ends meet". The entry into working life, the individual professional career, the daily confrontation with the regional job market, which does not offer much security and stability — here these problems are faced with realistically engaged and sceptical thoughts. The danger is seen much rather in too quick and too early commitments, in choosing dead—end streets, or in spending too much of one's energies and resources in the areas of work and career.

There are ambivalent concepts of short—term and long—term life management. A frequent phrase is "on the one hand — on the other hand" — doing something and finding out if it will develop into something meaningful, and if so, how and into what. Always ready to start something else as well; taking one direction and still keeping alternatives in mind — be it professionally or privately. The reproductive areas of life are an important part in this pattern: building social networks and making as many different contacts in the "scenes" of the city as possible, creating an independant life by having an apartment of one's own. Leisure time is not a remainder but rather an important constituent of everyday life. The attempted balance of the productive and reproductive orientation leads to choices among the available opportunities: not always the most advantageous ones in reference to long—term income and a career, since the goal is seen in keeping all or almost all alternatives available and choosing only those opportunities that allow the combination of work—related and private interests. We find a utilitarian orientation toward the constituents of the urban social infrastructure, and subjective momentary needs are the criteria for the selection from the variety of possibilities.

"Conventional adjustment"

"I have been living by myself for 3 years now; I do a lot of sports, I'm doing this and that, right now I'm taking a master class. I have a lot of things going on, and presently I have a girlfriend. To be honest, this confines me most, that's almost like living with my parents again... Okay, once you have made something happen, well, then you can talk about children, but before that? No way." (24 – years – old, employed in public enterprise).

The pattern "conventional adjustment" is shared by young women and men who give their professional training, their education, and their profession high priority. The goals to be achieved are good grades at graduation, a secure job with a sound company and in an expanding field, sufficient income, and a career. The nonprofessional areas of life are dominated by these goals. Within this pattern it is important to lead a stable and organized life and to avoid risks related to experiments and the untimely satisfaction of material and immaterial needs. A frequently used line expresses this principle: "Everything has it's right time and place".

The postgraduate phase, experienced in the present, is considered important as the time for setting future directions. This way it serves in a rather traditional way as a period of preparation for adult life and conforms largely with the expectations of the older generation. Qualifications and professional placement are clearly in the foreground, peer group relationships, personal development, and dating are just a part of life, not priorities. We find very consciously planned moves in the biographies, and there are hierarchies in the life – styles: professional training comes first, then the entry into a professional career with a positive outlook, including possibilities for further qualifications, and only then or parallel with this, the young adults admit time and space for their private lives, for friendships, and their social life.

Among the women and men who follow the conventional pattern the perspectives for the future clearly differ depending on gender: While the period in their lives in which they will live with a wife and children is imagined by most young men as a natural, almost automatic sequence after having performed all prior biographical tasks, young women have much more differentiated thoughts and concepts about combining a career with a family. They also attribute priority to higher education and/or professional training as a specific and biographically relevant stage. After they have successfully entered their career, however, they often insist on the traditional distribution of roles. Once they are married and have children, it is they, and not their partners, who are responsible for the family household. They do not describe this traditional pattern with any undertone of regret or complaint against gender – specific disadvantages, they rather make a point of seeing the advantages of a life around the house.

"Ritualization"

"I couldn't even imagine that I would have to look for an apartment myself, it seemed an unmanageable thing to me, and also I thought that my parents would somehow take care of this." (23 years, furrier; she lives by herself in a studio apartment for DM 500 a month, with a monthly income of DM 1,300 net).

We call the third pattern of life management in the postgraduate phase "ritualization". By this we understand the behavioral patterns in which certain biographically necessary steps are performed and untimely ones postponed, without prior reflection, however, on the conditions or consequences of these steps. The "social clock" is more decisive than spontaneous ideas or unorthodox plans of life design. These young adults rather willingly accept the common patterns of behavior adequate to age and status and are not very eager to shape them individually. They would, for example, move into the apartment provided by their parents without liking it, just as they would stay with their parents without really being satisfied. As students or young professionals they fulfill the requirements, trying to stay out of areas of competition and special pressure. They arrange themselves with the role of the unobtrusive, "good" student and/or employee. Their level of achievement is sufficiently honored by a mediocre standard. The point of their lives lies neither in "higher" goals, hopes for social rise, escape, or redemption, nor in "having fun" in the present, or optimistic plans for the future, it's simply about coping with the "ever stingy reality".

Even under the condition of a stable income, these young adults are only able to make ends just meet, they do not see much possibility for extra spending. They hardly ever explore available reproductive opportunities, their social and communicative networks are only rudimentarily developed, but they often do not have committed relationships with one partner either. Socializing does not seem to be a priority. They prefer to join activities they are invited to, without insisting on own preferences, mainly in order to keep up with the Joneses. Compared to their age and to the fact that they — legally at least — are already adults, they seem rather young. They frequently leave to their parents the responsibility for decisions that they could easily make themselves, and they also rely on them in matters like dealing with official institutions, contractors, and so forth. In other ways they seem old compared to other adolescents, like complaining, established petits bourgeois, who have somehow arranged themselves with life as it is, and who, looking at it, are rather inclined to see the negative aspects before any conceivable perspectives. Their concept for a realistic life management seems to be based on an attitude of "wait and see". But if there are decisions to be made, not much time is wasted on comparing the available alternatives with their own wishes and ideals, they prefer to decide quickly and subject themselves to the consequences of the new situation.

"Withdrawing"

"At the moment I am an apprentice, a trainee. I'm not sure if I will continue this kind of work afterwards or if I'll do something else, because I don't like it at all. In there (with the company) I also don't have anyone to relate to. They all can't stand it, but nobody speaks up. Okay, everybody tells you that it would be the same everywhere, but I think that's bullshit... I'd like to get out of here, to Canada or somewhere else. We're already five who want to split together. We decided we're going to work until we've got the money together, and then we want to leave." (Single parent, 19 years, after an interrupted education at the vocational college she is a trainee in an office.)

The life management of young adults categorized by this pattern can be described as follows: The access to the potentials of their own Lebenslage is blocked. Life management is reduced to a minimalist coping and to "withdrawing": Withdrawing from the demands of parents, the instructors, the work place, from the confrontation with objectively restricted opportunities in the professional world and in the reproductive areas, like independent living or participation in society or the urban environment.

"Minimalism" is certainly an applicable term here. Only the absolutely necessary effort is made at school, during professional training, and at work, and little energy goes into the daily share of private life. At the same time we observe the retreat into the private sphere, which, however, is not experienced as satisfying. On the other hand, we see the tendency to escape into dreams, into a temporally or geographically remote and better life — "emigration", a composed existence in scenes, "getting out", and a life in the subculture.

Subjectively this life—style is brought about by frustrations and a general feeling of dissatisfaction, by the self—evaluation of being a failure. Early negative conditioning at school like failing class and learning problems, difficulties in finding a good job or an acceptable training program are mainly responsible for the attitude described by this pattern. A professional training, theoretical instruction, and the job itself are considered imposed by others, only endured as a necessary dread. They do not really expect ever to get out of this confinement, they do not see a challenge, and they already anticipate a negative outcome of the endeavor. Daily life is in a shaky balance. Because certain stages in the process of growing up have not been resolved, the entire structure of life is very unbalanced, and these young adults fear that under the given circumstances their entire life might not have a very good chance.

Withdrawal is mainly a result of the entry into working life. But also other areas of life as well as any activity toward possible short— or long—term perspectives are dominated by this attitude, be it in their dreams or through the symbolism of "emigration". Peers play an essential role in keeping this dreamworld alive. They help to endure, repress, or deny the contradictions between the "other life" and the persistence of the daily requirements of city life. In order to make it day by day, to have a place to stay, and to coordinate work and recreation, a large circle of friends and a support system are as crucial for everyday life as recreational activities and subcultural urban "scenes".

Money and how to get it are central within this pattern. "No money, no life" — if money is available it is mainly spent to satisfy the numerous momentary needs. But although normally available sources are not sufficient for the realization of the "withdrawal", the circumstances and situations of gainful employment are looked at as "visits" in reality. These young adults' opportunities are obviously below the desirable and unclear perspectives of the future. The adolescents interpret momentary inconveniences as transitional costs or just part of a dry period. "Withdrawal" does not mean active, politically motivated refusal of social participation. As a life pattern it manifests itself individually instead of aiming toward collective changes of the group—specific life situation.

5. Conclusion

Our surveys of "peer groups" during the decade from 1977 to 1987 have shown that the changes in the structure and content of these settings of relations are intertwined in the sequence of biographical stages with changes in the significance and the relevance of peer group networks. As such they are an expression of the deep "structural transformations" of adolescence, which takes place against the background of the transformations and relocations of the work—oriented society.

Peers and the network of social relations take on new and for the life management often indispensable functions. For some adolescents and young adults they become the compensating agents for a lack or insufficient supply of institutional services in the process of growing up. At the same time they maintain their function of emotional support, of providing partners for recreation, and of offering a frame of reference for the confrontation and the experiments with generation – specific norms and values.

Our surveys also show the socioecological differentiation of peer groups: Peer groups in a modern suburban housing area have probably a different significance from peer groups in a small rural town. These regionally specific differentiations themselves become concrete in various patterns of the life management of adolescents and young adults. Their impact remains significant, next to the gender – and class – specific design of the peer group.

In the context of the sociopolitical function of peer groups as elements of Lebenslagen, a youth policy is required that aims to support and expand the action scope and resources for the life management of adolescents and young adults. In concrete terms it would have to improve housing, opportunities for professional qualification, employment, and income, as well as the social infrastructure in a complex sense, including the supply of youth – related social work. An acceptable kind of infrastructural design would have to respond to the specific functions of the peer groups of adolescents and young adults.

References

Bertram, H. (1988): Risiko oder Chance — Jugendliche im Wandel der Arbeitsgesellschaft. In: Deutsches Jugendinstitut. Report of the Year 1987, 132 – 146

Böhnisch, L., & Schefold, W. (1985): Lebensbewältigung. Soziale und pädagogische Verständigung an den Grenzen der Wohlfahrtsgesellschaft. Weinheim: Juventa

Böhnisch, L., & Funk, H., (1988): Jugend im Abseits? Zur Lebenslage Jugendlicher im ländlichen Raum. Munich: Deutsches Jugendinstitut

Gaiser, W. (1985): Ausbildungszeit: Lebensbeschränkung oder Eröffnung neuer Perspektiven? Thesen und Materialien zum Verhältnis von Arbeitswelt, sozialökologischem Kontext und Biographie. In Friebel, H. (Ed.): Berufliche Qualifikationen und Persönlichkeitsentwicklung. Opladen: Westdeutscher Verlag, 181 – 204

Gaiser, W. (1988): Hürden fürs Erwachsenwerden. Probleme der sozialräumlichen Verselbständigung in der nachschulischen Jugendphase. In Wiebe, H. – H. (Ed.): Jugend beim Übergang in den Beruf. Bad Segeberg: Akademie Verlag

Gaiser, W., & Müller, H. – U. (Eds.)(in press): Junge Erwachsene. Lebenslage und Lebensbewältigung im regionalen Kontext. Munich: Deutsches Jugendinstitut

Hornstein, W. (1985): Jugend. Strukturwandel im gesellschaftlichen Wandlungsprozeß. In Hradil, S. (Ed.): Sozialstruktur im Umbruch. Opladen: Westdeutscher Verlag, 323 – 342

Hübner – Funk, S., Müller, H. – U., & Gaiser, W. (1983): Sozialisation und Umwelt. Berufliche Orientierungen und Gesellschaftsnormen von Hauptschülern im sozialökologischen Kontext. Munich: Deutsches Jugendinstitut

Hurrelmann, K., Rosewitz, B., & Wolf, H. (1985): Lebensphase Jugend. Eine Einführung in die sozialwissenschaftliche Jugendforschung. Weinheim: Juventa

Keupp, H. (1988): Auf der Suche nach der verlorenen Identität? Paper presented at the Berlin Kongreß für klinische Psychologie und Psychotherapie

Lutz, B. (1987): Zukunft der Arbeit und soziale Integration. Neue Praxis, 5, 387—391

Müller, H.—U. (1983): Wo Jugendliche aufwachsen. Umweltaneignung in verschiedenen Lebensräumen. München: Juventa

Olk, Th. (1985): Jugend und gesellschaftliche Differenzierung — zur Entstrukturierung der Jugendphase. Zeitschrift für Pädagogik, 19, 290—301

Sinus—Institut (1985): Jugend privat. Verwöhnt? Bindungslos? Hedonistisch? Opladen: Leske and Budrich

Zinnecker, J. (1981): Jugend 1981: Portrait einer Generation. In Jugendwerk der Deutschen Shell (Ed.): Jugend '81. Lebensentwürfe, Alltagskulturen, Zukunftsbilder. Vol. 1. Hamburg: Jugendwerk der Deutschen Shell, 80—114

Zinnecker, J. (1987): Jugendkultur 1940—1985. Opladen. Leske and Budrich

18.
Milieu Attachment and − Erosion
as Problems of Individual Socialization

Wilhelm Heitmeyer and Kurt Möller
University of Bielefeld, Federal Republic of Germany

The central task of the present paper is to describe and substantiate the milieu − theory approach and to distinguish it from other sociostructural, analytical concepts. The relevance of this approach for empirical, sociostructural socialization research will be dealt with in closing. Based on qualitative material gained in our 5 − year long − term study (1985 − 1990) concerning the political orientation of male working − class youths born in 1967/1968 and its relationship to the threat of unemployment, we outline shifting tendencies of the functions of two distinct milieus in which youths live: peers and the family. The goal hereby is, on the basis of the qualitative analysis undertaken, to contribute to the development and differentiation of the theoretical discussion concerning milieu and individualization.

1.   Milieu − Theory Approach − Why and How?

Our suggestion of a milieu − theory approach can be explained on the basis of the development of new orientations in the analysis of social structures which aim to "grasp" scientifically the observed diversification in causes, forms, and combinations of social inequality and in the plurality of life styles (for a review of their various positions, see Berger, 1987). It is evident that both of the traditional model concepts of "rank" and "class", being based on the premises of structurality, regularity, and durability of social organizations, have failed in their attempt to meet this challenge (Hradil, 1987). As a rule, they fail to incorporate the increasing significance of new sources and dimensions of social inequality which, besides the classic factors of power, money, and prestige, seem to be more and more influential: working conditions, leisure conditions, living and environmental conditions, social security, relationships and disparity in social intercourse. Unlike the "old" dimensions of inequality, the "new" dimensions do not represent resources of social skills; rather, they describe more or less favourable opportunity— or risk structures. They no longer describe particular positions of status which can be connected with vocational status in a causal sense; instead, they are factors of so—called "horizontal inequality": gender, age—groups, cohorts, nationality or race, skin color, neighborhood, and family status. Such categorization of characteristics which are, in part, "natural" inequalities cannot be graded in one—dimensional degrees of a purely vertical, hierarchical nature, nor can they simply be traced back to economic — in particular, vocational — factors; above all, they cannot be regarded as individually acquired positions of status. Nor can the new dimensions of inequality be related to underprivilege with the universality assumed by the premises implicit in the concepts of rank and class. They do not affect all members of society equally — above all, in terms of their effect; they are not manifest in all situations, nor at all times.

Studies on status inconsistency indicate that older manifestations of status are dissolving for a majority of society's members, and that accumulated underprivilege frequently adds to the stigmatization experienced by society's minorities (e.g., foreign workers, large families): "The typical constellation is one of simultaneous privilege and deprivation" (SFB 3, 1984, 31). Within the middle class, life styles have also become more heterogenous (Bertram, 1976; Grüneisen and Hoff, 1977; Steinkamp and Stief, 1978; Uttitz, 1984). In light of such de—structuring tendencies, it proves increasingly difficult to maintain causal explanations of cognitive—symbolic representations of objectively existing patterns of inequality based on class or rank. Systems of interpreting social inequality also show increased differentiation, as shown by the difficulties encountered in tracing class—related styles back to social class, or in defining the relationship between "class consciousness" and the influence of or adherence to a particular class (Huch, 1975; Gottschalch et al., 1975; Abrahams and Sommerkorn, 1976, Bertram, 1976; Kern and Schumann, 1982; Kaase and Klingemann, 1983; Berger, 1984). In addition, global risks (e.g., rearmament, nuclear technology) resulting from technological modernization are generalized and are in no way distributed according to class or rank.

The consequences for the general process of socialization, particularly for adolescents from working—class families, is that this process no longer takes place "spontaneously" within the framework of class, nor is it mediated by class—related institutions; instead, "the overlapping bands of experience and control inherent in a class—culturally characterized social milieu have, in many cases, been dissolved" (Beck, 1986, 129); and, "the individual has become a social reproductive unit within his or her own living space" (Beck, 1986, 209); or — more illustratively — "a planning office in regard to his or her own life course, capabilities, orientations, partnerships, etc." (Beck, 1983, 59). Within this tendency toward individualization — and this proves especially important for our question — the family loses its socializing influence: For example, increasing numbers of children grow up in so—called "broken homes" or one—parent families, or in changing family constellations which result, for example, from divorce (Olk, 1985; Olk and Heinze, 1985; Walker, 1985; Griffith, 1985). At the same time, peer groups seem to gain in importance (Allerbeck and Hoag, 1985).

What is needed, therefore, is an analytical model which can accomodate the changes in social structure and modus of socialization described above, without completely losing the dimension of social inequality being viewed as a factor of "functional differentiation" that leads not to vertical ranks, but only to differences. Above all, for our purposes, this model must incorporate the interplay and the contextual combination of all important dimensions of social inequality relevant to the individual case, as well as the new interpretative "treatment inequality", and its consistency creating, complementary, and reciprocally relativating components. Inasmuch as the problems of socialization that are manifest within the framework of the socialization processes focused on can be grasped on the basis of the theory of individualization, such a model must, on a microlevel, be able to grasp longitudinally the long—term changes in the socialization modi which are described on a social macrolevel. In terms of research methodology, this comprehensive assessment leads to the abandonment of expectations that causality analyses will prove fruitful in explaining interpretation patterns and behavior of individuals and social groups; and, in the face of the relative "freeing" of subjective interpretation based on family—conferred class situations or rank—related obligations, result in an orientation toward methods which provide an understanding of the subjective relevance of living conditions (Hradil, 1987). Such a model must, therefore, at least make provision for a qualitative research design.

With reference to the writings of Durkheim, who, by viewing the milieu analysis as the search for the "first source of each social event" (1965, 194), established the term "milieu" within sociology, and with reference to distinct traditional paths of sociological phenomenology (Schütz, Scheler, Gurwitsch), milieu can be defined as the historically determined social aggregate of continuous social everyday interactions within primary zones of operation, limited in time and space, that also by virtue of the milieu's own value system has a socializing effect on the physically and bodily present fellow persons.

Milieus are thereby more than, for example, "life situations", inasmuch as these are distinctly separate from subcultural forms of expression and life styles

(Böhnisch, 1980); more than "sociotopes" which are oriented toward restricted areas (Kuthe et al., 1979; Bargel et al., 1982); more than "social ecologies" which are centered around the subject (Baacke, 1980; Lüscher, Fisch and Pape, 1985); more than the actual, subjectively held view of the universe manifest in the form of a "life—world" perspective (Schütz, 1980); and more than "networks" which are characterized more by socialization norms than by structural constraints, and in which a kind of "social capital" (Bourdieu) becomes manifest. It is not only the historical specificity of existing objective living conditions and "social opportunities", the territoriality, the structure of social relationships, the economic—material opportunity structure, a supposed relative value homogeneity, and the subjective view of these factors that is important; instead, it is all of these aspects taken together that form the definitory reference points of this version of the milieu concept.

The construction, maintenance, and destruction of a milieu is thereby viewed in the context of its relevance for the individual in terms of socialization. That which makes this version of the milieu concept predestined to be a reflective microscopic instrument, used for diagnostic purposes of societal individualization tendencies as applied to individual cases, is the definitory restriction of the term "milieu" to small—scale social organizations within the individual's primary zone of operation. It is just this organization of social life, incorporating traditional bonds, that purports the individualization theory to be in a process of dissolution, in that it points out general societal developments such as the internationalization of dependencies, increasing fiscal influences, generalization of legal aspects, processes of the institutionalization of welfare—state type services, urbanization, increasing media influence, the expansion of transportation systems, the consequences of expanded educational facilities, and other aspects of increasing demands on mobility and flexibility, as well as tendencies toward increasing abstractions in social relationships.

Thus, problems of individualization can reveal themselves in their individual—biographical characteristics if manifestations of such tendencies can be stated in particular forms and combinations within the subjects' life—areas over a period of time. In respect to the individual case, the congruence or noncongruence with the ideal type of a milieu—influenced social bond or the emerging new form of social bond still containing residual aspects of the milieu and new elements of social identity can be described, if the classic areas of socialization — including the family and peers — are regarded in relation to the qualitative aspect of their existing and potential milieu function. In a concrete sense, the aim is to examine the extent to which such life situations are separated from one another as small, social "part—time" life—worlds (Luckmann, 1978), the extent to which their traditional aspects are still cordoned off from external influences, the extent to which they retain their small — scale, day — to — day reality, the extent to which they are still constituted on the basis of social interactions within primary zones of operation, the extent to which they guarantee and/or convey a certain constancy and sense of belonging; and, by compensating for milieu loss, which horizons may be important for socialization.

Socialization can be regarded as a learning process which takes place within the context of the subject's attempts at coping with the environment (Hurrelmann, 1983, 1988), during which the attempts to control reality — or that which is regarded as reality — are undertaken through orientation and activities, as well as through the construction of an identity — constituting self — concept and a corresponding external, social representation of personality. As such, within the context of socialization, the relevant effecting factors which protrude from the network of innumerable elements that act upon the life experience can be sought on four levels:

1. At the level of the orientation potential of the predominant systems of milieu values, norms, and interpretations — including the external threat of sanctions inherent in these systems;

2. at the level of the spectrum of behavior and action which determines the motivations, intentions and opportunities for realization that are determined, above all, by the extent of material resources, applicability — structures of milieu material, space and time patterns, networks of social relationship, and the above — mentioned orientation potential;

3. at the level of offers of self — image constructions relevant for establishing identity, including their reflective and ritual and/or habitual elements of rationality constructions;

4. at the level of opportunities for the subject's external representations in relation to milieu members and milieu — external persons. Such opportunities are essentially dependent on the provision and social acceptance of their forms in the milieu.

A differentiated milieu analysis must therefore offer a detailed description of the milieu in its physical — material, "everyday — time oriented", social, functional, normative, and historical — processual determining aspects — all of which can only be separated in an analytical sense.

The physical — material basis of such an analysis is undertaken on the basis of a description of the milieu "inventory". This includes persons and objects in their spatial (al)location, and the corresponding rights of ownership and use, questions of providing for and servicing the milieu, as well as the respective coupling with or differentiation from other social milieus. The "everyday — time" element (for a differentiation between "everyday — time" and "life — time", compare Fischer, 1982, 1983) refers to the temporal order that depicts the day — to — day milieu in its uniformity, its cyclic, repetitive impulses, and its idealized continuities (of "and so forth" and "I can always do it again"; Schütz, 1980). It generates a routine, temporal sensation of a continuing "expanded present". The social aspect is directed toward the specificity of the communal form of life in the milieu, that is, the point at which the emphasis is on the analysis of the network. From a functional viewpoint, interest lies primarily in the utility structures of milieu inventory and the variety of their utility justification.

The observation of normative impulses inherent to the milieu represents an analysis of that which Scheler described as the milieu value — structure. This refers to the combination of knowledge elements, ideologies, moral concepts, and other cognitive — symbolic representations of the social situation. As a mastic of communality and of its self — description these present themselves as opportunities for interpretation patterns of reality that are offered within the milieu and which lead some authors (Lepsius, 1973; Reulecke and Weber, 1978; Mooser, 1983; Beck, 1983, 1986) to refer to as "social — moral" milieus. From a historical — processual viewpoint, the focus is on the temporal organizations that are not intraphasic everyday — time aspects, but rather, are irreversibly progressive life — time factors of interphasic linear movement (Rammstedt, 1975). Thus, on the one hand, the milieu's historical growth and orientation toward the future is taken into account, and, on the other hand, the uniqueness of biographical orientation schemata and positional sequencing is refered to (Kohli, 1986).[1]

2. The Family and Peer Groups: Milieu Erosions, New Sozialisation Horizons, New Social Identities

That which has so far been developed as a research program is operationalized within the framework of large — scale research into the political socialization of adolescents, whereby an attempt is made to combine qualitative and quantitative studies. The theoretical premises presented in this paper are based on extracts from the following three studies:

1. In a quantative study on political orientation, interviews were carried out with 1,330 male and female adolescents between the ages of 16 and 17 who were about to make the difficult transition from school to the employment sector (Heitmeyer, 1987).
2. A second quantative study was undertaken in regard to the youth culture of soccer fans. The focus hereby was on the importance of peers and violence. Interviews were carried out with youths between the ages of 15 and 27, most of whom were male (Heitmeyer and Peter, 1988).
3. In a qualitative long−term study, the process of political orientation of youths from working−class families was examined, which, in a theoretical sense as well as in terms of the selected population, is related to the above−mentioned studies. In the long−term study, youths are observed from their 17th to 22nd year of life. In addition to the quantative studies on the political socialization of West German youths, methods are employed that, by attempting to understand the subjects' concepts of self and reality, are oriented toward achieving a valid evaluation of the way in which social processes evolve. The approach is therefore not oriented toward external, sociostructural factors: Instead, the selection of cases combines the method of "theoretical sampling" (Glaser and Strauss, 1967; Glaser, 1978) with a strategy of searching for "deviant" cases which demonstrate distinct contrasts. Problem−centered interviews form the basis of the study methods, as they give greater yield than "narrative" interviews in terms of population and subject matter. The evaluating methods are based on the theme−centered evaluations as suggested by Witzel (1982), who used the latter in an attempt to achieve "collective validation".

In the following we refer to three cases of youths who were accompanied beyond the second and third year of apprenticeship. These youths show almost no differences in regard to the degree of objective, acute vocational insecurity and had had no dramatic experiences in this respect, having experienced no difficulties in being accepted for vocational training on completion of their general education. Partial differences between the youths exist only in respect to their anticipation of insecurity, so that an explanation of their differences in their orientation toward socialization contexts and opportunities for social identity can be excluded, which interprets them, for example, as a result of more or less dramatic experiences of failure in vocational biography, such as unemployment. Bearing in mind Beck's premise of the individual as a "planning office" for the life course, the following extracts from youths' individual interpretations are used to show which actual combinations of work−plan relevant orientations and anticipations of vocational insecurities or hopes can be recognized in the individualization problematic of working−class youths, the extent to which milieu adherance to a family or peer groups is recognizable, and whether new forms of socialization horizons and new opportunities for social−identity patterns can be stated.[2]

Case 1: "Doing something in the community for the workers' cause"

Leonard, a youth born in 1968, who, after an untroubled school career in which he gained a secondary school leaving certificate, is motivated by a content – based work orientation (above all, in terms of specific concrete tasks, preferences for cooperative work relationships, opportunities for self – actualization), has made the transition to an aspired to vocational field with bright future prospects: that of energy – plant electronics. In respect to work and training, he sees his situation as stressful only – although increasingly so – in respect to momentary financial restrictions and to varied hierarchical dependencies, the latter disturbing his predominant desire for more independence in structuring his work.

In an almost classic manner, Leonard feels himself integrated into the workers' milieu from which he has come, and within which he has always lived. In addition to his activities in the volunteer fire brigade, in which he serves as an alternative to military service, he has been engaged for several years in the Social Democratic Party in a conventional, organizational sense, in his union, a workingman's sports club, and, in recent years, in a community initiative against a Neonazi center within his neighborhood. He professes to maintaining a consistent political "line" in respect to the "cause of the worker", which "concerns everyone, whether 'left –' or 'right – wing'". The spontaneous, natural attachment toward the milieu in terms of social orientation, political and other activities, self – definition, and self – representation which he demonstrated in the encounter with the interviewer illustrates his attempts to account for its relevance for his socialization: "Why that is, I cannot say. Of course, first of all, we come from a working – class family, and from a working – class area. All of our family are Social Democrats who are fairly active politically. I mean, when you think about it carefully, and then you have one or two friends or collegues with whom you can talk, then you really have no other choice but to adopt this line, or at least, to be left – wing. We are, after all, the guys from the working – class. Not that I ever wanted to be something better!".

However, he does have problems with the conventionality of a lifestyle that is a prerequisite for the integration within this type of milieu. In his orientation toward work, he recognizes the necessity of a "must" that he would actually rather reject. The idea that he had nourished at the beginning of his training – that is, to later have work of an autonomous nature that would also be socially useful – is "over and done with": "I wouldn't like to end up here in Germany as a pensioner at 65 and have slaved in one company all of my life!". He attempts, therefore – on a daily basis and in the long term – to keep opportunities open which allow him to "get out": "On Monday, the week begins; on Friday it's over, and then I live a little bit". There is, however, no tendency to "flip – out". Leonard toys with the idea of emigrating to Finland or – encouraged by a recent holiday – to Greece; at the same time knowing that "nothing will come of that in the near future!". Doubts about the meaningfulness of an existence which is centered around work are evidently not substantial enough to loosen the ties to the milieu, or to initiate a move toward new horizons of socialization.

Case 2: "Anything to get out of here. Life as an action video"

Otto is a youth born in 1967, who, despite bad marks in his junior secondary school leaving certificate, has, owing to fortunate circumstances, entered an apprenticeship as a turner. He regards this vocation as a substitute choice for which he shows little practical motivation or interest. ("It doesn't mean shit, what kind of work I do!; the main thing is I am not unemployed and can earn money!"). Now in his third year of training, he is completely convinced, on the evidence of verbal assurances, that he will be retained by the company, even though his future prospects are dimmed by problems within the trade school and by the effects of technological modernizations (CNC — machines) in his field of work. He is forced to stand by idly while other, more able apprentices in the trade school are introduced to the new technologies which are gradually being introduced into his firm.

Otto's familial integration is burdened by the fact that, since her divorce, his mother has been living with a new partner with whom Otto does not get along. The same applies to his father's new girlfriend. During the course of our observations, the family lost its function as a source of feelings of emotional security and as a place where personal problems can be dealt with. His relationships to peers, which are centered around weekend meetings with a clique of soccer fans who display violent behavior and neonazi tendencies, today only contain a nostalgic myth of stability and homogeneity. The local bar frequented by the group has changed ownership and is oriented toward a clientele which is better situated financially. The automobiles with which the youths drive into the city are frequently full. In other words, he "has had a lot of friends", "there was a lot happening"; but at the same time, "things are not the way they used to be". Otto has no girlfriend. He is forced to deal with his problems on his own.

He sees the homogeneity of his neighborhood, and the possibility of living an untroubled life in Germany, being threatened by the influx of foreigners: "You don't feel at home anymore...foreigners everywhere. That's shitty, when you are walking along the street and along comes a Tamil or a Turk. They are all so dark — skinned; it's disgusting. When you are walking around the city after 10 o'clock, all you see is blacks, it's really disgusting. I find that sickening, honestly. The country is finished. Foreigners everywhere, Tamils and such, or whatever you call them. They come from all over. You take a look, 4 more years or so... if this continues, North — Rhine — Westphalia, for example, is finished. And then, slowly, the other counties; none of us is left. Wham, they should gas 'em all!".

According to Otto, National Socialism is "a system,... that we could really use". A mandatory "pro forma" union membership resulting from pressure at work cannot have any effect on this view. Altogether, Otto views his upbringing as being heavily influenced by his family— and living conditions. It seems that Otto feels as if important factors within the context of his life that are relevant to his milieu ties are disintegrating. He feels himself simply — as he puts it — "no longer at home" in his neighborhood. As his employment only has instrumental interest for him, it too does not offer him a place of refuge.

As a result, he attempts to find positive experiences in daily life by "frequently having a drink", and, within the context of conflicts between his soccer clique and other fans, by utilizing his hobby of pottering and playing with makeshift guns; an activity that is otherwise pursued in solitude. As he feels persecuted in this respect by state restrictions on weapons, and, as an admirer of the military, having experienced the shame of being rejected for military service, his dreams are centered on escaping the narrow confines of his employment situation, and, in his eyes, the "occupation" of his country by foreigners: "I see myself as a dreamer...I am always having new ideas — for example, emigrating to the United States, being a professional boxer, or a soldier of fortune on a Columbian opium farm...with a machine gun...it feels great when you blast the whole magazine!"

It is remarkable, that, the greater the erosion of the peer group during the course of the biography, the more the dreams shift toward freedom and adventure in America: from the image of a "fantastic" freedom for street — gang action to fantasies of complete freedom to own weapons, even to a media—conveyed conception of the individual citizen's duty to carry weapons.

One hardly need know of this adolescent's extensive video and television viewing habits, of the fascination for "Rambo", and of the regular readings of weapon journals, in order to recognize that we are dealing here with media—induced fantasies. The spatial—temporal, material, social, and — most likely — the normative controlling bands of Otto's real day—to—day life have been destroyed. The fictitious reality presented by the media serves as a blueprint for a fantasy lifestyle. Is this a case of unrealistic media—socialization instead of milieu—socialization, perhaps? Not quite: The relevant factors offered by media contents evidently stem from daily life: the forms of violence which still determine the erosion—plagued peer milieu, Otto's weapons hobby, and his dreams of the freedom to hold weapons, which are set in contrast to the German weapon laws he regards as being too restrictive. "You have to be able to attack those people that attack you. The pressure that you feel, you have to let out somewhere else". — Such is Otto's maxim and its explanation in the context of his socialization experience.

Case 3: "I attach a fair bit of importance to brand names"

Sammy is an adolescent of the same age as Leonard. He is in the same year, type of apprenticeship, and firm as Leonard, has had a similarly untroubled school career, did particularly well in his secondary school leaving certificate examinations (entrance qualifications for a technical college), and does his work with a specific task—oriented motivation. He has little sense of being burdened by problems, except perhaps for the low chances of future employment in his company and his disturbed relation to tutors and fellow apprentices, who regard him as arrogant and "stuck up". His vocational ideal is to be a helicopter pilot in the army. Sammy is of the opinion that "...the future is more or less ruined. You must have plans, maybe even illusions. You don't think about the whole mess the world is in". In his eyes, the most predominant and acceptable method of distributing opportunities is through a "natural selection"..."based simply on the principle of achievement".

In contrast to Leonard, Sammy stems from a family that is oriented toward upward mobility and which resides in a neighborhood of mixed social structure. The father has worked his way up from unskilled worker to skilled tradesman; the mother, presently a housewife, was previously a bank saleswomen. The parents watch over the future opportunities of their only child. During the course of the investigation, they prove to be consistent discussion partners with whom he could discuss his problems; they can be expected to give substantial help in situations of need, and project a feeling of "something like emotional security". Mutual activities are undertaken frequently. For example, the father, who incorporates Sammy's ideal of achieving vocational status, often takes him horse riding. Politically, Sammy conforms to the line of his parents, which he characterizes as "more or less conservative", "right—wing", "Christian—Democrat oriented". Among the relatives, only one uncle is conspicuous as a "socialist". Sammy's friends, whom he regards as dependable and accepting of him, are similarly oriented — some being active in the Christian Democrat youth organization. According to Sammy, it is, above all, the politically engaged youths who "babble a lot of fancy talk", and for this reason he has been spending less time with these persons recently, preferring to be with aquaintances who are not aware of each other's political preferences.

Sammy's girlfriend is very important to him. He is a member of the union only because he would otherwise, as the only exception in an all—union company, be the subject of social ostracism. In his leisure time he "kicks up a storm", and "enjoys himself". Most of his leisure time is spent listening to New—Wave—Music, reading magazines on New—Wave fashion and youth culture, working part—time as a waiter in a fashionable bar, riding his moped, and, in recent times, driving a car. He makes frequent visits to discos and the local dancing school, eats in restaurants, goes to the cinema, and makes extensive efforts to acquire conspicuous and stylish clothes. His extremely "flipped—out" style of dress, his preference for make—up, and his extravagant hair style have been modified with time, owing to the problems which this had caused with his "proletarian" oriented "jeans and tennis shoe" wearing fellow apprentices and trainers: "Let's say, I've modified the flippiness a bit and have gone over to the nobility". By paying attention to the "right brand of clothes", and by wearing a fashionable but less conspicuous hairstyle, he is able to win acceptance by indicating a readiness for integration, within as well as beyond the place of work, without having to feel as if he must distance himself from an idiographic external presentation: "At the moment things are quieter with me... I look more respectable these days. I still wear cowboy boots with my jeans — that's something some people don't really appreciate, but it is accepted".

The pluralizations of a synthetic, youth—culture—producing consumer world affords him a socially accepted modus of social living without making him appear "the same as all the others" — a thing he hates: here we have a consumerism—oriented youth culture instead of a subculture based on class.

We now will compare the three case analyses in respect to particularly relevant individualization—theory factors:

1. It is apparent that, according to traditional criteria for class or rank membership, all three youths would be classified within the same category of social—structure analysis. At the same time, they differ greatly in respect to their attachment to the orientation classically associated with such categorization. Such models once again reveal their inability to deduce

forms of class consciousness or forms of activity on the basis of such abstract classifications. In addition, the youths have the same vocational status. The differences in their orientations can therefore not be explained by this factor.

2. All three youths are members of the classical workingman's organization: the union. However, this fact does not have the same meaning for all of them. For Sammy and Otto it is meaningless in terms of social orientation. They are only pro forma members who joined as a result of social pressure. Other cases in our study could also verify that formal membership in (vocational –) political organizations is seldom an indication of the importance of the corresponding positions for socialization.

3. All of the youths conformed to the political opinions of their (working – class) parents. In no way can one refer to one youth having a similar orientation toward the other two youths. It is, therefore, no longer possible to assume a stability of orientation within a homogeneous working class not even for the parent generation, unless one is prepared to dismiss the cases reviewed here as "renegades" – a view which is not in the least supported by our study.

4. The substantial work – biographical insecurity of the three youths is not characterized by failure in school, acute or previous unemployment, periods of unskilled labor, and so forth. Otto, who seems himself as a victim of impending, sweeping technological change, is increasingly more pessimistic about the future and, unlike the others, is not able to secure his motivation for his vocational and further – educational future through an interest in the content of his work. Although he feels secure in the immediate future, due to his belief that the company will retain him after training, in the long term he feels himself more or less pressured into a position of passively defending his vocational status. In contrast, the other two youths make attempts to increase their capabilities, also in the vocational field: the one youth essentially through gaining further qualification and attempts at upward mobility, the other through engagement in traditional, politically oriented organizations. It seems that integration into normal work and training relationships alone does not guarantee protection from a Machiavellian orientation and from neonazi tendencies. In this context, it would seem that the presence or absence of a content – based orientation toward work play a key role – a finding that could receive substantial support from other cases in our study.

5. The three youths differ greatly in respect to milieu factors. Otto is affected by biographical and acute milieu erosions. Neither the family nor the peer relationships are stable or constant over time. The family increasingly loses its function as an institution of social support. Otto feels himself partly isolated and left on his own. The integration into the peer group of soccer

fans disintegrates, and a substitute group is not available. Occasional experiences of violence and "action" during weekend skirmishes in the context of soccer stadiums serve to partially conceal the gradual disintegration of group cohesion. Other qualitative experiences of collective solidarity, which, in theory, would be accessible within the framework of union activities, are not available to Otto. A tendency to atomization seems to characterize the current direction in Otto's lifestyle. In comparison, Sammy and Leonard show more attachment to their milieu, although in structurally different ways. Traditional values of a working—class culture can neither be found in the milieus of Sammy's family nor of his peers living within a sozialisation horizon based on the principle of an orientation toward individual upward mobility without changing the societal status quo, and accepting the principle of achievement. So he deals with the vocational insecurity through fantasies of individual success (in the state—supportive institution of the army) in the future, and through idiographically motivated preferences for a consumer—oriented youth culture. In contrast, Leonard lives within conditions in which working—class culture and a corresponding identity have been preserved. He relates to collective activities oriented toward political organizations, whereby the traditionally evolved subculture continues to have a socializing influence. Individualizing tendencies, which lead to atomism in Otto and to pluralization in Sammy, have had no effect in Leonard's case.

3. Perspectives for Socialization Theory

What are the consequences of our study for socialization research that takes account of constituted sociostructural changes that lead to the gradual separation of the individual from hierarchically formed social classes? From a socialization—theory standpoint, aside from methodological aspects, the dual question arises, as to what are the conditions on which the emergence of "new" socialization horizons depend, and which consequences for the quality of socialization processes arise from particular socialization horizons.

Otto's socialization horizon is, in our sense, "new" inasmuch as the "milieu", consisting of the effects of social interactions in the operation zones of daily life, loses its influence. Abstract figures that are neither inherent in daily life nor integrated into the immediate individual's interactive operation context become relevant to orientation, behavior, self—image, and self—presentation. In comparison with the other two cases, his case shows several noticeable deviations in respect to milieu factors, vocational orientation, and future assessments, all of which can be considered as factors which contribute to the development of new socialization horizons:

1. An increasing erosion takes place in the influence of the family and peer groups (in regard to soccer fans, compare Heitmeyer and Peter, 1988) in their function as systems of support and emotional refuge that can convey a sense of belonging. Feelings of having a home, of belonging to the place where one lives, increasingly come under pressure as a result of the influx of foreigners, who, by occupying living space and public facilities, are regarded by Otto as endangering homogeneity, restricting living space, and threatening the stability of orientation. He increasingly has a sense of being ostracised and left alone.
2. Owing to the lack of content–based interest in his field of work, possibilities for identification are not available here.
3. Otto anticipates substantial problems with his own achievement abilities in respect to his future when seen in the context of the threat to his vocational activities represented by sweeping technological changes in his field. He regards himself as a victim of rationalization.

It would appear, therefore, that these three points contribute toward the emergence of "new" socialization horizons — at least as far as male apprentices in the early phases of their work biography are concerned: the dissolution of established, biographical, milieu factors that previously were important aspects of socialization, combined with the sense of loss in respect to feelings of belonging, the absence of content–based orientation toward the chosen vocation, and scepticism in respect to one's own ability to assert oneself in the field of employment, this being the central area of social achievement.[3)]

In another sense, Sammy's socialization horizon is also "new". Although he is much more influenced by his attachment to his milieu than is Otto, and, in consequence, is not "new" in terms of a milieu rejection in comparison with Leonard, he lacks the traditional embedment in established working–class values; however, this would seem to be at least a "second generation" deficit. Its distinguishing charactistics would appear to consist of an orientation toward social and vocational advancement on the basis of individual efforts, corresponding free space for activity which accepts norms, and a concept of self and others that is essentially constructed around consumerism. Observations secured by social research in the course of the last decades concerning changes in the area of social inequality suggest that the disassociation from class–related socialization factors can generally be equated to the increasing permeability of vocational and educational systems in respect to individual advancement and to the levelling of individual consumer–culture lifestyles. In Sammy's case, the admiration for his father's upward mobility from unskilled laborer to skilled tradesman is of additional explanatory value.

The incorporation of milieu values is also suggested by Sammy's content–based interest in the chosen field, and by his confidence in his own capabilities. Sammy's case suggests that the lack of "class consciousness" — or however one chooses to designate traditional class–cultural interpretation and orientation patterns — can be associated with the father's upward mobility and the social orientation of parents, particularly in relation to consumerism, in respect to the assessment of his own capabilities and chances of fulfilling content–based orientation toward work. Of additional importance is the fact that Sammy need not fear the dissolution of his idiographic interests within the uniformity of an undeveloped mass–consumer market. In contrast, the consumer–cultural differentiation of an expanding leisure–style market offers sufficient material for an individualized self–(re–)production.

Although in Leonard's case also the content–based interests in relation to work and confidence in his own capabilities dominate, a different milieu tradition exists regarding the aspired to modus of socialization. In his family–, peer–, and living–milieu, attempts at individual social advancement and the ensuing suspicion that one intends to desert the milieu are rejected. It is possible that the relative homogeneity of this orientation throughout all areas of life is responsible for its continuing influence. From this, the following provisional hypothesis can be deduced and tested: In respect to the individual, traditional working—class milieus remain effective for socialization as long as they form a comprehensive band which encompasses all important aspects of life and provide social control as well as social integration within the framework of the immediate environment.

The three cases which we have discussed indicate more than constellations of factors which explain the "newness" of socialization horizons or the retention of obvious milieu orientation. As "prototypes", they each reveal distinct qualities of socialization prozesses. Within the spectrum of possible ways of constructing social identity, we can distinguish the following variations:

1. A continuous collective—solidarist orientation (by Leonard);
2. a shift to forms of idiographistic orientation toward consumerism (by Sammy); and
3. a tendency toward atomistic Machiavellism (by Otto).

Behind these three variations of predominant socialization horizons, at least one of the three factors can be easily recognized: milieu, market, media. Admittedly, this does not allow for statements as to the quality of the constellation of factors which can be found within these three concrete formations. However, there are a number of criteria which could contribute toward identifying their "quality". Inasmuch as we examine the efforts which contribute toward the construction of social identity, for us the quality criterion for the respective concepts is the individual's interest in social participation as conveyed by social opportunities — this being part of a comprehensive, identity—constructing need for reality control.

In this respect, we can therefore attempt to describe the following: the orientation pattern that is made salient by the potential for orientation within the socialization horizon; the type of actions that emerge from the opportunities for behavior and activities associated with the latter; the concept that determines the construction of the self—concept, and the medium of external presentation that is realized.

The most conspicious characteristic of the pattern of "consumerist idiographism" is its orientation toward the rules of a capitalist economy — within the areas of work as well as leisure. Correspondingly, the "achievement principle" and the consumer culture form the central value systems relevant to orientation. Within the framework of such orientation—relevant factors, vocational scope emerges within the framework of an acceptance of and adaptation to existing rules of commerce regarding exchange and barter. Therefore, in the vocational field, those opportunities must gain preference that not only secure a position within "normal" careers offered by society, but, in addition, offer possibilites for upward mobility through a demonstration of abilities. Within the area of reproduction, which is distinctly separate from the latter, behavior dominates which projects a partially hedonistic consumption of individual gratifications received for achievement activities into the foreground, and which thereby can enjoy cultural differentiations of the consumer market.

In respect to self — concept and external representation, this, in turn, can serve as a compensating counterpart to a person's self — conceptualization as a conforming and functioning individual (within the area of social achievement: work) by setting idiographic accents in ways which are socially accepted and which are desired by and supportive of the capitalist reproduction economy. They create "identity propagation" by means of brand names and manufacture individual "styles" through market products. The historically evolved milieus with their tradition of homogenizing subcultural value — and interpretation systems are replaced by a short — lived, ever changing "scene", which regulates membership by virtue of the identifying labels of consumerism, and which is dependent on the laws of a capitalist free — market economy. Such a system finds a fertile breeding ground wherever the family and the peer groups have already adapted to it, and when the neighborhood is socially mixed.

This type of social — identity formation responds to individualization by accepting exactly those roles offered to individuals by the existing economic system. It appears only consistent when the areas of political thought and action are determined by considerations of securing the status quo. It is evident that this formation's high degree of social acceptability and functionality is responsible for its degree of resilience.

The construction of social identity on the basis of a pattern of "atomistic Machiavellism" resembles the type described above in that it evidently appears as a reaction to societal tendencies of individualization. However, in the case of "consumer idiographism", the advantages of the increase in the importance of the vocational area can be utilized in the formation of the individual biography while transcending the attachment to the developmental conditions of the milieu and its limitations on vocational status (Beck — Gernsheim, 1983). In contrast, the displacement from a biographical family — orientated schema to the vocation — which takes place within the context of tendencies toward individualization — proves precarious inasmuch as lifelong idealized continuity in respect to the maintenence of a "normal" vocational career is questioned; at the same time, the dissolution of milieu support in the form of a sense of belonging, sanctuary, acceptance, dependability, and support within the family and peer group is undermining feelings of "being at home", and, in addition, changes are taking place in the availability of possibilities for sheltered seclusion in the neighborhood due to the fluctuation of inhabitants – in particular as a result of the influx of other nationalities and cultures. When the "basic securities" (Schelsky) provided by the family and vocation break up – especially just during adolescence –, and an adequate guarantee of continuity is absent, the emergence of a feeling of threat in respect to internal control of one's own living conditions cannot be "buffered", neither milieu – internally nor (vocational –)biographically, it comes as no surprise that fictitious opportunities for identification offered by the media enter into this gap in the system of social integration and in consequence offer a new socialization horizon.

In such cases of separation experiences and/or anticipations, the absence of other experiences of community solidarity, and the simultaneous existence of infrequent, rudimentary milieu attachment based on the aggressive habitus of a peer group, it must appear plausible when fictional identification processes are attached to such residual milieu orientation, and that under such conditions, media – projected individual heroes a la Rambo emerge as effective socializing factors. When structural opportunities for communal coping forms begin to disintegrate, idols appear who ostensibly, in foreign territory – whether in a jungle or in the thick of a strange land that is seemingly occupied by foreigners –, show themselves to be resilient and assertive "tough guys" who prove to be efficient and flexible models for behavior – particularly as their fascination and orientation for many adolescents can be integrated with a practical interest in weapons, symbolizing a ruthless, assertive individualism.

Atomism, in the above – mentioned constellation of factors, seems to activate a potential for orientation toward Machiavellianism. When the individual can only conceive of social participation in terms of asserting partial interests, feels himself to be externally controlled, and the self – image of personal strength is functionally identified with a ruthless, self – assertive individualism that is free of moral and ideological scruples, then it is to be expected that in experiencing insecurity in the process of constructing social identity as a background for behavior, he will act in like manner: with partial power interests. If, in the course of attempting to actuate these interests, he – for whatever reason – does not have access to means of achievement in socially accepted, functional activities, forms of personal demonstration and utilization of violence can prove useful – whether, for example, of peripheral points of a media – transported dream reality, or of real, concrete nature. A potential for orientation and behavior inherent in such patterns can then reflect a self – image of a strong personality, who, through assertive acts, is able to single – handedly

314

W. Heitmeyer and K. Möller

box himself through life also with methods that are beyond the limits set by
"normality". Strength, in the sense of a "deterred by nothing" attitude, is then
interpersonally representable by a "macho" image. The uniqueness of the
individual can then be documented on the basis of violent behavioral styles.

This type of social identity calls forth individualization tendencies in the form
of atomization, inasmuch as that which is subjectively experienced as a
substantial determinant of societal organization — the fight of one against all —
lacking in concepts of morals, ideological convictions, or an opportunistic way
of dealing with these, accompanied by a functional attitude to violence, becomes
a real or fantasy — world strategy of constructing social identity. Machiavellism
need not be accompanied by organized political extremism; as such, Burnham's
(1949, 81) statement on the proponents of this pattern is applicable: "All that
they want is a minimum of security and the chance to lead their own lives and
deal with their own affairs".

In contrast, the collective — solidarist orientation draws its potential from an
orientation which combines central, traditional, community values, criticism of
the ruling classes, and reservations in respect to interindividual inequality in
material resources — how ever it has arisen — combined with an interest in
protecting against social risks and in utilizing and developing content — based
vocational orientation. This can be found, for example, in traditional
working — class milieus. The scope for activities which is available here is, on
the one hand, determined by the attempt to procure social security and a
modest prosperity — in this respect it is similar to the point of departure of
Machiavellism — and, on the other hand, through the preference for collective,
organized, authority — resisting — in some cases explicitly political — activities.
This allows for the construction of a self — image which perceives the self as
existing within the ambivalence of necessary social integration into the existing
system on the one hand, and in opposition to this system on the other hand. As
a medium of external representation, a utility — value oriented competence is
manifest in the area of interpersonal relationships, and, above all, in the area of
vocations; it appears to determine the quality of interpersonal utility — value as
an ideal of "solidarist colleagues and comrades".

Social identities of this nature can only survive as long as societal
individualization, conveyed through diversification tendencies, does not destroy
or make obsolete the general possibility of handing down traditional values and
their forms of generation transference within the everyday context of
milieu — type organizations; that is, also within the essentially neighborhood —
bound "homogeneity" between the socialization instances of the "family" and
"peers".

4. Summary and Prospects

Societal individualization tendencies bring on consequences for the individuals' socialization process and opportunities for focusing their social interests within the context in which they live. Firstly, according to our knowledge, new formations of *socialization contexts* arise. Not only the spatial limitations and concrete daily conditions of social interactions − which are encompassed by comprehensive homogenous milieus and which cover various socialization fields − are eroding in various specific ways by pressure from societal individualization tendencies. In addition, the socialization fields as such, being limited within the framework of the spatial conditions of everyday life, seem to be losing their socializing effect. A new quality of socialization contexts is emerging, which we attempt to describe with the term "socialization horizons". It becomes increasingly difficult to describe such contexts in terms of "fields". They are spatially diffuse, polymorphic, and highly fluctuant in their constituent elements and personal consistency. Membership can therefore no longer be a reliable definitive variable; cohesion proves changeable. Within socialization horizons, common bases of understanding do not construct themselves as such, but rather, through abstract symbolism.

The emergence of socialization horizons is the result of a societal development which not only results in the increasing dissolution of milieu borders, but also serves to dissolve the small−scale, concrete, everyday relationships with their idealized continuity and resulting dependability through demands for mobility and flexibility, as well as urbanization, media expansion, traffic expansion, increasing judicial and fiscal influence in social relations, and so forth. In this respect, it seems worthwhile to pursue the thesis whereby the socializing influence of the "family" and "peers" is being reduced, particularly in respect to attempts to cope with vocational−biographical insecurity and the accompanying unpredictability of long−term planning. This should correspond to the extent that milieu character vanishes and that competitive socialization horizons particularly conveyed by factors containing individualized behavior strategies that are relevant to the media and commerce with their potentials for orientation, opportunities for activities, opportunities for self−image construction, and modes of self−presentation prevent a "penetrative effect" of the milieu by contributing to its dilution.

Secondly − and this follows from the above−mentioned − new ways of constructing *social identity* and corresponding new qualities are emerging. Because the "new" patterns are essentially directed toward the atomized individual, it seems logical to assume that within this context the motives for continuous collective strategies will lose importance in respect to changes in the "dark side" of individualization tendencies, as well as to the utilization of the advantages of individualization processes in view of the pluralization of opportunities for creating an autonomous lifestyle. From a sociopolitical viewpoint, the question arises as to whether this development is inevitable and irreversible, or whether new contextual conditions of collective — solidarist orientation can be created.

Notes

1. The methodological problem of measuring relevant factors becomes obvious here. Between individual subjects (i.e. also between the researcher and the subject of research), the attribution of factors relevant to orientation can be divergent owing to the enmeshment of the individual with his/her position and its corresponding perspective. As a result, based on the work of Sprout and Sprout (1965), a distinction can be made between the levels of the psychological milieus, operational milieus, and "real" milieus. The latter represents the milieu as it actually exists, and as it would be experienced by a fictitious, "all—knowing" observer. In contrast, the psychological milieu represents that part of the real milieu which is perceived by an individual. Finally, the operational milieu consists of that group of factors which are regarded by a particular observer as relevant for the activity of the individual in question.

2. In order to maintain perspicacity, we must, at this point, condense the results of the milieu analysis; we cannot demonstrate the case analyses in the above mentioned steps (in respect to theme — centered evaluation methods and exact, detailed individual interpretations, compare Heitmeyer and Möller, 1986, 1988). We hereby do not answer the question of how milieu analyses are to be approached, but rather, how milieu categories of individualization theory can make a contribution toward sociostructurally oriented research into socialization.

3. These relationships are still rather approximate. It would be expedient to differentiate them through further research. Questions which arise are, for example, the following: Does the probability of the emergence of new socialization horizons grow in accordance with the strength of insecurity in respect to vocational biography? Are one, two, or three conditions — possibly in combination with other factors — sufficient in order to explain a tendency toward "new" socialization horizons? Must the milieu disintegration have an equal effect on both the family and the peer group? Is the objective milieu disintegration sufficient, regardless of the subjective perception of loss of a sense of belonging? What happens when content — based interests beyond the vocational field can be utilized? Do rationalizations exist which can compensate for experiences or anticipations of one's own performance in capabilities, etc., etc.? Due to lack of space, the answers to such questions, which could be formulated on the basis of our research material, cannot be presented here.

References

Abrahams, F., & Sommerkorn, J. (1976): Arbeitswelt, Familienstruktur und Sozialisation. In Hurrelmann, K.(Ed.): Sozialisation und Lebenslauf. Reinbek: Rowohlt

Allerbeck K., & Hoag, W. (1985): Jugend ohne Zukunft? Einstellungen, Umwelt, Lebensperspektiven. München/Zürich: Piper

Baacke, D. (1980): Der sozialökologische Ansatz. Deutsche Jugend, 11, 493−505

Bargel, T., Fauser, R., & Mundt, J. W. (1982): Lokale Umwelten und familiale Sozialisation: Konzeptualisierung und Befunde. In Vaskovics, L.A. (Ed.): Umweltbedingungen familialer Sozialisation. Stuttgart: Enke, 204−236

Beck, U. (1983): Jenseits von Stand und Klasse? Soziale Ungleichheiten, gesellschaftliche Individualisierungsprozesse und die Entstehung neuer Formationen und Identitäten. In Kreckel, R. (Ed.): Soziale Ungleichheiten. Soziale Welt, Sonderband 2, Göttingen: Schwartz, 35−74

Beck, U. (1986): Risikogesellschaft. Auf dem Weg in eine andere Moderne. Frankfurt: Suhrkamp

Beck−Gernsheim, E. (1983): Vom "Dasein für andere" zum Anspruch auf "ein Stück eigenes Leben". Individualisierungsprozesse im weiblichen Lebenszusammenhang. Soziale Welt, 34, 3, 307−340

Berger, P. A. (1987): Klassen und Klassifikationen. Zur "neuen Unübersichtlichkeit" in der soziologischen Ungleichheitsdiskussion. Kölner Zeitschrift für Soziologie und Sozialpsychologie, 39, 59−85

Berger, R. (1984): Zusammenhänge und Abhängigkeiten zwischen Lebensbereichen. In Glatzer, W., & Zapf, W. (Eds.): Lebensqualität in der Bundesrepublik. Frankfurt: Campus, 249−263

Bertram, H. (1976): Probleme einer soziostrukturell orientierten Sozialisationsforschung. Zeitschrift für Soziologie, 5, 103−117

Böhnisch, L. (1980): Jugendpolitik und Sozialpolitik. In Böhnisch, L., Müller−Stackebrandt, J., & Schefold, W.: Jugendpolitik im Sozialstaat. München: Juventa, 193−233

Burnham, J. (1949): Die Machiavellisten. Verteidiger der Freiheit. Zürich: Pan

Durkheim, F. (1965): Die Regeln der soziologischen Methode. (2nd ed.). Neuwied: Luchterhand

Fischer, W. (1982): Alltagszeit und Lebenszeit in Lebensgeschichten von chronisch Kranken. Zeitschrift für Sozialisationsforschung und Erziehungssoziologie, 1, 5−19

Fischer, W. (1983): Zeit und chronische Krankheit. Eine Untersuchung zur sozialen Konstitution von Zeitlichkeit. Darmstadt/Neuwied: Luchterhand

Glaser, B.G. (1978): Theoretical Sensitivity − Advances in the Methodology of Grounded Theory. Mill Valley: Sociology Press

Glaser, B.G., & Strauss, A.L. (1967): The Discovery of Grounded Theory. Strategies for Qualitative Research. Chicago: Aldine

Gottschalch, W., Neumann−Schönwetter, M., & Soukup, G. (1975): Sozialisationsforschung. Materialien, Probleme, Kritik. Frankfurt: Fischer

Griffith, I. (1985): Social support providers: Who are they? Where are they met? The relationship of network characteristics and psychological distress. Basic and Applied Psychology, 6, 41−60

Grüneisen, V., & Hoff, E. (1977): Familienerziehung und Lebenssituation. Weinheim: Beltz

Gurwitsch, A. (1977): Die mitmenschlichen Begegnungen in der Milieuwelt. Berlin/New York: De Gruyter

Heitmeyer, W. (1987): Rechtsextremistische Orientierungen bei Jugendlichen. Empirische Ergebnisse und Erklärungsmuster einer Untersuchung zur politischen Sozialisation. Weinheim: Juventa

Heitmeyer, W., & Möller, K. (1986): Die politische Sozialisation von Jugendlichen aus Arbeiterfamilien im Zusammenhang mit der Bedrohung durch Arbeitslosigkeit und neofaschistische Orientierungsmuster. Unpublished manuscript, University of Bielefeld

Heitmeyer, W., & Peter, J.—I. (1988): Jugendliche Fußballfans. Soziale und politische Orientierungen, Gesellungsformen, Gewalt. Weinheim/München: Juventa

Hradil, S. (1987): Sozialstrukturanalyse in einer fortgeschrittenen Gesellschaft. Von Klassen und Schichten zu Lagen und Milieus. Opladen: Leske & Budrich

Huch, K. J. (1975): Einübung in die Klassengesellschaft. Über den Zusammenhang von Sozialstruktur und Sozialisation. Frankfurt: Fischer

Hurrelmann, K. (1983): Das Modell des produktiv realitätverarbeitenden Subjekts in der Sozialisationsforschung. Zeitschrift für Sozialisationsforschung und Erziehungssoziologie, 3, 1, 91—103

Hurrelmann, K. (1988): Social structure and personality development. New York: Cambridge University Press

Kaase, M., & Klingemann, H.—D. (Ed.)(1983): Wahlen und politisches System: Analysen aus Anlaß der Bundestagswahl 1980. Opladen: Westdeutscher Verlag

Kern, H., & Schumann, M. (1982): Arbeit und Sozialcharakter: alte und neue Strukturen. In Matthes, J. (Ed.): Krise der Arbeitsgesellschaft? Verhandlungen des 21. Deutschen Soziologentages in Bamberg 1982. Frankfurt: Campus, 353—365

Kohli, M. (1986): Gesellschaftszeit und Lebenszeit. Der Lebenslauf im Strukturwandel der Moderne. In Berger, J. (Ed.): Die Moderne — Kontinuitäten und Zäsuren, Soziale Welt, Sonderband 4. Göttingen: Schwartz, 183—208

Lepsius, M.R. (1973): Parteiensystem und Sozialstruktur. In Ritter, G.A. (Ed.): Deutsche Parteien vor 1918. Köln: Kiepenheuer & Witsch

Luckmann, B. (1978): The Small Life—Worlds of Modern Man. In Luckmann, T. (Ed.): Phenomenology and Sociology. Harmondsworth: Penguin

Lüscher, K., Fisch, R., & Pape, T. (1985): Die Ökologie von Familien. Zeitschrift für Soziologie, 14, 1, 13—27

Mooser, J. (1983): Auflösung der proletarischen Milieus. Klassenbindung und Individualisierung in der Arbeiterschaft vom Kaiserreich bis in die Bundesrepublik Deutschland. Soziale Welt, 34, 3, 270—306

Olk, T. (1985): Jugend und gesellschaftliche Differenzierung — zur Entstrukturierung der Jugendphase. In Heid, H., & Klafki, W. (Ed.): Arbeit — Bildung — Arbeitslosigkeit. Beiträge zum 9. Kongreß der Deutschen Gesellschaft für Erziehungswissenschaft. 19. Beiheft der Zeitschrift für Pädagogik. Weinheim: Beltz, 290—302

Olk, T., & Heinze, R.G. (1985): Selbsthilfe im Sozialsektor. Perspektiven der informellen und freiwilligen Produktion sozialer Dienstleistungen. In Olk, T., & Otto, H.—U. (Eds.): Gesellschaftliche Perspektiven der Sozialarbeit, Vol. 4. Neuwied: Luchterhand

Rammstedt, O. (1975): Alltagsbewußtsein von Zeit. Kölner Zeitschrift für Soziologie und Sozialpsychologie, 27, 47—64

Reulecke, J., & Weber, W. (Ed.)(1978): Fabrik, Familie, Feierabend. Beiträge zur Sozialgeschichte des Alltags im Industriezeitalter. Wuppertal: Hammer

Scheler, M. (1966): Der Formalismus in der Ethik und die materiale Wertethik. Bern: Francke

Scheler, M. (1960): Die Wissensformen und die Gesellschaft. Bern: Francke

Schütz, A. (1980): The phenomenology of the social world. London: Heinemann Educational Books

SFB 3 (1984): Mikroanalytische Grundlagen der Gesellschaftspolitik. Unpublished manuscript, SFB 3, University of Frankfurt

Sprout, H., & Sprout, M. (1965): The ecological perspective on human affairs: With special reference to international politics. Princeton/New York: University Press

Steinkamp, G., & Stief, W.H. (1978): Lebensbedingungen und Sozialisation. Die Abhängigkeit von Sozialisationsprozessen in der Familie von ihrer Stellung im Verteilungssystem ökonomischer, sozialer und kultureller Ressourcen und Partizipationschancen. Opladen: Westdeutscher Verlag

Uttitz, P. (1984): Von den vertikalen Spannungslinien zu den horizontalen Gegensätzen: Wandel des Freizeitverhaltens als Indikator. Unpublished manuscript, University of Cologne

Walker, A. (1985): From welfare state to caring society? The promise of informal support networks. In Yoder, J.A. (Ed.): Suport networks in a caring community. Dordrecht: Nijhoff

Witzel, A. (1982): Verfahren der qualitativen Sozialforschung. Überblick und Alternativen. Frankfurt: Campus

19.

The Role of School, Family, and Peer Group in the Sexual Development of the Adolescent

Georg Neubauer and Wolfgang Melzer
University of Bielefeld, Federal Republic of Germany

The theoretical considerations and empirical findings presented in the following have been developed within the context of a current project on adolescence and sexuality in the time of AIDS. They relate to the concrete investigation of the status of early adolescence (14 to 18 years) as a life phase between childhood and adulthood in the process of sexual development.[1]

The project stands in the research tradition of socialization theory, but also in part of developmental psychology, that investigates the course of personality development in its confrontation with the social and material environment and how the human organism develops into a subject who is capable of action. In other words, we are concerned with the question of how the process of socialization and the process of individuation are interwoven and interlinked (Hurrelmann, 1988; Oerter and Montada, 1982).

1.   Adolescents and Sexuality − An Outline of the Problem

Adolescents very often are situated in an "orientation dilemma" (Baacke and Heitmeyer, 1985, 16) in solving their developmental tasks. This also applies to the area of sexuality, on which they can collect information, knowledge, and experience in their parental home, at school, and above all, in peer groups. The greater permissiveness toward questions of sexuality that can now also be seen in the parental home and school is, however, counteracted by the control function of these authorities. The greater degrees of freedom obtained are thus contrasted with a higher dependency in particular areas. The increased duration of education in particular means a postponement of the material independence which is an indispensible requirement for an autonomous lifestyle.

This increase in duration of education in the adolescent phase not only relativizes the importance of the parents but at the same time raises the relevance of the peer group. Both in the school and the clique, adolescents are separated from other age groups and social groups. These processes contribute to the emergence of images of the world and of the self that are specific to adolescence. Through their connection to school and information and communication networks of peer−groups, adolescents are confronted with tensions and inconsistencies, as well as new forms of demands and problem states that they increasingly have to endure and solve alone, outside of traditional certainties and often without collective supports. An example is the conflicts in value areas, as school and profession demand discipline, planning, achievement, and delay of gratification; while leisure time, in contrast, calls for the spending of money, hedonism, and an immediate orientation.

In the present societal conditions and risk constellations, such individualization processes are frequently evaluated as being threatening and stressing for the personal biography. For instance, adolescents have to experience that the transfer to employment is uncertain, the natural foundations of life are threatened by the destruction of the environment, and even the continuation of humanity is uncertain because of the threat of atomic war. In their confrontation with these potential dangers, they experience that demands are not only placed on them on an abstract, societal level, but also on a very personal level, for example, in the question of consumer behavior, of peacefullness, but also in the intimate sphere, and here specifically in the question of "natural" and "artificial" contraception. They have to "integrate" these demands into their life. With the arrival of the acquired immune deficiency syndrome (AIDS), there is even a virus directly attacking their intimate sphere in everyday life.

Even this short outline of the current life situation of adolescents shows that they are not without practice in confronting a "risk society" (Beck, 1986). Although they have more freedom compared to the past, they are under an increased pressure to find their own way. The available theories and empirical findings from adolescence research show that the demands on the competences of adolescents to cope with problems have changed qualitatively and increased quantitatively as a result of the above−mentioned societal changes. It is questionable whether adolescents can alone summon up the necessary action competences. The question of which supports − particularly in the field of the tasks of sexual development − can be expected from the parental home and school requires a precise scientific analysis.

We do not want to discuss the state of research in this field at this point. However, we wish to point out here that adolescent sexuality and its development have received little attention in West German research on adolescence within the social sciences. One reason for this appears to be the higher social estimation of school and career; in the concept that adolescents should give priority to educational and occupational qualifications, as this area of life remains a focus of central future decisions on their professional and social status as adults (Hurrelmann, Rosewitz, and Wolf, 1985). This trend is further reinforced by the uncertain employment situation in West Germany that heightens the career aspirations of both parents and children, with the consequence of an increased pressure on the children (Melzer, 1987).

Whether parents and school were able to fulfill their task of sexual education in the past has not been the object of comprehensive scientific evaluation. However, it can be assumed that important informations and values were conveyed in the context of both socialization authorities and were effective in a diffuse manner. Yet it has to be noted that adolescents question the plausibility of these authorities and subject them to reflective processing. This is even more the case when adolescents experience that the adults' blueprints for lifestyles cannot always serve them as models. The 1985 Jugendwerk study in the FRG has even shown the opposite: that parents have frequently adopted the habits of adolescents; they visit discotheques, are fashion conscious, and in this respect no longer offer any mentionable points of conflict against which adolescents can shape their own contours.

The style of parental upbringing has become more permissive: Parents possess less authority, and the relationships with adolescents are tending to become more like partnerships (Fend, 1988, 108). At the same time, these social relationships are defined through individual options and no longer through sociocultural definitions (Beck, 1986). This means that each network of relationships in which adolescents are now situated is an individual one, and, in all, there is a multitude of constellations of relationships in which the parents play, or can play, an important role.

In this chapter, we shall pay particular attention to the question of to what extent the parental home and the school accept the sexual questions of adolescents, and are in a position to provide the necessary support. A further focus is the role played in this process by the peer group and whether it functions as a part of the support network.[2]

After looking at the individual socialization authorities in the sequence of parental home, school, and peer group, possible consequences and considerations for sex education will be presented on the basis of these observations. This should also clarify the relationship between our empirical studies and the whole of our work, and the status of such basic knowledge for our educational work.

The empirical basis of the following observations is a survey study from 1987. In this study we used a standardized questionnaire to carry out a written survey of 14−to 18−year−old adolescents in North Rhine−Westphalia (Neubauer, 1987b). This questionnaire contained 78 questions or blocks of questions on the subject of sexuality and particularly recorded sexual behavior.

In the first phase of assessment, college students distributed the questionnaire to 14− to 18−year−old adolescents whom they knew personally. In addition, team leaders from youth groups or youth travel groups were asked to distribute the questionnaire to adolescents in youth clubs or during their excursions. We consciously selected this assessment technique in order to avoid bureaucratic restrictions in schools that we had previously experienced in another project dealing with this subject.

Furthermore, it became noticeable that when the questionnaire was filled out in groups outside of schools, adolescents were more highly motivated to reply to the questionnaire individually and without controls. For this reason, at the end of the assessment phase, we selected a procedure in which the adolescents should have the opportunity to fill out the questionnaire at home and return it anonymously to the research group in prepaid envelopes. For the above−mentioned reasons, we distributed the questionnaire *in front of* schools instead of in schools in the Bielefeld district. The proportion of girls in the total sample was 56%, and that of boys 44%. A total of 344 adolescents filled out the questionnaire.

2.   Socialization Authorities and Their Influence on the Sexual Behavior of Adolescents

The parental home

The importance of parental upbringing for the sexual development of children is sufficiently acknowledged in both scientific and legal contexts. On the one hand, it is confirmed that important dispositions that determine later sexual behavior are already formed during childhood; on the other hand, it is also legally ordained that sexual education is the responsibility of parents up to the 18th year of life, and only the parents can tranfer this responsibility to other persons.

Nevertheless, a great many studies have shown that parental sexual education is completely insufficient. The most recent comprehensive study was presented by Schmidt−Tannwald and Urdze (1983). Their explanation for this state of affairs was that "parental education is hampered or prevented by a generally reserved relationship between parents and adolescents, through the parents' lack of sexual knowledge, and through a taboo against sexual questions in the parental home" (Schmidt – Tannwald and Urdze, 1983, 68)[3]. However, at the same time they confirmed that the majority of adolescents have an open, trusting relationship with their parents. It must therefore be postulated that this reserve and silence has its roots in the specific subject of sexuality.

The taboo in this area is also shown when the interaction problems between parents and adolescents are investigated. In our study, we asked adolescents which of the following situations had at some time led to conflicts with their parents. The following response preferences in Table 1 were reported by the adolescents on a 4 – point Likert scale ranging from *never* (1) to *very often* (4). The table presents mean responses in an ordinal ranking.

Table 1: Conflicts with parents

Response categories	Means
Because of my untidiness	2.38
Because I didn't want to help in the home	2.25
Because of going out in the evenings	2.12
Because of my school work	2.08
Because of my bad manners	1.76
Because of my clothing	1.72
Because of my hairstyle	1.60
Because of smoking	1.53
Because of my friendships with girls/boys	1.50
Because of the music I wanted to listen to	1.48
Because of differences in political opinion	1.35

Untidiness, not wanting to help in the home, going out in the evenings, and school work are the situations that most frequently led to conflicts. The first two categories are everyday conflicts that arise in the network of relationships (e.g., social behavior in shared accomodation) and should not necessarily be interpreted as points of conflict with parents that are specific to adolescence. Going out in the evenings and school work are directly related to one another. "Someone who is out a lot in the evenings can't do well at school" is a statement from parents that we have all heard at some time or another. It is certain that this pressure from the parental home is expressed because a good school – leaving certificate is a *conditio sine qua non* for career success. This constellation leads to a higher level of aspiration regarding school – leaving certificates and occupational expectancies.

It is possible that uneasiness about their children's friendships with the opposite sex plays a role in some parents control of going out in the evenings. However, as Table 1 shows, this is hardly a direct point of confrontation between adolescents and parents. In contrast, "appearances" such as manners, clothing, and hairstyle, as well as smoking, music, and political opinions only play a subordinate role in the conflicts with parents.

When we look at communication as a form of support, we see that only 13% of the adolescents in our study reported that their parents were primary communication partners on questions of partnership and sexuality. They predominantly discussed such matters with their mother, and hardly at all with their father. More adolescents also reported that they got on either very well or well with their mothers (83%), compared to their fathers (69%). A further finding was that girls more frequently turned to their parents than boys to discuss partnership and sexuality (15% compared to 9%). However, they did not get on significantly better with their mothers than the boys.

In our study as well, 12% of the boys compared to 4% of the girls reported that they did not talk to anybody about partnership and sexuality. In addition, 30% of the boys and 16% of the girls disapproved of discussing this with further persons. The girls preferred to discuss it with their boyfriend (35%) or their girlfriend (33%); boys, if at all, with their girlfriend (21%) (cf. Table 3).

Before we deal more closely with the communication structure of the peer group for the subject of partnership and sexuality, we want to discuss the position of adolescents' sexual behavior within the family. Here too, we will first refer to the above—mentioned study from Schmidt—Tannwald and Urdze (1983). In their parent survey, they found that only circa 5% of parents had nothing against their children engaging in sexual intercourse between the ages of 13 and 17; circa a further quarter would not mind as long as safe contraception methods were used (Schmidt—Tannwald and Urdze, 1983, 76). One—fifth of the parents who found out that their children had previously engaged in sexual intercourse attempted to dissuade their children from further coital activity; one—half of the mothers attempted to advise their children on contraception. In contrast, almost two—thirds of the fathers kept out and did not concern themselves. More than one—third of the parents of daughters with experience of coitus and almost one—half of the parents of sons with experience of coitus were not aware of their child's experience of coitus. Sex—specific differences between girls and boys regarding their willingness to discuss sexual matters with their parents were also found here. If one compares the parental statements on girls with those on boys, it can be seen that parents more frequently attempt to restrain their daughters from further sexual intercourse than their sons (22% compared to 15%). In the latter, they more frequently tend not to get involved (Schmidt—Tannwald and Urdze, 1983, 79).

A similar result is shown in one of the questions in our study. The adolescents were asked to report whether they were allowed to spend the night at home with their girlfriend or boyfriend. The results are presented in Table 2.

Table 2:   Permission to sleep together in the parental home (percentage distribution)

Response categories	Sex		Age			Total
	M	F	14	16	18	
They would not allow it	15	32	49	21	5	24
They would insist that we slept apart	17	34	18	28	12	21
They would allow it with hesitation	48	33	27	36	45	25
They would allow it without hesitation	20	11	6	15	38	15
Total	100	100	100	100	100	100
N	143	184	51	91	56	327

Our table shows distinct sex — specific differences: Boys were more frequently allowed than girls to sleep together with a potential sexual partner in the parental home. At the same time, it can be seen that the parents' permission was dependent on age. However, this relationship also persisted when age and sex were controlled reciprocally. This was necessary, as girls were overrepresented in the younger age groups in our study. From the adolescents who had already had experience of sexual intercourse in our study (circa 40%), more than half reported that they had had their first sexual experience in the parental home or the parental home of their partner. There were no significant sex — specific or age — specific differences in this. If this finding is compared with older studies from the 1960s and 1970s, it would appear that the parental control over the home either no longer functions as a prevention of adolescent sexuality or that the parents are to some extent more prepared to either permit or tolerate the sexuality of their children in the parental home.

This change in parental behavior must, however, also be traced back to changes in material and social conditions. For instance, adolescents nowadays, on the one hand, more frequently have their own room into which they can withdraw, while, on the other hand, their right to sexuality is more widely accepted by the entire population, so that reproaches from neighbors and other persons have become less common. In particular, there is a widespread concept among adolescents themselves that the expression of sexuality belongs to their everyday life, so that parents who apply sanctions here generate a conflict, and parental bans would construct barriers between themselves and their children.

School

Both the Jugendwerk study (1985, 236) and the study from Schmidt—Tannwald and Urdze (1983, 62) come to the conclusion that sexual education in schools has increased in significance in recent years. This role could increase, because sexual education has been made obligatory in schools since 1968, that is, sexuality can be taught within the respective disciplines.

Nevertheless, there are still controversies for and against sexual education and regarding concepts and methods. With "yes, but ..." reactions, sexual education is only practiced in a half—hearted manner; it is also an expression of the teachers' problems with dealing with sexuality in the classroom (Neubauer, 1987a, 141).

Thus, in practice, sexual education is restricted to biology and the teaching of biological knowledge. Thus, a self—image of the school is expressed that completely limits its task to the conveyance of cognitive learning contents (Melzer, 1987, 100). The most important finding in our context is that there has been a general increase in information on the treatment of sexuality. But this knowledge only provides a minimum of assistance to adolescents in coping with their everyday problems.

Two examples may clarify this point: If, for example, one treats the subject of homosexuality in sexual education outside of schools, it becomes apparent that adolescents have "learnt" a cognitively tolerant understanding toward homosexuals particularly through the school. As a rule, they express the opinion that homosexuals should live out their sexuality and that homosexuality should be tolerated in society. However, if one asks adolescents how they would actually behave toward homosexuals in youth clubs, they mostly answer, "We would throw them out".

There is a similar discrepancy on the subject of contraception: Adolescents are certainly mostly able to name forms of contraception and point out that one should act responsibly and take preventive measures. However, if you place condoms in boys' hands, they tend to find them disgusting; they frequently do not trust themselves to use them. The situation is similar among girls, who, although they know the structure and function of their bodies, have still never inspected or touched their genitals; although the latter is necessary for the application of alternative forms of contraception to the pill, such as the diaphragm. Thus it becomes understandable that many adolescents fall back on the most "pleasant" form of contraception;

the pill (66%). For other forms of contraception, it is pointed out that they interfere with sexual intercourse and feelings, although they have never been tried out.

The last example makes it clear that although adolescents know about sexuality, they are unable to integrate this knowledge into their lifestyle and often engage in sexual intercourse without any form of contraception (circa 10%); an excessive feeling of shame and an incompetence in the application of forms of contraception also contribute to this. A further aspect is that despite "equal" knowledge, there can be a great variation in reactions. These starting conditions must also be taken into account in the development of preventive measures to deal with AIDS. Although schools can disseminate abstract knowledge, the communication of knowledge must always be accompanied by practical experiences. However, in our opinion, adolescents can only obtain this if in addition to explanation in sexual education they, for example, practice the putting on of condoms.

Thus teachers could encourage male adolescents to try out condoms at home, initially without a partner; adolescents could be encouraged to sit in front of a mirror and explore themselves in the comfort of their own homes − without feeling guilty about it. Even such proposals would cause many teachers and school directors to shake their heads and object that it is simply not possible to carry out such measures of sexual education in schools. Although, legally speaking, there would be no problems with the above − mentioned proposals, we know that schools make heavy weather with sexuality in general. Even today, students of both sexes have to experience that, for example, even caresses and friendships are often not allowed in the school; adolescents behave correspondingly and mostly hide their intimate areas from the school. In this way they learn that practiced sexuality belongs to the private sphere, has no place in school, and is for this reason insufficiently discussed in school on a practical level. As the following table shows, the school has a correspondingly low status as a source of information and experience in the consciousness of adolescents.

Table 3 shows yet again the importance of the parental home and the mother for girls in particular in a counseling process on sexuality. Professionals (e.g., doctors or psychologists) are rated higher than parents as counselors. However, peers rank in first place. It has to be assumed that these various groups also represent very different levels of interaction (symmetry, complementarity, competence, experience), and that the interaction partners change according to problem situation or state of interest, and several of these authorities can be drawn on simultaneously for advice according to an individual plan. Table 3

Table 3:   Percentage distributions of persons or institutions from whom or which one would
           want to learn more about partnership and sexuality (multiple answers)

Persons/Institutions	M	F	Total
Do not want any further information	30	16	22
Mother	9	24	17
Father	5	6	6
Professionals	15	29	23
School	7	7	7
Brother or sister	2	12	8
Boyfriend	13	35	26
Girlfriend	21	33	28
Other boys	15	19	17
Other girls	17	23	21
Books, newspapers, films	14	21	18

makes it clear that if adolescents in any way want to know more about sexuality, they particularly want to learn this from peers.

Peer group

Allerbeck and Hoag (1985, 39) come to the conclusion that the personal social network of adolescents is more dense in 1983 than it was in 1962. Adolescents increasingly organize themselves in cliques in which they spend their leisure time. In our survey, almost two−thirds of both girls and boys were integrated into such groups. It is noticeable that 70% of girls found themselves in informal groups that were made up of girls and boys in equal proportions; in contrast, 40% of boys mainly kept to male groups and only 44% were in mixed groups. In all, these adolescents reported that they did a great deal together in the clique, and that they met several times a week (70%).

It can be emphasized that the boys are concerned with recognition from other boys; their interest in relationships is directed toward boys. Relationships to girls tend to be more the means to this recognition, and therefore tend to be of secondary importance (Fricke, Klotz and Paulich, 1980, 37).

In our survey, 17% of the boys reported that a steady partner was important for recognition in the clique; this proportion was 6% in girls. Girls more frequently reported that a steady partner did not play any role for recognition in the clique (72% compared to 62% of the boys). Related to the forming of relationships between boys and girls, this means that both sides tended to have different interests when taking up a heterosexual relationship.

Girls most frequently talked about partnership and sexuality within the clique (54%). Only half as many boys did this. They prefered private discussion with the girlfriend (27%) or with a male friend (24%). These findings agree with the Jugendwerk study (1985, 245). This study concluded that, particularly for men, male peers play by far the most important role; in contrast, for the girls, the girlfriend suffers a loss of importance in the explanation of sexuality. In general, boys appear to be less communicative on the subject than girls (cf. Table 3). This is possibly also due to the fact that girls more frequently reported this question to be more important than, for example, school and career, than boys did. Thus 46% of the girls reported school and career to be the most important for them, in contrast to 57% of the boys (46% of the girls reported sexuality and partnership to be most important compared to 41% of the boys).

The results presented so far suggest that adolescents also receive different orientations in the field of sexuality. We have already shown that the parental home and the school set the demands placed on the adolescents by school and career at the focus of their interest. Adolescents feel themselves to be controlled by adults in this respect and treated as nonadults. The link to the peer group thus opens up more freedoms, but simultaneously means the confrontation with another system of values and norms that generally strongly deviates from the system of norms of the parental home or school.

The norms of the clique are predominantly recruited from youth culture and are mostly conveyed by the mass media. In this the clique represents a quasi – coordinating point: It communicates the latest norms of the youth culture to the individual. At the same time, it is the authority that takes care that norms are complied with and it controls this, although this is mostly not experienced as control (Fricke et al., 1980, 36).

Because of the restrictions in both the school and the parental home sketched above and the positive evaluation of the peers by the adolescents themselves, sexual education has principally and increasingly applied itself to youth work outside of schools. Through this work, sexual educators also have the opportunity to be able to share the experience of the direct expressions of everyday sexual experience, to observe, and apply their measures directly there (Marburger and Sielert, 1984, 128).

In the following discussion, we will consider whether this perspective of sexual education is correct in its exclusiveness, and/or what support can be provided by the family and school with regard to an interaction process in questions of sexuality and partnership.

3.   Consequences for Sexual Education

According to the above findings, we must place great emphasis on the importance of the peer authority as an interaction system, as a relatively free space with opportunities for (self−) experience in the field of sexuality − the one field that is either the subject of taboo or is only dealt with in a one−sided manner (e.g., only cognitively) in the other socialization contexts.

This is also the reason why we offered corresponding "forums" in public youth centers and evaluated the processes we found there in a sexual education project.[4] In this practical youth work, we experienced − rather like Allerbeck and Hoag − that peer groups are becoming increasingly important for leisure−time−related life practice, and that the cliques are, socially speaking, relatively homogeneous (Allerbeck and Hoag, 1985, 13). This makes it possible to fall back on similar backgrounds of experience and opinion. It is particularly these conditions that make sexual education outside of schools an increasingly important supplement to training in the school and family. For it is not just the experience of life and opinions of parents and teachers that guide adolescents, but, in addition, the experiences and opinions of the clique. Sexual education in youth work must therefore be located where adolescents tend to self−define and experience their everyday life. This is particularly: on the street, in youth clubs, in commercial adolescent meeting places (discotheques), on vacations, and so forth.

Here there is hardly any access threshold to adolescents, and they can also express themselves more freely even at low pain and problem levels (both are indeed also frequently repressed and covered up). The counseling educator must participate in these adolescent environments much more strongly than before, if adolescents are not to be totally abandoned in the subcultural ghetto.

The intent is not to "colonialize" adolescent environments, that is, to check and break social pluralization and individualization processes by educating and taking away the rights of adolescents, but to help design and accompany these processes in a self−controlled and counseling manner.

The open and voluntary principles used in sexual education find a way between two extreme poles: one that takes complete influence on the design of youth work or the second that withdraws from it completely. In both cases, youth work outside of schools must start with the interests and demands of the adolescents, take up their impulses and suggestions — quite simply: take adolescents seriously. However, the open and voluntary principles produce a range of educational problems. For example, as a rule there is no set group of participants but rather an unspecified one. The same ambiguity applies to the curriculum. A certain continuity and commitment can consequently only arise in the concrete work. In this process, patterns of behavior have to develop that are expected and supported by the group, so that adolescents can gain trust. It is understood that these frameworks cannot simply be educationally predetermined and set. It is far more the case that they have to be negotiated with adolescents. In this sense, sexual education outside of schools could be conceived as a forum in which the participants can voice, investigate, and work out their ideas, problems, and solution strategies with educational and other professional support (e.g., doctors, psychologists, family planning, AIDS self—help groups).

This form of sexual education is in no way concerned with splitting up parental home, school, and peer group. It must, however, be noted that adolescents find themselves in a process of separation from the parental home even during the early phase of adolescence, and — particularly as far as the process of sexual development is concerned — they require a freedom that is only partially provided in the lap of the family. Familial restrictions often arise from a parental awkwardness and incompetence in questions of sexuality. Sexual education outside of schools can in contrast present support and offers of educational self—regulation less awkwardly and with the necessary distance and competence so that adolescents are not left alone with their problems (Neubauer, 1986).

One criticism raised against the approach of sexual education outside of schools is that it only reaches a subgroup of adolescents while schools reach all adolescents. The current discussion on AIDS prevention also confirms this tendency to prefer school education despite the previous experiences in sexual education. But if we look at the curricula on AIDS published by the ministries of culture and the national center for health education in West Germany, we again run into the same dilemma: Both students and teachers are trained to become professional virologists; the transfer into life—related, social, interpersonal relations, the critical assessment of panic—raising media reportage, and so forth, receive far too little attention and, as expected, can in no way be performed by the teachers. The national center touches upon this in AIDS teaching material for the 9th and 10th grades: One of the difficulties is, that the conditions under which there is a particularly high risk of infection relate to forms of behavior that normally are not dealt with in the classroom (e.g., oral and anal intercourse, homosexuality, bisexuality, promiscuity). This can lead to the teachers developing reservations and insecurities about the subject that permit them to distance themselves from dealing with it in the classroom.

The measures of sexual education in *some* West German states partially recognize this problem. For example, Berlin implemented a "School Worker Program" in 1987. In this program, sexual education is taught by external experts. North–Rhine Westphalia launched the "Youth Worker Program" in 1988, in which sexual education is planned both inside and outside of schools. Both programs are based on the estimation that the teachers' opportunities for dealing with sexuality and AIDS within the normal school curriculum are problematic. At the same time, this also shows that the subject of sexuality is still a "hot potato" for many of those who are concerned with the educational process. The parents often feel overwhelmed because they have difficulties in dealing with the subject and themselves do not know enough about it. The teachers share their difficulties and take cover behind the dissemination of facts. The adolescents see and experience these difficulties and do not expect any further support from these authorities of socialization in this form – not least because of the control they exercise and the adolescents' subordinate status (Neubauer, 1986).

Despite the recent growth in the discussion of "sexuality and AIDS", the scene appears to an observer as a shunting yard of competences and responsibilities. The problems are only shunted between the authorities, but not solved in a concentrated action as would be sensible. Once again, it should be stated distinctly that this is not a plea to leave adolescents to cope by themselves. This would only encourage a further segregation of adolescents and isolate them even more from the milieu – specific experiences of adults. With the present state of knowledge, the question whether sexual education outside of schools can be the only didactic answer has to be kept open. In our opinion, there must be a further discussion of concepts, such as treating the school as a social meeting place.[5] For instance, sexuality could be mentioned openly in the classroom (also by involved teachers) so that it is not a "secret curriculum" that is conveyed and discussed, for example, in the "underlife" of the school yard.

Furthermore, it would be conceivable to use the school to provide parents with the opportunity to approach this subject at parent – teacher meetings in order to also help reduce their own (feelings of) incompetence (Melzer, 1985). The inclusion of the parental home is not only supported by our research finding that the presentday relationship between parents and adolescents can be rated good (Jugendwerk, 1985). Parents still have an influence on their children (Kandel and Lesser, 1972), particularly in decisions with long – term effects (e.g., career and marriage/partnership). In contrast, a higher estimation should be made of the influence of peers in questions dealing with current status and immediate problems (Brittain, 1969). A link between school and peer socialization does not only exist, however, because school is also a social meeting point, but because this general network of relationships with its largely formalized and alienated interaction (student – teacher relationship as an asymmetric relationship; student – student relationship as a competitive relationship) also contains informal relationships to fellow students that extend beyond the field of school and lead to the formation of cliques. Most students find their best friend among their circle of classmates. This is a further indication of the necessity to support the availability of an integrative system of support in every kind of prevention measure and to consider how to realize the support potential of family and school as well (Hurrelmann, 1987).

Notes

[1]   The members of the project team are Wilfried Ferchhoff, Wolfgang Melzer, and Georg Neubauer from the Department of Educational Science at the University of Bielefeld. It is intended to use the results of the planned main study for a comparative study of adolescent sexuality in West Germany and Israel. For this purpose, we have formed a research group together with two Israeli colleagues (Dr. Ronny Shtarkshall, University of Jerusalem; Dr. Michael Nathan, University of Haifa).

[2]   The mass media remain important sources of information and explanation. However, "In total the significance of the media is also limited for adolescents" (Jugendwerk, 1985, 236). In this study, circa 8% of adolescents named adolescent magazines as their source of information. In our survey, 18% of the adolescents desired further information through books, magazines, and films (see Table 2).

[3]   We have translated all quotations from German for this article.

[4]   The following considerations are taken from a project on sexual education and AIDS prevention in youth work that we have been running since April 1988. This is being financed by the minister for work, health, and social welfare in the state of North – Rhine Westphalia. The project is testing and evaluating forms of sexual education outside of schools (cf. also Neubauer, 1984, 1986).

[5]   The American examples of youth counseling services show that schools can function as a support network (Coleman, 1974). In particular, Scandinavian experiences with the treatment of sexuality in schools provide important indications (cf. for Sweden: Bergström – Walan, 1984, 301; for Denmark: Mollerup, 1984, 340). In West Germany such programs are only just beginning – but there are scientific considerations that take a similar direction (Hurrelmann, 1988).

References

Allerbeck, K., & Hoag, W. (1985): Jugend ohne Zukunft? München/Zürich: Piper

Beck, U. (1986): Risikogesellschaft. Frankfurt: Suhrkamp

Brittain, C.V. (1969): A comparison of rural and urban adolescents with respect to compliance. Adolescence, 4, 59 – 68

Fend, H. (1988): Sozialgeschichte des Aufwachsens. Frankfurt: Suhrkamp

Fricke, S., Klotz, M., & Paulich, P. (1980): Sexualerziehung? Köln: Bund

Hurrelmann, K., Rosewitz, B., & Wolf, H. (1985): Lebensphase Jugend. Weinheim/München: Juventa

Hurrelmann, K. (1987): The importance of school in the life course. Journal of Adolescent Research, 2, 111–125

Hurrelmann, K. (1988): Social structure and personality development. New York: Cambridge University Press

Jugendwerk der Deutschen Shell (1985): Jugendliche und Erwachsenen '85. Opladen: Leske & Budrich

Kandel, D.B., & Lesser, G.S. (1972): Youth in two worlds. San Fransisco: Jossey–Bass

Marburger, H., & Sielert, U. (1984): Sexualerziehung in der Jugendarbeit. In Kluge, J. (Ed.): Sexualpädagogik Bd. II. Düsseldorf: Schwann–Bagel

Melzer, W. (1985): Objektive und subjektive Bedingungen für Elternpartizipation in Schule und Lehrerschaft. In Melzer, W. (Ed.): Eltern – Schule – Lehrer. Weinheim/München: Juventa, 129–157

Melzer, W. (1987): Familie und Schule als Lebenswelt. Weinheim/München: Juventa

Neubauer, G. (Ed.)(1986): Sexualpädagogik in der offenen Jugendarbeit. Bielefeld (unpublished manuscript)

Neubauer, G. (1987a): Jugend und Sexualität. In Neubauer, G., & Olk, T. (Eds.): Clique – Mädchen – Arbeit. Weinheim/München: Juventa, 123–145

Neubauer, G. (1987b): Jugend und Sexualität. Bielefeld (unpublished manuscript)

Oerter, R., & Montada, L. (Eds.)(1982): Entwicklungspsychologie. München: Psychologie Verlags Union

Schmidt–Tannwald, I., & Urdze, A. (1983): Sexualität und Kontrazeption aus der Sicht von Jugendlichen und ihren Eltern. In Schriftenreihe des Bundesministeriums für Jugend, Familie Bd. 132. Stuttgart: Kohlhammer

Part V
Educational and Occupational Careers

20.

Parents' Management of Adolescents' Schooling: An International Comparison

David P. Baker and David L. Stevenson
The Catholic University, Washington, USA
Department of Education, Washington, USA

In studying the lives of adolescents, researchers often examine the separate and distinct influences of school and parents. There are, however, linkages among schools, parents and adolescents. In this paper, we examine one of these linkages. We focus on the relationship between the organization of schooling and how parents manage their adolescent's school career in three countries: the United States (USA), the Federal Republic of Germany (FRG), and Japan.

In the educational systems of these countries, as in the formal educational systems of most countries throughout the world, adolescents are "sorted" during secondary schooling. They may be divided into different levels of a curriculum, different types of curricula, or different schools. The sorting of students may be related to future educational and labor market opportunities. For instance, an academic curriculum track is designed to prepare students for attending university while a vocational curriculum is designed to prepare students for entry into certain occupations. This allocation of students into different types of secondary schooling often has life long consequences for an adolescent's occupational status and general social status.

Parents recognize and respond to these significant educational allocation decisions. We argue, however, that differences in the organization of allocation processes shape parents' management of their adolescents' school careers. To examine several implications of this argument, we conducted a series of studies in three national educational systems.

1. Parental Management of School Careers

One way to assess the continuing role of parents in the adolescent's life is to examine parental involvement in the day – to – day activities of secondary schooling. Parents who are motivated and informed may manage their child's school career to help their child obtain important school credentials. The parental management perspective expands other family – school perspectives (Dornbusch et al., 1987; Majoribanks, 1979; Scott – Jones, 1984; Steinberg et al., 1988). First, this perspective examines what parents do at each stage of schooling. Second, it examines how the requirements of schooling over the school career influence parental actions (Epstein & Becker, 1982):

Educational attainment in modern school systems requires both academic achievement and a skillful approach to the organization of schooling. At each successive stage, schooling becomes more complex in terms of the institutional procedures, such as the manner by which students are placed into different courses, as well as the substantive academic material. By considering the parent as a manager of the adolescent's school career, we examine an additional link between allocation within schooling and family influences on educational opportunity.

2. School as an Allocative Context

Allocation theories of education depict schools as sorting, selecting, and credentialing students (Meyer, 1977). Schools group students by age and require them to develop social and cognitive skills. Advancement within schooling is based on allocation rules that govern educational transitions. These rules, however, change according to the stage of the student's school career. In the primary grades, school advancement is dominated by rules based on social and cognitive development (Parsons, 1959; Entwisle & Hayduk, 1983). Young children must display certain standards of behavior, cognitive competencies, and social maturity before beginning the next stage of schooling. In the secondary grades, competitive selection is an additional allocation rule. The competitive rules governing school transitions during adolescence have implications for how and when parents manage the school careers of their child. Different educational systems use different allocative rules, especially during the important transitions to postsecondary education or the labor market.

In his classic article, Turner (1960) distinguishes between two general methods of allocating students: contest and sponsored mobility. In educational systems stressing contest mobility, "elite status is the prize in an open contest and is taken by the aspirants' own efforts" while in those stressing sponsored mobility, "elite recruits are chosen by the established elite or their agents, and elite status is *given* on the basis of some criterion of supposed merit and cannot be *taken* by any amount of effort or strategy" (Turner, 1960, 856–857).

The three educational systems that we examine have different allocation mechanisms: Secondary educational allocation in the U.S. is a "continual contest", since there are many competitive academic situations over the years of high school. Allocation to secondary schools in the FRG is generally low in competition, occurs at one point in time and has many sponsored qualities. Allocation in the Japanese educational system is a unique mixture of contest and sponsorship mechanisms that we describe as "contested sponsorship." Japanese students compete for admission to secondary schools and university and upon admission to a prestigious university students are sponsored into an elite.

Another important institutional characteristic of schooling is the school charter. Schools may have distinctive charters and therefore the ability to "define people as graduates and as therefore possessing distinctive rigths and capacities in society" (Meyer, 1977, 59). In some educational systems, such as in the FRG, different types of secondary schools have different charters and therefore the graduates have different occupational and educational opportunites. In other educational systems, such as the U.S., most secondary schools share a common charter.

3. Empirical Studies

The United States

Two distinct institutional characteristics of U.S. schooling have an impact upon how parents manage the school careers of their adolescents. One is the method by which students are allocated to schools. In the U.S., entrance into public secondary schools is not based on entrance examinations or competitions, but rather all students in a residential area have equal access to the public high school. Although there may be tracks within a high school, the curriculum of the track is defined locally rather than nationally. Also, the boundaries between these tracks are very permeable as students select and take courses in different tracks. In fact, many students can not properly identify their curriculum track (Rosenbaum, 1980). Rules governing school transitions within U.S. public secondary schools are based on teachers' evaluation of the students' cognitive and social performance. In general, such allocation procedures can be influenced by student and parental actions.

During secondary education a student's progress is not marked by irrevocable decisions that fix future educational possibilities. For instance, students are more likely restricted from attending college by their failure to apply than by their high school grades (Stevenson & Baker, 1988a).[1]

U.S. secondary schools do not have distinctly different charters, and graduates receive the same credential regardless of the school they attend. Individuals with only high school diplomas appear to have similar labor market experiences regardless of the high school they attended. And, whether the student has been enrolled in an academic or general curriculum is not related to the prestige of their future occupation (Kerckhoff & Everett, 1986). Many state university systems accept almost all high school graduates, and, therefore, admission to postsecondary education in the United States approaches a general entitlement with about one half of graduating high school seniors continuing to postsecondary education (Stevenson & Baker, 1988a).

In a system of undifferentiated secondary schooling in which school promotions are based upon teachers' evaluation of school performance, in which allocation approaches a semi-voluntary process, and in which secondary schools do not have distinctly different charters, what do parents do to manage the school career of their adolescents?

In several studies of American parents' management of adolescents' school careers, we predicted that parents would have a constant, long-term interest in their adolescents' daily school performance and in motivating their adolescents to do well in the academic activities of the local school. Since no single school transition dominates the life chances of the American student, parents are compelled to remain involved throughout their children's school careers. The sponsor-less, loosely coupled character of schooling in the U.S. requires parents to remain informed about their child's schooling to assure appropriate management strategies.

To be an effective parent for educational success in the U.S. requires relatively demanding and continuing effort. Parents who know more about the educational system and who have more resources will be more likely and able to manage their child's school career. Also, since the institutional structure of American schooling favors those who take a direct and proactive role, informed parental management ought to yield educational benefits to students.

Findings from our studies of parental management in the U.S. lend support to these claims. Parental management of schooling, particularly among parents of young adolescents, was identified by most parents as an important parental activity. The American parents that we interviewed, consistently described a set of actions about managing their child's schooling that appeared to be a commonly known "script" of what parents should do about their adolescent's schooling (Baker & Stevenson, 1986). Knowledge of this script did not vary across parents of different socio−economic statuses or between parents of sons and parents of daughters. Management of a school career was closely tied to the American parents' definition of a "good" parent.

We did, however, find differences among parents in whether they acted upon the common script for management of their child's schooling. For example, mothers of higher socioeconomic status were more likely to have greater knowledge about their child's schooling and more contact with the school in a variety of ways (Baker & Stevenson, 1986; Stevenson & Baker, 1987). Also, college educated parents, whose adolescents were performing poorly in school, were less likely to follow the curriculum recommendations of the school and more likely to have arranged for their child to be admitted to the advanced courses. Parents with less education tended to follow the track placement recommendations of the school. Parental management also appeared to be associated with higher school grades across elementary and secondary schooling (Stevenson & Baker, 1987), and such effects are similar to the results of other American studies (Porter, 1968; Lareau, 1985). The openness of the American school system emphasizes that individual students and their parents decide the direction of student's school career relying upon persistence, performance in local school settings, and knowledge of the educational system. This institutional quality of the educational system also places greater responsibility on parents to manage their child's school career.

The Federal Republic of Germany

The institutional structure of secondary schooling in the FRG differs from secondary schooling in U.S., and so does the pattern of parental management of adolescents' school careers. The most salient institutional difference between the two secondary educational systems, and the characteristic which dominates the family−school relationship within the FRG, is a set of differentiated secondary schools. There are four different school types, each with a distinct charter to different educational and labor market opportunities. The different types of secondary schools are physically separated and confer different social statuses upon their graduates. We argued that this institutional characteristic of the secondary system shapes important dimensions of the family — school connection in the FRG. Specifically, parents' management of their adolescents' schooling is influenced by which type of secondary school their adolescents attend.

The four types of secondary schools are the *Gymnasium*, *Realschule*, *Hauptschule*, and *Gesamtschule*. The first three make up the traditional hierarchical system of secondary education and the fourth is a relatively recent reform.

— The *Gymnasium* is the secondary school that serves as preparation for the *Abitur* degree which grants entrance into the university system. Lasting until grade 13, the *Gymnasium* has a rigorous traditional academic curriculum and has been tightly linked to higher positions in the labor market, such as professionals, politicans, and academics. Its elite position in the educational system is reflected by the fact that it is relatively difficult and rare to enter the *Gymnasium* from other types of secondary schools or to drop out before completion.

— The *Realschule* is the secondary school that leads to the *Mittlere Reife* degree, which is based on students' grades and final examination performance. Lasting until grade 10, the *Realschule* has a mixed curriculum stressing academic, vocational and business skills that are training for a range of skilled blue — collar occupations and business apprenticeships. The *Mittlere Reife* is more loosely tied to the labor market and unlike the *Abitur* does not guarantee postsecondary education. *Realschule* students are managed in a more openly competitive mode, intensified by the tension to complete the *Mittlere Reife*, which is necessary to be a "modern German" (Hearnden, 1976).

— The *Hauptschule* is the minimum compulsory secondary schooling leading to a certificate after grade 9 or 10. This vocational form of schooling leads to low — level jobs in industry, service and agriculture.

— The *Gesamtschule* is fashioned after a comprehensive high school model. Students can earn any of the three secondary degrees and often take a mixture of courses from the traditional *Gymnasium*, *Realschule* or *Hauptschule* curricula. The *Gesamtschule* was developed to weaken the traditional demarcation among the three traditional schools. There is no compulsory curriculum tracking within the *Gesamtschule* and students are encouraged to choose their curriculum as they strive for one of the three traditional degrees.

In the FRG, differences among secondary school types play an important role in defining the contours of the adolescent's world and in shaping how parents can influence their world. Specifically, we investigated whether parents differed in their management of *Gymnasium, Realschule,* and *Gesamtschule* school careers.[2] We expected that the type of secondary school that the student attended would be associated with different patterns of parental management (Oswald, Baker, & Stevenson, 1988). For example, we predicted that the comprehensive organization of the *Gesamtschule* encouraged parents to do more managing of school than parents of students in either the *Gymnasium* or the *Realschule.* The organization of the *Gesamtschule* influenced parents to become more involved by motivating them to act on behalf of their adolescents in a school where course selection and curriculum management are directly related to the attainment of different secondary degrees. We also expected parents of students in *Realschule* to do more management than parents of students in the *Gymnasium* for several reasons. One is that, compared to the *Gymnasium,* the *Realschule* has a less – clear charter and presents the students with a wider range of occupational choices, and therefore may raise the demand for parental help in selecting various paths for the student. Another reason that we expected greater parental management was that the less sponsored *Realschule* may facilitate informal parental participation, while the elite sponsorship of the *Gymnasium* may discourage informal parental participation. Finally, since completing the *Realschule* has become the cutoff for entering the expanding German middle class, parents of *Realschule* students may be more involved in order to prevent their child from dropping to the *Hauptschule.*

From a large sample of parents and adolescents in West Berlin we collected data similar to those collected in the American studies. To test these school type hypotheses, we added a school charter (school type) variable to a multivariate model of parental management which was developed in previous work with U.S. samples and with German samples (Barsch et al., 1976; Freese, 1976; Baker and Stevenson, 1986).

As we predict, the type of secondary school the adolescents attended was associated with distinct patterns of parental management of schooling. Parents of *Gesamtschule* adolescents were the most involved and also were most likely to be informally involved in such activities as helping with homework, discussing course selection, and speaking to teachers. There were less sharp contrasts between *Realschule* parents and *Gymnasium* parents, but the former were more informally involved (helping with homework, discussing course selections with their child) and the latter were more formally involved (attending Parent – Teacher Association and serving as school representatives).

We did not find a separate and consistent association between the level of family background and parental involvement. This finding was different from our findings in the American studies. We speculated that there was a lack of social class effects for two reasons. First, the major point of school allocation in their German educational system occurs at the end of elementary schooling when school officials place students in different types of secondary schools. At this point there are notable effects of social class in both the decisions of school personnel and the likelihood of parents attempting to influence the allocation process on behalf of their child. Once students are placed in secondary schools, we found that the institutional characteristics of the secondary school were more important determinants of parents' management than was the social class of the parents.

A second reason for a lack of social class effects on parents' management was the sponsorship qualities of the German secondary educational system. In a non—sponsored educational system, like that found in the U.S., allocation is a long—term and continual process. Therefore, differences in the abilities of parents of different social classes to influence the allocation process are diffused throughout the school career. In the sponsored educational system of FRG, the charters of secondary schools are so clear and meaningful to the future of the student that the social class effects on parental management are lessened.

Japan

Secondary schooling in Japan has a different type of institutional arrangement and, therefore, different patterns of how parents manage their adolescents' school careers. The primary school allocation point occurs at the end of high school. Most Japanese universities require applicants to take university entrance examinations. Admission is based almost entirely on a student's performance on the entrance examination. This practice significantly diminishes the importance of high school grades for students with college aspirations (Rohlen, 1983).

Most secondary schools in Japan, like those in the U.S., have the same charter, and their academic curriculum is oriented towards preparation for the university entrance examinations. Japanese universities, unlike those in the United States, do have significantly different charters. Graduates of a set of prestigious universities have access to careers in the most prestigious firms and departments of the civil service. These graduates have life—long advantages over graduates of lesser universities. Gaining admission to prestigious Japanese universities is, therefore, a key to later life success (Amano, 1986; Brinton, 1988; Cummings, 1980).

What do parents do when the educational allocation process is dominated by an openly competitive and performance based decision point? One thing that Japanese parents do is to invest in a wide variety of school examination preparation activities. In our study we described such preparation activities as part of "shadow education" (Stevenson & Baker, 1988b). We define shadow education as a set of educational activities that are not part of the formal educational system but whose expressed purpose is to enhance the student's school career. Shadow education is shaped by the institutional rules governing school careers in the formal educational system. A change in the institutional criteria, such as decreasing the significance of university entrance examinations and increasing the significance of grades, would bring a corresponding change in the activities of shadow education. During the high school years, shadow education consists of activities such as correspondence courses, practice university examinations, tutoring, and private cram schools. Also, students who fail the university examinations and wish to reapply can spend an additional year or two after high school in full-time preparation for the next annual round of examinations.

In Japan, shadow education is one way in which parents can attempt to influence and manage their adolescent's school career. In our study of shadow education and the transition to university, we examined which parents purchased several types of preparation activities and what influences these services had on the adolescent's school career (Stevenson & Baker, 1988b). We found that sons rather than daughters were more likely to engage in these preparation activities. We also found that students with parents of higher socio-economic status were more likely to use these strategies. The effects of participation in shadow education for an adolescent's education can be significant. For example, there was a large advantage in spending an extra year or two after high school preparing for the university entrance examinations. Such students were more likely to gain admission to a prestigious university. By supporting their adolescents' participation in shadow education, parents directly influenced their adolescents' educational and occupational opportunities.

4. Discussion

We have described the relationship between characteristics of educational systems and how parents manage the school careers of their adolescents in three educational systems. In the loosely coupled American educational system, consisting of schools with generally undifferentiated charters, parents tend to manage the daily school activities of their children. We found that parents who do this type of parental management raised the academic standing of their children. In the more tightly coupled West German system, consisting of secondary schools with highly differentiated charters, parental management differed according to the type of secondary school. Parents engaged in less management in the sponsored *Gymnasium* than in the less—sponsored *Realschule* or the comprehensive *Gesamtschule*. Finally, in the Japanese educational system, which has a competitive selection process and universities with different charters, we found that parents invested in a set of schooling activities outside of formal schooling. By supporting the adolescent's use of examination preparation activities, parents influenced the adolescent's educational and occupational opportunities.

In three educational systems, we have shown a relationship between the organization of allocation and parents' managerial actions. The differences in the ability and motivation of parents to undertake successful managerial strategies has implications for a general theory of educational stratification during adolescence. Stratification by social class may move through the educational system, in part, because of a specific type of parent—school relationship that is shaped by the institutional character of the educational system.

Stratification occurs to varying degrees in all modern educational systems. In many educational systems, adolescents from families of higher socioeconomic status obtain more or better education than adolescents from families of lower socioeconomic status, and males have better educational opportunities than females. Speculations about these findings have focused either on family based differences in children's learning capacities, socialization, and motivation, or on school—based practices. Our research suggests additional mechanisms behind educational stratification. Educational systems differ in how schooling is organized and in what rules govern school transitions. Such institutional features of schooling can permit, encourage, and channel parents' managerial actions about their child's schooling. The managerial actions of parents can help to create patterns of educational stratification by social class, gender, and other social characteristics. A better understanding of how institutional characteristics of schooling influence the family—school relationship would lead to a comprehensive theory of educational stratification during adolescence.

Notes

The research reported in this article was supported by a grant to Dr. Baker from the Spencer Foundation, National Academy of Education. The authors thank Dr. Hans Oswald of the Freie Universität Berlin for his collaboration on the study of adolescents in Berlin (West) and Sally Flanzer, Klaus Hurrelmann, and Maryellen Schaub for comments on earlier drafts. A version of this paper was presented at the Annual Meeting of the Sociology of Education Section of their German Sociological Association in Arnoldshain, Federal Republic of Germany. The views expressed here do not necessarily reflect the position or policy of the U.S. Department of Education and no official endorsement should be inferred.

[1] While it is relatively easy to gain admission to some legitimate institution of higher education, it does require, at the minimum, that students remain in the system and this is often a question of persistence and parental support. Approximately one fourth of American high school students drop out and, at least temporarily, end their pursuit of more education.

[2] The data were collected only from West German citizens living in West Berlin. Because Hauptschulen in Berlin enroll such a large number of foreign (guestworker) students, the sample did not yield enough German Hauptschule parents to include in our analysis.

References

Amano, I. (1986): Educational crisis in Japan. In Cummings, W.K., Beauchamp, E.R., Ichikawa, S., Kobayashi, V.N., & Ushiogi, M. (Eds.): Educational policies in crisis. New York: Praeger, 23 – 43

Baker, D.P., & Stevenson, D.L. (1986a): Mothers' strategies for children's school achievement: Managing the transition to high school. Sociology of Education, 59, 156 – 166

Barsch, W., Gehrken, K., & Janowski, A. (1976): Wechselwirkung zwischen Schule und Familie. München: Deutsches Jugendinstitut

Brinton, M. (1988): The social – institutional bases of gender stratification: Japan as an illustrative case. American Journal of Sociology. Forthcoming

Cummings, W. (1980): Education and equality in Japan. Princeton: Princeton University Press

Dornbusch, S., Ritter, P., Liederman, P., Roberts, D., & Fraleigh, M. (1987): The relation of parenting style to adolescent school performance. Child Development, 58, 1244 – 1257

Entwisle, D., & Hayduk, L. (1983): Early schooling. Baltimore: The John Hopkins University Press

Epstein, J., & Becker, H. (1982): Teacher practices of parental involvement. Elementary School Journal, 83, 103 – 113

Freese, H.L. (1976): Schulleistungsrelevante Merkmale der häuslichen Erziehungsumwelt. Studien und Berichte des Max – Planck – Instituts für Bildungsforschung, Vol. 35. Berlin

Hearnden, A. (1976): Education, culture and politics in West Germany. Oxford: Pergamon Press

Kerckhoff, A., & Everett, D. (1986): Sponsored and contest education pathways to jobs in Great Britain and the United States. In Kerckhoff, A. (Ed.): Research in sociology of education and socialization, Vol.6. Greenwich: JAI Press, 133 – 164

Lareau, A. (1987): Social class differences in family – school relationships: The importance of cultural capital. Sociology of Education, 60, 73 – 85

Marjoribanks, K. (1979): Families and their learning environments. London: Routledge and Kegan Paul

Meyer, J. (1977): The effects of education as an institution. American Journal of Sociology, 83, 55–77

Oswald, H., Baker, D.P., & Stevenson, D.L. (1988): Secondary school charters and parental management in West Germany. Sociology of Education, 61, 4.

Parson, T. (1959): The social class as a social system: Some of its functions in American society. Harvard Educational Review, 29, 4, 297–318

Porter, J. (1968): The future of the upward mobility. American Sociological Review, 33, 5–19

Rohlen, T. (1983): Japan's high schools. Berkeley: University of California

Rosenbaum, J. (1980): Track misperceptions and frustrated college plans: An analysis of the effects of tracks and track perception in the National Longitudinal Survey. Sociology of Education, 53, 74–88

Scott–Jones, D. (1984): Family influences on cognitive development and school achievement. In Gordon, E. (Ed.): Review of research in education. Washington: American Educational Research Association Press, 259–304

Steinberg, L., Brown, B., Cider, M., Kaczmarck, N., & Lazzaro, C. (1988): Noninstructional influence on high school student achievement report: National Center on Effective Secondary Schools

Stevenson, D.L., & Baker, D.P. (1987): Family–school relations and the child's school performance. Child Development, 58, 1348–1357

Stevenson, D.L., & Baker, D.P. (1988a): Transition to postsecondary education in the United States. In Greene, A.L., & Boxer, A.M. (Eds.): Transitions through adolescence: Research and theory in life–span perspective. Hillsdale/New Jersey: Erlbaum

Stevenson, D.L., & Baker, D.P. (1988b): Shadow education and the transition to university in Japan. Paper presented at the American Sociology Association meetings, Atlanta

Turner, R. (1960): Sponsored and contest mobility and the school system. American Sociological Review, 25, 855–867

21.
Social Reproduction and School Leavers: A Longitudinal Perspective

Claire Wallace
Plymouth Polytechnic, Great Britain

1. Theoretical Approaches

From the 1960s onward, a number of studies have looked at the transition from school to work (which in England began at the age of 15 and after 1972 at the age of 16). The main problematic was to explain how young people from different social class backgrounds willingly entered the same sorts of jobs as their fathers. This was particularly difficult to account for in the case of young working – class people who were destined to enter the sorts of employment that had the worst prospects and working conditions — although at the age of 15 or 16 these jobs also paid the most.

Some explained this by reference to the kinds of values imparted by the workplace to different groups of workers and the ways in which these were reflected in child rearing practices and in educational experiences (Ashton and Field, 1976). For example, those in more middle – class and professional jobs encouraged autonomy and independent thinking in their children, which was in turn rewarded at school. The children of those in clerical and skilled manual jobs were more instrumental in their school orientation and were likely to enter "short term careers". Those from unskilled and semiskilled working – class backgrounds, on the other hand, experienced little sense of power or control at work, had very negative school experiences, and in turn entered "career – less" jobs at the earliest possible opportunity.

Others explained these divisions by reference to the labor market, and the way in which the structure of opportunities served to determine young peoples' expectations, so that to talk of "choice" was nonsense (Roberts, 1968). The concern of many writers in the 1960's was with how to prevent young school leavers "wasting their talent" by entering "dead end" jobs.

Marxists, on the other hand, writing in the 1970s argued that what needed explanation was not the so-called "underachievement" of working-class youth, but the way in which a capitalist social order reproduced itself with the consent of those within it. This was explained either by the correspondence between the organization of the education system and that of the world of work (Bowles and Gintis, 1976) or through emphasizing the importance of the education system as a form of ideological state apparatus (Althusser, 1971), or its importance as a source of the reproduction of the dominant class culture (Bourdieu and Passeron, 1977). Hence, for the last 10 years, the most influential paradigm for looking at young people and the transition from school to work has been that of "social reproduction".

In England, empirical studies of young working-class men emphasized the fact that they too had a culture in contradistinction – and in opposition – to the dominant culture (Willis, 1977; Corrigan, 1979). Their entry into working-class culture, effected before they left school, helped to prepare them for working-class jobs, and their enthusiasm to enter working-class male adulthood – by drinking and smoking, for example – meant that they were keen to enter the workplace and earn a wage. In these studies, the peer group – rather than the individual or the family – was important as the site for the creation and transmission of this culture.

These paradigms were criticized from the late 1970s for their masculine bias (MacDonald 1980; McRobbie, 1980; Griffin, 1985). Feminist scholars argued that they had not adequately accounted for young women as a group – indeed many studies had explicitly ignored them – and the models of social reproduction had not taken patriarchal structures into account as well as those of class. Others argued that the more Marxist variants of these models had artificially polarised the social class orientations of respondents into middle-class conformists and working-class rebels. In so doing, "ordinary kids" had been ignored (Jenkins, 1983; Brown, 1988).

Those who started to look at young women explicitly, found that their aspirations were depressed by gender as well as class, with marriage and motherhood looming over their prospects and their expectations. However, the apparent upward mobility of working-class young women into clerical and white collar jobs needed different explanations in terms of gender stereotypes (Deem, 1980). Similarly, the experience of factory work was far more negative for young women than for the lads in Paul Willis' study, and it was rendered tolerable by escape through the ideology of romance (Pollert, 1981). The ideology of romance was important for young women also because it prepared them for their later roles as wives and mothers. This ideology was thought to preoccupy the subcultural activities of young women (McRobbie and Garber, 1976).

What all these studies did was to emphasize the essential *continuity* between home, school, and work. Entering work was not a shock for most people, because they broadly entered the sorts of jobs for which they had been prepared by their background and by their school experience. Furthermore, their aspirations were very realistic: They more or less expected to do the sorts of jobs that were available. Their peer group affiliations reflected this.

My own research began in the context of rising unemployment. It appeared — from this context — that arguments about the nature of social reproduction assumed a situation of full employment for men and marriage and motherhood for women. It went without saying that there would be jobs at different levels for young men and women to enter, and that marriage and children (in that order) were part of the normal biography of young women. However, this was no longer the case in practice.

Table 1 indicates the difference between 1976 and 1986. It can be seen that whereas the majority of school leavers went straight into work in 1976, only 15% did so in 1987. (This figure is inflated by the fact that in the official statistics all those whose destination is unknown are counted alongside the "employed"). A further 27% entered government schemes — which did not exist in 1976 — and the numbers remaining in education also increased between these years. A steady percentage were unemployed.

In addition, the career paths of young women do not necessarily follow the normal biography of work—family—work either. Changes in the family have resulted in its fragmentation through divorce and remarriage, and family formation has been postponed (1 in 3 brides were teenagers in the 1960s as against 1 in 7 now) whilst cohabitation and the establishment of nonfamilial households by young people has increased. Young women can expect to be workers rather than homemakers for most of their lives, although young men cannot necessarily assume that they will be "breadwinners".

What happens to social reproduction under these circumstances? I hypothesize that there may be a fracture in the reproduction of work roles and gender roles under these circumstances. My reading of official statistics indicates that young people were no longer likely to enter the same sorts of jobs as their fathers straight from school (the mother's occupation was never taken into account), because many of these jobs no longer existed or were not employing young people. They were more likely to be unemployed, in education, or on

Table 1:   Educational and employment activities of 16—year—olds in Great Britain

Percentage of 16—year—olds who were:	1976	1986
In full time education at school	28	31
Further education	12	14
In employment[*]	53	15
On Youth Training Scheme Programmes	0	27
Unemployed	7	12

[*] This includes unregistered unemployed and those seeking work but not claiming benefit and those neither employed nor seeking work.

Source: Social Trends, 18, HMSO

temporary government schemes instead. What parental and peer expectations were relevant here?

The main theoretical explanations in this area were implicitly or explicitly biased toward masculine experiences. It appeared from Willis' and Jenkins' work that masculinity depended crucially upon access to the workplace and the wage packet. What would happen when this was no longer possible? For girls, the family had been the main site of the reproduction of social relations, and evidence suggested that girls had to undertake substantial housework in addition to other labor (Griffin, 1985). Consequently, some had been lead to speculate that young women's positions would be strengthened by unemployment at the same time as young men's were weakened by it (Willis, 1984a, 1984b). Peer group relations are thus likely to change too.

My own work was therefore intended to document the social reproduction of work roles and gender relations in times of rising unemployment. My research, using participant observation, lengthy in—depth interviews, as well as more quantitative survey data, was carried out on the Isle of Sheppey in Kent. The island was originally chosen as a research base because it had suffered high unemployment — roughly twice the national average — since the naval dockyard had closed some 20 years previously. From a practical point of view, this provided a readily identifiable community and local labor market to study.

Moreover, there was one large comprehensive school containing 565 fifth formers at the time, and the staff there kindly gave me access to it.

There were three waves of surveys. In the first survey, in 1979, I contacted 153 16 — year — old school students, drawn from a mixed ability division at the local comprehensive school. This constituted approximately a quarter of that age group on the island divided evenly between boys and girls. In 1980, I reinterviewed 103 of these young people after they had been in the labor market for one year; and in 1984 I was able to carry out a third survey of the same young people, and at this point 84 were traced. The full account of this work is available in Wallace (1987) and Wallace (1988).

2. The Transition from School to Work

Since recent research has concentrated upon the school — work interface, and since this is a particular source of popular concern, I shall focus upon this transition for the purpose of this paper.

In my own research, respondents were asked what sorts of jobs they were looking for and how they would go about finding them. Apart from two exceptions (who wanted to be rock singers) they held broadly realistic expectations. Aspirations fell into distinct patterns, but these were not ones which necessarily corresponded with the Registrar General's (government) classifications nor with social — science status groups. Job aspirations and school experience broadly reflected social class origins, so that those seeking more middle — class jobs were likely to come from more middle — class backgrounds. However, since the workforce of the island consisted mainly of manual workers, and since I chose to concentrate primarily upon the minimum — age school leavers, the sample is skewed toward young people from manual working — class (skilled and unskilled) and lower white — collar backgrounds. Together these constitute the majority of the workforce in the United Kingdom. The social class origins need to be understood within the context of the local labor market, which is described more fully in Wallace (1987).

The first group aimed to do *professional and managerial* jobs (14%). In this group, I classified all those who were doing further academic qualifications and wanting to go into higher education. The second group were those who aimed to do *clerical work* (7%), and these were mainly girls for whom it conformed to images of respectable femininity. Roughly half of these aimed to do this by remaining in the education system and undertaking vocational courses, and the rest hoped to train on the job.

The most popular set of occupations for young men was that of *skilled work* (60% of all the boys), but nearly half of these hoped to learn their skills by picking them up informally whilst on the job. The majority, however, preferred formal apprenticeships with certificates. The reasons given for seeking out training of some kind was that it would provide security in an insecure labor market, a recognized status in the community, and access to self—employment or promotion. Skills were highly gender—specific with the girls wanting to train as hairdressers or in *caring* jobs such as nursing, which required them to continue at school or college for at least another year (caring and skilled work were sought by 43% of the girls and boys together). However, 6% of girls wanted the same training as boys in male apprenticeships such as mechanics. Another popular choice was to join the *Armed Forces* (9%), often as a way of avoiding unemployment; and finally there was *unskilled work*, mentioned by 29%, which included shopwork, factory work, and outdoor laboring among other things. Of these, shop work was by far the most important for girls, and outdoor laboring the most important for boys. Shop work offered opportunities for human contact and fitted images of respectable femininity. Outdoor laboring fitted images of independent masculinity, physical prowess, and control over the work process. Only factory work was mentioned consistently as the job that most school leavers would least like to do. The monotony, depersonalization, and lack of personal control were regarded with horror.

If we look at *Table 2* we can see that not all of these aspirations matched the first job that young people found. All those above the line were forced to pursue jobs of lower status to those to which they had aspired.

However, only a minority were able to fulfill such expectations, and 30% in fact finished up by working in factories as these were the main employers. These often had very negative experiences, as the following quotation makes clear:

"Well, I stayed 6 months, but I was so pissed off with it I left. I'm just not cut out for factory work. It was terrible doing the same thing all the time, and all those fiddling little bits you had to do (to make fuses). You couldn't stop for breath and I started getting headaches. It was just so boring — and the dirt and noise and that. It is like a rabbit hutch in there — no windows and it's so hot. I never thought it would be so awful."

Hence, the idea of the "smooth functional" transition into work was not borne out in this sample, at least on leaving school: The *discontinuities* between what they had hoped to do at school and what they actually entered at work were as

Table 2:   Aspirations by first jobs found: 1979 school leavers

Aspirations	First job found					
	Profess/ manage/ clerical	Formal skilled and caring	Informal skilled and caring	Armed forces	Un– skilled	Opportunity scheme
Professional/ managerial/ clerical	(8)				3	
Formal skilled and caring	2	(9)	10		11	2
Informal skilled and caring		1	(5)		10	3
Armed forces	1			(7)	3	1
Unskilled					(28)	5
%	10	9	14	6	50	10

Note: Ten of the 119 minimum age school leavers are not included here, having emigrated, fallen pregnant, or their destinations were not known. Total = 109

evident as the continuities. However, it is evident that they are still entering broadly the same type of jobs — mainly working class ones — and in this sense there was still some continuity. However, their routes into work were more uncertain or blocked altogether. This lack of opportunities reflected the steady decline in apprenticeship places generally up until the 1980s and the casualization of areas of employment, such as the construction industry which provided most of the outdoor laboring.

In response, young people took on jobs as temporary measures or entered special government schemes, or waited around unemployed until something suitable came up. At this stage they had not all fully entered the labor market.

Leaving school did not necessarily involve the transition from full–time education to full–time work, since some school–leavers were working both before they left school and afterwards in temporary, casual, and part–time jobs. Many undertook seasonal and casual jobs in preference to full–time work in a factory. Others took temporary or seasonal jobs, or spent a period "on the dole" as they termed it, whilst they waited for a suitable opportunity to come up. Indeed, for some sorts of jobs — such as hairdressing — part–time jobs were the way in which a full time job was secured, and altogether 19% of school leavers obtained jobs that were related in some way to things they had done before leaving school. Every single person in the sample had some experience of part–time work. It would seem that a whole sector of the local economy depended upon these casual jobs performed by juveniles. For boys, such jobs included casual laboring, digging for lugworms (fish bait), mending cars and motorbikes, or helping on boats. For girls, there was fruit picking, caring for children (for money), and working in shops and cafes.

Informal work had a number of functions for young people whilst they were in the process of leaving school. First, in some cases, it provided some extra income and a source of activity whilst they were unemployed or still at school or college. Secondly, it could be a strategy for learning skills informally; and thirdly, some young people took up this casual employment in the hope that they would be taken on permanently later. Some employers preferred to hire young people but not to declare it, and so some young people were unsure as to their official status. At this stage many said that they preferred casual jobs to full–time ones as they wanted to feel free from constraints.

In addition to this, many entered some sort of scheme rather than full–time employment. At the time that I began my field work in 1979 these schemes were temporary and intended only for the unemployed. However, Sheppey had a special status on account of its high unemployment, and so school–leavers were able to join the schemes as soon as they left school.

The study has identified a mismatch between school and work. This mismatch was due not to the fact that young people were underqualified and underexperienced — they had considerable work experience and did not appear to require qualifications for many of the jobs locally. The reason for the mismatch was that despite young people's own enthusiasm for certain jobs — especially skilled ones — there were few such jobs for them to fill.

Whereas the transition from school to work is usually imagined to be a smooth process, with a clean break between full–time education and full–time employment, it can be seen that in circumstances such as those on Sheppey it is a "ragged" transition stretching both sides of the official school–work divide. Some young people had effectively left school before they reached 16 and did not begin work until some time later: Theirs was a transition from not much schooling to no work. Others had found jobs which were extensions of the kinds of casual jobs they had already been doing: Theirs was a transition from part–time to full–time employment. In between there might be a whole variety of part–time and casual jobs interspersed with periods of doing nothing. This corresponds with work carried out by Finn (1984) too.

Moreover, young people were selective about the kind of employment they were prepared to take. The job needed to fit the self—image they had constructed, and these self—images were gendered ones. At this stage, most young people still held some hope of finding rewarding employment that would lead them toward excitement and adventure and would introduce them to a world of new and interesting people. For this reason they were critical of many local jobs. They rejected much of the "slave labor" locally because they hoped for something better.

At this time, young people were able to obtain supplementary benefits 6 weeks after leaving school if they were unemployed, and, hence, they were relatively better off than they had been at school even if they had no job.

A year later, roughly half the sample had experienced some spells out of work. Some of them adopted "rebel" stances; many obtained more dignity and status by rejecting low paid "slave labor" or by leaving jobs. To quote one young women:

"There's Tesco's, the shirt factory, and shit like that. Boring, repetitive jobs, sewing jeans and stacking shelves. I wouldn't do a lot of factory work unless I was really desperate because I would think it was a waste of my life. In a factory, doing the same thing all day. You need an awful lot of money to be able to stand that."

This is quite contrary to the passive and helpless images of the young unemployed that we are usually presented with. Many were still hoping to find better jobs and holding out for apprenticeships, although they were approaching the age limit for entry into apprenticeship training, which at that time was 17. Others had decided to go into the army instead.

For these young people, leaving school was an escape, and many of them did not expect much satisfaction from the sorts of jobs available locally. At this stage, they did not actually see themselves as unemployed, but rather, as waiting for jobs. Many of their friends were unemployed or on low paid government schemes, and they were able to see their friends frequently. They did not necessarily suffer from the loss of social contacts, because they were unemployed alongside many of their school friends. Indeed, they were able to see their friends more often if they were unemployed. Thirdly, they did not suffer from a loss of social status because unemployment was so common; many people were in the same position — at least it was better than being a school student. Furthermore, they had not yet fully acquired a work status in the sense that an adult man would do. They did not expect to be unemployed for very long.

What young people missed most at this stage was not the loss of the latent functions of work — such as status, a time structure, participation in collective purposes, and so forth (see Jahoda, 1982) — but rather the manifest function of employment: money. The wage packet was a source of status in itself, but also bought access to the adult world of entertainment and to a range of consumer goods such as stereos, motorbikes, and so forth, which young people were expected to acquire. They also feared the long—term consequences of being unemployed and sinking into an unemployed subculture or "vegetating" as they saw it.

"Most of 'em, it's not their fault, so you can't blame them (the unemployed). But some of 'em, they just don't *wanna* work. They've been like that for years and they won't ever change."

In fact, I never found any respondents who did not want to work, but this is obviously the impression others had formed.

By 1980, less than one third had been employed continuously in the same jobs, and these were either in particularly satisfying jobs or in jobs that were difficult to leave, like the army.

However, of the 97 job departures, 44% were voluntary in nature but more than half were involuntary — a product of the increasing fragmentation of the youth labor market. Temporary YOP (Youth Opportunity Programme) schemes and college courses contributed toward this process. Hence, redundancies, dismissals, temporary jobs, and low—paid schemes mean that it is often difficult to find a full time permanent job, and this, too, would serve to extend the period of transition.

Studies of female youth have emphasized the role of romance and motherhood in the reproduction of femininity. What it has been necessary to explain was how young women came to be so dominated by these ideologies. In my own study, however, I came across some resistance to traditional models of femininity amongst girls. Many did not want to experience the same fate as their mothers, and nearly all of them wanted to "live a bit" before "settling down". They also often resented the amounts of housework they were obliged to do (not all of them had to do housework). Young unemployed women became more dependent upon the family for emotional, financial, and social support as they could no longer go out. Some rebelled by getting pregnant — which they saw as a revolt against traditional respectable femininity; some became involved in masculine activities, such as bike riding, and some rejected conventional models of attractiveness through adopting a "punk" image. Others were simply verbally critical. Certainly, feminine roles were not passively accepted by young women:

(Question: What do you want to do?) "Not just stay on this island and get married and have a husband and a baby and get out to work; dinner on the table and 'What did you do today?' That's terribly boring. I want to do something different. Do something with my life. Families are boring altogether. You know, it's 'My family is better than yours, my baby is better than yours'. I live next door to a young family and it's all hassle all the time. The young girl up the road, she's got two children and she's worrying all the time about how she can pay the bills, because her husband's not living with her."

The ideology of romance could also be used instrumentally to legitimize a sexual relationship, since codes of sexual conduct and negative sexual labeling served to constrain the peer relations of young women (Lees, 1986).

Young men resorted to a different kind of romance. They embellished their status and roles in the community — especially if they were unemployed — with stories of their confrontations with authority — police, social workers, teachers, and so on — and their ability to get by economically. Many of them dreamed of becoming self–employed in order to control their own patterns of work and leisure time.

Hence, there was no universal response to unemployment, but a variety of responses. What is evident, however, is that gender roles were not unproblematically reproduced. For young men, where they lacked a secure economic and social status provided by employment, they created fantasized ones, and girls hoped that exciting jobs would save them temporarily from marriage and motherhood.

3. The State of the Transitional Process Five Years Later

It would appear therefore, that at 17 the transition was incomplete and fragmentary. Had this changed after 5 years? By this time, the downward trend in aspirations was confirmed, and many had finished up in worse jobs than the ones they had originally intended to do: 51% had been downwardly mobile in relation to their original expectations. Very few had been able to obtain training, and more than one third were presently working, or had last worked in unskilled manual jobs (*Table 3*).

Although in at least half the cases they were not doing the jobs they had originally wanted, at that stage they seemed to have forgotten many of their earlier aspirations — until I reminded them — and to generally accept the sorts

Table 3:   Most recent employment of young adults 1984

	Men	Women	%
College/university	6	3	11
Supervisory	5	2	8
Clerical	–	9	11
Skilled manual – formal	5	5	12
Skilled manual – informal	6	–	7
Unskilled manual	18	13	37
Armed forces	4	3	8
Never worked	–	5	6

Source: Survey of Young Adults on Sheppey. Total = 84 (44 male; 40 female)

of jobs they were in. Some of those who had obtained apprenticeships found that they were not signed up before they were 17 – despite promises from employers. Other businesses had collapsed or had had to cut back on training before the young person could be guaranteed a place. In still other places the young person felt exploited – used for menial tasks and paid very little – so that they had left. However, by 1984, it was evident that they had come to accept whatever work they were in. They were less critical of employment and more likely to accept factory jobs, they were less likely to leave or refuse them, and they no longer saw unemployment so much as a waiting period. They had "settled down" to accept work, like Dennis:

"Oh, it's lousy pay. Well, they can hire whoever they like, can't they? They can kick you out and they know they can get someone off the dole queue, so they don't have to pay so much, do they? They can find anyone, can't they? It's so simple, so they can keep the prices down, it's as simple as that. You can't earn no more."

Young men and women had become increasingly instrumental toward work. They increasingly thought that any job was better than no job, and a job that paid more was better than one that paid less. Whereas on leaving school they had emphasized more the intrinsic satisfactions of work, they now increasingly mentioned the extrinsic factors – security and money. It was not so much that young adults saw job satisfaction as being any less important. It was just that they were more likely to have given up hope of finding it. Thus, whilst outdoor and casual work were still seen as preferable to factory work in many ways, young men also complained that it was irregular and unstable – the very things that they had seen as advantageous when they left school.

What were the reasons for this "settling down"? The first reason was that unemployment itself (which had risen by 1984) was a labor discipline. Young men and women had come to realize their poor labor market position, as Dennis, quoted above, makes clear.

The second reason was that an increasing number of respondents had domestic reponsibilities and were therefore no longer in a position to leave jobs; as Dennis continues:

"It's a real crusher, especially if you're out of work 2 years like I was. In the end. You're so hopeful at first. When I first got unemployed, I remember, it was when Thatcher first got in and you could see the jobs disappearing then... Oh, it's a real killer being unemployed for 2 years. See, it's not just me now, it's them (indicating his girlfriend and child) I got to think of."

For young women, those who were single or in partnerships building a home expressed similar sentiments, but those with children were more likely to be working part – time or to have temporarily given up work.

The third reason was habituation. If a person was in a job for long enough, then they simply became accustomed to it, developing various techniques of survival in order to cope rather than wasting time wondering what they might have done otherwise.

Thus, the rate of voluntary job turnover declined by this time, although about 35% had undertaken temporary and casual jobs and 14% had been on temporary government schemes at some point. A further 12% had been working part – time. Hence, the fragmentation of the juvenile labor market and of young people's work careers continued, but largely for involuntary reasons. Hence, much of the job turnover was involuntary.

At this stage it was the cumulative experience of unemployment that was important, and so I classified them according to the length of time out of work: 49% had been regularly employed for the entire period, 33% had been long term unemployed (for at least a year altogether), and 17% had been unemployed for only short periods. Unlike at 16, there was a great contrast between the mainly employed and the mainly unemployed. Those who were regularly employed had been able to buy houses and accumulate goods, and were confident of their future. Those who were unemployed were desperate to obtain work of any kind and were unable to accumulate the objects and symbols — such as cars, motorbikes, stereos, and so forth — by which transitions into adulthood were measured. Regular employment was associated with getting married and owning one's own home, both statistically and in the minds of these respondents; Andy, for example:

(Question: What do you think you will be doing in 5 years' time?) "I reckon if I had a decent job I'd want a nice house and a decent job, then I'd start saving up, something to look forward to. Otherwise, you haven't got much to look forward to, have you? Yeah, yeah, when you come back in 5 year's time I'll have my house, I'll have a decent job, a little kid to cause me lots of trouble. I should think we'll be married by that time too."

These sentiments echoed those expressed at 16 and 17. However, it was evident that those who already had families or were wanting to start a home were particularly desperate to get jobs and would work even for very little reward.

Informal work was still important as a subsidiary activity, but was no longer a substitute for full−time employment (39% had done some at some point) − indeed, it was more often performed by those in full−time work.

It was evident that the long−term unemployed were drifting more and more apart from their employed peers in terms of social contacts and lifestyle. They often appeared to form distinctive subcommunities and subcultures, as they were not able to maintain the same consumption patterns as the employed, and, in response to questions on the questionnaire, they were more likely to say that their friends were unemployed and that they felt ashamed of their status.

It is popularly supposed that the work ethic may be eroded by rising unemployment. If this is the case, we might expect the younger generation to be evolving different attitudes toward work. It appeared from responses in 1980 that this might be happening. For this reason I included a number of questions about the work ethic in the questionnaire in 1984. From their responses it appeared that the work ethic was still strongly espoused by these young people, as 36% of the 53 who were asked the question said that they would work for less money than "the dole". Indeed, many had worked for less money already, and 80% said that they would do any job rather than be unemployed. Those who did not fit this pattern were often those with families, who pointed out that they could not afford to work for less money than was offered on social security. Hence, although the government schemes were mostly regarded as "slave labor", they were at least better than being unemployed.

The degree of family support that a young person received was important too, since those who were generously supported by parents were not in general as badly off as those who were not. Young people were more dependent upon the home, often in domestic situations that they would have liked to have escaped, and this led to domestic tensions so that young people often left home − or were thrown out — after rows. In a recent secondary analysis of a large—scale survey of Great Britain as a whole, Jones (1987) found that 11 to 12% of young people's reasons for leaving home were "negative ones", including being thrown out. In my sample, young people left home from the age of 15 onward, staying with relatives, friends, in squats, or sleeping rough for a while.

In the introduction, I argued that unemployment may lead to a "fracture" in the reproduction of work roles. After 5 years, young people had "settled down" to meet the demands of employment to a far greater extent than they had just after leaving school. Hence this fracture, which appeared to be taking place at the immediate work—school interface, had become a process of adjustment later on.

4. Conclusions

It would appear that until the mid—1970s, the majority of young people left school at the minimum age and followed fairly well—defined tracks into work. In the 1980s, their career paths are more fractured and confused. The period of transition from school was becoming fragmented and extended; indeed, for the long—term unemployed it could go on indefinitely.

It could be argued from this study that indeed there is a fracture in the processes of social reproduction as they have been described here. There was a fracture in both the reproduction of work roles and the reproduction of gender roles during high unemployment, at least when compared with traditional models derived from other studies. At 16 and 17 young people were simply waiting for the right opportunities to come up, and so they were in a strong position to reject the more degrading work, to remain unemployed, and to take on odd jobs or an antiwork posture. However, at 21 this was no longer possible. They accepted the sorts of work available and desperately searched for work. Their position in the life course was relevant at this stage, since those with accumulating domestic responsibilities were further pressured to find work, and there was an increasing division between the cumulatively employed and the cumulatively unemployed in terms of lifestyle.

This may lead us to question models of social reproduction more generally. It is possible that they have overemphasized the smoothness of the process and concentrated more upon the subordination of young people to dominant structures than upon young people's responses. Hence, the resistance of young people to many kinds of work, and the resistance of young women to feminine ideology have been overlooked.

Since this research was carried out, the situation for young people has moved on. The direct employment of school leavers is now negligible, as more and more are recruited directly through the youth training scheme or after having completed college courses. The entitlement to supplementary benefit if they are under 18 is being removed, thus encouraging recruitment onto the youth training scheme. The Youth Training Scheme (YTS) itself — introduced in 1982 — has become a permanent 2 – year bridge between school and work. The dependency of young people upon parents has been reinforced through lower rates of benefit for those under 25 and changes in housing benefits. It would seem that nearly all those under 18 from now on will be either trainees or students. This has the effect of extending some of the trends described here and already discernible in 1980. The transition from school to work has been extended, become more uncertain, and less obviously tied to jobs. Although it might be argued that the YTS offers a more protected transition into work, thus counteracting the fragmentation of the career paths of young people, we have yet to find out young people's responses to this situation and what their long – term prospects are.

References

Althusser, L. (1971): Lenin and philosophy and other essays. London: New Left Books

Ashton, D.N., & Field, D. (1976): Young workers. London: Hutchinson

Brown, P. (1988): Schooling ordinary kids. London: Routledge

Bourdieu, P., & Passeron, J.C. (1977): Reproduction in education, society and culture. London: Sage

Bowles, S., & Gintis, H. (1976): Schooling in capitalist America: Educational reform and the contradictions of economic life. London: Routledge and Kegan Paul

Corrigan, P. (1979): Schooling the smash street kids. London: MacMillan

Deem, R. (1980): Schooling for women's work. Milton Keynes: Open University Press

Finn, D. (1984): Leaving school and growing up: Work experience in a juvenile labor market. In Bates, I., et.al. (Eds.): Schooling for the dole?. London: MacMillan

Griffin, C. (1985): Typical girls? London: Routledge.

Jahoda, M. (1982): Employment and unemployment. A social psychological analysis. Cambridge: Cambridge University Press

Jenkins, R. (1983): Lads, citizens and ordinary kids. Working class youth life – styles in Belfast. London: Routledge

Jones, G. (1987): Leaving the parental home: An analysis of early housing careers. Journal of Social Policy, 16, 49 – 74

Lees, S. (1986): Losing out. Sexuality and adolescent girls. London: Hutchinson

McDonald, M. (1980): Socio – cultural reproduction and women's education. In Deem, R. (Ed.): Schooling for women's work. London: Routledge and Kegan Paul

McRobbie, A. (1980): Settling accounts with sub−cultures. Screen Education, 34, 37−50

McRobbie, A., & Garber, J. (1976): Girls and sub−cultures. An exploration. In Hall, S., & Jefferson, T.: Resistance through ritual. London: Hutchinson

Pollert, A. (1981): Girls, wives and factory lives. London: MacMillan

Roberts, K.A. (1968): The entry into employment. An approach toward a general theory. In Williams, W.M. (Ed.): Occupational choice. London: Allen and Unwin

Social Trends 18 (1988): Central Statistical Office. London: HMSO

Wallace, C. (1987): For richer, for poorer. Growing up in and out of work. London: Routledge

Wallace, C. (1988): Value change and inter−generational comparison. In Bertram, H. et. al. (Eds.): Young people and their parents. München: Deutsches Jugendinstitut

Willis, P. (1977): Learning to labor. Farnborough: Saxon House

Willis, P. (1984a): Youth unemployment 1. A new state. New Society, 29 March, 475−477

Willis, P. (1984b): Youth unemployment 2. Ways of living. New Society, 5 April, 13−15

22.
Recent Changes in the Pathways from School to Work

Kenneth Roberts and Glennys Parsell
The University of Liverpool, Great Britain

In 1974, just after the last raising of the statutory school—leaving age, almost two—thirds of Britain's young people completed their full—time education at 16, then nearly all obtained jobs immediately. Unemployment was an issue only in chronically depressed regions. The quantity and quality of the training offered to young workers was a perennial issue. Another concern was that so many teenagers lost all contact with formal education on leaving school at age 16. However, the young people themselves did not appear to share these worries. The quality of the available employment seemed to satisfy the overwhelming majority. Had 16—year—olds' wishes been decisive, there can be little doubt that the majority would still be entering full—time employment. The catalyst leading to the restructuring of their pathways has been the withdrawal of their former jobs. Nowadays, in many parts of Britain, most 16—year—olds' only scope for choice is between educational programs and training schemes. Access to adult employment has been delayed, maybe for ever in some cases.

Today's 16—year—olds face labor markets that are poorer than ever in terms of jobs, though richer than ever in schemes and courses. They are being offered more opportunities to obtain training and further education, and some of the new provisions are enabling beginning workers to qualify for the expanding number of higher—level, skilled occupations that are being created by economic growth, technological change, and occupational restructuring. However, other new "opportunities" look more like waiting rooms or warehouses than routes toward any kinds of adult employment. By the late 1980s, Britain's army of unemployed young adults was better educated and better trained than ever before.

Every new educational course and qualification, and every new training scheme, has been introduced amidst talk of improving young people's skills and enhancing their employability, thereby enabling them to contribute to, and to benefit from Britain's economic growth. However, another motive behind all the initiatives has been to offer young people alternatives to unemployment. Despite overall economic growth, 16— and 17—year—olds seem to have become literally surplus to economic requirements in many parts of Britain. It is also the case that educators have vested interests in the expansion of their industry, and, likewise, those whose own employment is now in Britain's new youth training industry. Youth unemployment has become a base for new business sectors and occupations.

The Economic and Social Research Council (ESRC) has launched the "16—19 Initiative" in response to, and to investigate the broader and longer—term significance of young people's new social condition. The core of this on—going research consists of longitudinal studies in four parts of Britain with contrasting economic histories and current labor market conditions (see Bynner, 1987; Roberts, 1987). These inquiries are designed to identify typical movements between various positions in old and new educational programs, conventional jobs, and new training schemes, and to explore how the opportunities of young people following different routes vary by sex, home background, educational attainment, and according to local employment conditions. The intention, then, is to relate individuals' progress along different pathways through education and youth labor markets to the development of their self—concepts, social beliefs and attitudes, political orientations, family and peer group relationships, and leisure activities.

The following section outlines the new educational programs and training schemes that have been introduced in attempts to plug an otherwise yawning gap in Britain's youth labor markets. Evidence from the initial stages in the ESRC inquiries is then used to distinguish five main career trajectories that 16 to 19—year—olds now follow. Finally, comparisons are drawn between the old and new pathways from compulsory education toward employment, and the implications for adolescent socialization.

1.   The Restructuring of 16—Year—Old's Opportunities

This is not the place for a thorough analysis of the economic and occupational restructuring that has removed most jobs that Britain's 16— and 17—year—olds once entered. Suffice it to say that the changes have been rapid and dramatic. To state that young people have felt the full force of recent economic changes is an understatement. Some groups of workers have been sheltered. The impact has been amplified among other groups, especially young people.

One response to the contraction of 16−year−olds' job opportunities has been to create new educational programs, thereby encouraging them more to delay their entry into the labor market. Nearly all of Britain's 16−year−olds now have the option of remaining in full−time education.

There was a time when school sixth forms in England were dedicated to GCE A−levels (General Certificate of Education, Advanced level, examinations normally taken at age 18), the qualifications that lead to higher education, and when good performances in the GCE O−level (General Certificate of Education, Ordinary level, examinations normally taken at age 16) were a precondition for entry. This long−standing academic route remains intact. It has certainly not been undermined by recent economic trends, but neither has it grown much broader. Since the 1950s there have been trends toward higher proportions of 16−year−olds with good O−levels enrolling for A−levels, and toward higher proportions of those who gain two or more A−levels proceeding to higher education. By the end of the 1970s, however, this trend toward a broader academic mainstream was nearing exhaustion. GCE O−levels were administered to, and the GCSEs that replaced them in 1988 continue to be governed by standards that prevent more than a third of young people gaining sufficient passes in the grades deemed necessary to continue in the academic mainstream.

Since the 1960s the trend toward staying on in full−time education has been reinforced by the arrival of "new" sixth formers as they were once called. Increased numbers of 16−year−olds have been staying on to improve their O−level or Certificate of Secondary Education (CSE) results, or to take technical and vocational courses. (GCE O−levels are normally taken at age 16. These examinations are designed for the most able students. Others take CSEs. Only 13% of 16−year−olds in England and Wales today fail to pass in at least one subject.) In the 1960s and early 1970s virtually all postcompulsory students had the option of immediate employment. They stayed on not because unemployment was the sole alternative, but rather to improve their qualifications and, thereby, their longer−term job prospects. Then during the late 1970s the trend toward staying on was reinforced by rising unemployment. Jobs ceased to be available, so by 1983, forty−five percent of 16−year−olds in England and Wales were continuing in full−time education. Throughout Britain less than one half of all the young people who now stay on study for the A−levels that are normally required for higher education.

In general, Britain's schools and further education colleges have become keen to retain as many 16−year−olds as possible. Teachers' careers, even their jobs, can depend on their succeeding, particularly in an era when the size of the secondary age group is declining. Some local education authorities (LEAs) have developed particularly attractive options for less academic 16−year−olds. However, even the most innovative schools, colleges, and LEAs operate within constraints. There is simply no way, given the prevailing examination regimes, in which the prospect of earning the most prestigious qualifications at 18—plus, GCE A—levels, can be offered to the majority of 16—year—olds. Nor do educators have the decisive say over whether these or any alternative qualifications will be valued by employers.

During the 1980s the emphasis in state responses to youth unemployment has not been toward persuading still more 16—year—olds to remain in full—time education, but on expanding firm—based training. This is what the *Youth Training Scheme* (YTS) normally offers. This scheme has evolved from earlier efforts to plug the gap in Britain's youth labor markets. Job Creation Projects were introduced in 1975, from which a Work Experience Programme for 16 to 18 year olds was detached in 1976. This was absorbed into the larger Youth Opportunities Programme in 1978, which was superseded in 1983 by the still larger YTS. The intention is to guarantee opportunities to receive systematic "quality" training to all 16— and 17—year—old school—leavers; thereby making two—step transitions into the labor market into the norm, as in West Germany where apprentice training has long been offered to virtually all young people who complete their full—time education at 15 or 16.

Britain's youth training schemes are administered, but are not actually operated, by the Training Agency, a central government body. The front—line training providers are known as Approved Training Organizations, formerly managing agents. Most trainers are firms in mainstream business sectors, and other schemes endeavor to place trainees with such employers for work experience. An inevitable result is that large segments of the YTS have been absorbed into firms' normal recruitment and training practices (Roberts et al., 1986). In some enterprises the YTS is the initial phase in longer training to which most entrants are expected to proceed. The proportions of schemes offering such prospects vary from area to area. Nowadays 16—year—olds seeking access to "good jobs" in certain organizations have little option but to enter the relevant training schemes. Entry to schemes with prospects can be intensely competitive, and the better—qualified applicants tend to win the places (Lee et al., 1987). Other schemes are far easier to join but confer vastly inferior prospects, which gives the trainees every excuse for treating the YTS primarily as a waiting room. Some still enter only because they are unable to obtain proper employment.

Since the mid—1970s schemes have been introduced in response to, and have then accelerated the disappearance of school—leavers' former jobs. Why should employers offer straight jobs when the YTS will cover most of their induction and initial training costs? Firms that do not wish to train under the YTS now have the option of hiring scheme—leavers instead of school—leavers. The YTS was launched as a 1—year scheme in 1983 and became a 2—year scheme in 1986 thereby pushing many 16—year—olds' prospects of real employment still further into their futures.

Yet there is still some employment of 16− and 17−year−olds in all parts of Britain. Some firms still hire the age group for a variety of reasons (Roberts et al., 1987). Firstly, some believe that it remains necessary to offer "untainted" employment in order to attract the quantity and quality of youth labor that they require. The strength of this consideration varies according to local labor market conditions. As explained below, in areas of relatively full employment, relatively large proportions of 16−year−olds are still able to make direct transitions into jobs. Where unemployment is higher and youth labor more abundant, then training places are more likely to prove a sufficient attraction. However, firms do not always synchronize their recruitment and training with local labor market conditions. National companies may wish to avoid internal anomalies in their terms and conditions of employment. Another reason why some firms continue to recruit and train outside the YTS is to retain full control, instead of having to comply with, or even having to learn about this latest scheme's requirements. This may or may not be because the firms have no intention of offering systematic training. A desire to attract 16−year−olds with the ability to cope with training, and to benefit from the longer−term prospects, is among the motives of some firms that still recruit and train outside the YTS.

However, another reason why youth employment is not disappearing altogether arises from 16− and 17−year−olds having become so cheap and plentiful, and being just as able to perform certain jobs as individuals who prolong their education or pass through the YTS. High unemployment has led to a revival of low−paid, literally dead−end youth occupations. The YTS, and the further incentives to hold down youth wages under the Young Workers Scheme 1982 to 1986, and subsequently under the New Workers Scheme, have contributed to the recasualization of substantial segments of Britain's youth labor markets. (These schemes have offered subsidies to firms that employ young people in the age group immediately following eligibility for youth training. The subsidies are conditional on the rates of pay being beneath a ceiling that is set below the average for the age group). Low−paid entry−jobs can sometimes be stepping−stones, but in other instances they are literally blind alleys. Some dead−ends are open to 16−year−old school−leavers. Others await scheme−leavers. Meanwhile, other straight jobs that remain open to 16−year−olds are anything but menial.

The educational and training options for 16 to 19−year−olds that have been introduced since the 1970s have reduced, but they have certainly not eradicated Britain's youth unemployment problem. During 1988 the "option" of unemployment was withdrawn from most 16− and 17−year−olds, meaning that they ceased to be able to register as unemployed and claim social security. The young people directly affected are the unemployed who refuse to enter the YTS, a very small minority, plus the larger numbers who quit prematurely, fail to obtain jobs, and refuse to re−enter the scheme. The points that have to be made in these young people's defence are, firstly, that the majority opt for unemployment only because employment is not among their options, and secondly that for many the chances are that a spell on the YTS would simply defer their unemployment. Withdrawing their entitlement to social security seems certain to pressure more of these young people onto, then keep them aboard the YTS. However, it seems equally certain that a hardcore will remain unemployed, but will become officially invisible, since they will not be registered with any statutory agencies unless they encounter "trouble" with the police and courts.

Britain's youth unemployment has not been eradicated, but its shape has changed since the 1970s. The problem used to be unemployment among school – leavers at whom special measures were therefore targeted. In the 1970s unemployment rates gradually declined as each cohort progressed toward adulthood, but this trend has now been reversed. This is partly because there are now enough schemes and courses to accommodate all 16 – to 18 – year – olds, and partly because some employers have begun adjusting to, and taking advantage of the abundance of cheap teenage labor. Risks of unemployment now increase as each cohort moves beyond the YTS and outgrows juvenile jobs and wages. YTS – refusers and quitters are then joined by young people who become unemployed only because there are just not enough jobs.

2. 16 – to 19 – Year – Olds' Career Routes

The ESRC Initiative is based on representative samples from the 1984/5 and 1986/7 fifth form (15 – to 16 – year – old) cohorts in the local authority schools in three English areas – Swindon, Sheffield, and Liverpool – and their counterparts in the Scottish district of Kirkcaldy. Both cohorts are being surveyed through three mailed questionnaire sweeps in 1987, 1988, and 1989, thereby generating evidence on their career development from age 15/16 to 19/20. However, the evidence presented below is from the first sweep only, and from just the older cohort from which 2,158 individuals responded. They were 78% of the achievable sample. The following passages focus on their responses to just one set of questions that asked whether they had been mainly in full – time education, full – time employment, part – time employment, on the Youth Training Scheme (YTS), unemployed, or doing something else during successive 3 – month periods from Spring 1985, when the respondents had reached or were nearing the end of their compulsory education, until the time of the survey in April – May 1987.

Table 1 plots the sample's positions at each of these points in time and the trends in the proportions in different situations. This information does not amount to a complete record of the respondents' careers because only "main positions" during each 3 — month period were identified. Short spells in and out of work were not recorded, which means that our evidence will understate the number of separate occasions when individuals were unemployed, in employment, and so on, and likewise the proportions of respondents who had been in each position at some time or another, however briefly. The advantage in discounting brief episodes is that main patterns of career development are thrown into sharper relief.

Table 1: Main positions at 3 — month intervals (percentages)

	1985		1986		1987
	April May June	October November December	April May June	October November December	April May June
Full — time education	73	49	40	32	30
YTS	7	27	23	17	13
Full — time employment	6	13	21	33	36
Part — time employment	3	4	4	5	5
Unemployed	11	7	10	12	15
Other	—	1	1	1	1

Table 2 focuses on the sample's main positions between October and December 1985, when those who were continuing in full — time education had returned to school or college, while others had found jobs, joined the YTS, remained unemployed, or, in a few cases, dropped out of both education and the labor market. Altogether 49% of the sample were continuing in full — time education, 27% were on the YTS, 13% were in full — time jobs, 4% were in part — time employment, 7% were unemployed, and 1% were doing something else. These proportions, however, varied considerably depending on the individuals'

educational attainments and home backgrounds, between boys and girls, and according to where they lived.

Table 2:   Main positions during October – December 1985 (percentages)

	Area				Sex	
	Swindon	Sheffield	Liverpool	Kirkcaldy	Male	Female
Education	45	40	47	61	46	52
YTS	18	38	34	21	27	27
Full – time job	28	10	8	7	16	11
Part – time job	5	2	2	6	4	4
Unemployed	3	10	9	4	7	6
Other	1	–	–	1	1	–
n	532	499	457	561	1031	1018

The main difference between the four areas was that 61% of the Kirkcaldy sample had remained in full – time education against just 40 – to 47% elsewhere, while the Swindon respondents had been the most likely to obtain full – time jobs (28% compared with just 7 to 10% in the other areas). The higher proportion of 16 – year – olds obtaining employment in Swindon is easily explained. Swindon is an expanding labor market, sharing the prosperity of most of Southern England in the 1980s and with an unemployment rate well below the national average. The higher stay – on rate in Kirkcaldy is a general feature of Scottish education. Scotland's school calendar, school – leaving regulations, and the ages at which students have tended to start primary schooling result in substantial numbers of Scottish students completing the fourth year in secondary school (the equivalent to the fifth form in England and Wales) before they are eligible to terminate full – time education. These individuals, who amount to approximately one half of all who enrol in Scottish fifth forms, take postcompulsory courses, but as compulsory students. Staying – on in Scotland has rather different educational and social meanings than south of the border (Raffe and Courtenay, 1988).

Overall stay – on rates in the English areas did *not* vary with the general educational attainments of the local 16 – year – olds. Scottish and English schools enter their students for entirely different examinations, which makes it difficult to compare their results. However, we can compare the educational achievements of respondents from the three English areas. The Swindon respondents had been the most successful, followed by those in Sheffield, then Liverpool. Differences in overall attainments between the areas reflected their social class compositions. However, among the three English areas Liverpool had the highest stay – on rate, followed by Swindon, then Sheffield.

For as long as information has been collected, parental social class has been a splendid predictor of young people's educational performances, and of their likelihood of staying in full—time education as opposed to leaving at the first opportunity. This applied within our samples. *Individuals from the highest status families had the best examination results.* Also, the higher their social origins the greater the likelihood of the young people having remained in education beyond Summer 1985, and the lower their origins the greater their likelihood of having entered the YTS or obtained jobs. Unemployment was highest among those from nonskilled, manual families (see *Table 3*).

Table 3: Main positions according to social status (percentages)

	Ed. attainments			Parental occupational class				
	High	Medium	Low	1/2	3	4	5/6	Total
Education	75	40	14	66	57	46	42	49
YTS	11	37	41	17	21	30	29	27
Full—time job	9	15	24	9	14	15	14	13
Part—time job	3	3	3	3	3	4	4	4
Unemployed	2	5	18	5	5	5	9	7
Other	–	–	1	–	1	1	1	1
n	515	537	436	258	317	929	451	2049

The stay—on rate in an *area* used to be a good indicator of its social class mix. Until recently, Britain's more middle class areas, in which students have the best achievements at 16—plus, also had the highest stay—on rates, but it seems that this no longer applies, assuming that the areas covered in the ESRC Initiative are representative in this respect. Local retention rates in education now depend on other things apart from the general levels of 16—year—olds' academic attainments, together with their educational and occupational aspirations. Staying on may be encouraged or discouraged by entirely different considerations, such as the range and appeal of syllabuses offered to less academic students, and the wealth or paucity of local job opportunities for early school—leavers.

The routes that our samples had taken at age 16 were related to their home backgrounds and places of residence, and, most strongly of all, to their own educational attainments. Within the English areas, 75% of the highest achieving third had remained in full—time education beyond 16. The middle and lower bands had similar proportions on the YTS (37 and 41%), but the lowest achievers were well ahead in both their employment and unemployment rates. Interestingly, it was the least qualified among all those who left full—time education at age 16 who were tending to obtain the full—time jobs that were available. This is a sign of opportunities at 16—plus forming new hierarchical relationships during the 1980s. When special measures were first introduced in Britain they tended to recruit the least qualified school—leavers who were at the back of the job queue (Jones et al., 1983). Among the 1984/5 fifth form cohort in the areas covered in this research, the best qualified had tended to remain in education, as was the case in earlier decades. Then, judged by the qualifications possessed by entrants, the YTS was proving the next most attractive option, followed by jobs.

The main difference between the sexes that is apparent in Table 2 is that the girls were the more likely to have remained in full—time education after age 16 (52% against 46% of the boys), while more boys had obtained full—time jobs (16% against 11%). However, these figures will understate the importance of gender. Boys and girls tend to be divided not so much according to whether they obtain any education, training, or employment, so much as by the types of courses and occupations that are involved.

The variation shown in Table 1 in the proportions in full—time education, on the YTS, and in employment indicate considerable movement between these positions during the 18 months covered in this survey. The point we want to emphasize, however, is that these movements were far from random. Movements between different positions, in given directions, tended to have occurred during specific periods, and the strength of the flows varied according to the points of origin and destination. Forty—nine percent of the cohort were in full—time education at the outset of the 1985/6 academic year, and 40% at the end. By the next academic year the proportion in full—time education had fallen to just under one third. There was plenty of movement out of full—time education, whereas only 1% of respondents who were in full—time jobs, 2% who were unemployed, and 4% who had joined the YTS by Autumn 1985 had returned to full—time education up to the time of our survey. So the overwhelming majority of full—time students in Spring 1987 had been in full—time education without interruption, apart from vacations in some cases.

By late 1985 and early 1986, 27% of the cohort, the peak figures, were aboard the YTS. The proportion of the sample on these schemes then declined gradually to just 13% at the time of the investigation. The YTS was normally a 1—year scheme when the cohort completed compulsory education. Some individuals who were still on the scheme nearly 2 years later would have been allowed to remain for "bolt—on" periods due to the shortage of suitable jobs in their areas. Others were late entrants. Thirteen percent of the individuals who had been in full—time education in Autumn 1985, 2% of those who had been in full—time employment, and 15% of the unemployed had joined the YTS subsequently. However, all these late entries had been before Summer 1986.

The percentage of the cohort in full—time employment rose progressively with two sharp surges during the summer school—leaving periods, and more slowly throughout the intervening months. The numbers in work remained well beneath the combined totals on the YTS and unemployed until Summer 1986, whereas by early 1987 those in employment were the majority of all who had entered the labor market, though still only 36% of the total sample. A noteworthy feature of full—time employment among our sample was that, once individuals achieved this status, they had tended to stick to it. Of those in full—time employment in Autumn 1985, eighty—six percent had retained this status up to the time of the survey. Most of the remainder were unemployed. The proportion of the entire cohort in employment rose gradually as individuals left education, the YTS, or unemployment and joined those already in work; but whatever their ports of departure and times of entry, once in full—time employment the young people had nearly all held on, though not necessarily to their initial jobs. If they wanted to leave, or had to do so, their work experience was likely to have proved an asset when seeking fresh jobs. Any qualifications, contacts, and self—presentation skills that had helped them to obtain their first jobs were likely to have been useful in subsequent job—changing. Also, needless to say, many young people must be reluctant to leave any job unless and until they have substitutes arranged.

The ability of individuals who gained jobs to hold on to them contrasted sharply with the difficulties that the unemployed were obviously experiencing in breaking into employment. Fifty—three percent of those who were unemployed in Autumn 1985 were still in the predicament 18 months later. The outflow from unemployment into employment was exceeded by the numbers who became unemployed as they left education, the YTS, and jobs in far fewer cases. This is why the percentage of the entire cohort that was unemployed rose gradually, if the peaks during the summer school and college vocation periods are ignored, from 7 % in Autumn 1985, to 8, 10, 14, then 15% at the time of the research. Risks of unemployment were increasing, not diminishing, the further the cohort progressed beyond compulsory schooling.

Up to the time of our investigation, employment and unemployment had been concentrated among different groups of respondents. Just 35% had unemployment as their main position during any 3—month period, while 43%, mostly entirely different individuals, had been in full—time jobs on any such occasion. Surveys among out—of—school youth in the late 1970s and early 1980s produced rather different findings. They stressed the extent to which young people on schemes, young workers, and the young unemployed could be exactly the same individuals at different points in time (Roberts, 1982; Church and Ainley, 1987). The greater part of youth unemployment was then being absorbed in subemployed early careers. By the time that our cohort completed their compulsory education in 1985, Britain's youth labor markets appeared to be settling down, and divisions among out—of—school youth were hardening.

The best predictors by far of the positions individuals would occupy 18 months later were their positions in Autumn 1985 — whether they had stayed on in full–time education, obtained jobs, entered the YTS, or were unemployed. As we have seen, which first steps individuals took beyond compulsory education depended on their family backgrounds, sex, educational attainments, and places of residence; and all these predictors remained operative as the young people's careers progressed. At age 16 girls had been the more likely to remain in full–time education, while more boys had made direct transitions into paid employment. Males continued to be the more successful in obtaining full–time jobs throughout the next 18 months whether from education, unemployment, or the YTS. Moreover, those females who were in full–time jobs in Autumn 1985 proved less successful than employed males in holding onto the status. By Spring 1987, more girls than boys had settled for part–time jobs, especially girls who were formerly unemployed. However, girls were no more likely than boys to have withdrawn from both education and the labor market.

Place of residence was related to two main kinds of difference as the 16–year–olds' careers subsequently developed. Firstly, the areas with the highest stay–on rates in education at 16 had the highest drop–out rates between 16 and 18. As a result, there was little difference among the areas in their proportions still in full–time education in Spring 1987 — between 28 and 31% in all the localities. Secondly, Swindon retained its reputation as the best area for obtaining employment. Direct transitions straight from school into jobs at age 16 had been most common in Swindon. And this was also the area in which those who were unemployed in Autumn 1985 had been the most likely to obtain jobs during the next 18 months — 67% compared with only 12 to 28% in the other areas. Similarly, 66% of the Swindon respondents who were on the YTS in Autumn 1985 had obtained employment by Spring 1987 compared with 37 to 45% elsewhere.

Family background was continuing to make a difference to the young people's career development whether they stayed in or left full–time education at age 16. Those from nonmanual homes who continued in education were the most likely to have persisted up to the time of this research. Repondents from middle–class homes who held jobs in Autumn 1985 were also the most likely to have stuck to these positions. Among respondents who entered the YTS, those from middle–class homes were the most likely to have progressed to employment by the time of the research. However, among those who were unemployed in Autumn 1985, individuals from nonmanual homes had *not* been the more successful in escaping from this predicament.

Educational qualifications held at age 16 were related to the young people's next steps and also to their subsequent career propects. The highest achievers among those who continued in education were the most likely to have stayed there until Spring 1987. The best−qualified among those who moved straight from compulsory education into jobs were the most likely to have held onto employment. The best−qualified entrants to the YTS were the trainees most likely to have progressed to jobs. And it was the least qualified among the unemployed in Autumn 1985 who were the most likely to have remained in the predicament throughout the next 18 months.

We can compare the subsequent progress of otherwise similar groups of 16−year−olds according to where they placed their first steps after compulsory schooling. A particularly interesting comparison is between those who remained in education and those who entered the YTS. Overall, among those who had subsequently entered the job market, the former postcompulsory students had the higher employment rate − 77% against 70% among former trainees. However, the apparent superiority of the educational route was entirely due to its entrants being the better−qualified, on average. Well−qualified 16−year−olds were enjoying relatively good employment opportunities whatever routes they subsequently took, while in the below−average attainment band it was the former trainees, rather than those who had remained in education beyond 16, who were experiencing the greater success on entering the job market. Even so, it would be extravagant to describe the YTS as opening good employment prospects for 16−year−olds with low educational attainments: only 49% of the bottom third who entered the scheme and subsequently left had progressed to full−time jobs. However, a mere 30% from the bottom third who had remained in postcompulsory education and then entered the labor market had established themselves in employment.

By combining our evidence on links between 16−year−olds' points of departure, their experiences during the next 18 months, and the positions they had then achieved, it is possible to distinguish five main career trajectories that the sample had followed. These are listed in *Tables 4 and 5* together with the proportions of males and females from each area, from different home backgrounds, and (in the English areas) with different levels of qualifications, who had followed each track.

Firstly there is an *academic track*. This contains those young people who had remained in full−time education up to the time of the survey, and who were studying for, or had already taken the examinations that would qualify them for higher education − A−levels in England, and Highers in Scotland. Our evidence shows that, in England, entry to this track had been rare among all but the better−qualified 16−year−olds. Just under one half of the best−qualified third in the English areas had followed the academic track. Well−qualified 16−year−olds had other options, but very few of those with inferior qualifications had proceeded along the academic route. Family background was also related to entering this track.

Table 4:   Career trajectories by area and sex (percentages)

	Area				Sex	
	Swindon	Sheffield	Liverpool	Kirkcaldy	Male	Female
Career trajectories						
Academic	20	21	20	17	17	22
Other educational	20	15	20	27	19	22
School to jobs	32	9	11	10	19	13
YTS to jobs	12	18	11	12	14	13
Unemployed	16	37	38	33	31	31
n =	518	488	444	548	1010	988

Table 5:   Career trajectory by social and educational background (percentages)

	Parental class		Educational groups			Total
	m.c	w.c.	High	Med	Low	
Career trajectories						
Academic	28	14	48	8	1	20
Other educational	23	19	20	23	7	21
School to jobs	14	16	11	17	21	16
YTS to jobs	11	13	7	18	12	13
Unemployed	23	38	14	34	60	31
n =	470	1425	518	549	512	1998

Table 6: Career trajectories by area, education and family background (percentages)

	Ed−/Parental class+			Ed−/Parental class−		
	Swi	She	Liv	Swi	She	Liv
Career trajectory						
Academic	2	−	−	1	2	2
Other education	17	4	10	10	10	14
School to jobs	33	11	8	42	11	14
YTS to jobs	19	29	8	11	15	16
Unemployed	29	57	74	36	63	54
n =	52	56	50	172	185	179

	Ed+/Parental class+			Ed+/Parental class −		
	Swi	She	Liv	Swi	She	Liv
Career trajectory						
Academic	41	55	49	25	27	34
Other education	23	13	30	24	23	22
School to jobs	23	5	5	23	7	11
YTS to jobs	6	10	5	11	19	8
Unemployed	6	17	12	18	25	25
n =	133	94	66	187	170	143

Table 6 permits an examination of the interactive effects of place of residence, family backgrounds, and educational attainments, though in the English areas only; and in this table respondents are divided into just two educational groups according to whether their attainments at 16 were above or below average. The lower achievers were rarely entering the academic track whatever their family

backgrounds, but the higher achievers from middle−class homes were much more likely than working−class 16−year−olds with equal qualifications to have remained in full−time education on the academic track. Sex and place of residence was making relatively little difference to the likelihood of respondents following this route.

Our second career route is labelled *other education*. It comprises the careers of respondents who remained in full−time education beyond age 16, but not on the academic route. The evidence previously presented has shown that when they eventually entered the labor market the job prospects of young people who stayed on were generally good, though this was largely attributable to the abilities and qualifications that they had already demonstrated and earned by age 16 rather than any exceptional value added by their postcompulsory education. Sex was making only a slight difference to the sample's likelihood of proceeding down the "other education" trajectory, as was also the case with the academic route. Family background was unrelated to the likelihood of individuals staying on for "other" educational programs, and in this respect the "other education" route was different in being less socially selective than the academic trajectory. Qualifications were related to the likelihood of the young people being retained on the "other education" track, but here it was just the bottom third, not the bottom two−thirds as in the case of the academic trajectory, that was underrepresented. There was little variation by area in the proportions proceeding down the academic track, but substantial variations in the breadth of the "other education" route. The percentages of respondents who had followed this latter trajectory ranged from 27% in Kirkcaldy where, as previously explained, some of those who continued had no legal alternative, through 20% in Swindon and Liverpool, to just 15% in Sheffield. Opportunities to continue on "other" educational courses vary considerably according to the efforts of different LEAs, schools, and colleges to cater for less academic 16−year−olds, and for specific target groups within this broad category. However, the wealth or paucity of the alternative opportunities for 16−year−olds in an area, especially the jobs, is probably just as important in accounting for geographical variations in the proportions who remain on "other" educational courses.

Traditional transitions *straight from education into jobs* comprise our third trajectory. We have already seen that those 16−year−olds who obtained jobs had usually been successful in maintaining their employed status throughout the next 18 months. Family background was unrelated to whether respondents had accomplished such traditional trasitions at age 16, but boys were more likely to have done so than girls. Traditional transitions had been most common among the least qualified because higher proportions of the better qualified were remaining in education. The other substantial variations in the proportions stepping directly from compulsory education to employment were by area. Thirty—two percent in Swindon had done so against just 9 to 11% in the other localities. The 16—year—olds' chances of making traditional transitions had clearly depended very heavily on the strength of labor demand in their home areas.

Two—step transitions from education to the YTS, then into employment, are our fourth trajectory. The proportions of respondents who had completed two—step transitions did not vary by family background or sex so much as by area and qualifications. In Sheffield 18% had already completed two—step transitions compared with 11 to 12% in the other areas. This difference is most easily explained in terms of the kinds of training places available in Sheffield, where the local council was a prominent training provider, responsible for nearly one half of the city's provisions, and was guaranteeing continued employment to as many trainees as possible. None of the local councils in the other areas covered by the ESRC Initiative had embraced the YTS so vigorously and constructively. Two—step transitions had been most common among respondents with average qualifications because the best—qualified were more likely to have remained in education on the academic trajectory, while the least qualified tended to have gone straight into jobs or unemployment at 16, or had failed to obtain employment following youth training.

Our *fifth trajectory* contains all cases that did not resemble any of the other patterns. However, the majority of the individuals placed in this fifth group did not fit elsewhere either because they had been unemployed for too long to qualify, or because they were still on the YTS at the time of the research, which would normally have been due to their inability to obtain jobs. This trajectory, therefore, groups together those career histories that had already led into, or appeared to be leading toward unemployment. Similar proportions of males and females were on this *unemployment track*, but there were wide differences between the areas according to educational qualifications and family backgrounds. The obvious explanation for the main difference between the areas — just 16% on the umemployment trajectory in Swindon against 33 to 38% elesewhere — is in terms of the relatively buoyant economy in Southern England. The higher proportion, 60% of the bottom third in terms of educational attainment, on the unemployment trajectory will be a product of their difficulties in obtaining jobs whether they entered their local labor markets immediately on completing compulsory education, after further spells at school or college, or following youth training. Family background was associated with variations in the proportions of the sample who followed the most and least prestigious routes, the academic and the unemployment tracks, but not with any of the intermediate trajectories. Thirty−eight percent from manual families compared with 23% from nonmanual homes were already in the predicament, or were apparently heading toward unemployment. Working−class origins were associated with increased risks of unemployment in all areas, and among both better qualified and less qualified young people.

3.   Transitions to Adulthood

Even if the number and range of old and new educational, training, and job opportunities were sufficient to keep all Britain's 16− to 19−year−olds fully occupied, and if all the pathways from age 16 led eventually to adults jobs, the process of becoming adult in the late 1980s would still be very different than in the 1950s and 1960s. *To begin with, for the majority, though still far from all young people, entry into adult employment is now being delayed beyond the ages at which other adult rights are conferred, including the right to marry without parental consent, and to vote.* Economic self−sufficiency is customarily one of the last stages in the transition to adulthood in those social strata in which it has been normal for young people to proceed through higher education, but it is not customary in working−class families. Many are simply unable to make sense of the delay when the jobs, if any, that are to be entered eventually, do not appear to justify immediate sacrifices.

The consolations for educational failure and modest long−term job prospects used to include rapid progress to adult earnings and immersion in commercialized youth cultures during a "brief flowering period" before marriage and family formation. Recent cohorts of such school−leavers have often been disappointed and angry when confined to the margins of the labor market. Many of their parents have been equally outraged at their children being denied the right to work (Allatt and Yeandle, 1984). Most such parents sympathize with their children's predicaments and offer such support as they are able in attempts to ensure that grown−up members of their families can feel adult at home and are not excluded from out−of−home recreation by poverty (Hutson and Jenkins, 1987). However, there are inevitable strains when both sides resent the young adults' enforced dependence and their inability to proceed through the customary processes of courtship and family formation. There could be profound long−term consequences if substantial numbers of young adults stabilize adult identities that involve neither economic self−sufficiency nor customary family responsibilities.

A second change is that some earlier divisions among young people have been blurred, while other schisms have widened. The academic high—fliers are less separate than formerly, partly due to the spread of comprehensive secondary schools, and also because increasing numbers of those who proceed to A—levels share institutions, and often some courses as well, with new sixth formers in schools and adults also in many further education colleges. The new division is beneath all young people who continue in postcompulsory education, whatever their courses and eventual attainments. Their day—to—day routines, levels and sources of income, and access to education—based social and recreation facilities, set them apart from the rest of their age group. It is doubtful whether we can still meaningfully describe most young people who remain in postcompulsory education as deferring gratifications. It is not just that, for many, the longer—term rewards are now uncertain. It is no longer so obvious as in the past that they are sacrificing immediate gratifications. *Most early school—leavers now enter training schemes and receive allowances that are well beneath adult wage levels.* Meanwhile, there are more opportunities than ever for students to obtain part—time and temporary jobs in service industries, especially retailing, and hotels and catering. Many employers look specifically to student labor markets to fill these vacancies. They are impressed by the quality labor of the students who are willing to take low—status jobs. And many are equally attracted by students' instrumentalism — their willingness to work simply for immediate cash without any longer—term commitment on either side (Roberts et al. 1987). Students' part—time and vacation earnings often exceed the allowances paid to youth trainees and sometimes rival wage rates in full—time youth jobs.

The YTS has blurred the former division between young people training for skilled jobs and the rest, especially when set alongside the new cleavage between all young people who "stay afloat", whatever their schemes or jobs, and the "new underclass" as those descending toward long—term unemployment have been described. *Despite economic growth, and despite higher than ever spending on youth education and training, more young adults than formerly are slipping through all the nets, settling into claimant roles, becoming accustomed to lives without regular employment, gravitating into their own social networks, and devising their own ways of passing time.* By age 19/20 or so, these young adults' own histories of joblessness become additional handicaps when approaching employers. By their mid—20s they are rearing another generation in impoverished and often chronically unstable domestic circumstances, which is how the underclass is beginning to reproduce itself down the generations. Meanwhile, other long—standing divisions seem to be surviving all the turbulence of the 1980s. Gender remains as divisive as ever in employment, in education, and on the YTS (Blackman, 1987; Cockburn, 1987).

Ethnic advantages and disadvantages also seem to be surviving all the surrounding changes (Cross and Smith, 1987).

A third difference between the old and newer pathways is that the latter are less clearly linked to adult occupations. In Britain the destinations to which all routes at 16 – plus once led were clear to all and well understood. There was an obvious hierarchy. Young people who remained in full – time education could anticipate higher status and better paid jobs than 16 – year – old leavers were likely to achieve. This may still apply when young people take A – levels and proceed to higher education, but Britain's new sixth formers are in very different situations. Seventy – seven percent of respondents in the ESRC inquiries who had stayed in education after age 16, then subsequently entered the labor market, were in employment by the time of our survey. The majority had obtained jobs, but few could have been certain, when deciding to stay at school or college for an extra year or more, that they would not eventually be part of the unemployed minority. Nor could they have known which occupations, if any, they would obtain on entering the labor market. They may have hoped, but they could not have been sure, that their eventual jobs would be any better than those open to 16 – year – olds or following youth training. Secondary school examinations that can be passed at age 16 do not appear to carry quite the same weight when taken to the labor market at age 17 or 18 (Roberts et al., 1987). Many employers confess their ignorance and protest that they simply do not know what value, if any, to attach to the newer vocational qualifications that many of today's postcompulsory students earn. Some advantages of becoming better qualified by staying on seem to be cancelled by the lost opportunities to enter training in firms in which recruitment is still geared to 16 – year – old school – leavers (Lee and Wrench, 1983).

The types of jobs that 16 – year – olds used to enter were easily classified. Most girls were employed in offices, in retailing, or in unskilled occupations in manufacturing or service sectors. Very few were apprenticed. Only the best qualified and ambitious girls entered nonmanual jobs with either the training or opportunities for continuing education that would lead to management or professional status. Boys who gained nonmanual employment usually expected, and were granted these propects. The rest of the lads were divisible into apprentices, mainly in engineering and construction, then the remainder who obtained other manual employment. All these types of jobs were clearly linked to adult occupations. This is not to say that school – leavers used to be placed in occupational castes within which they would remain for life. Their jobs were certainly not always long – lasting. Nevertheless, a typist, for example, could be confident that her experience would enable her to obtain a similar job elsewhere. Some apprentices dropped out before serving their time. It was sometimes possible for individuals who never served apprenticeships to acquire skills informally, and eventually to establish themselves in skilled occupations by "dilution". The status of skilled workers could be threatened by the contraction of their industries, but short of such uncontrollable and largely unpredictable events, and provided they were neither grossly imcompetent nor ambitious, young people had assured prospects.

Virtually all youth jobs once led, via paths that were visible to the entrants, to adult occupations with adult pay. The YTS rarely offers equivalent security. Even young people who enter "good" schemes are normally granted only probationary, trainee status to begin with. Their destinations are less certain than beginning workers' prospects in the 1950s and 1960s. Many young people in transit in the 1980s cannot be certain where their trajectories are heading. This does not mean that the socio—occupational structure has become more fluid, and that social mobility has increased. Links between social origins and eventual destinations are probably as tight as ever. Rather, *the new situation is that fewer of the individuals who will ascend, descend, and maintain their status can be identified or can know their own fates as early or as confidently as formerly.*

It was once possible to divide beginning workers into broad categories such as those whose jobs offered extended careers, short careers, and no progression at all (Ashton and Field, 1976). The types of careers on which school—leavers embarked were related to their success or failure in education, and also to their family backgrounds, and the net result was that the majority entered the labor market with levels of ambition and expectations that matched their prospects. School—leavers who were unable to obtain the particular jobs they had said they wanted mostly found sufficiently similar employment to adjust their aspirations with minimal discomfort. Of course, there were always exceptions who became problem cases for the Careers Service and other agencies, but the main problem that occupied researchers was why the vast majority, even among those with the most limited prospects, were so acquiescent (Willis, 1977).

There is now a mass of evidence, and not only from the ESRC inquiries, of out—of—school youth in the 1980s clinging to ambitions that they are unable to fulfil (Church and Ainley, 1987; Furlong, 1987; Roberts et al., 1987). There are two very obvious reasons for this change. Firstly, the majority of today's out—of—school youth have no certain adult destinations with which they could identify. Secondly, adjusting their ambitions to their early labor market achievements would involve settling for far less, not just slightly different positions than they had been aiming for.

Young people have always been liable to change their occupational goals, but at any point in time the vast majority have been able to express definite ambitions, which remains true today. Most 16—year—olds know what they would like to become, but few can take immediate steps that will set them firmly on course toward these destinations. Worse still, there is often a huge gap between the kinds of jobs and schemes that 16—year—olds can enter, and the types of employment that they eventually want to obtain. Rather than abandoning their ambitions and settling for far less, it seems that a more common response is for the individuals to dissociate their real selves from their current schemes, jobs, or lack of any employment. Young people who remain in education on the academic trajectory have always been denied certainty as regards their occupational futures, but they have been able to adopt "student" as a credible status. Until recently, being a postcompulsory student has carried connotations of past educational success and splendid occupational prospects. New sixth formers and youth trainees, not to mention the unemployed, have far less incentive to identify with their immediate positions.

This new situation has potentially profound implications for the development of young people's self—concepts which the ongoing ESRC Initiative is exploring. To what extent can "wannabee", knowing the kind of adult that one would like to become, operate as a satisfactory basis for identity formation when a person has no assurance of ever becoming that kind of individual? How many young people who enter the new trajectories are turning to ascriptive statuses based on sex and ethnicity to define their selves and their positions in society? How many girls (and boys) are using domestic roles in this fashion? These are among the questions posed by the restructuring of young people's opportunities.

Note

This research is supported by a grant from the Economic and Social Research Council.

References

Allatt, P., & Yeandle, S.M. (1984): Family structure and youth unemployment. Bradford: Paper presented to British Sociological Association Conference

Ashton, D.N., & Field, D. (1976): Young Workers. London: Hutchinson

Blackman, S.J. (1987): The labor market in school: The new vocationalism and issues of ascribed discrimination. In Brown, P., & Ashton, D.N. (Eds.): Education, employment and labour markets. Lewes: Falmer Press

Bynner, J. (1987): Coping with transition: ESRC's new 16—19 Initiative. Youth and Policy, 22, 25—28

Church, A., & Ainley, P. (1987): Inner—city decline and regeneration: Young people and the labor market in London's docklands. In Brown, P., and Ashton, D.N., (Eds): Education, unemployment and labour markets. Lewes: Falmer Press

Cockburn, C. (1987): Two—track training: Sex inequalities and the YTS. London: Macmillan

Cross, M., & Smith, D.I. (1987): Black youth futures. Leicester: National Youth Bureau

Furlong, A. (1987): Coming to terms with the declining demand for youth labor. In Brown, P., & Ashton, D.N., (Eds.): Education, employment and labour markets. Lewes: Falmer Press

Hutson, S., & Jenkins, R. (1987): Coming of age in South Wales. In Brown, P., & Ashton, D.N. (Eds.): Education, unemployment and labour markets. Lewes: Falmer Press

Jones, P., Williamson, H., Payne, J., & Smith, G. (1983): Out of school. Sheffield: Manpower Services Commission, Special Programmes, Occasional Paper 4

Lee, D., Marsden, D., Hardey, M., & Rickman, J. (1987): Youth training, life – chances and orientations to work. In Brown, P., & Ashton, D.N. (Eds.): Education, employment and labour markets. Lewes: Falmer Press

Lee, G., & Wrench, J. (1983): Skill seekers. Leicester: National Youth Bureau

Raffe, D., & Courtenay, G. (1988): 16 – 18 on both sides of the border. In Raffe, D. (Ed.): Schooling and scheming: Education and the youth labour market. Lewes: Falmer Press

Roberts, K. (1982): Contemporary youth unemployment: A sociological interpretation. Liverpool: Paper presented to the British Association for the Advancement of Science

Roberts, K. (1987): ESRC – Young people in society. Youth and Policy, 22, 15 – 24

Roberts, K., Dench, S., & Richardson, D. (1986): Firms' uses of the youth training scheme. Policy Studies, 6, 37 – 53

Roberts, K., Dench, S., & Richardson, D. (1987): The changing structure of youth labour markets. London: Department of Employment Research Paper 59

Willis, P. (1977): Learning to labour. Farnborough: Saxon House

23.

Uncertain Career Prospects and Problem Behavior in Adolescence

Uwe Engel
University of Bielefeld, Federal Republic of Germany

1. Introduction

A major aim of the present study is to contribute to the understanding of the social and cultural foundations of what might be termed problem behavior in youth. The term is solely used for heuristical purposes to conveniently refer to four types of "behavioral" reactions: the concepts of (1) symptoms of stress, (2) negative (or low) self−esteem, (3) substance use, and (4) delinquency. The main goal of the model reported below is to permit a *simultaneous* empirical analysis of all four types of behavioral reactions. Each form of problem behavior is therefore simultaneously traced to the same set of social and cultural factors in order to obtain unconfounded estimates of the relative effects involved. We shall start with a description of both the theoretical concepts and the assumptions established to connect them.

2. Concepts and Propositions

One way of looking at "youth" is to see it as a period of status transitions comprising vertical mobility in various dimensions. In modern societies youth is closely linked to the basic societal allocation process, in the course of which the job−related positions held by adults are taken over or filled by the rising generation (Kreutz, 1974). Youth is characterized by both the promise of intergenerational upward mobility and the risk of moving downward, especially in terms of status dimensions such as education, occupation, and income.

The underlying ideological conception of achievement−oriented societies implies that it is the level of formal education completed in youth that provides the basis for the social positions subsequently gained. Accordingly, after having entered the school career, social assessment of the child and adolescent will primarily be in terms of his or her own achievement, rather than based on family status or class of origin. Since this implies the chance of eventually getting ahead as well as the risk of not getting anywhere at all, the adolescent is under heavy pressure to meet the achievement—related role expectations and to achieve a social position in adult society that befits his or her social background.

It is precisely the possibility of long—term career patterns such as decline or rise that causes status insecurity to be a basic feature of youth. Status insecurity primarily springs from an interaction between a culture that is strongly dominated by the values of success, status, and competition, and a social organization of youth established to − in a formal sense − provide the option of becoming successful through acquiring the respective educational requisites.

The experience of "uncertain career prospects" (taken as a partial indicator of perceived status insecurity) is, however, but one mechanism through which, in particular, long—term decline functions. "Social conflict with parents" is also a most probable event because of the fact that an unfavorable educational career not only carries the risk of failing to get a socially approved and privileged position in adulthood; it also carries the risk of failing to reproduce the social status of the family of origin. Scholastic failure is "costly" for both the students who fail to meet the scholastic demands and for their parents. The scholastic success of the offspring lies therefore in the parents' most vital interest, and, consequently, this will affect their attitudes toward what constitutes intolerable scholastic failure. When now the scholastic performances of the child do not come up to the parents' expectations, the parents will in turn emphasize these very expectations, in this way considerably raising the probability of even serious social conflict in the home as well as, on the side of the child, the probability of subsequently induced insecurity.

Figure 1 displays the basic structure of effects assumed to be operating in adolescent societies. The model serves to provide estimates of effect that are subsequently described in some detail. In *Figure 2*, we document the variables that we take as "risk factors" and symptoms of "problem behavior".

The following indicators were used for the exogeneous factors:

Educational background: The subjective anticipation of successfully continuing the educational career is expected to be a core element in the process of social selection at school that in part serves to account for the fact of a differential

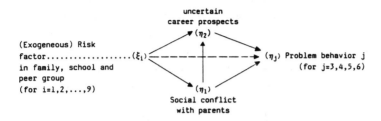

effects $\xi_i \rightarrow \eta_1$, not for ξ_1

effects $\xi_i \rightarrow \eta_2$, not for ξ_5 and ξ_7

effects $\xi_i \rightarrow \eta_j$ only for some of the possible relations (cf. the structural equation model)

Fig. 1: General structure of effects*

SOCIAL ORIGIN	AGE AND SEX
ξ_1 Education of father	ξ_8 Sex (female)
ACHIEVEMENT-RELATED EXPEC-TATIONS IN SCHOOL AND FAMILY	ξ_9 age
	CONFLICT AND CAREER-UNCERTAINTY
ξ_2 Scholastic strain	η_1 social conflict with parents
ξ_3 Failure to meet scholastic demands	η_2 Uncertain career prospects
PEER GROUP	PROBLEM BEHAVIOR
ξ_4 status deprivation (regarding requisites for conspicious consumption)	η_3 symptoms of stress
	η_4 negative self esteem
ξ_5 Clique integration	η_5 substance use
ξ_6 social integration of the friendship circle (weak)	η_6 delinquency
ξ_7 Degree of overlap of the friendship circles of respondent and best friend (low)	

Fig. 2: The variables included in the study

risk of degrading: In West Germany, students of lower social origin are not only much more likely to be allocated to the very types of secondary school that themselves carry only poor career prospects, but are also more likely to drop out of the system or to be downwardly mobile to a lower—graded school after having entered the educational track in secondary school for the first time.

In this process, the perception of uncertain career prospects may function like a self — fulfilling prophecy in that an unfavourable educational background favors the anticipation of an uncertain future, which in turn raises the probability of school failure due to this very form of perceiving unfavorable opportunities. Distinguishing three background levels, we expect the lower the educational background the higher the perceived degree of uncertain career prospects.

Scholastic strain and failure to meet scholastic demands: We shall consider three common instances of unfulfilled educational demands: (1) Scholastic success is endangered by (the risk of) having to repeat one or more school years or of being transferred to a lower graded school. (2) The student attends a type of school not designed to prepare for the school — leaving certificate that the parents desire for their offspring; and (3) The parents regard the scholastic performance as not coming up to their expectations, although none of the conditions mentioned above might actually apply.

The concept called "failure to meet scholastic demands" covers exactly these possibilities (that accordingly have been mapped into one single index). It is supplemented by a concept that throws light on the accompanying perceived strain (as measured on an 11 — point — scale) to come up to the scholastic demands, and it seems reasonable to assume that this perceived degree of "scholastic strain", as well as an increased risk of failing to meet the educational demands placed on the student, will strongly contribute to the occurrence of the problem behavior at issue.

Status deprivation: There are some peer — group — related risk factors to be brought into the picture. The first one to be considered is termed "status deprivation". Stated more precisely, this concept, as measured in the present study, should be termed status deprivation regarding the requisites for "conspicious consumption" (Veblen, 1899), since it measures the degree to which the adolescents believe that they do not possess the goods desirable for social life among their peers. Every student was asked to indicate on a 4 — point scale (1: You have everything you want; 2: You have not got everything, but quite a great deal of what you want; 3: You lack some things; 4: You lack a great deal) his or her answer to the question: "If you think of the things you, as a girl or boy, would like to buy to go down well with others (e.g., fashionable clothes, records, and so forth), do you have all you are wishing for? Or do you lack some things?"

In a culture strongly dominated by the values of success and competition, the topic of social rank naturally plays a basic role not only in terms of the above — described large — scale comparison regarding family background and the social position the offspring will probably be attaining in later adult life. Long – term decline and rise, is just one topic that affects individual and collective behavior. Social rank, however, is much more pervasive in that corresponding values advance in nearly every part of social life. That is to say that social status governs the behavior of individuals by virtue of both the positions attained in the broader social structure and the more informal positions the individual holds within its significant reference groups.

Viewed this latter way, status to a large extent depends on conspicuous behavior. This means that whether or not a person attains, say, a high social status, depends on all his/her features that can be observed by the members of the respective social circle. For instance, status is not simply social appreciation by significant others, since this may remain a totally private experience. But it will serve to contribute to social status to the extent to which it becomes a collective experience sufficiently shared by the members of the collectivity at hand. The crucial point is that a person may win or lose status solely by the fact that others focus attention to observable aspects of his/her behavior. This is a widely acknowledged fact in everyday life, and so most people try to gain control of the very impressions they produce in their reference persons.

To accomplish this task of acquiring status through forms of what is often called impression management, a variety of means are observable and presumably well – known in higher – educated groups. To designate them all as forms of impression management may, however, be misleading in that the term "management" suggests that it covers rational, self – initiated, that is, planned activities. To carry out a particular course of action in a rational way, however, presupposes skills that by no means are evenly distributed over the whole society, and so a lot of attempts to produce certain impressions seem to represent rather a highly reactive type of behavior, that is to say: role – taking behavior primarily governed by a literal and rigid reading of the underlying cultural norms.

Though it is intended to be a more general proposition, this is in particular applicable to the gender roles and the social process through which these very roles are taken over by the rising generation. However, adopting the social values and stereotypes associated with the gender roles as well as the corresponding male and female behavior is but one aspect of this socialization process. Gender roles not only represent statuses in that they are positions toward which specific role expectations are directed. Supposing the strong emphasis put on success and competition, they also represent positions embedded into a stratification system of social ranks, since culture suggests, so to speak, not only becoming a male or female, but also becoming an attractive male or female person. The process of socialization into the gender roles not only shapes a consciousness in terms of differences between the sexes, but also in terms of superiority within each gender group.

In this process, conspicuous consumption and visible signs of lifestyle (Lipset and Zetterberg, 1966) play a central part, since to become approved of by peers, usually requires serious attempts to correspond to social images and stereotypes enforced by publicity and the mass media. These images and stereotypes usually imply a lot of goods, that is, articles of commerce, that are strongly tied to the social role at issue, and that in this way become the requisites for conspicuous consumption.

As outlined above, in competitive social systems, the primary function of this type of behavior is displaying social status as well as succeeding in the competition for the favor of peers, either with respect to gender role behavior or with respect to social behavior in youth in general.

The main assumption, then, is that feelings of deprivation of these very requisites for conspicuous consumption are a strong source of problem behavior in youth. In particular, we expect a lowered self−esteem and delinquency to be probable responses to the pressure exerted upon the adolescents by a widely shared value system.

Clique integration, social integration of the friendship circle, and degree of overlap of the friendship circles of respondent and best friend: Since the impact of culture is to a certain extent transmitted through the social life in microgroups, it matters how strongly these very groups tie together their individual members. The degree of social integration of the peer group is expected to be a relevant condition also on grounds of the assumption that it influences the opportunity structure not only for becoming acquainted with special elements of the cultural system, but also for becoming involved in certain courses of activities. In particular, a high degree of social integration of the peer group is assumed to favor both delinquent activities and substance use, while the very opposite is expected to lower the self−esteem.

Therefore an attempt was made to assess the structural integration of the friendship circle of the respondent by means of three network concepts (operationally measured in a subjective fashion). The first one is labeled "clique integration" and simply carries the information on whether or not the respondent spends his leisure time within a clique. The second concept provides a cognitive map of the social structure of the friendship circle in terms of closeness of interaction structure ranging from a clique structure in which everyone has contact with everyone else (high integration) to friendship circles characterized by a series of otherwise unconnected peer dyads (weak integration) (trichotomous scale). The third concept grasps the perceived degree of overlap of the friendship circles of the respondent and his or her best friend (of the same sex) respectively. As in the previous case, the concept categories rise numerically as integration becomes weak, that is in the latter case, when there is a low degree of overlap.

Age and sex: Finally both age and sex of the respondent are regarded as attributes that serve to reflect the impact the cultural and social system can impose on adolescent societies.

The following indicators were used for the measurement of the endogeneous concepts ("problem behavior"):

Social conflict with parents ($R^2 = .368$): Every student was asked to indicate on an ordinal 4 — point — scale how often he or she quarreled with either their father or mother (two separate scales).

Uncertain career prospects ($R^2 = .241$): Information was obtained regarding the subjective probability, in terms of a 5 — point — scale ranging from very sure to absolutely unsure, of both (1) getting the desired educational qualification, and (2) realizing the occupational plans (2 separate scales).

Symptoms of stress ($R^2 = .515$): Based on a preliminary confirmatory factor analysis, the concept was measured by two separate indices, summing the number of "frequently" or "sometimes" (as opposed to "seldom" or "never") ratings for either psychosomatic or emotional symptoms of stress. The concept includes the following items: (a) Psychosomatic complaints: loss of weight due to worrying, spells of dizziness, heart beating hard, nausea, sleeplessness, troubled sleep, trembling hands, loss of appetite, stomach trouble, profuse perspiration, difficulties in breathing, nightmares, headache, nervousness, restlessness, lack of concentration. (b) Emotions: Helpless, useless, lonely, sad, meaninglessness, anxious, sense of guilt, discontented.

Negative (or low) self esteem ($R^2 = .426$): The concept was measured by two separate indices, each combining a set of four items on positive and negative self — evaluations in terms of, for example, self — related contentedness, pride, desire to be another person, feelings of uselessness, and feelings of not being a person of worth. Each index counts the number of responses indicating "low" self — evaluation.

Substance use ($R^2 = .503$): Three separate 4 — point scales for (a) alcoholic beverages with low alcohol content (wine, sparkling wine, beer); (b) highly alcoholic beverages (liquor, wisky, etc.); and (c) cigarettes were used to record responses with the points: (1) never; (2) only tried; (3) sometimes; and (4) regularly.

Delinquency ($R^2 = .474$): The concept is based on three separate indices combining the responses to the events (a) truancy (on own initiative), staying away from home at night, theft, forging a signature; (b) intentionally inflicting damage or purposively destroying public or private property, purposively inflicting bodily harm, "robbery"; (c) inflicting bodily harm during a brawl or fight, armed threat (knife, brass knuckles), burglary (from a house, car, or automatic vending machine), member of a delinquent "gang", bill dodging. Each index counted the number of events that occurred once or more during the last 12 months.

3. Sample, Data Analysis, and Findings

The data are from the first wave of a longitudinal youth survey conducted in the late autumn of 1986, by means of a self – administered questionnaire. The population is defined as 7th – and 9th – grade students in the main types of secondary schools: secondary vocational school, intermediate secondary school, grammar school, and comprehensive school. Based on a proportionally stratified cluster – sampling device, samples were drawn independently within three geographical regions (statistical areas) of the state of North – Rhine – West-phalia, where each of these regions represents one type of socioecological area according to the official returns. The total sample size amounted to N = 1,717 students aged 13 – 16 years.

A path analytic design with the above – described concepts as latent variables seemed to be most suitable for obtaining unconfounded and disattenuated estimates regarding our assumptions. Hence, a structural equation model combined with the pertaining measurement models for the x and y indicators was set up and estimated by means of LISREL VI (Jöreskog and Sörbom, 1986; Jagodzinski, 1986). It turned out that the initial model could be improved by means of setting some very weak paths equal to zero, while removing such restrictions from other parts of the model. The final model is displayed in *Figure 3* (Goodness – of – fit GFI = .982; RMSR = .04).

Since most of our indicators were on ordinal scales, it seemed appropriate to avoid computing product – moment correlations. Instead of this, the estimation of effects was based on a matrix of polychoric/polyserial correlations. As recommended (Jöreskog and Sörbom, 1986) for the analysis of nonnormally distributed, ordinal – scale indicators, this matrix of polychoric/polyserial correlations was then analyzed by the method of unweighted least squares (ULS). The corresponding maximum – likelihood – (ML –) solutions were taken into account only for comparison purposes. Chi^2 – and/or t – values (in the case of ML) were not regarded as valid, given the skewed distributions involved. Hence, no conclusions were drawn from those figures (Jöreskog and Sörbom, 1986).

$$
\begin{pmatrix} \eta_1 \\ \eta_2 \\ \eta_3 \\ \eta_4 \\ \eta_5 \\ \eta_6 \end{pmatrix} =
\begin{pmatrix}
0 & 0 & 0 & 0 & 0 & 0 \\
\beta_{21} & 0 & 0 & 0 & 0 & 0 \\
\beta_{31} & \beta_{32} & 0 & 0 & 0 & 0 \\
\beta_{41} & \beta_{42} & 0 & 0 & 0 & 0 \\
\beta_{51} & \beta_{52} & 0 & 0 & 0 & 0 \\
\beta_{61} & \beta_{62} & 0 & 0 & 0 & 0
\end{pmatrix}
\begin{pmatrix} \eta_1 \\ \eta_2 \\ \eta_3 \\ \eta_4 \\ \eta_5 \\ \eta_6 \end{pmatrix} +
\begin{pmatrix}
0 & \gamma_{12} & \gamma_{13} & \gamma_{14} & \gamma_{15} & \gamma_{16} & \gamma_{17} & \gamma_{18} & \gamma_{19} \\
\gamma_{21} & \gamma_{22} & \gamma_{23} & \gamma_{24} & 0 & \gamma_{26} & 0 & \gamma_{28} & \gamma_{29} \\
0 & \gamma_{32} & 0 & 0 & \gamma_{35} & 0 & 0 & \gamma_{38} & 0 \\
0 & \gamma_{42} & \gamma_{43} & \gamma_{44} & \gamma_{45} & 0 & 0 & \gamma_{48} & \gamma_{49} \\
0 & 0 & \gamma_{53} & 0 & \gamma_{55} & 0 & \gamma_{57} & \gamma_{58} & \gamma_{59} \\
\gamma_{61} & 0 & \gamma_{63} & \gamma_{64} & \gamma_{65} & \gamma_{66} & 0 & \gamma_{68} & 0
\end{pmatrix}
\begin{pmatrix} \xi_1 \\ \xi_2 \\ \xi_3 \\ \xi_4 \\ \xi_5 \\ \xi_6 \\ \xi_7 \\ \xi_8 \\ \xi_9 \end{pmatrix} +
\begin{pmatrix} \zeta_1 \\ \zeta_2 \\ \zeta_3 \\ \zeta_4 \\ \zeta_5 \\ \zeta_6 \end{pmatrix}
$$

Direct and indirect effects (standardised solution)

Effects from...

...toward:	η_1	η_2	$\eta_3...\eta_6$		ξ_1	ξ_2	ξ_3	ξ_4	ξ_5	ξ_6	ξ_7	ξ_8	ξ_9
η_1	0	0	0...0	η_1	0	.10	.23	.38	.19	.09	.11	.10	.12
η_2	.05	0	0...0	η_2	−.15	.13	.31	.20	0	.08	0	.14	−.14
η_3	.38	.22	0...0	η_3	0	.20	0	0	−.06	0	0	.42	0
η_4	.28	.32	0...0	η_4	0	.08	.07	.15	−.22	0	0	.23	−.06
η_5	.31	−.13	0...0	η_5	0	0	.16	0	.33	0	−.07	−.13	.27
η_6	.32	−.04	0...0	η_6	−.07	0	.14	.06	.27	−.10	0	−.45	0

Figure 3:   Structural equation model and estimates of effect obtained

The list of endogeneous concepts shown above provides a general view of how the endogeneous concepts are related to their respective y − indicators. All indicators of the above − described exogeneous concepts were included in the analysis as fixed − x − variables, thereby assuming a fixed, one − to − one relation between the theoretical concept and observed indicator. In such a case, the x indicators may even be coded dummy variables (Jöreskog and Sörbom, 1986). A more detailed description of the measurement models together with panel − data − based tests of the causality assumptions underlying the present model may be obtained from a (forthcoming) monograph (Engel and Hurrelmann, 1989).

Figure 3 displays the structural equation model and the estimates of effect obtained through it. Accordingly, the main findings can be stated as follows:

1.   Failure to meet scholastic demands turns out to be a strong source of both substance use and delinquency mainly in either of two ways: directly or through the path via social conflict with the parents. It also contributes to negative self − esteem and to symptoms of stress; however, mainly through the transmitter effects of conflict and uncertain career prospects respectively. Comparing this result with the one obtained for the second factor, that is, scholastic strain, an interesting difference can be noticed:

Contrary to the finding just reported, no direct effect on substance use and delinquency was found — a difference that is possibly due to the fact that being under strain is an event compatible with both failure and nonfailure to meet scholastic demands in the sense described above. What we did find, however, is the strong direct effect scholastic strain has on the number of symptoms of stress, as well as the moderate effect it has on negative self—esteem. This, too, emphasizes the important role that is played by school and the achievement—related role expectations in the genesis of both low self—esteem and symptoms of stress.

2.   A low educational background favors uncertain career prospects.

3.   Status deprivation lowers the self—esteem of adolescents to a great extent in either of three ways: (a) directly; (b) indirectly, by means of causing social conflict, which in turn leads to a lowered self—esteem; and (c) indirectly, by means of causing uncertain career prospects, which in turn cause a lowered self—esteem. Additionally, status deprivation causes delinquency in either of two ways: (a) by leading to conflict, which in turn causes delinquency; or (b) directly, but with moderate strength only. This finding therefore yields evidence for the assumption in conflict sociology (Coser, 1967) that destructive activities are particularly likely to arise in cases in which constructive and socially approved ways of obtaining social status are blocked, so that the individuals are tempted to attain status through the conspicuous use of physical strength and even violence.

4.   Regarding the structural integration of the friendship circle, the main findings can be stated as follows: (a) To be a member of a clique strongly supports both substance use and delinquency. This is shown by all three measures on substance use, delinquency, or both types of problem behavior. Hence, it is strong peer—group integration that makes for substance use and delinquency. (b) Just the reverse is true for negative self—esteem, which is favored by weak peer—group integration.

5.   This leaves us with sex and age as the remaining conditions. Stated briefly, there is a strong tendency for females to show symptoms of stress and a somewhat weaker tendency toward a lowered self—esteem. Just the opposite is true for males who are most likely to become involved in delinquent activities. Finally, it should be noted that substance use rises with age.

The analysis yields some evidence for a differential impact exercised by cultural and structural conditions upon the four types of problem behavior at issue. The societal value system appears to play a major role in the genesis of the behavioral reactions studied. This is a conclusion that is also supported by a more detailed empirical analysis of the value orientations in the field of achievement, status, and social justice held by our sample of respondents (Engel and Hurrelmann, 1989; Engel, 1988a). Finally, structural conditions in either the friendship circle (as shown above) or the peer community at school (Engel, 1988b) prove to exert a substantial influence upon the types of individual reactions studied.

6.   References

Coser, L.A. (1967): Continuities in the study of social conflict. New York: Free Press

Engel, U. (1988a): Youth, mobility and social integration. In Hazekamp, J., Meeus, W., & Poel, Y.te (Eds.): European Contributions to Youth Research. Amsterdam: Free University Press, 81—92

Engel, U. (1988b): Status inconsistency and criss—cross in an adolescent society. International Sociology, 3, 283—300

Engel, U., & Hurrelmann, K. (1989): Psychosoziale Belastung im Jugendalter. Berlin: De Gruyter

Jagodzinski, W. (1986): Pfadmodelle mit latenten Variablen: Eine Einführung in das allgemeine Modell LISREL. In Koolwijk, J.v., & Wieken—Mayser, M. (Eds.): Techniken der empirischen Sozialforschung. Band 8. München: Oldenbourg, 77—121

Jöreskog, K.G., & Sörbom, D. (1986): LISREL. User's guide (4th edition). Mooresville: Scientific Software, Inc.

Kreutz, H. (1974): Soziologie der Jugend. München: Juventa

Lipset, S.M., & Zetterberg, H.L. (1966): A theory of social mobility. In Bendix, R., & Lipset, S.M. (Eds.): Class, status, and power. Social stratification in comparative perspective (2nd.ed.). New York: Free Press, 561—573

Veblen, T. (1899): The theory of the leisure class. An economic study of the evolution of institutions. New York

Subject Index